The Gift of Responsibility

The Gift of Responsibility

The Promise of Dialogue among Christians, Jews, and Muslims

Lewis S. Mudge

continuum

NEW YORK • LONDON

The Continuum International Publishing Group Inc., 80 Maiden Lane, New York, NY 10038

The Continuum International Publishing Group Ltd., The Tower Building, 11 York Road, London SE1 7NX

www.continuumbooks.com

Scripture quotations are from Revised Standard Version of the Bible, copyright © 1946, 1952, and 1971 National Council of the Churches of Christ in the United States of America. Used by permission. All rights reserved.

Printed in Canada

Mudge, Lewis Seymour.
The gift of responsibility : the promise of dialogue among Christians, Jews, and Muslims / Lewis S. Mudge.
p. cm.
Includes bibliographical references and index.
ISBN-13: 978-0-8264-2839-4 (pbk. : alk. paper)
ISBN-10: 0-8264-2839-8 (pbk. : alk. paper)   1. Christianity and other religions.
2. Judaism—Relations.   3. Islam—Relations.   4. Religion and civilization.
I. Title.
BR127.M83 2008
201'.5—dc22
2008017816

Contents

Foreword

This book concerns the responsibility of the Abrahamic faiths to their traditions, to one another, and to the modern world. It has been a long time coming to fruition. Hints of the insights to which I have come in this gestation process can be found in at least three of my earlier writings: *The Sense of a People* (Trinity, 1992), *The Church as Moral Community* (Continuum, 1998) and *Rethinking the Beloved Community* (University Press of America, 2001). But it was not until I came across the work of Rabbi Jonathan Sacks that I began to realize what these previous forays toward other faiths could mean if, instead of being left as isolated references in works on other subjects, they could be brought together and sufficiently thought through to became the main event.

But this does mark for me a change in focus. How does one move from where one has lived theologically by heritage and training to take on a project such as this one? I have been a Christian theologian and ethicist, and I intend to remain both. Furthermore, I reaffirm my long-standing commitment to Christian ecumenism, the shared effort of the churches together to rediscover and affirm the meaning of Christian faith for the world through a shared recovery of unity and purpose. This personal history and these commitments obviously color what it is possible for me to do in this book. Every such argument will come from somewhere. There is no argument from nowhere. If this is a limitation, at least I have stated it. It cannot be otherwise.

Besides, I think that the question of inter-Abrahamic relationships is about to become, if it is not already, a divisive issue within the Christian ecumenical conversation itself. In fact it could soon become the central issue. Christian ecumenists had better be ready for this encounter. Indeed I suspect that the fact that interreligious issues have been in the room for some time, yet insufficiently recognized programmatically up to now,[1] accounts in part for the sense of theological and organizational malaise one feels across much of the Christian world. We have not truly seriously approached the challenge of religious pluralism in a common search for understanding. The inquiry I am making in this book could help lead to what I have called "the next ecumenism" in which such an effort would be made. This would mean not

merely a new subject-matter for ecumenical conversation but an approach to
what Christian theology in a pluralistic world now needs to be and seems at
present so ill-equipped to become.

One way to probe this sense of shortcoming and malaise is to ask where
one's own faith tradition, conventionally understood, begins to seem inadequate to the challenges around it. One starts with situations in which familiar
formulas seem less and less persuasive. Musing on these things, I remember
a byword spoken years ago by my former mentor, the scripture scholar W.D.
Davies: "When you find yourself stuck, try enlarging your categories." This
was the advice that "W.D." would give his students as we struggled to find
our way through the complexities of biblical interpretation. When insights
cease to come, he implied, when arguments seem to be losing their traction,
we should suspect that the paths being followed are too narrow for us to
avoid muddy patches and ruts, whether inherited or of our own making. We
should consider reframing our projects in larger landscapes.

Whether or not certain Christian theological projects today literally
qualify as "stuck" is for those involved to say. Some are and some are not.
But it does seem that Christians (and others as well) are almost paralyzed by
a number of diversionary internal debates that seem to defy resolution. Too
many of our fields of contention seem bogged down in political and cultural
polarization. To suggest enlarging categories to take in new horizons may in
fact be an unwelcome suggestion to many battlers who draw energy from
their struggles and do not want to see them end too soon. And I certainly
do not think that seeking a responsibility covenant among Abrahamic communities will solve many, if any, of the problems wracking our communities
from within. Many of these internal questions are, after all, worth contesting
because they are both theologically and humanly important. But the initiative
I am suggesting might nevertheless divert the attention of some of the combatants to wider horizons for pursuing their continuing concerns. It could
certainly raise new points of contention, leading to still more comprehensive
struggles between those willing to entertain proposals such as this one and
those abhorring the very idea. The resulting fracas could help resolve many
of today's dilemmas simply by dwarfing them. It could also help dramatize
what is truly at stake as we struggle to understand what it means to be people
of faith in a world such as ours.

All well and good. But what justification can there be for a book that
covers so much territory as this one tries to do? Few people know enough
to be confident in bringing so many concerns together, and I am not one of
them. I am in awe of the learning of specialists in the many fields on which
this book touches, and I have freely drawn on their work. But I also think that
our time needs attempts at synthetic thought, so long as these efforts do not

overreach. As Rebecca Chopp has recently said, "The twenty-first century may be about disassembling information, but it is always and everywhere about recreating. Synthesizing will be as important as the specialization of knowledge which has dominated since the 1950s."[2] One *can see some* things better by standing back from them instead of being constantly up close with a magnifying glass.

A word is needed about my use of the terms "I" and "we." I was once taught that such words should be sparingly, if ever, used in formal writing. But it has seemed wiser to indicate straightforwardly that these pages contain what "I" have come to think about the matters concerned. I feel a personal responsibility for these opinions and their possible consequences. I want to acknowledge that fact throughout. But who, then, do I mean by the "we" who appear from time in this account? Writers can be notoriously vague about the reference of this word. I use it here most often simply to mean "we human beings," indicating my strong feeling that "we" share, as Hannah Arendt put it, a common "human condition."[3] There exists today a certain comradeship among contemporary cosmopolitans who wrestle with similar scientific, governmental and economic problems around the world. "We" also today face certain common threats to life. In these ways, at least, humanity is one. But "we" human beings are also deeply divided along lines of gender, race, class, nationality, religion, and many other factors. Many fellow travelers on this planet will not easily consent to being included in any "we" spoken by me. They will articulate their own sense of "we." So, when I use this word, I use it both cautiously and hopefully, knowing its limitations but looking forward to the "covenantal humanism" with which my argument concludes.

I am indebted to many colleagues who have helped me, as well as to organizations at whose meetings I have given papers anticipating these chapters and learned much from the ensuing discussions. It is not by accident that the scholars from whom I have learned most on this long journey have been two Orthodox Rabbis, Peter Ochs and Jonathan Sacks, two Muslim imams, Farid Esack and Rashied Omar, and a Christian ethicist concerned with pluralism and "theological humanism," William Schweiker.

I single out Rabbi Sacks for special mention because his book, *The Dignity of Difference* (Continuum, 2002), combines a clear vision of the way political and economic forces have set faiths against one another with what I have called making space for the "Other" at the heart of our own religious identities. This book, as I read it, urges a step beyond "interreligious dialogue" as we have known it by being a call for mutual moral commitment. The Abrahamic faiths can thereby recover their identities, ceasing to fight against one another and beginning to struggle, this time together, for the integrity of the human race in the modern age.

Many other sources and influences have also flowed into this work. While offering a very great deal that is new, the present book includes thoroughly reconsidered versions of materials that first saw the light of day in previous writings of mine. I mention my paper "Faith, Ethics, and Civil Society," given at the 1995 Consultation on Theology and Civil Society sponsored by the Evangelische Akademie, Loccum, Germany, published in *Loccumer Protokolle* 23/95, and also published in a different form as "*Les théologiens et le débat sur la societé civile*" in *Cahiers de l'Institut Romand Pastorale*, Lausanne, Switzerland, 1996; *The Church as Moral Community* (Continuum, 1998); the lecture "Moral Hospitality for Public Reasoners" given at the Fourth Visser't Hooft Memorial Consultation under Julio de Santa Ana's direction at the Ecumenical Institute, Bossey, Switzerland, and published in *Democratic Contracts for Sustainable and Caring Societies*, edited by Lewis S. Mudge and Thomas Wieser (WCC Publications, 2000); a chapter "Ecumenical Social Thought, 1968–1998," in *A History of the Ecumenical Movement*, Vol. III, edited by John Briggs, Mercy Oduyoye, and Georges Tsetsis (WCC Publications, 2004); "Poverty and the Poor in Recent Ecumenical Social Thought" at the 2001 Cape Town, South Africa, meeting of the International Academy of Practical Theology (IAPT) and published in *Poverty, Suffering and HIV-AIDS*, edited by Pamela Couture and Bonnie J. Miller-McLemore (Cardiff Academic Press, 2003); the Graduate Theological Union "Distinguished Faculty Lecture" for 2003 titled "The Gift of Responsibility: Fostering Global Social Contracts" and published online[4]; a chapter "Covenanting for a Renewing of Our Minds: A Way Together for the Abrahamic Faiths" in Julio de Santa Ana's *Beyond Idealism: A Way Ahead for Ecumenical Social Ethics*, edited by Robin Gurney, Heidi Hadsell, and Lewis Mudge (William Eerdmans, 2006); two as yet unpublished papers given at the Society of Christian Ethics, "Conditions of Trust" (Pittsburgh, 2003), and "Practicing Parallel Hermeneutics: In Search of a Covenantal Humanism" (Miami, 2005); and finally "José Casanova on Secularization Theory" at the IAPT, Humboldt University, Berlin, 2007.[5] With two exceptions, to the best of my knowledge, none of the above material is reproduced or closely paraphrased here from publications under copyright. I thank The William B. Eerdmans Publishing Company for permission to rearrange and reframe materials from my above-mentioned essay "Covenanting for a Renewal of Our Minds" in chapters 1, 3, and 6. I thank the Continuum Publishing Corporation for permission to rework a few paragraphs from *The Church as Moral Community*, to which I hold copyright, in chapter 9.

Many colleagues helped me by commenting on parts of this book in early stages of its development. Martin Conway and Leslie Houlden scanned a primitive proposal and guided my steps in the right direction. Clare Fischer was unfailingly gracious in lending me her aid, twice acting as respondent to public lectures at the GTU: the first in 2001 on ecumenical social ethics based on my Cape Town presentation, and the second my GTU faculty lecture of November 2003. Philip Wickeri, Robert Coote and Christopher Ocker of the SFTS faculty have never failed to respond when I needed them. I also thank the Association for Religion and Intellectual Life, sponsored by the CrossCurrents Foundation under the direction of Charles Henderson, for naming me a "Coolidge Fellow" at Columbia University/Union/Jewish Theological Seminary in New York during the summer of 2004 at which time these ideas were further aired. Thanks particularly to Farid Esack, Pamela Eisenbraun, and Mark George, who commented in detail on early versions of two of my chapters. More recently, a Colloquium on Contemporary Ecclesiology sponsored by the Institute of Reformed Theology at Union Theological Seminary, Richmond, Virginia, spent much of a day discussing my work in contrast to that of Stanley Hauerwas. The materials dealt with included first drafts of several other chapters. Thanks especially to George Telford for his invitation, and to Douglas Ottati, Dawn DeVries, and Laird Stuart for their trenchant comments.

Through much of the period of writing I have also been in debt for thinking on these subjects to the members of the colloquy on "Accelerated Economic Globalization" sponsored by the WCC Ecumenical Institute led by Julio de Santa Ana with funding from the Nathan Soderblom Foundation. Thanks especially to Bob Goudzwaard, Ninan Koshy, Leopoldo Niilus, Joanildo Burity, and Heidi Hadsell.

More recently I offered chapter drafts as assigned reading for jointly taught seminars on ecumenism, globalization and ethics at the Graduate Theological Union, Berkeley, in the years 2004 to 2006. Thanks to my Newhall Fellows Tamara Nichols Rodenberg and Eileen Harrington, and my teaching colleagues Clare Fischer, Rosemary Ruether, and Philip Wickeri, as well as to our many students, for stimulating responses.

And, still more recently, colleagues in addition to those already mentioned have most helpfully commented on parts of my manuscript in the latter stages of its development or helped me with references. These have included Heidi Hadsell, John Hadsell, Karen Lebacqz, Jane Smith, Larry Rasmussen, William O'Neill, William Schweiker, Abdul Rashied Omar, Jay Rock, Marianne Farina, Hans Ucko, Thomas Best, Lukas Vischer, Monawar Hussain, William Saint, Walt Davis, Herman Waetjen, and Ingrid Creppell.

I must not forget either to mention a down-to-earth local experience that has encouraged me greatly. The Montclair Presbyterian Church of Oakland, California, in 2005 began to build relationships with the Kehilla Synagogue of Piedmont and the Northern California Islamic Center of Oakland. From these ties there has emerged a group calling itself a "Faith Trio," devoted to ongoing and ever more searching, conversations. I am grateful to be a participant in this continuing experiment. I thank Rabbi David Cooper, Imam Ali Sheikholeslami, and Pastor Karen Stokes for their colleagueship.

Finally, I want especially to mention Norman Hjelm, former Director of Fortress Press, whose initiative, support, and friendship have helped bring to birth both this and several previous writings of mine. He has done this with unfailing patience in ways too numerous to recount here but always to be thankfully remembered.

My wife, Dr. Jean McClure Mudge, with writing and film projects of her own to attend to, read parts of this book with a keen editorial eye, and responded patiently to my endless talk about problems and possibilities. She has been my comrade in the "Faith Trio" adventure, and in many other shared projects and conversations, some of which have flowed onto these pages. This book is dedicated to her in the year of our fiftieth wedding anniversary.

But the advisory burdens cheerfully borne by all these wonderful people must come to an end at some point. Once in print, I am on my own, and some readers may find what I have written controversial. All conceivable rhetorics of absolution to colleagues have been tried already. Choose the expiatory liturgy you prefer. I do absolve all those whom I have mentioned, and any I have culpably forgotten, from responsibility for what now appears in these pages.

I close these acknowledgments with words from Rabbi Sacks. He is commenting on the words of Deuteronomy 30:19: ". . . therefore choose life, that you and your descendants may live . . ."

> That is still the choice facing humankind. Will we endlessly replay the hatreds of the past? Or will we choose differently this time, for the sake of the world's children and their future? As our capacity for destruction grows, so must the generosity of our moral and spiritual imagination. I pray that this affirmation will be answered by many voices from many faiths.[6]

Certainly I understand mine as one of those answering voices. To "the dignity of difference" I respond with "the gift of responsibility." I trust that Rabbi Sacks, should he come across this book, will recognize, despite inevitable differences in perspective and method, an ally.

Lewis S. Mudge
The Graduate Theological Union, Berkeley
March 2008

Notes

1. The World Council of Churches has for years had a department dealing with inter-religious issues, headed by such excellent scholars as Stanley Samartha and Hans Ucko. But the Council has repeatedly failed to give such matters any serious programmatic centrality. The recent Ninth Assembly of the WCC (Porto Allegre, 2006) failed to take any action on the subject despite the enthusiasm of the then-moderator of the Central Committee, Catholicos Aram I of Cilicia, Lebanon, where interreligious issues are a part of daily life. The current reorganization of the Council appears to be further subordinating these concerns.

2. Rebecca Chopp, as interviewed in *Religious Studies News* for October 2007, 26.

3. Hannah Arendt, The *Human Condition: A Study of the Central Dilemmas Facing Modern Man* (New York: Anchor Books, 1959), *passim*.

4. See http://gtu.edu/news-events/events/lectures-and-addresses/distinguished-faculty-lectures/the-gift-of-responsibility-fostering-global-social-contracts.

5. "José Casanova on Secularization Theory," The International Academy of Practical Theology, Humboldt University, Berlin, March–April 2007.

6. Jonathan Sacks, *The Dignity of Difference: How to Avoid the Clash of Civilizations* (London: Continuum, 2002), viii.

Introduction

We spiritual pilgrims of the early twenty-first century live with a growing awareness of the ambiguous portents of religious pluralism in our midst. On the one hand, faith communities, and particularly the "Abrahamic" ones, have found or currently find themselves convulsed with various forms of both internal and intercommunal violence. Some of these religious groups are prematurely acting out their own eschatological narratives. Others are allowing themselves to be caught up in the ambitions of competing national, cultural, or economic interests. Or they are doing both at the same time. On the other hand, a deepening understanding of pluralism's peaceful potential has encouraged increasingly numerous attempts to bring these faiths together for serious interaction and forms of mutual commitment. Thus we have an apparent paradox: rising levels of angry confrontation coexist with deepening dialogical relationships, if not always exactly at the same time or place or with the same participants. The resulting situation is both urgently threatening and remarkably promising.

It is hard to name any previous historical epoch in which such a combination of contrary impulses has been so salient. The same religious traditions living in the same global world at the same moment of time are producing both violent and peacemaking versions of themselves. Two distinct, yet possibly interconnected, narratives are being acted out on the world stage. Which story is the *real* story? Which is more likely to sway the long-term human future?

If one consults the media, the violent story wins out. Reporters and editors prefer news of bloody confrontations to accounts of patient efforts to foster mutual forgiveness, trust, and solidarity among the faiths. But constructive relationships among Jews, Christians, and Muslims are being built in some of the same venues where conflict is at its worst. A signal instance has been the city of Jerusalem and Israel-Palestine in general. In that fraught situation, to name just one example among many, an umbrella organization calling itself the Interfaith Encounter Association headed by a rabbi of Russian origin, Yehuda Stolov, sponsors a vast array of dialogues, debates, shared activities, public manifestations, and the like. Such gatherings go on continuously throughout this territory, involving persons of all three faiths (plus the Druze)

1

in their different ethnic versions. And this organization is far from being the only one of its kind. The numbers of events sponsored by such groups greatly exceed the number of reported terrorist incidents and retaliatory air strikes. What sort of promise—even a promise for humanity itself—could lie in such reconciling encounters in the midst of violence, not only in Israel/Palestine, but all over the Middle East and the world?

This question of promise is crucial. Do such dialogical efforts have a constructive force of history behind them? The overwhelming majority of these peacemaking activities are not self-interpreting. That is, their leaders and followers generally do not pause to ask what is going on in an "upstream" sense. They are too busy following the advice of Tariq Ramadan, a Swiss-born Muslim scholar now teaching at Oxford. He says, in effect, don't ask too many questions. Just get together and act![1] But it is important to raise the fundamental issues as Ramadan also does. In a world-historical sense, what is going on here? Do these peacemaking activities and others have any purchase on the future? Are they, in the end, the effective story of our times, or are they not? Could they carry with them the Abrahamic promise of blessing to all the families of the earth (Gen 12:3)?

Framing a Discussable Hypothesis

The purpose of this book is to offer a hypothesis capable of provoking constructive argument about what the real story is and what it means. In a world filled with religious strife, members of the Abrahamic faiths—and not only they—have been building dialogical and practical relationships. They have built on, and moved beyond, history-of-religions scholarship, beyond dialogues about practices and beliefs, beyond mutual spiritual exploration, even beyond internal debates about how such relationships can be justified (all of which need to continue), to various kinds of substantive ongoing relationships that involve specific mutual responsibilities and commitments. These pages seek to construct a frame of reference for understanding what is going on, in world-historical terms, in such relationships. But the number of these committed intercommunal links is by now so great, their situations so various, and their perspectives and methods so diverse that no single conceptual framework for understanding them just jumps out from the data. So I will try to explore the question of their underlying promise by exploring what conditions, what attitudes, what presuppositions may be functioning to make such underlying relationships between the Abrahamic faiths *possible* in such a world as this. I will try to make my findings "discussable," in that participants in these relationships will find my questions relevant and my responses to them plausible, and hence appropriate for serious consideration, even if they prefer other interpretations of the same phenomena. Along the way, I will draw on the results of my inquiries to suggest elements for a shared agenda that, properly adapted and appropriated, could give these inter-Abrahamic relationships more promising direction and bite.

By conditions of possibility I do not mean such things as formulas of doctrinal agreement or a rise of religious syncretisms. Rather I mean the mostly unspoken but very real qualities or principles of intercommunal relationship that, however variously they may be grounded in the different traditions, make possible ongoing mutual commitments across continuing difference. Such assumptions do not often find their way into organizational by-laws or programmatic projections. The sorts of language, the kinds of subject matter, actually in use in these relationships is so dependent on who the participants are and on the concrete contexts they face that it does not seem feasible to treat the language of any single dialogical situation as normative. Our postmodern sensibilities in any case militate against any such generalizing efforts. But one can ask, both from inside and from outside such contextual conversations, what fundamental background assumptions are needed to make such relationships practically possible. And, looking toward the future, one can also ask whether these relationships point to some larger historical agenda whose full significance is yet to appear. Probing assumptions and possibilities in this manner could lead to a cross-culturally discussable hypothesis, even if it too can only be stated in different religiously situated ways.

I will try to show that such commitments as those described arise because those involved find themselves gifted and motivated by a sense of shared responsibility to one another and to the world. In the case of the Abrahamic faiths, this means responsibility *to* a covenantal promise of blessing to humanity, of the sort described in Genesis 12:1–3 and its several parallels (Gen 18:18, 22:18, 26:4, 28:14; Acts 3:25; Gal 3; and less exact, that is, more originally conceived, Qur'anic echoes). Members of each of the three faiths living in mutual relationships are able to *recognize* such a gift of responsibility to covenant in the lives and traditions of those of the other faiths. In no way am I speaking of agreed theological formulae. I am speaking of mutual recognition of a certain resonance across cultural and religious difference that is a sign of the presence of such a gift of responsibility that each can understand in his or her own way, just as the different "families of the earth" come to "bless themselves" in ways corresponding to their own traditions of faith.

But two questions immediately arise. First, why is it important to reflect— and in academic terms no less—about all this? Why do we need a *theory* about what is already happening? Is not the fact of such growing relationships enough? Will such relationships not grow and prosper, as they have up to now, without any such "upstream" analysis? In fact, might not inter-Abrahamic communities more easily prosper without the too obviously professorial analysis of their relationships that I am proposing? Quite possibly so. But I think, in the midst of such diversity on the ground, that it is useful to offer a conceptual model aiming to account for what already seems to be going on in order to be able to offer a model for assumptions that might be needed to steer its future flourishing—in short, a model for a conscious agenda. A purely descriptive account of different inter-Abrahamic relationships would also be worthwhile. In fact, this sort of thing is already available in several different forms. But that is not what I am trying to provide here. Put it this way: if the relationships we are trying to account for should unaccountably cease, might we not suspect that certain formerly present assumptions or attitudes accounting for their possibility had also ceased to exist? And we could not ask or answer this question without having named, in some language or other, the assumptions we thought had been present in the first place. In short, those actively involved in what is going on, including the present writer, need conceptual resources, however tentative, for discerning and naming the meaning of all this interfaith activity.

And there is a second fundamental question needing at least a provisional answer. Given the kind of analysis I am proposing, why not include faiths other than the Abrahamic ones? I am well aware of the riches for humankind offered by the Hindu, Buddhist, Confucian, and many other religious cultures. I do not mean to denigrate any of them by omission. But the three Abrahamic faiths have characteristics that urge us to ask what their new relationships might mean and what they might do together for such a world as this. These faiths have been among the worst religious troublemakers through the centuries. Just to achieve a world without their involvements in religio-political violence would be more than well worth doing. But the fact that these three faiths are historically interrelated and look to overlapping scriptures strongly suggests that there is potential, some of it already beginning to be realized, among them for something new, for what Hannah Arendt calls "natality,"[2] to arise on the stage of history. Already many Jews, Christians, and Muslims are working in various ways to bring this about. This book seeks to join this ongoing conversation and to make a distinctive contribution to it by asking what it means that the conversation is going on at all and seeking to discern where it might lead.

Constructive theology has of late been insufficiently engaged with the problems of modernity in a religiously pluralistic world: one in which much that is vital to faith itself is radically threatened. Reaching out and deciphering the evidence for this, we find that Jews and Muslims, as well as others too, are grappling with many of the same issues that face Christians. The forms taken by these questions are inevitably diverse, but not mutually incommensurable or incommunicable. Facing similar dilemmas about the nature of their being-in-the-world, these communities, particularly the Abrahamic ones, have so much in common that it becomes inconceivable that they would willingly continue to wrestle in isolation. It is time for the different religious traditions to reach out to connect together with the human condition in each particular situation where they live, and, in doing so, to connect with one another.

What kind of a common theological project would this likely to be? It would not be a simple matter of accommodating our thinking to "the spirit of the age." Nor would it be a simple theological postmodernism either, determined to undermine secular certainties in the interest of letting every flower, including theological flowers, bloom. Rather it would be a shared effort to bring newly recovered and appreciated traditions to bear on modernity's self-betrayals without seeking to translate religious messages totally into modernity's categories. Postmodernism has placed theology in a position to do this, so long as we do not forget that modernity is still with us as a material and spiritual culture that has deeply shaped our identities and continues to do so.

For two centuries and more, most religious responses to modernity have been either self-protective or apologetic in nature. Nearly all of these responses have been worked out within the limits of particular religious traditions struggling to survive the onslaughts of secularism, either intellectually or institutionally or both. But today these relationships have changed. Religion as such, however defined, has made a significant comeback in the public world, even as religious communities are being forced to recognize the reality of radical pluralism among themselves, even as different faiths jostle for position and preferment in myriad public arenas. And modernity as such, having ridden high, is now, as we have said, deeply troubled as its economic engines fuel divisive political ambitions and broadly ignore the welfare of persons and cultures.

Yet modernity has helped to bring Western religious consciousness to a point at which serious interaction between faith traditions is conceivable. The historical-critical method has saved many of us from fundamentalism and exclusivism. This same method has helped us see the appropriate response to the scriptural promise of universal blessing as at least in part a human enterprise subject to the false starts, mistakes, and distortions of all things earthly. Entering responsibly into the actual history of responses to this gift convinces us that we in our generation need to enter this process alongside Abrahamic companions who are now trying to do the same thing. Such a perspective, of course, now includes the use of human-science resources—those of sociology, anthropology, political philosophy, and the like—to illumine the character of our religious origins and our religious prospects. Many prophetic oracles and gospel parables, for example, take on new meaning when they are studied with a knowledge of ancient Near Eastern agricultural economics and the debt-system of Palestine in the time of Jesus. Modern hermeneutical attitudes, moreover, illumine the ways in which texts take on new meanings in their passage through different conditions and cultures on their way to contemporary readers.

The postmodern critique of Western consciousness has in turn liberated such texts and their interpretations from having to justify themselves before the secular thought-police. Religious affirmations can now be what they want to be, while simultaneously exercising the inner freedom to reach out toward the affirmations of other faiths. Critical methods—perspectives that have helped us see our interpretative responsibilities as fallible historical beings—are now subject to questioning about their own pretensions to finality. The claims of human language to be able to grasp reality independent of itself have themselves been called in question. Modernity's achievements for human well-being are being justly celebrated even as its secular certainties and absolutist reasoning styles are under challenge. This means that scriptural narratives of all three faiths have their own validity simply by being what they are, without submitting to any extraneous logical or epistemological claims.

This book's argument displays a number of these modern and postmodern traits. It stands apart from modernity to find leverage for helping to save modernity from itself. It sees religious texts not merely as products of social-historical circumstances, but also as worlds of discourse within whose unique "logics" we can come to live and act. It puts a premium on practices rather than propositions as carriers and conveyors of religious truth. It learns from Emmanuel Lévinas that faith resists ideological "totalization" and that ethics is "first philosophy."[3]

Yet, all this said, we continue to live in the epoch we call "modernity," our name for the stage of history we are all passing through. I mean by this the whole material and cultural civilization that has followed on the Enlightenment, now more obviously religiously pluralist than ever before. Modernity does not look the same everywhere, but its manifestations are linked together economically and communicatively so that, for better or worse, it is rapidly creating a single global civilization. The achievements of modernity are great, but its injustices and other shortcomings are enormous as well—so much so that the latter threaten to undermine the very conditions of religious freedom and flourishing, not to speak of broadly shared human well-being. We need to criticize this modernity simultaneously with defending its best features.

In sum, then, we owe thanks to the historical-critical method that has saved, and continues to save us from literalism. We owe thanks to postmodern critique for insight into the power of sacred texts to be what they are and to speak for themselves, as well as insight into the communicative power of practices understood to function like texts to be interpreted. We owe thanks to modernity itself for maintaining the freedoms and material conditions needed for all this to happen. To another of my mentors, Paul Ricoeur, who honored all these perspectives and built bridges among them, we owe thanks for his emphasis on the power of symbol and metaphors, for the sense that these things mediate realities of a kind that can be shared.

The proposed common inquiry into presuppositions in the hope of finding an agenda will inevitably pose a challenge to each faith to rethink the *way* it holds its animating beliefs, including core affirmations. Such rethinking of the manner of believing for our time is already happening. Many responsible religious leaders and thinkers (I think of Rabbi Jonathan Sacks) now seem ready to reframe at least one core presupposition: the application of the Platonic-Aristotelian law of contradiction where religious language is concerned. More and more of us refuse to believe now that if our own formulations of faith are "true," all formulations that appear to say something different must then be "false." Some of us are abandoning religious exclusivism not only as contrary to the nature of faith language as such (powerfully symbolic and metaphoric, not literally descriptive), but also as contrary to the substantive convictions that our faith languages seek to express.

Such questions would not have been even formulable at the heart of Christian (or any other) faith without years of history-of-religions scholarship, interreligious information sharing and exchanges of friendship. But such a query clearly makes a new demand on us. This demand constitutes the essence of the critical moment in which we now live and to which we need to be alert.

The "Gift of Responsibility" as Pivotal Category

I have introduced the idea that the new relationships among the Abrahamic faiths can be understood in the light of a shared, if incompletely expressed, presupposition: that they have a common gift of responsibility to a shared covenantal promise to one another and to humanity. It will be well to dwell for a moment more on what I take this to mean. What, in a world created, redeemed, and being brought to its fulfillment by God (to speak in Christian terms), is it the responsibility of human beings to be and to do? Scripture sees this capacity for responsibility as a gift before it is a task, as a gift in order for it to be a calling. I am aware, of course, of the paradoxical significance of the notion of "gift" in the work of Jacques Derrida.[4]

The notion of responsibility has been seen by some as the threshold of ethics generally. To be responsible is first of all to identify oneself with one's own acts or deeds: to "own up" as the saying goes. But there are other definitions. An enormous literature exists on this subject, some of which will be touched upon in the pages ahead.[5] But a few directional indications can be given now. "Being responsible," for example, sometimes is taken to mean endorsing social gradualism, going slow, having patience, conforming to common wisdom, acceding to entreaties from authorities not to rock the boat. It also sometimes is taken to mean planning the lives of people deemed incapable of caring for themselves (i.e., taking on the "white man's burden"). Or it sometimes represents a demand that others "shape up," i.e., reasoning that people are poor because they do not manage their lives better than they do, and insisting that they do so before being helped (i.e., "self-reliance" as a conservative mantra). Or a notion of responsibility may be derived from its often forgotten tie to human rights, as when one speaks of "rights and responsibilities." This thought can turn "rights" into something one *earns* by being "responsible," whatever that means, instead of something God-given with the evolutionary emergence of self-conscious personal agency. Or one can say that being responsible is being accountable to humankind for wrongs that have been done in the name of religion through the ages. This last insight comes closer to my point.

The core of the responsibility theory at work in this book derives from the story of a particular actor, Abraham, the patriarch of all three "Abrahamic" faiths. The notion of Abrahamic, rather than mere arbitrary, responsibility runs throughout the argument and is elaborated in a variety of ways. In many of these ways it is an example of enlarging the usual categories of ancient thought and of our own thinking as well. Abraham is the model of responsibility before God in ways that go beyond the usual meanings of the word, i.e., doing one's assigned tasks, being accountable, bringing one's integrity and competency to handling complex challenges. It is not that Abraham is represented as free of personal moral flaws. In the Hebrew account, he lies about Sarah to Abimelech, calling her his sister (Gen 20), and summarily sends away "the sons of his concubines," separating them geographically, "eastward to the east country," from Isaac and his line (Gen 25:6). But Abraham also undertakes responsibilities never before given in any job description for a nomad chieftain of the ancient Middle East. He extraordinarily helps foreign monarchs make peace with one another. Furthermore I will argue that in Genesis 22 (the *Akedah* or "binding and unbinding of Isaac") he comes to grasp that his responsibility is not to obey what he can only receive as a sheer, irrational command. It is, rather, responsibility to a gift: the gift of a promise to him and his descendants. And hence he comes to know that true obedience to God requires him responsibly to exercise the gift of discernment of what obedience requires.

He must ask himself what is the real nature of this gift, and what it calls on him to do.

As Walter Brueggemann puts it, obedience to "the demand of YHWH" confers on Israel "a responsibility, given in the same breath, given in this initial utterance of generosity."[6] This is the "gift of responsibility" to be discerned at the origin of all three Abrahamic faiths. Taking on such responsibility is included in the scope of appropriate human response to the divine command. We are summoned to do those things that make us free to be instruments of the promise of "blessing" extended to all human beings. In the Abrahamic scriptures, this "blessing" is both an act of giving and a gift that conveys the responsibility to be what we will be, in ourselves and for others. The Israelite father (yes, these texts are very patriarchal) affirms the son's (or, we say daughter's) responsibility to fulfill the covenant promise that is in him or her. The giving and receiving of blessing confer a deep well-being that, far from being an esoteric religious state, is thoroughly understandable in terms of common human experience. It is food and drink, it is "blessings of the breast and of the womb," again a sexist image (Gen 49:25). Above all it is the blessing of being *capable,* of being able to fulfill human purposes that can be fruitfully shared for the deep well-being of everyone.

What the philosophers of the Enlightenment thought was a calling they could take over from traditional institutions and *reinvent* by refashioning the human essence according to rational principles turns out, as interpreted here, to be a responsibility already *given* to human beings in the evolution of their nature to the point of self-conscious agency. This is responsibility for building the blessed or beloved community. The gift already given is the blessing of *having* such a responsibility, together with the "capabilities" (see Amartya Sen and Martha Nussbaum, whose work I consider in chapter 9)[7] needed for fulfilling it.

In this vision, extended and developed, lies the promise: the possibility that the three Abrahamic faiths can come to comparable, compatible (although far from identical) interpretations of the gifts of worldly responsibility for sharing blessing that they have received, while maintaining their own traditional understandings of the divine authority that has given them such a gift. The exercise of this divine gift of responsibility is the appropriate in-depth response to God's summons to obedience or "submission."

Among the requirements of realizing this Abrahamic responsibility for blessing of the human community is the need responsibly to interpret sources, words, and actions *in the presence of one another.* Abrahamic responsibility becomes the key constant or touchstone of this interpretative process. Much more is involved than the interpretation of *written* texts. Scholars such as Paul Ricoeur and Clifford Geertz, as well as semioticists such as Roland

Barthes, have shown that our words, actions, cityscapes, monuments, and all the rest are textlike: subject to interpretations that have consequences.[8] Our behavior with one another and toward the human world depends very much on how we read one another's words and actions, and on how we present our own actions to be interpreted. The opportunities for mutual misinterpretation are enormous, and we have responsibility as human beings to strive to understand one another.

It makes a difference, for example, if we are interpreting our own texts alongside others who are interpreting their texts in relation to ours. Such a situation warrants a higher than usual demand for integrity and attention to the consequences of what we say our scriptures mean. The mere fact that interpretation is done together with mutual responsibility for integrity and attention to consequences is vital to our argument. We need also to admit the difficulties we encounter, to acknowledge to one another the lines of argument that do not work out as we had hoped. I will develop the notion of "parallel and interactive hermeneutics" (meaning interpretation done together) of ancient texts and of contemporary patterns of symbolic communication among our three faiths as a resource for reconstructing the ancient scriptural notion of covenant. To live in "covenant" is to live in a community of mutually communicated expectations, including responsibility to God's expectation for all.[9]

The responsibility agenda at the heart of this book thus summons Abrahamic scriptural interpreters into the center of today's debates over human purposes and meanings. Those who live by the conviction that their responsibility to humanity is a divine gift could possibly make the difference between a modernity apparently bent on self-destruction and a modernity purged and preserved to bless us on the way to the achievements of tomorrow.

A Synopsis of the Argument by Chapters

Part I of the book, comprising chapters 1 through 4, seeks to characterize the potential of inter-Abrahamic discourses in relation to "what is going on" in the modern world.

Chapter 1 begins with a critical tour of the landscape. It explores the present situation with regard to the Abrahamic faiths and their relationships. These faiths, given the violent ways some interests among them have behaved over centuries and continue to do so today, seem unlikely sources from which to expect serious contributions to human well-being. Too much mutual enmity, too much violence, too many exclusive claims, seem to mark their public profiles. Yet many Jews, Christians, and Muslims long for their faiths to mean something positive to humankind. This chapter seeks to show how that yearning might be fulfilled. A century of interreligious dialogue has created conditions which could help. But such dialogue has raised new questions *within* religious communions. A recent World Council of Churches conference[10] has called this a "critical moment" in relations among the faiths. The need is to move from useful dialogue to a common agenda: to bring out of all this talk some sense of a common way forward.

Yet in seeking such a way we become aware of the enormous complexity of each of these religious traditions, and hence the enormous complexity of such a task. Which Jews, Christians, and Muslims are we talking about? An increasingly large class of persons from all three faiths, people whom Kwame Anthony Appiah calls "rooted cosmopolitans,"[11] seem suited to be carriers of the emerging agenda we need. With what sort of proposition could they be approached? The Abrahamic faiths have a vital scriptural resource in common, namely the Abram-Abraham traditions that mark out their common origins. These passages are traditionally interpreted by our three faiths in different, yet overlapping, ways. This chapter's intuition is that these "rooted cosmopolitans," if challenged, will interpret the Abraham stories in new, not quite traditional, ways corresponding to their experience of living in secular yet religiously pluralistic worlds. Their new interpretations will move them away from literal obedience to scriptural commands toward the possibility of responsible obedience as a divine gift. This would mean that God gives human beings a capacity for grasping the underlying point of such commands and for actively living out their larger meanings: I will show that this could well be the direction taken by cosmopolitan readings of the call to covenanting in Genesis 12:1–3, and of Genesis 22, the *Akedah* or "binding" or, better, the *unbinding* of Isaac. Abraham may have been the first genuinely "rooted cosmopolitan," moving from being a typical Bedouin chieftain (but not forgetting what that meant) to being the father of "blessing" to "all the families of the earth."

Chapter 2 develops some contemporary implications of these findings. It traces religion's increasing "publicness" in the contemporary world, and suggests that this may offer opportunities for rooted cosmopolitans to become long-term instruments of Abrahamic "blessing" or deep human well-being. Modernity makes claims of its own to confer blessing, as economic, educational, medical, and other forms of globalization bid fair to create the first genuinely global community. Yet, paradoxically, there is a high price to be paid for these achievements. Religious protests against injustice are negated in the common mind by religiously generated strife. Public religions seem bent on getting control of polities and cultures, whether in Afghanistan or in Middle America. Religious assaults on the findings of science are seen as threatening to take us back to the premodern, if not the "Dark Ages." In this situation we may well reconsider the striking thesis put forward by the sociologist José Casanova: that religion might paradoxically prove to be a more effective carrier of Enlightenment promises than Enlightenment institutions themselves, institutions that have often betrayed such promises.[12]

Casanova's hypothesis is based on a number of elegant case studies, largely of Roman Catholicism in relation to governments and other secular institutions in the late 1980s. These studies are suggestive for our purposes. Yet they can be faulted on a number of counts. The question is whether they nonetheless provide models for rooted cosmopolitans who seek to take responsibility for promoting human well-being in late modernity. To do this, Casanova says, religious groups need to have internalized the "Enlightenment critique of religion,"[13] which I interpret as meaning adopting an historical consciousness in which people of faith are responsible to one another and to the world around them. How might an "enlightened" Abrahamic, yet cosmopolitan, religious consciousness help to make possible such a redemption of modernity's self-betrayals? Several possible models are considered.

To answer this question more fully, we must go deeper into how Western culture got to be the way it is. This is the work of chapter 3. What, exactly, is modernity's self-betrayal? How did it happen? The essence of the Enlightenment was a human determination to "take responsibility"—away from traditional institutions—for a project of remaking human nature and community along rational lines. The key notion was "autonomy." We enlightened human beings decide who and what we will be, and are confident that we have the resources to make ourselves so. It is often forgotten, however, to what an extent the emergence of Enlightenment consciousness took place within and was beholden to an ongoing religious culture and among continuing religious institutions. John Locke's *Second Treatise on Civil Government* and Ernst Becker's *Heavenly City of the Eighteenth-Century Philosophers* both show how this was so from the seventeenth through much of the eighteenth century. In a different and less obviously confessional way, so does Adam Smith in his *Theory of Moral Sentiments*. The Enlightenment theme of autonomy was saved from being self-destructive by being wrapped in conscience maintained through religious teachings. When the power of these teachings declined, autonomous reasoning gradually transformed itself into today's cost-benefit analyses and "rational choice theory."

The result is that we have a global political and economic world driven by competitive ideological values rather than by concern for the well-being of human life. Religious traditions have been co-opted to legitimate violence whose purpose is to achieve competitive advantage in global struggles. Secular moralists struggle with these questions, but seem to find virtually no agreement as to sources or method. A host of resistance groups, non-government organizations and the like, are at work on various aspects of the problem.

What could Abrahamic responsibility, as exercised by Jewish, Christian, Muslim, and other cosmopolitans, mean in such a world? We are here on the brink of deepening the very idea of responsibility: from routine responsibility, which means simply doing one's job, to complex responsibility (i.e., management), which means dealing with many interacting factors all at once, to transcendental responsibility, which I interpret to mean taking on that which is no individual's or institution's responsibility as culturally understood but yet urgently needed to fulfill the obligations that now go with human capabilities. The demands of transcendental responsibility thereby generate the ultimate conditions of possibility for ethics as such. Such responsibility reaches out across categories and expectations to think what has not been thought before, to do what has not been done before. It is the capacity for transcendental responsibility that is the divine gift, Enlightenment thinkers supposed that they needed to "take" responsibility away from "tutelage" by traditional institutions. Now, ironically, we say that responsibility is, and always was, not something to be grasped, but a free gift beyond ordinary human capabilities. Now it is indispensable for saving today's modernity from itself. Transcendental responsibility is based not only on analysis and reasoning. Our understanding of it is also based on religious narratives of risky commitment. God's conventionally understood will is defied in favor of deeper conceptions of God. Adam eats of the fruit of the tree of the knowledge of good and evil. Noah believes the rainbow sign. Abraham transcends his culture's legitimation of divine commands received in dreams, in this case the command to cut Isaac's throat, because God, by providing the sacrificial ram, gives him the possibility of responsible wide-awake choice.

But what about actual instances of Jews, Muslims, and Christians acting together to address the forms of irresponsibility that are eating away at modernity's well-being and undermining its future? Chapter 4 offers three examples of inter-Abrahamic coalitions that have attempted to do something about this. These cases describe (a) the rise of Islamic, Christian, and to a minor extent Jewish, liberation theologies in the struggle against apartheid in South Africa, as interpreted by the Sunni Muslim imam, Farid Esack; (b) Abrahamic groups exploring "scriptural reasoning" for the repair of modernity's failed logics, as interpreted by the Orthodox Jewish scholar and rabbi Peter Ochs; and (c) modern "reflexive" cultures in which faiths continuously influence one another by being challenged to affirm a "hermeneutical realism" as a riposte to moral relativism that affirms self-cultivating individualism combined with the pursuit of power, as interpreted by the Christian theological ethicist William Schweiker. Why these instances in particular? Most of the many cases of inter-Abrahamic commitment with which this book is concerned are preoccupied with the contextual human concerns that have brought them together and devote little or no time to theological reflection as such. These three cases stand out because in each case the interpreter combines action and reflection, taking full part in the activity in question *and* interpreting it in an illuminating conceptual framework. Our interpreters are chosen not because they are accredited representatives of their faiths, but because they offer their own fascinating frames of reference for understanding what is going on around them. Their views probably do *not* reflect majority opinion in the communities from which they come. Rather they seek to understand the new thing that in their view is happening as their faiths encounter one another over common human concerns.

Furthermore, each of these studies addresses only one form of modernity's betrayal of its promise among many that could have been chosen. Each, while grasping the whole human picture, does so through only one of many possible conceptual lenses. These cases and interpretations differ markedly from one another. One wonders whether they represent a single phenomenon in many guises or a collection of apples, oranges, and persimmons. But there are significant shared insights that seem to apply across the board. Such insights have to do with (a) the manner of responsibly interpreting scriptural sources; (b) the manner of interpreting our responsibilities to one another; and (c) the manner of interpreting the public situations in which we live and the meaning of our actions with reference to them. These are "hermeneutical" concerns, one and all. Whatever our situation or our ways of understanding, we are dealing, in some form, with a parallel hermeneutics of interactive responsibility. The differences among our cases remain important. One cannot fasten any single template upon them. But one can ask similar questions and offer similar answers in other contexts.

Part II of the book, comprising chapters 5, 6, and 7, models contexts of three kinds for such questioning and answering. Instead of describing actual cases, these chapters offer accounts of inter-Abrahamic discourse that might be called, after Max Weber, "ideal-typical."[14] They offer tentative models for dialogue. Actual dialogues would inevitably differ in the light of contexts, issues, and participants.

Chapter 5 opens the discussion, foregrounding the practice of reading our overlapping Abrahamic scriptures together. Interpretation of sources, from whatever perspective, is fundamental to worldly action. This is as true of suicide bombers such as Mohammed Atta as it is for those with peaceful intentions. I choose, once again, the Abraham narratives, but this time to open up the profound differences of perspective in which the three faiths come to this material. The covenant with Abraham and Sarah, or Abraham and Hagar, to bring forth descendants through whom the families of the earth will find "blessing" (Gen 12:1–3 and parallels) and the *Akedah* or binding-unbinding of Isaac (Gen 22) are again chosen, but now with full attention to the distances, as well as areas of overlap, between Jewish, Christian, and Islamic interpretations. The comparison of these interpretations does not tempt us to syncretism, but rather may lead us to changes in the ways we see ourselves as interpreting communities. We become less stiffly self-sufficient. We come to realize that scripture interpretation has always in each faith been an ongoing argument, and that the argument now begins to involve all three faiths together. Argument about the meaning of the binding and unbinding of Isaac is a prominent case in point. I have already suggested how today's "rooted cosmopolitans" may interpret this passage as signifying the move from rote obedience to obedience as worldly responsibility. But such an interpretation, or any other, becomes illegitimate if it is not seen as part of the long history of hermeneutical arguments in each tradition, becoming now an interfaith argument. Questioning and answering lies *inside* scripture as well as in arguments *about* scripture. And we citizens of modernity are not the only questioners. But we see that our questioning of scriptural meanings today has to do with the meaning of our responsibility to the Abrahamic promise. If this be true for ancient Israel, it is equally true for today's Judaism, Christianity, and Islam.

Then, with chapter 6, the discussion turns to the ethical-relational yield of such parallel-hermeneutical study. Groups devoted to such study take on characteristics of the institutional arrangements—graduate schools, seminaries, congregations, movements, organized intellectual projects—that support or make room for them. But such publicly available self-understandings quickly prove inadequate for either containing or conveying these dialogues' deeper subject matter. The covenantal gifts of responsibility that the texts associate with the stories of Noah and Abraham, Hagar and Sarah, Ishmael and Isaac also govern the emerging relationships among the dialoguers themselves. Certain "covenantal virtues" are needed, behind the institutional settings as it were, for such dialogues to begin, continue, and succeed.

I frame the needed virtues in gerund-based expressions: giving and receiving forgiveness, fostering conditions of trust, and acting in mutual solidarity. These expressions employ words that belong today in the vocabularies and patterns of understanding of Western languages. They are indispensable in those roles, but each of them also, when pressed to say more, runs into what philosophers call *aporias,* places where the processes of rational explanation lose their way. Writers such as Jacques Derrida, Adam Seligman, Emmanuel Lévinas, and Paul Ricoeur in different ways help us understand these limitations in the transparency of meaning. Forgiveness in modernity tends to stop at being amnesty or pardon, trust is watered down into "system confidence" or calculated risk, and solidarity becomes only strategic alliance. Words so reduced in reference need to be rejoined with meanings derived from scriptural sources. It is such scriptural derivations that justify such relationships being called "covenantal."

But the writers and redactors of Abrahamic scriptures and traditions did not have our modern problems in mind. Merely consulting our roots does not bring about the dynamic bilingualism we need. To realize a covenantal social reality in with and under our given empirical social realities requires not merely exegesis of ancient texts but theologically constructive hermeneutics, understood in the Ricoeurian sense of exploring the new action-worlds our texts, read today, open up for us. Into our *given* understandings of social reality, borrowed to make our dialogues practically possible, we bring the *gifts* of responsibility to promise. The social givens of modernity, as we have argued, need the gifts that covenantal communities can give them in order to not to self-destruct from irresponsible use of our modern scientific, industrial, economic, and military capabilities.

The social locations in which covenantal gifts of responsibility can begin to help save our social-structural givens from such self-destruction themselves belong to what political philosophers call "civil society." Chapter 7 discusses how Abrahamic thinkers, as well as modern philosophers, view this notion, seeking to imagine what could happen if such Abrahamic covenantal communities, functioning in civil society and sustained by the covenantal virtues of forgiveness, trust, and solidarity, could contribute something to fostering just social contracts in society at large. Both "civil society" and "social contract" are familiar notions in Western political thought. The Abrahamic faiths have been exposed to these Western notions in different degrees and in different ways befitting their diverse historical experiences. But now there is need for a global, yet inwardly diverse, civil order or polity. The notions of civil society and social contract need broad religious, as well as philosophical, justifications. To what extent can Judaism, Christianity, and Islam begin to internalize the philosophical questions in order to add religious understandings that will help them participate productively in a just public order? What would such an internalization and participation mean to these faiths?

The philosopher John Rawls is author of the most widely accepted Western account of justice in the public realm. His picture combines "justice as fairness" for all with room for the "reasonable comprehensive doctrines" of different groups, whose moral visions overlap to support (but should not seek to define) the values of the public order. Dare the Abrahamic faiths come to understand their possible public contribution in Rawlsian terms? Or does Jürgen Habermas offer a superior philosophical matrix for understanding the contribution to the public world of religions in dialogue? The works of both philosophers have been subject to serious criticism as to their applicability to a pluralistic and fragmented social world. It may be that the Jewish philosopher Michael Walzer offers a more applicable picture. For him, "thin" justice principles applicable to all emerge from the interactions of "thick" traditions that know one another through reciprocal acts of moral imagination. I argue that "thin" or minimal principles can then function as "armatures," in the sculptural sense, for more filled-out communal flesh to grow on. Covenantal substance can then grow in, with, and under relationships that already belonged to all by virtue of existing social contracts, and could influence the shaping of new elements in these arrangements to meet new historical contingencies.

Part III of the book, finally, has to do with concrete and ideational consequences. Chapter 8 is a case study testing the concrete applicability of the conceptions developed throughout the volume. It asks if a cross-border presence of inter-Abrahamic covenantal communities could have helpful consequences in so difficult a situation as that of today's Israel-Palestine. I take for granted that the parameters of this situation and of the projected "peace process" are well known. I focus on the uneven presence, yet future potential, of "civil society" in these lands as they rely on international diplomacy to help them devise "social contracts" on a range of issues—borders, contiguity, refugees, security, and the like—for peace. Pockets of civic discussion that resemble the "civil society" paradigm exist in widely varying forms in both nations and between them. This is most obvious, of course, in the westernized Israeli regions of Tell Aviv, Haifa, and West Jerusalem, and less obvious in more traditional religious neighborhoods on both sides of the border. Some of these dialogue communities intentionally bring the faiths together; others are secular. Either way, they represent many distinctive arenas of ferment and potential political will. The rise of covenantally based inter-Abrahamic communities among the many other elements in the civic life of both nations could well open opportunities for peaceful social contracts to be devised and find broad support.

This study then maps the possibilities for such discourse in various sectors of both territories, also weighing the chances for cross-border civil society institutions. It also probes the strengths and weaknesses of international diplomacy as addressed to forming peaceful social and political arrangements. Real difficulties emerge in both arenas, needing the most creative sorts of solutions. We have nowhere else to turn. Undoubtedly, dialogical ties among the faiths, increasingly expressed in covenantal terms, can make things easier for the diplomats while informing them more adequately about the cultural and religious realities with which they have to deal.

Clearly a "two-state solution" offers the most promising way forward, but what does that mean? The "wall" or "security barrier" no doubt needs to remain provisionally in place, although relocated to follow the Green Line, for the sake of initial security. And the resulting diplomatic partition of the two territories may be the most that can be accomplished for the foreseeable future. But both Israel and Palestine exist in already religiously and culturally pluralistic territories. Changing that by any sort of mass population exchange (or mutual "cleansing") would bring about upheavals and recriminations. Is it possible to imagine Arab Islamic groups to grow in numbers and remain Israeli citizens, while Israeli settlers in Palestine maintain themselves and become Palestinian citizens? Or can one imagine members of both groups remaining citizens of their homelands while "living abroad"? With either understanding, the two populations will continue to be mixed. In that case, the very reality of an ongoing and growing civil society—maintaining cross-cultural, interreligious, and transborder ties—may be that which saves the "two state solution" from shipwreck. One can imagine, sometime in the future, the two nations at peace and the wall coming down.

The wall-free solution would be, humanly speaking, by far the greater achievement. Two nations, two administrations, two of everything, existing in the territory of a single interconnected civil society. Further terrorism restrained not by a wall but by the strength of growing interfaith and intercultural relationships. The whole direction of this book's argument moves toward this second possibility, while being thoroughly aware of the difficulty of achieving it.

Chapter 9, finally, considers consequences in the realm of ideas. It argues that the pursuit of parallel-interactive hermeneutical practice, with all the ramifications described, could begin to constitute a "covenantal humanism," a lived understanding of common life supporting not merely efforts to achieve an Israel-Palestine solution but also the search for a just global polity. I use the term "humanism" in such a way as to avoid implications of total secularity or godlessness. There have been, and still are, religious forms of humanism that answer to the conviction that God's purposes are for the entire human race and that different religious faiths are instruments of this purpose, yet far from being full or exclusive expressions of it. Others have developed very similar ideas, notably William Schweiker with his notion of "theological humanism." I prefer the term "covenantal humanism" because of its link to the notion of divine promise to "all the families of the earth." The word "covenantal" catches up the many interacting meanings of mutual responsibility expressed in the virtues of forgiveness, trust, and solidarity. The notion of responsibility to a covenantal promise is an eschatology, or vision of history's goals, much to be preferred to eschatologies of violence and victory found in differing ways in all three Abrahamic faiths. One can, following Lévinas, find "traces" of covenantal promise-fulfillment in the midst of life experience, and center one's interpretation of human existence around them. Still, I do not mean to *substitute* such a notion for the fullness of existing, distinctive, religious narratives. These narratives, with the communities they support, are needed to give continuing substance to the covenantal idea. "Covenantal humanism" as an idea standing alone without communal or narrative support would not stand for long.

I see this sort of humanism in contrast to the humanism of Enlightenment thinkers and their successors who conceived of themselves as reinventing humanity along autonomous lines. Theirs was a defiant humanism of self-determination over against the teachings of traditional institutions. By contrast, the notion of "blessing" or giftedness stands at the heart of the "covenantal" humanism I find to be so much more fruitful for human life. The moment at which a father (or mother) communicates God's blessing (Abraham to Isaac or Ishmael, Isaac to Jacob or Esau) is the moment a young Jewish Israelite, a young Palestinian Muslim assumes the responsibilities of adulthood and becomes an autonomous person by receiving the gift. The responsibility to be a self is *given* in this moment to the new generation, not *taken over* in an act of rebellion. Yet the resulting self, as Genesis 49 shows, is far from being rigidly or predictably determined by tradition or parental demands. The heart of the matter is "promise keeping"[15] where the promise is the great one of Genesis 12:3. This human capability needs to be added to the list of capabilities definitive of the human in the theories of Amartya Sen and Martha Nussbaum.[16] Each person's gift of promise-keeping capability, of self- and world responsibility, works itself out in a unique way. Personhood becomes a matter of *relationships* within the family and the community that unfold as the history of the community unfolds. The being of such a person is a being-to-others in ever-new situations, hence inherently "covenantal." Covenantal humanism is not based on the genetic characteristics of the human organism, nor is it an expression of our capacities for self-recreation. It concerns what the person gifted with mature responsibility has the capability of *becoming* as life goes on and relationships become richer and more complex. The human person is the one who *becomes* what he or she is to be, in communities of creative interaction contributing to the presence of God's "image" in the universe, undertaking ever more deeply the vicegerency of which Muslims speak. This human way of being thus ultimately has to do with eschatology, with citizenship among the "traces" (Lévinas) even now, of the Holy City that is to come.

But Can Thinking Such Thoughts Make a Difference?

I am about to launch, with chapter 1, into a full exposition of the argument just sketched. But it may be well to pause a moment to ask whether this exercise can possibly make a difference either for the Abrahamic communities or for the wider human spheres in the midst of which they live. Early in his career, my mentor, the philosopher Paul Ricoeur, faced a challenge from colleagues to direct his thinking toward practical results. He was surrounded by Marxists and others (and likewise by intellectual activists such as Paul Mounier, founder and editor of the journal *Esprit*), urging him to take political actions commensurate with his words. In fact, Ricoeur later on did so on many occasions. But here he speaks of following "the philosophical way of being present to my time."[17] He notes that this amounts to saying "that one need not be ashamed of being an 'intellectual' as is Valéry's *Socrates in Eupalinos*, doomed to the regret of having made nothing with his hands."[18]

I do not, myself, belong in such company. But I can resonate to Ricoeur's further thoughts:

> ...I believe that man's greatness lies in the dialectic of work and the spoken word. Saying and doing, signifying and making are intermingled to such an extent that it is impossible to set up a lasting and deep opposition between "theoria" and "praxis." The word is my kingdom, and I am not ashamed of it.[19]

One wonders today what sorts of historical experience we must now live through to harvest the possible fruits of such "saying and doing, signifying and making." This book, like every other, is written without knowing what form the human dénouement will take. These pages are intended, throughout, to offer a theory for the praxis of inter-Abrahamic responsibility in and for the human world. Its perspective will need to be tested in possibly very difficult circumstances alongside other efforts to think such matters through. But now the need is to think these particular thoughts as clearly as possible. And so we begin.

Notes

1. These words are my paraphrase of Tariq Ramadan's remarks as I heard them in conversation at the "Critical Moment" conference sponsored by the World Council of Churches, June 7–9, 2005.

2. See Hannah Arendt, *The Human Condition* (Chicago: University of Chicago Press, 1958), 10–11, 157–58.

3. Emmanuel Lévinas, *Totality and Infinity: An Essay on Exteriority,* trans. Alphonso Lingis (Pittsburgh: Duquesne University Press, 1969), and "Ethics as First Philosophy," in *The Levinas Reader,* ed. Sean Hand (Oxford: Blackwell, 1989), 75ff.

4. It is significant that the notion of "gift" is one of the ideas Derrida, late in his life, exempted (along with "justice" and "forgiveness") from his program of deconstruction. So restored, as I see it, "gift" becomes for us a transcendental idea that remains an "impossible possibility." See Derrida's *Given Time* (Chicago: University of Chicago Press, 1992) and *The Gift of Death* (Chicago: University of Chicago Press, 1995). To put the matter too simply, for this philosopher a gift ceases to be a genuine *gift* if it is involved with social conventions like acknowledgment, reciprocity, self-interest, or calculation of advantage. Yet, in ordinary human language and experience, the notion of "gift" remains encumbered with such expectations. We cannot, in this human context, access what Robert Frost called the "gift outright." Language and thought here encounter an *aporia,* i.e., a point of impasse or paradox where reasoning fails (see Chapter 6). One is tempted to say that for the genuine outright "gift" to be operative in human life it must be given by a Giver with power to break through the aporetic limitations of language and thought through some form of transforming worldly *presence.* This brings us close to the theological concept of gift as "grace," which is always in the background of my use of the word in these pages.

5. For a most helpful treatment of the theme of responsibility in relation to Christian ethics in particular, see William Schweiker, *Responsibility and Christian Ethics* (New York: Cambridge University Press, 1993).

6. Walter Brueggemann, "Law as Response to Thou," in *Taking Responsibility: Comparative Perspectives,* ed. Winston Davis (Charlottesville: University of Virginia Press, 2001), 91. Italics in the original.

7. See Amartya Sen, *On Ethics and Economics* (New York: Blackwell, 1987) and *Development as Freedom* (New York: Knopf, 1999), and Martha Nussbaum, *The Fragility of Goodness: Luck and Ethics in Greek Tragedy and Philosophy* (New York: Cambridge University Press, 2001) and *Women and Human Development: The Capabilities Approach* (New York: Cambridge University Press, 2000).

8. I mean by this that the ways we "name" our surroundings produces a metaphorization of our action-world that shapes the sorts of actions we take in dealing with that world. Derogatory speech about certain groups leads to discriminatory behavior toward them. See George Lakoff and Mark Johnson, *Metaphors We Live By* (Chicago: University of Chicago Press, 1980), and, on "framing," George Lakoff, *Moral Politics: How Liberals and Conservatives Think* (Chicago: University of Chicago Press, 2002).

9. I am well aware that the word "covenant" has different meanings in the different religious traditions. I am also aware that its signification differs in different parts of my own Christian tradition. I cannot make my argument rest on any supposed or given univocity of sense for this or any other leading idea: "gift," "responsibility," "promise," "blessing," or otherwise. Indeed, this argument has the audacity of trying to *lend* such words commensurable meanings across traditions and situations by projecting what inter-Abrahamic discourses may come to be. Such terminology can gain shared meanings in the very process of the discourses this book describes and seeks to understand.

10. I refer again to the Geneva "Critical Moment" Conference, June 7–9, 2005, involving representatives of a dozen or more world religions.

11. See Kwame Anthony Appiah, *Cosmopolitanism: Ethics in a World of Strangers* (New York: W. W. Norton, 2006).

12. See José Casanova, *Public Religions in the Modern World* (Chicago: University of Chicago Press, 1994), and the extended treatment of Casanova's thesis in chapter 2.

13. Ibid., 205.

14. The term "ideal typical" has been used to characterize Max Weber's method in *The Protestant Ethic and the Spirit of Capitalism,* trans. Talcott Parsons (New York: Charles Scribner's Sons, 1930).

15. Arendt, *Human Condition,* 219ff.

16. See Sen and Nussbaum in note 7.

17. Paul Ricoeur, *History and Truth,* trans. Charles A. Kelbley (Evanston, IL: Northwestern University Press, 1965), 5.

18. Ibid.

19. Ibid.

Part I

Abrahamic Communities and the Traumas of Modernity

1

Exploring the Lay of the Land
Searching for a Common Agenda

Can the Abrahamic faiths—Judaism, Christianity, and Islam—make any serious contribution to the well-being of a humanity now threatened by global economic aggrandizement, environmental depredation, and religiously motivated or legitimated violence, while people everywhere substitute the pursuit of personal fulfillment and the lust for power for the values of public responsibility? Many well-informed observers, including many who generally wish these religious bodies well, are currently inclined to doubt it.

These three faiths face what seem to be disabling liabilities. Whatever else they may stand for now, they appear too uncritically open to fundamentalist distortions, too engaged in games of institutional positioning and defensive efforts at self-preservation, too implicated in supplying self-righteous legitimization for conflict among competing interests and cultures, and too mesmerized by opportunities for proximity to power, to be of much use to the future of humankind. Above all, even those among their members who are most alert to such failings seem to have no coherent approach—and certainly none in common—to overcoming them.

Yet in each of these communities there are both leaders and followers who yearn for their traditions of faith to fulfill their historic destinies by coming to mean something affirmative to humankind. Such faithful ones, whether prominent or obscure, try to express their identities in acts of dual responsibility; responsibility to their religious roots and to the processes of public reason. They long for ways to be responsible *to* (not "for," which would claim too much) a vision of the future of the human race under God. They also recognize that today such a vision can only be acted out by members of Abrahamic and other faiths acting together.

But before going further, we need to pause to see the lay of the land. Before taking such an affirmation as self-evident, it is important to pause for an acknowledgment of the difficulties any such proposal must face as well as pointing to the peaceful possibilities it might foster. Religious communities thinking themselves justified by literal, unreflective obedience to selected scriptural passages have done far too much damage in the world over the centuries and continue to do so now. An agenda such as this one needs to confront some of the underlying reasons for the Abrahamic faiths' apparent paralysis in the face of, and sometimes vulnerability to being used by, the destructive forces now on the loose across the globe. I write at a moment in which little of what has just been sketched would seem likely to happen anytime soon. At the same time, constructive dialogue among Jews, Christians, and Muslims grows impressively in scope, as well as in depth of mutual commitment.

Imperial Ambitions and Religious Violence

Christian-Islamic relations remain confused and clouded by a long history beginning with the Crusades and culminating in the events of September 11, 2001. Subsequent American military adventurism in Afghanistan and Iraq, with oil supplies and political positioning as primary goals, has made matters worse. Terror bombings on commuter trains in Madrid and in the London Underground are likely to be repeated elsewhere before this book reaches print.

What lies behind these events? Two interconnected things. First, the Abrahamic faiths' seeming inability to live in peace with one another: hence the issue of religious violence. And second, the proclivity of corporations and nations to irresponsible imperial behavior that threatens the very viability and sustainability of what we call "modernity" and, in certain situations, provokes religious violence as a covert instrument of policy.

The central issue is whether such violence results mainly when religious communities are used by various political and economic interests to provide ideological cover for their purposes, or whether a tendency to violence is generated from within religious symbol systems themselves. The answer must be both. Undoubtedly religions are used by secular interests. We may wonder what makes them so vulnerable to such use. The desire to emerge from marginalization to proximity to power is a powerful motive. But the interplay in our modern world between religious and secular forces is extremely complex. Religiously motivated violence is often encouraged against the demonized opponents of given power-interests. The rage of the people is thus directed away from those who actually oppress them toward their oppressors' adversaries. What is really a matter of economic justice at home is turned into a religious crusade against the religious or cultural Other far away.

Clearly the violence is both between different faiths and between different expressions of the same faith. Examples of both are very numerous. Terrorism against Western interests by radical Islamists is rooted in economic injustice, and the sense of humiliation that goes with it, exacerbated by religious grievances. Oil-rich Saudi Arabian royalty and other Muslim elites condone such activity if they sense that it can weaken their Western competitors without destroying markets for their oil. The Jihad is allowed to go on, and Saudi schools are allowed to teach hatred of the West on religious grounds, just so long as these activities are thought to confer competitive advantages in the real game, which is political and economic.

Intra-Islamic violence has been of late even more lethal, with Iraq the prime example. Are the dynamics here the same, or different? Sunnis and Shi'a both perceive themselves to represent authentic Islam and may engage in civil war on that ground alone. But other factors are generally needed to touch off conflict. The American presence in Iraq is one such factor because it upsets the long-standing hegemony of the minority Sunnis, and supports a Shi'a-led government. But Sunnis and Shi'a also represent the power interests of Saudi Arabia and Iran respectively, and so their struggle reflects the larger geopolitics of the region, including control of oil fields. Again, proclivities to violence are already embedded in religious ideologies. But they can be fanned into flame by initiatives reflecting competitive political and economic interests.

The corresponding phenomenon in the West is hardly symmetrical, but it offers some interesting parallels. The present (2008) United States administration is interested in projecting American economic power around the globe and is willing to protect its markets and oil supplies by military means. Those who actually profit from these tactics form a very small elite of the super-rich. But the many poorly informed persons who support these policies politically, and particularly the young men and women who bear the brunt of battle, are encouraged to believe that they are on a great religious or moral crusade. George W. Bush himself is allowed to (and certainly does most earnestly) believe this, while many of his advisors probably do not.

And of course, the West is not free either of serious tension, or actual conflict, between different expressions of the same faith. Sometimes these differences cut across confessional lines. Sometimes they follow those lines. The Protestant–Roman Catholic conflict in Northern Ireland simmered for centuries with periodic outbreaks of violence. Behind the two sides, of course, were the political interests of Great Britain and the Republic of Ireland. Two generations ago, European Christians fought against one another in World War II.

All things considered, it appears that tensions between different versions of the same faith can be as great or greater than the tensions between different faiths. To be confronted by a different *version* of one's own faith can be more unsettling than being confronted by a different faith altogether. But always there are political, economic, and cultural factors that turn tensions into various forms of "ethnic cleansing" that in turn generate resentments that escalate the battles even more, inviting outside forces, often with different interests of their own, to intervene not only to help make peace but to take advantage of opportunities to broaden their spheres of influence.

The conflict between Israelis and Palestinians is a point where these internally complex Eastern and Western problematics meet. Israel is seen by Arabs as an outpost of American power competing for spoils with other powers. Israel with Western help shores up its own security by taking over Palestinian land. The Palestinians see the Israeli presence as far from being purely religiously motivated. It is, rather, seen as a military and economic occupation. But both sides are willing to exploit peoples' convictions in order to portray the conflict as one between good and evil seen in religious terms. The training of Palestinian suicide bombers is a case in point. Muslim young men and women are allowed to believe that they detonate themselves for righteousness sake when the real point is rendering the Israeli occupation unsustainable and gaining control of an economic asset, the land of Palestine.

But, on the other side, consider the placement of very conservative Jewish families in some of the furthest-out West Bank settlements. These are people, as the assassination of Yitzak Rabin and other events have made clear, who believe that the biblical accounts of the gift of land to Abraham and his descendants remain literally valid today, and who are willing to fight for that original territory. While the real issue is the clash over land between two economic and cultural worlds, those inclined to do so are encouraged to believe in religious crusades. (That word in this place, I know, is ironic.) This game, of course, is dangerous. The Palestinian authority may not be able to stop its religiously motivated (or other) terrorists even if it wishes to do so. If Ehud Olmert or one of his successors were to wish to withdraw from the West Bank, the religious settlers could, and might well, use their weapons to fight him. And religiously motivated violence by Jews is not confined to threats by the settlers. At least a few Israelis have been guilty of terrorist acts against Palestinians. In one case a Jewish man sprayed bullets around the interior of a West Bank mosque full of Muslim worshippers, killing many. In another case, bombs were attached by Israeli extremists to the ignitions of several cars driven by Palestinian officials, resulting in severe injury to at least one.

And religious violence is not confined to the Middle East. African nations, particularly ones already divided between Islamic majorities in the north and Christian majorities in the south, are possible future battlefields as well. Already there have been Muslim-Christian skirmishes in certain locations. The danger is that both Islamic and Christian politicians will use the people of these respective faiths as foot soldiers in conflicts billed, once again, as religious struggles, when the actual issues have to do with political and economic power. On the Islamic side, Africans are recruited into broader Islamic agendas, including those devoted to Jihad. On the Christian side, one finds increasingly conservative churches whose people simultaneously succumb to advertising that leads them to covet Western consumer goods and can be led to see themselves militantly on the side of religious truth in a struggle against religious falsehood. A series of violent struggles between these forces for control of African nations and territories has already begun, and could well spread.

In all three cases, the Jewish, the Christian, and the Islamic, the religious traditions in question are being exploited and distorted for hegemonic purposes that are expertly hidden from the ordinary citizens involved. The question, then, is why these faiths are so vulnerable to such misuse? Not all of these phenomena, of course, are direct results of economic and political projections of Enlightenment logic. Some proclivity to violence comes from internal features of the Abrahamic traditions themselves.

Mark Jürgensmeyer has written of these faiths' moralistic tendency to polarize light and darkness, virtue and evil that, in turn, are derived from dualisms encouraged by their respective creation narratives. He speaks of cosmic battles joined on the playing fields of human history though images of struggle and transformation. Religion becomes fused with violent expressions of social aspiration and nationalism. All this is exacerbated by the renewed role that religion plays in many lands at the heart of ideologies of public order.[1]

René Girard, still more complexly, writes of a primordial state of "mimetic" violence pitting all against all that eventually becomes religiously transformed by the collective sacrifice of a scapegoat. This sacrifice halts violence for a while; ritual repetition of the act suffices to absorb belligerent impulses. But soon enough an inner need arises to substitute new, actual victims for the ritualized original victim. Others—those of different ethnicity or different faith—then answer to this need. Original violence then repeats itself, this time with the religious legitimation it has acquired along the way.[2]

Quite apart from such theories, it is plain that groups that feel marginalized and humiliated can be vulnerable to believing themselves invited, on almost any beguiling terms, into anything represented as a world-historical crusade or campaign to protect home values against foreign values, good against evil. Such involvement confers on the co-opted ones an instant sense of importance or significance that is otherwise denied them by the sophisticated powers that be. Religious leaders, motivated by their own desires for personal importance and proximity to power, often give full cooperation to this co-optative process. Such vulnerability to being used, combined with the tendency to intensify otherwise secular struggles, makes religion one of the most dangerous forces in the world today.

It has been the view of *New York Times* columnist Thomas Friedman, and others, that what is needed is the sort of "modernization" of religion that has gone on for two centuries or more in the West. For Friedman, religions and religious teachings need to come to terms with modern economic and scientific reasoning.[3] Religiously dominated communities need to be drawn further into the present cosmopolitan world order, where amassing profits seems a more attractive option than making war. But, if the Western secularization model is followed, this means the neutralization of religion by privatization and marginalization. And, as we will see in chapter 2, the modern Western culture that Friedman sees as our salvation is itself in serious trouble and, if anything, needs to *be* saved from its betrayals of its own promises to humanity.

What is needed, then, is not the mere "modernization," i.e., neutralization of religion by assimilation to modern secular goals. The tendency today is, if anything, the opposite. Religions East and West are becoming, if anything, more intrinsic to the different civilizations of humankind rather than less so. Certainly they are increasingly at the heart of many competing national ideologies. Hence they must take on a new sort of responsibility for determining what they are to *be* in the public world. The Abrahamic faiths in particular need to become far more critically aware of the roles they are often being asked to play. They need to find in their own traditions, and not merely in the blandishments of modernity, resources not only for resisting exploitation but for making positive contributions to human well-being. And, above all, they need now to do so together.

Burgeoning Interfaith Relationships: Foundations for Future Possibilities

One hopeful sign that such a positive agenda might be feasible lies in the multitude of interreligious studies and initiatives now in progress with significant achievements to their credit. These go on simultaneously with all the sorts of religious violence just described. Without existing interfaith initiatives, proposals of the sort made in this book would have little traction. Despite inevitable setbacks and roadblocks, interfaith dialogue is today an impressive growth industry. I do not have to argue for its already remarkable reach or for its importance. The present book swims in that stream, and would be impossible to conceive without it. It is worth pausing to look at the kinds of possibilities that lie in such relationships. The connections concerned are of at least four kinds: discussions of practical issues of life in the modern world, formal academic studies, organized dialogues on issues of faith per se, and outreach efforts by the leaders and scholars of particular religious bodies and institutions.

Dialogue begins with the sheer fact of meeting and getting to know one another. Partners in discussion want to be sure that their faiths are held in respect by their interlocutors and that participants are *both* valid representatives of their religious communities *and* sufficiently open-minded for the discussion to be fruitful. "Theological" issues as such are likely to come up only after many practical questions of religious life in the modern world have been aired. Very often the animating question is how to live faithful lives in the midst of secular, materialistic societies. This question often then turns to the question of raising children to be likewise faithful members of their faiths and good citizens as well. Or discussion may focus on ways in which the media, not to speak of governmental authority, misunderstands and distorts religious faith and its social roles, and what might be done together about this. Jews, Christians, and Muslims are eager to talk about practical relationships where they live, and also to hear how members of their faiths relate to one another in other parts of the world. They are also eager, with honesty about scriptural sources, to talk about ways of overcoming religiously motivated violence. Above all, it is clear that Jews, Christians, and Muslims today are interested in forming partnerships and coalitions involving mutual support and common approaches to the whole range of pressing issues where they live. At some point, given enough trust and sense of solidarity, they are willing to talk about sending their most promising people to study together, in appropriate institutions, to train sensitive, well-informed religious leadership for the next generation.[4]

All this typically goes on in interfaith groups apart from much study of the academic literature on interfaith matters. Yet that literature is indispensable, especially for more advanced leadership training. The work of scholars antedates by many decades the proliferation of dialogue groups as we know them today. But these groups have added great impetus to scholarly studies, building on the patient work of the past. At least four quite distinct sorts of interreligious studies are going on now in Western academic settings. Diana Eck, Mark Heim, Willard Oxtoby,[5] and many others share a concern for how we should understand the *history* and *phenomenology* of religions, including a concern for the manner in which clergy should be educated in the nature of religions other than their own. Another group of authors has been concerned with a theology of religions, that is, with the question of how, in this case Christians, should account for the very existence of other faiths in categories derived from their own faith. This last-mentioned concern has produced the well-known categories of exclusivism, inclusivism, and pluralism, recently most helpfully reconceptualized by Paul Knitter.[6] Among these alternatives, John Hick[7] has taken a consistent position for principled pluralism. An important, more conservative, study in this genre is *Pluralisms and Horizons* by Richard Mouw and Sander Griffioen.[8] I would characterize the latter book's position as "limited pluralism." And finally there are the numerous works focusing on the *historical and scriptural relationships* of the Abrahamic faiths as such, among them works by Kenneth Vaux[9] and F. E. Peters,[10] to name two of the more prominent and profound.

In a class by itself, perhaps, is the work of Jonathan Sacks, already mentioned, an Orthodox Jew, the Chief Rabbi of the United Hebrew Congregations of the British Commonwealth. In his Rieth Lectures of 1990 titled *The Persistence of Faith*,[11] he urged us all to become "bilingual": first learning thoroughly the language of our own religious tradition, then also learning to speak the language of the public world. In 1997, Sacks published *The Politics of Hope*[12] dealing with many topics, including surviving catastrophe and the politics of responsibility. In 2002, he published a highly controversial work, *The Dignity of Difference: How to Avoid the Clash of Civilizations*,[13] and in 2004, *To Heal a Fractured World: The Ethics of Responsibility*.[14] In all these works Sacks seeks to show how religious values can unite rather than divide us, and calls for a priority of covenantal over merely contractual relationships. For him, a covenant is a bond, not of interest and advantage, but of belonging.

These insights are already well-established in significant sectors of academe. The ongoing interreligious effort sponsored by Hartford Seminary under the leadership of President Heidi Hadsell is a case in point. This is a Christian seminary with a Jewish board chair, Islamic and Jewish faculty members, and innovative interreligious educational programs. This institution sponsors the MacDonald Center for the Study of Islam and Christian-Muslim Relations under the direction of Professors Ibrahim Abu-Rabi and Jane Smith. Besides its academic research and teaching, the MacDonald Center is dedicated to overcoming stereotypes and developing mutual respect and cooperation between Muslims and Christians. Hartford Seminary is also now authorized to help prepare Muslim chaplains for college and university campuses as well as the U.S. armed forces. It has been involved in inter-Abrahamic encounters all over the world. Its Board of Trustees recently met in Istanbul on the invitation of Islamic authorities in that city.

Comparable activities go on at the Graduate Theological Union in Berkeley, California, where nine Christian seminaries—six Protestant and three representing Roman Catholic orders—offer a doctoral program in which ecumenical, interreligious, and intercultural studies represent a public institutional commitment. The GTU sponsors research and teaching institutes devoted to Jewish, Muslim, and Buddhist studies respectively, all linked to the appropriate departments of the University of California at Berkeley. An effort is made to integrate these perspectives into the work of doctoral students of all these faiths, bringing them into contact with theology and with different human-science approaches to the study of religious institutions.

There are also groups bringing together scholars from many institutions. Some concentrate on joint reading of the Jewish, Christian, and Muslim scriptures. Foremost among these is the Society for Scriptural Reasoning, led by Peter Ochs of the University of Virginia, that meets annually at the American Academy of Religion. This Society has spawned a number of offshoots and parallel efforts. This effort tries to get seriously at fundamental issues of scripture interpretation and seeks to develop a method of shared interfaith reasoning that can confront the forms of positivism and rationalism otherwise predominant in the academic world. A profile of this program and of Ochs's vision for it will be found in chapter 4.

Still other inter-Abrahamic projects with academic connections have been in progress for even longer. The recent book *Abraham's Children: Jews, Christians and Muslims in Conversation*[15] records papers from the Oxford Abrahamic Group, begun in 1992 and continuing to the present day. Here one finds papers by members of the group on Abraham, Moses, Jesus, and Muhammad, as well as issues such as the image of God in humanity, pluralism, gender, the environment, and life after death. While these are individual writings, they have been influenced and shaped by the ongoing conversation to reach their present forms. A mine of information on the three faiths and their relationships is available here. And at a more popular and hence probably influential level one finds such recent publications as *The Tent of Abraham: Stories of Hope and Peace for Jews, Christians and Muslims*[16] and *Abraham, A Journey to the Heart of Three Faiths.*[17]

Many practical initiatives drawing on academe but operating beyond it also foster dialogue among the Abrahamic, as well as other, faiths. One thinks, of course, of the Parliament of the World's Religions, in which all four of the named interreligious research projects—and more—are being simultaneously pursued. A multitude of such interfaith organizations, numbering at least in the hundreds, exists across the Western world and beyond.

One of these deserving mention is the United Religions Initiative founded in 1996 by Bishop William F. Swing of the Episcopal Diocese of California and chartered in 2000. The URI is in some respects modeled on the United Nations through which nations are called to cooperate for peace. The structure of the URI is decentralized, emphasizing local "cooperation circles" of representatives of world religions, as well as other voices less often heard, in eight regions of the world. As of December 2005, more than three hundred of the circles were in active existence. The URI tries not to compete with other interfaith initiatives, but rather to complement and collaborate with organizations such as the Council for a Parliament of the World's Religions.

And finally one thinks of religious communions that reach out to others from standpoints within their own self-understandings. In 1962, Pope John XXIII excised from the text of the Catholic liturgy for Good Friday the words "*perfidies Judaeis*" and the prayer that Jews might convert to the truth. The Catholic Church now prays "for the Jewish people, first to hear the word of God, that they may continue to grow in the love of his name and in faithfulness to his covenant." Such moves bring to mind also the efforts of Pope John Paul II to establish unprecedented connections both with Jews and Muslims. This Pope's meetings with world religious leaders at Assisi, his visits to synagogues and mosques, his journey to the Holy Land to pray at the Western Wall and visit the Holocaust Memorial at Yad Vashem, his sensitive dealing with the question of the Carmelite convent next to Auschwitz, his calling the Jewish people "our elder brothers," and many other significant gestures all brought about a fundamental change in Catholic-Jewish relationships. It is still uncertain what legacy regarding such matters his successor Pope Benedict XVI will leave.

Deserving mention also are the "Building Bridges" seminars sponsored by the Archbishop of Canterbury. Founded by Archbishop George Carey in response to the 9/11 terrorist attacks and continued by his successor Rowan Williams, these events have since taken place yearly, alternating between majority Christian and majority Muslim settings. Meetings have so far taken place in New York, Qatar, Washington, Sarajevo, and London. A meeting scheduled for Malaysia in May 2007 was cancelled, possibly temporarily, by the government of that country. The seminars have brought together "religiously committed Christian and Muslim scholars who know and trust each other," and who, through the study of the Qur'an and the Christian scriptures "can explore themes of relevance to the contemporary world."[18]

One wonders whether there are examples of such relationships that do not owe their existence to some sort of initiative from the West. I have found little or nothing of the kind without at least *some* Western involvement.

Yet I am sure that dialogues under totally indigenous sponsorship do exist below our radars, producing results that do not reach publication in our journals, but yet could be enormously important. Two initiatives that do register in Western awareness are carried on very largely by people resident in the areas concerned and are devoted to interfaith issues in their local forms. One of these is the Interfaith Encounter Association in Israel-Palestine, led by Yehuda Stolov, a rabbi of Russian descent. I will have more to say about Rabbi Stolov's enterprise in chapter 8. Something quite different is happening in Indonesia, the world's most populous Islamic nation, with a non-Arab Muslim culture that opens doors to many possibilities. Here there has emerged an interreligious, international doctoral program jointly sponsored by three universities, one Muslim, one Christian, and one national-secular, under the direction of Dr. Bernard Adeny-Risskotta.

This short, and admittedly rather arbitrarily compiled, list of enormously varied inter-Abrahamic and interreligious activities is designed only to give some impression of the extent and sheer momentum of efforts of this kind, not only in the West but around the world. Countless other initiatives exist, many of them focused on and adapted to particular areas such as the Middle East, Indonesia, and sub-Saharan Africa. What I have described must represent no more than a tenth, or even less, of activities going on that have international connections and therefore some visibility. There are no doubt hundreds, perhaps thousands, more. These arise from meetings of neighbors of different faiths in myriad localities. They may engage each other over scriptural and doctrinal issues, but they are more likely to consider their diverse yet overlapping perspectives on issues representing the quality of life for people where they live. Such gatherings are as likely to be found in sophisticated university communities as they are in primitive villages. The world is genuinely blanketed today with such relationships at every level and of every sort. One's impression is that such activity exceeds in quantity the amount of discourse once devoted to purely Christian ecumenism at the height of the popularity of that movement.

Finding ways to bind the three faiths together in a single covenantal vision would in itself be a major step forward in world civilization, *provided* such togetherness did not in turn become oppressive to the many who could not see themselves as part of it. It has been pointed out to me[19] that members of the Abrahamic faiths—not to speak of citizens of the cultures significantly informed by them—represent a potential power bloc of huge proportions on the global stage. This fact and others related to it will need to be kept in mind throughout the argument that follows. Yet I do not think that the formation of such an oppressive power bloc is likely to happen in the conceivable future. The existing differences, both of outlook and interest, among the Abrahamic faiths are too great for that. The question is whether it will be fruitful to look into the potential for solidarity among these faiths afforded by their partly overlapping scriptures as a step worth pursuing in itself. I believe that it will be.

Learning about Complexity

One learns much of a practical nature both from studying religious violence and from participating in this wide range of interreligious studies and relationships. Things are never so simple as they seem at first. Christians and Jews, reading with fresh interest the spate of new books on Islam in particular, can only be struck by the radical pluralism and complexity of that faith and of the present global religious situation. One learns to be aware of the enormous internal diversity and complexity of each of the three faiths in question. One needs to speak in the plural: Jewish communities, Christian communities, Islamic communities. The same goes for nationalities. It can make a huge difference to whom one is talking and what tendencies or groups one's interlocutors represent. Each faith is represented by different subgroups (what Christians call "denominations" or "communions") whose tendencies also differ according to culture of origin.

Of course, Christian relations with Jews and with Muslims respectively are often quite different things, calling for distinct approaches and assumptions. Sometimes these interchanges cannot realistically be framed as coherent three-way discourses. Often the relationships that emerge are the result of many two-way conversations reflecting varying perspectives, somehow bundled together to simulate a common result. Furthermore, the scriptural approach advocated here runs the danger of forgetting the complex history of textual interpretation in each faith. Over the years, each tradition has looked at its foundational writings through multiple lenses. Some of these provide more useful perspectives on our project than others do. The search for a coherent inter-Abrahamic agenda is also a scripture-reading lens (in technical terms, a "hermeneutic") in its own right, learning from past history but creating its own. Each faith will read it differently.

Most striking, the character of potential interfaith relationships and their capacity for influencing public affairs depends on the nature of each situation. In a given time or place, possibilities may be promising, or very limited. Rabbi Stolov's Interfaith Encounter Association operates very successfully in Israel-Palestine under difficult conditions. Another variation appears in several ongoing dialogues in Istanbul, the ancient capital of the Eastern Roman Empire and still the seat of the Orthodox Patriarch, a multi-faith city yet predominantly Muslim from the time of the Turkish conquest of 1453. Here one encounters secularized Muslims anxious to lead Turkey into the European Union, and traditional Muslims anxious to turn their nation into a traditional Islamic state. If, on the other hand, one forms a dialogue group in Jakarta, Indonesia, another set of circumstances applies. Here Muslims form a large majority, but their culture differs radically from that of the Arab Muslims of the Middle East. And one could mention the already highly pluralistic city of London with its large population of Muslims from Pakistan, and the immensely complex city of New York, in which religious Jews of every persuasion follow their own rites and practices, while they and many secularized Jews are also highly influential in finance, the arts, the professions, and political life. To a lesser extent this is also true of Los Angeles. Generally across the United States one makes a distinction between Jewish congregations as such and Jewish organizations following particular political agendas. The character of the dialogue possible in any one of these locations or countless others heavily depends on the particular configuration of communal and political circumstances that exists in that place and calls for attention by the dialoguers. Furthermore, in most of these places, if not all, the Abrahamic faiths encounter additional religious communities: Hindu, Buddhist, Sikh, Zoroastrian, Bahai, Confucian, and so on. A study of Islamic religio-politics in India-Pakistan, for example, would require careful attention to Islamic differences and relationships with both Hinduism and Buddhism.

Everywhere we look today our neat categories are challenged. In 1968, Clifford Geertz published a book titled *Islam Observed*,[20] contrasting the ferocious, sectarian Islam of Morocco with the easy-going, tolerant Islam of Indonesia. But today, matters do not yield to such simple and illuminating comparisons. In a recent essay "Which Way to Mecca," Geertz tells us that

> many of the large-scale concepts by means of which we [have] been accustomed to sorting out the [religious and cultural] world have begun to come apart. [They] have lost much of their edge and definition, and we are left to find our way through vast collections of strange and inconsonant particulars without much in the way of assistance from finely drawn, culturally ratified, natural kinds.[21]

Geertz's quirky language can serve as a mirror in which we see ourselves: to realize that "Which Way to Mecca" is also a question for Jews and Christians. Which way to Jerusalem? Which way to Rome? Which way to Geneva, or Moscow, or Istanbul? The pluralism and conflict of interpretations of tradition, the variety of circumstances and historical narratives, and above all, perhaps the tendency—for Jews, Christians, and Muslims alike—to ideologize and politicize religious faith, make this a dangerous moment in which some alternative way of seeing things is urgently needed.

All this raises what must be a crucial question for any book with the objectives of this one: are *any* generalizations about such relationships, inter-Abrahamic or otherwise, possible? Can any "model for," even a very flexible and evocative (rather than prescriptive) one, apply to a very wide range of situations? I give only a very cautious "yes." In his book *The Idea of Civil Society,*[22] Adam Seligman, a secular Jewish author remarkably sensitive to religious issues, offers case studies of Jerusalem, Budapest, and Los Angeles. He clearly thinks that the notion of responsibility in "civil society" has descriptive value in all three cases. But the way this works out in one setting is far different from the way it works out in another. A certain "family resemblance" (Ludwig Wittgenstein) among these situations justifies cautious generalizations. But one also needs to know the details of each situation. Similarly Robert Schreiter in *The New Catholicity*[23] speaks of "global theological flows" that today link diverse experiences and vocabularies. But the point of his book is that this global "catholicity" or wholeness is shot through with differences that need to be respected. That is why one talks of "flows" of recognizably similar concerns rather than conceptual accords as such. I think that this is also true for interreligious dialogues going on in a host of different cultures and situations. Each is in one respect or another unique. The data does not support the notion of concepts, even in this field, alleged to be literally universal. But neither does it argue for total incommensurability between such different cultures and situations.

Responses within Participating Faith Communities

Meanwhile faith communities respond to all these contacts and activities with internal struggles about how they are to be understood in relation to long-held confessional traditions and theological positions. Here again the body of literature is enormous. Such efforts to understand go on in a great variety of settings from local congregations of all three faiths trying to decide what their attitudes to neighboring faiths should be, and why, to professors seeking to achieve book-length clarity about these matters for their scholarly colleagues. Several of the books mentioned earlier take up such internal-reaction questions.

Within Roman Catholicism, for example, the debate has already gone on for millennia. It began (on the basis of Rom 1:18–25) by asking whether revealed truths are also accessible to outsiders through the use of reason alone, and, if so, on what terms. More recently, the question has arisen in a new form from the fact that the Catholic Church clearly wants to offer respect to other faiths and indeed to partner with them in building a peaceful and just world. But how does one make theological sense of such a stance? The old position that no salvation could be had outside the church will not do in the world as we now know it. Vatican II, in the document *Nostra Aetate,* acknowledged that non-Catholics, even non-Christians, could be "saved."[24] Since that time, the Catholic Church has engaged in intensive internal discussions, marked particularly by contributions from the Pontifical Council on Interreligious Dialogue such as the document "Dialogue and Proclamation."[25] The heart of the question has been not whether the salvation of non-Christians takes place, but how. Is it because saved outsiders, as Karl Rahner once argued, were already "anonymous Christians" or had undergone an invisible "baptism of desire"? Are non-Christians saved through the agency of their non-Christian faiths, or are they saved in spite of these faiths?

My firsthand knowledge of this sort of internal debate is focused on the largely Protestant sectors of Christian ecumenism, hence more detailed attention to that history in this space. For more than a century, efforts have gone on in ecumenical circles to grasp and enact the unity Christian churches in principle have with one another. Now the status of, say, inter-Abrahamic dialogue becomes increasingly a new topic of interchurch contention. The fundamental question of what relationships with other faiths should *mean* comes to the fore, generating in new terms the question of where other faiths *belong* among the usual categories of Christian self-understanding. Does the interreligious dimension raise divisive issues that could bring Christian unity efforts to a halt, or at least slow them down? Could these concerns reopen old wounds, forcing painful revisits to lesions thought to have been healed long ago?

Perhaps the central ecumenical concern has focused on what these dialogues do to the validity of mission. Christian ecumenism has for well over a century been based on the proposition "that they may all be one ... so that the world may believe...." (John 17:21). Do not interreligious activities of the sort described raise difficult questions about traditional Christian relations to other faiths based on the conviction that the purpose of contact is conversion? "No one comes to the Father save by me," says John's gospel. Many would still say so, reminding us that Christianity's position in the world today is the result of the work of two centuries of faithful missionaries, many of whom did good works beyond bringing many to faith. But things have changed. There is less conviction that adherents of other faiths are lost without explicit personal relations to Jesus as the Christ. Attention shifts to the billions who have no faith at all and to the conviction that adding people to one's own membership rolls is less important than helping them receive the gift of their own forms of well-being, or blessing, before God.

One of many straws in the wind: in 1999, a group of Asian Christian missionary leaders issued a report that included (albeit buried in the middle of a long paragraph in the middle of a long document) this disarming question: "Can we understand the reign of God as religiously plural?"[26] The question, so expressed, is not further explored in the report in question. But it represents the sort of simple yet profound query whose answer is now being taken for granted by many religious progressives, and even by some of the more conventionally minded. The answer, in whatever context we ask the question, must be "yes." But what does this "yes" mean? Where does it lead? It is one thing to be genially open to any and all religious expressions while sending vague good wishes to the human race. It is another to deal responsibly with such a conviction—concerning, of all things, the "reign of God" in human affairs— within the central precincts of each of our traditions of faith that have, over the years, shown the world more than a small streak of religious exclusivism.

It makes a huge difference how such questions are asked and answered. What would constitute an ecclesially accountable Christian theological argument for a responsible sort of "yes" to a religiously plural vision of God's rule in human life and in the unfolding of historical events? How does one make such an affirmation seriously within a Christian perspective, if possible in a manner potentially open to other religious traditions? The heart of the matter concerns how Christian belief in salvation through Jesus Christ relates to God's activity in other, non-Christian, religious cultures. Some will say that they personally hold to Jesus as the only way but yet cannot limit God's freedom to be involved with human beings in other ways, including other faiths. The traditional distinctions of "exclusivism," "pluralism," and "inclusivism" no longer serve the debate very well, as Paul Knitter and others have shown.[27] Many in this debate are saying that the question now concerns the *kind* of inclusivism one favors. It concerns how one formulates one's belief that the God of Jesus Christ is also present in the experience and thought of persons of other faiths and perhaps persons of secular faith (a religion in its own right).

All this concerns what has been called the "theology of religions," an enormously involved matter in itself that relates to the different starting points in faith from which the matter of "other religions" may be approached. A key formulation for a Christian theology of religions has been given us by S. Mark Heim (author of the book *Salvations* mentioned above) who draws here on the work of M. M. Thomas and Gavin D'Costa:

> To make sense of the fact that God [is] as decisively in Christ as Christians [believe], it [is] necessary to hold that that God [is] elsewhere than Christ also. This is perhaps the key pivot point of the Christian

theology of religions. It balances the tensions such a theology must maintain: without such a decisive Christology, no Trinity; with Trinity, no understanding of Christ's uniqueness so extreme that it cannot fit within a wider economy of God's action. The reality of God's active relation to creation in ways distinct from the event of the historical Jesus is coded into the Trinitarian basis of the Christian faith. So, too, is the intrinsic connection of all of God's action with that historical event.[28]

A tightly packed statement of this sort has the potential to set off reconsideration of the ways in which many traditional Christian affirmations are formulated and understood. Along this way, Christians face three questions of fundamental importance. First, what is the nature of what has recently been called "God's mission to the human race"? Not our own confessional or institutional religious mission to other people, but rather the mission of God to all of us human beings, the communication to us, by the final Power with whom we have to do, of the covenantal promise under which we live? That mission may not be graspable at all in today's conventionally religious languages.

Secondly, what kind of need does each tradition of faith have for the collaboration of other faiths in answering such questions while maintaining its own authenticity? The underlying issue here concerns the sort of space that needs to be made by each faith, at the heart of its own self-understanding, for the religiously Other. Is this not a hospitable space of Other-welcoming needed for the full and genuine expression of each faith in a world of many faiths?

And finally, what, in the economy of God, are we as believing human beings responsible for? What is our human role in meeting the obligations that come with the gift of life and faith? Speaking in Christian terms, the issue is the perennial one of nature and grace. We are not responsible for achieving our own salvation. But by saving grace we are *given* the responsibility of making the world ready for the coming of God's rule. Combining the word "gift" with the word "responsibility" seems to me to catch that basic nuance. From here, I see the idea of a "gift of responsibility" ramifying into many different applications. Among these is the idea that if the Abrahamic faiths were together, in all their diversity, to appropriate such a responsibility, that would be a stupendous peacemaking gift to the rest of humankind. Hence the question: what are we therefore to do?

Such questions would not have been even formulable at the heart of Christian (or any other) faith without years of history-of-religions scholarship, interreligious information sharing and exchanges of friendship. But such a query clearly makes a new demand. This demand constitutes the essence of the critical moment in which we now live and to which we need to be alert. As Thoreau wrote in *Walden*, "Only that day dawns to which we awake. There is more day to dawn. The sun is but a morning star."[29] Our common consciousness of certain realities allows a day to dawn whose meaning we can work together to discern and act out.

But the obvious constraint in such a process lies just where it ought to be. All parties to the dialogue ask what, if any, fundamental theological concessions on the part of each faith might be required to give effect to such a new insight. Might mutual commitments among Abrahamic communities, so understood, reach the point of calling for changing basic articles of belief? If so, we will not go far. No faith is willing to contemplate such a thing, nor should it be expected to. Similarly, no agenda should call for an amalgamation of faiths, or of their terminologies. This proposal is not about syncretism. But suppose all are invited to reconsider the *ways* in which they believe. The *manner* of belief is not generally itself an article of faith, even if some would make it so. We might well reach the point of agreement with Rabbi Sacks that it is not true to say that only one formulation of any point of faith is the true one. Many expressions of faith may simultaneously be true in their own ways. I would add that this conviction is more a matter of attitude and practice than of theological definition. Probably no terms agreeable to everyone could be found. But if we could go along together at the level of attitudes and practices, there might grow enough mutual confidence among us to move to agenda-building of a practical sort.

In the early summer of 2005, the World Council of Churches sponsored a meeting at its Geneva headquarters with representatives of roughly a dozen world faiths, organized by Dr. Hans Ucko. This gathering's purpose was to deal with what the organizers called a "critical moment" in relations between the faiths.[30] Having been present at this event, I came away with the strong impression that the critical moment could be interpreted as involving the need to build upon growing mutual familiarity and trust to seek some sense of a way forward together: what I below call an agenda.

The Ninth Assembly of the WCC in Porto Allegre, Brazil, in February 2006 was watched by many for signs of whether the initiatives of the "critical moment" conference would gain some programmatic traction for the next period of the Council's life. The outgoing Moderator of the Central Committee, Aram I, Catholicos of Cilicia, Lebanon, had expressed his enthusiasm for the interreligious dimension of ecumenism at the 2005 Geneva conference but was unable to move Assembly delegates, who feared syncretism or diversion from the Council's historic goals or both. Yet Porto Allegre was the scene of a memorable address on this subject by Archbishop Rowan Williams, a key fragment of which is quoted here.

The language of anonymous Christianity is not now much in fashion, and it had all kinds of problems about it. Yet who that has been involved in dialogue with other faiths has not had the sense of an echo, a reflection, of the kind of life Christians seek to live?... If we are truly learning how to be in that relation with God and the world in which Jesus of Nazareth stood, we shall not turn away from those who see from another place. And any claim or belief that we see more or more deeply is always rightly going to be tested in those encounters where we find ourselves working for a vision of human flourishing and justice in the company of those who do not start where we have started.[31]

But will the ecumenical body that organized these meetings do what might be needed effectively to follow up their insights? Christian ecumenism has a long history of dealing with this issue rather peripherally. In the World Council of Churches, there has for many years been a secretariat for interreligious relations, staffed by a succession of extremely able, well-trained, and influential staff members. But never has this matter figured prominently on the public ecumenical agenda. Institutionally speaking, since Porto Allegre, it seems to be being thrust into the background once again, subsumed within another department with many other legitimate interests and concerns. Fears that this subject, made too prominent, could generate new inter-Christian divisions are not far-fetched. But my perception is that this is already happening and could willy-nilly become the principal ecumenical issue before too long, at which time it will need to be faced. Best to be prepared.

While a vast number of other sorts of institutions and initiatives are addressing these issues, the Christian ecumenical movement has one great advantage: Once any issue is open, ecumenism brings it rapidly into the heart of worldwide Christianity's most important theological forum, where it will then perforce be dealt with by a very wide range of thinkers speaking for their respective communions. Neither Judaism nor Islam has any comparable sort of worldwide organization. One is talking in both those cases only with individuals and local groups who desire to talk.

The question, then, is whether the Christian ecumenical movement and its major global expression, the WCC, will, despite its potential advantages for the task, choose a relatively minor role in the global sweep of interreligious dialogue or whether it will boldly take the matter on. If the latter is the choice, then a full-blown theological attempt to achieve agreement on where non-Christian faiths belong in the Christian theological scheme of things will be needed. This will not be easy, but it will be very important. The same question will inevitably be asked from the standpoint of the other faiths as well. Where do Christians and Muslims fit into a Jewish self-understanding?

Where do Christians and Jews belong in an Islamic self-understanding? Each faith should also want to be able to internalize, or at least come to some viable terms with, the other faiths' ways of regarding them in return.

Such reflections, in some form, go on among Jewish and Muslim scholars and within a variety of organizations representing these faiths. This usually happens without direct participation by outsiders. This Christian observer, for lack of firsthand experience, rightly has much less to say. But it is plausible to think that here, too, different sorts of commitments characterize different "denominations" of Judaism and Islam, depending very much on the cultures in which the discussants live. Very often the issue is not dealt with in theological terms, i.e., asking where other faiths belong within one's own religious self-understanding, but rather in survival or adaptive terms. For Jews, the fear, not entirely unfounded, is often that Christian advances toward them are in the end designed to make converts, thereby weakening Judaism's already beleaguered existence as a minority everywhere but in the State of Israel and soon to be a minority there too. Among Muslims, particularly those in the West, the issue is coming to terms with life in pluralist, secular, yet nominally Christian societies. For Muslims, the question is what dialogues with other faiths may mean for their project of learning to live adaptively but authentically in the West. In both cases, the question is whether talking to other faiths poses a danger to the integrity of one's own faith, particularly in situations where that faith is already under various kinds of challenge and pressure. Interfaith discussion, especially when conducted in academic terms, can easily be seen as a dangerous, diversionary luxury rather than a way forward from where these faiths stand. It is vital for all three Abrahamic faiths to be sensitive to one another's internal issues, especially where these questions of identity and even survival are concerned. The experience of Christians wrestling with their own "ecumenical" questions should sensitize them to similar internal issues within other faiths.

An Agenda for "Rooted Cosmopolitans"?

So while the inter-Abrahamic scene is complex, there are comparable issues and analogous debates across a wide variety of circumstances. There could also be a common agenda here worth pursuing. In all three faiths, there are both theological resources to be developed and persons around whom to build a shared way forward. If some groups among the Abrahamic faiths have tended to intensify, where they have not actually authorized, the violent confrontations among the "civilizations" they inform, it is also true that in many places today these faiths exist peacefully side-by-side. Each of these circumstances will be treated at greater length below. For now it is enough to note that here serious and continuing threats may now be beginning to be countered by new and creative possibilities just coming over the historical horizon.

The agenda we need will have to do not with abstractly comparing doctrinal formulations. It will have to do with holding such convictions as grounds for shared witness in the world. It will have to do with ways of *being* together in our continuing diversity, ways of shared being that offer something meaningful to humankind. In what terms might we frame such a notion of "being-to"? In terms of making gifts of our being to others? There are many sorts of gifts to the human race that we might find appropriate to offer: gifts fostering justice and peace and human rights, gifts of spiritual depth, gifts representing transcendence in a largely secular world. Above all, the gift of responsibility to the covenantal promise in the midst of the world, which begins by being a gracious gift to all human beings.

The most needed form of that gift is thinking and action that fosters the basic integrity of the human community. Humanity desperately needs help in the project of becoming one people welcoming many different beliefs and customs. It is easy to affirm that quality of oneness, but astonishingly hard to identify either an empirical or theoretical basis for it. No doubt what is attainable consists much more of shared assumptions and practices than it does of any common definition of the human essence. That continuingly *different* beliefs could be the basis of such a global community is a seeming paradox, but it is just what we propose.

Many thinkers and writers in today's religious situation are already envisioning some such common path for the "religions of the book," always conscious of their relationships to other faiths. The very idea is in the air we now breathe, with numerous variants both of broad conception and of detail. Can such thinking leap over the many obstacles and lay hold of the shared scriptural promise, allowing the "gift" to take hold? I believe that it can.

Jews, Christians, and Muslims can think about many things together today, despite differences of tradition and language. We of the West have been for some time in a cultural situation that William Schweiker calls "reflexivity." We constantly meet persons of other faiths as neighbors. Our different faiths react upon one another. Our lives are juxtaposed in ways that encourage influences to pass back and forth both in personal relationships and in the public world. Genuine isolation of these faiths from one another still exists, but it is increasingly rare. Any religious thinking we do today must somehow take the presence of the religious Other into account.

Furthermore, seldom if ever before have we lived in such a degree of global spiritual simultaneity. The Abrahamic faiths have had many similar concerns over time—usually over such matters as lines of legitimate authority, the dates of religious festivals, or relationships to temporal powers—but they have focused on these concerns at *different* times, sometimes centuries apart. It is still the case that different groups and nationalities within these faiths have different relationships to "modernity." Some live in premodern worlds; some adjust to a present represented by the evening news; some absorb the perspectives of postmodernity. But in many dimensions of life, all these faith communities inescapably share some relationship to human circumstances that are the same today for all. They are asking the same questions, struggling with the same dilemmas.

So why not try intentionally to think about these common contemporary matters together? Perhaps such thinking can be focused on building models that seek out regions of ideational overlap on the way to the shared agenda we seek. For such model-building, as already indicated, this book seeks to use the notion of a shared Abrahamic "gift of responsibility": the responsibility that we in our integrity of identity owe to humanity. We search together for an agenda that correlates this responsibility-gift with the human needs issuing from modernity's *ir*responsibility to its own ideals. Not only does the category of responsibility bring us to the threshold of ethics; it demands that we assume responsibility for our own religious identities and integrities as self-conscious actors. It calls us to bring these identities and integrities together with the further imperative of responsibility to the Other who shares with us this particular moment in time. What responsibility is about— the primordial demand of self upon self in the demanding presence of the neighbor who is different—must drive the efforts of Jews, Christians, and Muslims to think and act in moral collaboration.

But who will do this? What Jews? What Christians? What Muslims? Agendas presuppose a readiness by all, or nearly all, of a certain group to proceed in a certain way. Such readiness may or may not be present at any given time. Or it may be present for some contemporaries and not for others. The conditions for such readiness could be at hand, but the response to these conditions could take time to mature. Interest in these matters in all three faiths will probably remain for some time to come a minority concern. But increasing numbers will have reason to become involved.

What theological and sociological profiles might such early respondents represent? What schools of thought, allegiances, and interests within these faiths might eventually respond, and with what results? I believe that the first participants in such a venture would be persons and institutions open to certain new understandings of their traditions. And not necessarily persons who are pejoratively called "liberals," or doctrinal "revisionists." It may not be an accident that those who have given me the most help in thinking about these issues have been rather "orthodox" persons: very well rooted and yet open, out of conviction, to serious relationships with others.

Ideally, a response to this proposal needs to be made, at the very least, by well-informed persons representing each of the three faiths who are also able to function in the name of their faiths in the contemporary world of common human experience with its strong Enlightenment influences. Who might these people be? I have already referred to the notion of "traditioned" or "rooted" people whose religious traditions are part of their identities, and yet who are also full participants in, and adaptable, well-connected citizens of, the contemporary world. Such a combination of relationships and qualities is not unknown by any means. But it is very important that those who see themselves this way are not mere generalizers and assimilators who are willing to dilute their traditions. The impetus to a covenanting project of resistance to totalization and of a reframing of life together needs to come from within the deep integrity—the fullness—of each faith tradition that plays a role in this discourse.

Kwame Anthony Appiah, in his book *Cosmopolitanism: Ethics in a World of Strangers*,[32] following a usage that goes back some years, calls such people "rooted cosmopolitans."[33] These are people with deep roots in some particular faith or culture who also have the ability to function effectively in the modern world with deep concern for its well-being. This notion is suggestive for our purposes, but it does not get to the bottom of the matter. The term, after all, has overtones of elitism: as if one were interested only in those with "an infinite capacity for taking planes." Such world travelers are not the only ones who should be drawn into this conversation. Citizens of specific localities, rooted in their own faiths, may earnestly seek common ground with very different people who live only a mile or so, or even a few yards, away from them. The most important impulses toward an Abrahamic agenda may come, not only from world travelers, but from reports by people from many places, sharing their diverse experiences of such encounters and speaking in mutually recognizable terms.

What is needed is a rethinking of the manner in which the roots of faith support the sorts of cosmopolitanism one practices. This calls for more than the "bilingualism" Rabbi Sacks so strongly recommends in his Reith Lectures. It calls for more than the ability to edify Princeton philosophy students with homely illustrations from Ghana, or to function equally well whether one is in West Africa or central New Jersey. It calls for finding new meanings in one's religious roots that, far from distorting or misusing those roots, actually illumine them in the process of drawing out their wisdom for a cosmopolitan world.

Theological projects with such goals are well-known in all three faiths. One thinks of Jewish scholars like Maimonides, Moses Mendelsohn, Herrmann Cohen, Franz Rosenzweig, or Abraham Heschel. One thinks of Christian scholars like Thomas Aquinas, Karl Rahner, G. W. F. Hegel, Paul Tillich, or

Paul Ricoeur. One thinks of Muslim scholars like Averroes, Fazlur Rahman, Mohammed Arkoun, Farid Esack, and Tariq Ramadan. These names, of course, represent different eras. Not all of them are contemporary, and that is part of the point. There have been many instances of cosmopolitanism in the interpretation of historic faiths, each addressing distinct historical circumstances. Today the project of articulating an ancestral faith for a cosmopolitan world involves not merely assimilating the "spirit of the age." It also involves coming to terms with those of other faiths who are trying to do the same thing.

Rooted cosmopolitanism assuredly is not exclusively a "modern" achievement, as the above names show. One can even find examples of it in the scriptures of the three faiths. In a significant way, the first rooted cosmopolitan is Abram, who journeys from his homeland to what we now call Palestine. The region of Ur from which Abram came was part of the Babylonian Empire, already labeled in Genesis 11 as a failed cosmopolis for its ambition to unify humanity by force around a particular religio-imperial culture. Abram came from being a herdsman outside Babylon to a region of multiple Canaanite city states presided over by "kings," a different sort of cosmopolis in the sense of being a region of small tribally organized principalities, religiously pluralistic in the sense that each tribe had its own gods, and competing among themselves for territory and military power. What Abraham and his sons did in this situation is filled with more than a little ambiguity. But the legend has him called to found covenantal relationships not only among his own people but among these Canaanites as well. Not ceasing to be a Bedouin sheik, Abraham is pictured as mediating disputes between these Canaanite "kings," a feat that would have probably required him to be bilingual in a way of which Jonathan Sacks would approve.

It is true that the Abraham narratives as we have them have been worked over in various ways for centuries by scribes of the three faiths to produce the texts we have today. But it can also be argued that there are traces of tradition in these narratives from legends that predate the appearance of anything that could be called "Judaism," or much less Christianity or Islam. The figure of Abraham is not identified as Jewish, and the seemingly proper name "Hebrew" is thought to go back to a common noun for "outsider" or "wanderer." Hence in "Abraham" we have a point of departure for the genealogies of all three "Abrahamic" faiths, a point that long precedes the separation into the three branches we know today. We may refer to Abraham, then, not only as a figure revered in three contemporary "world religions" but also as a symbol of commonality among them. Hence we today can refer to dialogues among these faiths as "inter-Abrahamic," and the presiding perspective of these discourses as "Abrahamic" as well.

As the pages ahead will seek to show in some detail, Abraham is a figure who moves from mere unquestioning obedience to God's commands to an obedient kind of responsibility to a promise of blessing. Abraham is commanded to be free, and to share his freedom down the generations. To receive the responsibility of freedom as a *gift* is very different from taking or grasping that freedom, perhaps in the name of "autonomy," for oneself. The grasping move paradoxically imprisons the soul. Receiving and sharing responsibility as a gift in turn brings gifts to the human race.

I will not elaborate more at this point. I have said enough to show that there are persons and resources through which the Abrahamic faiths, first becoming reconciled among themselves, could take on a significant task of peacemaking and reconciliation among the worlds warring tribes. Whether such a thing can happen today in a world very much in need of it remains to be seen. The obstacles are great. The chapters ahead, seeking always to temper any impulses to naïve idealism, pursue the many aspects of this question.

Holding both questions and resources in mind, I try to see where certain avenues could lead. The chapters of this book develop the idea of an Abrahamic "gift of responsibility" for bringing blessing to earth's families. Despite our different beliefs, we consider one another, and all we meet, as members of a single human community. We seek to make our presence in the world as faithful people a gift rather than a curse. And we discover resources *within* each of our traditions that, when lifted up in our thinking and acting, enable us to be just that.

How, then, do we understand our common humanity alongside the humanity of all others in relation to the covenantal promises of blessing our respective scriptures convey? What *kind* of "blessing" might this be? It would involve frameworks for abundant life, for justice, peace, human rights, and for many other familiar values. But most of all it would mean a comprehensive human *polity* embodying responsibility to the civic values connected with overlapping Abrahamic visions of God's rule in human affairs. By "polity" I intend the meaning given first in most dictionary definitions, namely "civil order." A "polity" for the human race is not simply some "world government," some UN-like forum for interchange among sovereign states and their governments, although that difficult achievement needs to be continued and strengthened. A polity in the sense intended here would be a form of life together under God, a texture of acknowledged responsibilities to one another, a great community that recognized and included all other communities on earth without trampling on any of them. For there to be something like such a global civil order, a textured way of life embodied in institutions of every kind, we need some form of public moral imagination that is capable of including a great range of more particular moral narratives that bind humanity into a community of generous and expectant life. This reality, however institutionalized, is the goal of my argument.

Not surprisingly, such a comprehensive civic order would be inherently "religious": first in the content-neutral sense of *re-ligio,* meaning "binding together," and then in the intrinsically "covenantal," in the content-full range of senses given that word in the Abrahamic faiths. Again, I do not mean an amalgam or syncretistic combination of three faiths into one, but an ongoing civil discourse among the Mosaic, Messianic, and Islamic forms of Abrahamism. What we as Jews, Christians, and Muslims together owe humanity are our tradition-based gifts of responsibility for trying to help such a global polity into being, and to help its embodiment through appropriate and just institutions.

A Proposal for before, or after, the "War"?

Some shifts of theological consciousness come about only when violence or plague sweep a former world away. With many others, I take for granted that we are headed for events that will mark a major historical break in the human condition as we have known it since the dawn of modernity. What might such a break consist of? A global financial collapse? The use of nuclear weapons by terrorists and nuclear replies by the United States, Britain, France, or Israel? Or merely a more contemporary version of Oswald Spengler's "decline of the West," in which the United States would cease, out of its own folly and with help from Asian competition, to be a superpower and other powers would inevitably become realigned? One can pray for the latter sort of break. It would risk violence, but would not need to become violent. It could be a good thing for humanity.

The first duty of those who believe that religious communities might yet have some influence in the world is to do their best to help humanity to come to the softest landing possible, much as happened in South Africa in the nineties when most were expecting a bloodbath. But proposals such as this one may not (to say the least) be able to head off a catastrophe. They may not come into their own until some global paroxysm has brought the human race, or what is left of it, to its knees, or its senses. A lesson from a history I know well (others could give their own examples): from 1937 onward, as war in Europe drew near, Christian theologians and church leaders (others may have too) met repeatedly to gather up what they had learned over the preceding half-century of nascent Christian ecumenical effort, with the idea of launching a bold new initiative. Nearly simultaneously, theological works were underway that were later to prove enormously influential. Dietrich Bonhoeffer was already at work on his *Ethics.* Reinhold Niebuhr was giving the Gifford Lectures in Edinburgh, afterward published as *The Nature and Destiny of Man*. (German soldiers were marching into Poland even as Niebuhr neared his conclusion in September 1939.) The ecumenical thinking and planning subsequently continued underground, and in safe locations like Geneva.

Little of this activity was to bear fruit openly until after the war, with the formation of the World Council of Churches at Amsterdam in 1948 and a renaissance of theological studies in the West. These developments, of course, followed closely on the formation of the United Nations and the adoption of the Universal Declaration on Human Rights. No one in that postwar dawn could but be aware that in the conflict just concluded "Christian nations" had opposed one another in the trenches. Christian combatants on each side had fought against equally committed Christians on the other, just as Sunnis and Shi'a are doing in Iraq now. The mood at the war's close in 1945 was to say "never again." A network among the churches needed to be built that could remain intact across whatever new political and ideological chasms might open in the future. The interreligious dimension was, for most, not yet on the horizon.

Now, in the year 2008, much has changed, but much is also hauntingly familiar. Christian ecumenism has accomplished much, but some of its major goals remain unfulfilled. Adherents of the three Abrahamic faiths are already fighting among themselves and against one another in Israel-Palestine, Afghanistan, and Iraq. Such struggles, just though their objectives may be, threaten to ignite yet another global conflagration: financial, biological, nuclear, or otherwise. And once again we need to lay plans together—this time on an interreligious basis—that we pray will bear fruit in time to head off such a tragedy. Perhaps our present efforts will turn out to have been already too late for that. Perhaps our present thinking will turn out to mean more when the next war—this time an intercultural, interreligious war—is over, and again we say to each other, "never again," and again we try to weave a network of trust, solidarity, and responsibility, this time among the three faiths and others, a tissue of relationships that we hope can resist all ideological and political pressures to tear it apart.

Notes

1. See Mark Juergensmeyer, *Terror in the Mind of God: The Global Rise of Religious Violence* (Berkeley: University of California Press, 2000).

2. See René Girard, *Things Hidden Since the Foundation of the World* (Stanford: Stanford University Press, 1987).

3. Thomas L. Friedman's views on this subject have appeared in countless *New York Times* Op-Ed columns and in books such as *From Beirut to Jerusalem* (New York: Farrar Strauss and Giroux, 1989), *The Lexus and the Olive Tree* (New York: Farrar Strauss and Giroux, 2000), and *The World Is Flat: A Brief History of the Twenty-First Century* (New York: Farrar, Strauss and Giroux, 2005).

4. This description of the subject matter often pursued in typical local interfaith groups combines my own experience with that of Heidi Hadsell, president of Hartford Seminary, offered in private correspondence.

5. See Diana Eck, *Encountering God: A Spiritual Journey from Bozeman to Banaras* (Boston: Beacon Press, 1993); S. Mark Heim, *Salvations: Truth and Difference in Religion* (Maryknoll, NY: Orbis Books, 1995); Willard G. Oxtoby, ed., *World Religions*, 2 vols. (New York: Oxford University Press, 2002).

6. See Paul Knitter, *Towards a Protestant Theology of Religions: A Case Study of Paul Althaus and Contemporary Attitudes* (Marburg: N. G. Elwert, 1974); *One Earth, Many Religions: Multifaith Dialogue and Global Responsibility* (Maryknoll, NY: Orbis Books, 1995); *No Other Name? A Critical Survey of Christian Attitudes Toward the World Religions* (Maryknoll, NY: Orbis Books, 1985); *Jesus and the Other Names: Christian Mission and Global Responsibility* (Maryknoll, NY: Orbis Books, 1995); *Introducing Theologies of Religions* (Maryknoll, NY: Orbis Books, 2002); *The Myth of Religious Superiority: Multifaith Explorations of Religious Pluralism* (Maryknoll, NY: Orbis Books, 2005).

7. See John Hick, ed., *Truth and Dialogue in World Religions: Conflicting Truth Claims* (Philadelphia: Westminster Press, 1974); *Three Faiths—One God: A Jewish, Christian, Muslim Encounter,* ed. with Edmund S. Meltzer (Albany: State University of New York Press, 1988); *The Second Christianity* (London: SCM Press, 1983); *Problems of Religious Pluralism* (New York: St. Martin's Press, 1985).

8. Richard Mouw and Sander Griffioen, *Pluralisms and Horizons: An Essay in Christian Public Philosophy* (Grand Rapids, MI: Eerdmans, 1993).

9. Kenneth L. Vaux, *Jew, Christian, Muslim* (Eugene, OR: Wipf and Stock Publishers, 2003).

10. F. E. Peters, *Judaism, Christianity and Islam* (Princeton, NJ: Princeton University Press, 1990).

11. Jonathan Sacks, *The Persistence of Faith: Religion, Morality and Society in a Secular Age* (London: Continuum, 2005).

12. Jonathan Sacks, *The Politics of Hope* (London: Jonathan Cape, 1997).

13. Jonathan Sacks, *The Dignity of Difference: How to Avoid the Clash of Civilizations* (New York: Continuum, 2002).

14. Jonathan Sacks, *To Heal a Fractured World: The Ethics of Responsibility* (New York: Schocken Books, 2005).

15. Norman Solomon, Richard Harries, and Tim Winter, eds., *Abraham's Children: Jews, Christians and Muslims in Conversation* (New York: T&T Clark, 2005).

16. Joan Chittister, Murshid Saadi Shakur Chisti, and Arthur Waskow, *The Tent of Abraham: Stories of Hope and Peace for Jews, Christians and Muslims* (Boston: Beacon Press, 2006).

17. Bruce Feiler, *Abraham, A Journey to the Heart of Three Faiths* (New York: Harper Collins, 2002).

18. The Rev. Canon Guy Wilkinson, the Archbishop's interfaith advisor, in a press release May 21, 2007.

19. This point has been made by the Muslim liberation theologian Farid Esack.

20. Clifford Geertz, *Islam Observed* (New Haven, CT: Yale University Press, 1968).

21. Clifford Geertz, "Which Way to Mecca? Part II," *The New York Review of Books,* July 3, 2003, 36.

22. Adam B. Seligman, *The Idea of Civil Society* (New York: Free Press, 1992).

23. Robert J. Schreiter, *The New Catholicity: Theology Between the Global and the Local* (Maryknoll, NY: Orbis Books, 1997).

24. *Nostra Aetate* is the *Declaration on the Relation of the Church with Non-Christian Religions* of the Second Vatican Council, promulgated by Pope Paul VI on October 28, 1965. See Austin Flannery, ed., *Vatican Council II: The Conciliar and Post-Conciliar Documents* (Northport, NY: Costello Publishing Company, 1998), 738ff.

25. "Dialogue and Proclamation," a document produced by the Pontifical Council for Interreligious Dialogue, 1991, following on an earlier document *The Attitude of the Catholic Church toward the Followers of Other Religious Traditions: Reflections and Orientations on Dialogue and Mission,* May 10, 1984.

26. Philip L. Wickeri, ed., *The People of God among All God's People: Frontiers in Christian Mission* (London: Christian Conference of Asia/The Council for World Mission, 2000), 28. Report from a theological roundtable sponsored by the Christian Conference of Asia and the Council for World Mission, Hong Kong, November 11–17, 1999.

27. See Knitter, *Introducing Theologies of Religions.*

28. S. Mark Heim, "Sharing Our Differences: Koinonia and the Theology of Religious Plurality," in *Faith and Order at the Crossroads, Kuala Lumpur, 2004,* Faith and Order Paper 196 (Geneva: WCC Publications, 2005), 320.

29. Henry David Thoreau, *Walden,* in Joseph Wood Krutch, ed., *Walden and Other Writings by Henry David Thoreau* (New York: Bantam Books, 1981), 351.

30. This conference, brilliantly conceived and realized under the leadership of WCC staff member Hans Ucko, did not seem to me to reach much agreement about the "critical" nature of the moment concerned.

31. Address by Archbishop Rowan Williams at the Ninth Assembly of the World Council of Churches, Porto Alegre, Brazil, February 14–23, 2006, Document PLEN 02.1.

32. Kwame Anthony Appiah, *Cosmopolitanism: Ethics in a World of Strangers* (New York: W. W. Norton, 2006).

33. One may compare the contemporary usage of the term "rooted cosmopolitans" with the Nazi term "rootless cosmopolitans" to describe Jews for whom solidarity with Jews everywhere in the world was a value that transcended loyalty to the Third Reich.

2

Public Religions in the Modern World
Opportunity and Responsibility

Religious institutions functioning in modernity become what they become in part because they have seized, or failed to seize, certain situational opportunities. The core affirmations of faith remain, but expressions of faith can change as religious communities respond creatively to new situations. Such changes can in turn affect the ways in which core affirmations are eventually understood.

The religious situation described in the preceding chapter confronts world religions—and the Abrahamic faiths in particular—with significant situational opportunities to be either seized or ignored as the case may be. It is, of course, not as if global faith communities were organized to be able to make radical choices all at once. Genuinely historic turns have often begun by being local and modest, only later to be seen as the significant moves they turn out to be. Wisdom calls for careful analysis of options before directional decisions even begin to be made. Such an analysis of the possibilities of religion in modernity is the purpose of this chapter.

The importance of religious choices made to meet the challenges of particular situations is well attested in scripture. See Deuteronomy 30 or Joshua 24. But the very idea of faith communities maintaining their identities yet literally remaking themselves by their responses to historic opportunities would astound most sages and saints of the past, who have generally upheld the values of historical continuity across the ages. Indeed, in nearly every known society and culture up to now, religion has occupied a relatively fixed social location, and has performed a relatively fixed set of social tasks. Legitimating, ritualizing, giving moral instruction, connecting the orders of this world to the order of heaven: all such duties have been familiar parts of the priestly portfolio. The thought that religious institutions might at some moment reinterpret their traditions to call for being and doing something radically *different* has not occurred to many minds before the present time. It has been easier to exchange one religion for another than to rethink the fundamental social functions, and hence articulation of any given historic faith.

But today the latter sort of change is possible, if only because religious communities of the West are met with fewer *fixed* expectations than they used to be. As they emerge from various forms of Enlightenment-enforced marginalization, or take root in new cultures altogether, they have choices to make they have rarely had before. Some emerging religious bodies choose to replicate what they take to have been their traditional roles. Others claim freedom to become what they will be. The latter choice imposes a heavy responsibility for discerning opportunities clearly and for choosing means to pursue them wisely. Wise discerning and choosing not only can lead to new public responsibilities, it also can lead to new understandings of traditional affirmations and of the conclusions that can be drawn from them.

Such a reimagining begins to take place as we ask what responsibility Jews, Christians, and Muslims bear today, not only for the well-being of each clan, or tribe, or nation but also for the well-being of the whole of humankind. Acting together, how capable might these faiths prove to be in channeling covenantal "blessings" to "all the families of the earth"? Where might they find opportunities to exercise such responsibility, and how might they go about it? This chapter, as it unfolds, explores a series of case studies of changes in the recent roles of religious bodies in western societies and seeks to adapt the lessons these cases teach to the contemporary situation of the Abrahamic faiths.

Unquestionably, the hope that humanity might become a single peaceful, "blessed" community in some form (Gen 12:3) is now in the air we breathe, even as that very air is constantly polluted by the smoke of bursting bombs and shells. Many of us have not forgotten hearing Beethoven's Ninth Symphony with its *Hymn to Joy* played by the Berlin Philharmonic as the Wall came down in 1989. The hopes of humankind were for one instant tuned to that sound, only to hear it fade away, as nations and tribes fuelled by religious hatreds began again to enforce their rival interests by economic, political, and military means. What better role for the Abrahamic communities than to put aside their historic animosities, to cease legitimating violence, and try to discern together what might be needed to bring the idea of a global commonwealth at last within humanity's grasp?

Visions of a Peaceful Human Polity

It is not as if the notion of a single human community bridging historic differences were being proposed here for the first time. From the massive mud bricks of Babel to the infinitesimal electrical impulses of the Internet, imperialists and dictators, visionaries and prophets, philosophers and entrepreneurs, scientists and sociologists, programmers and proprietors have sought to conceive the notion of such a global commonwealth and, so far as they could, to act it out.

Nor is it as if there were not elements of such a global polity already in existence among us today. Such a proposal, as an agenda for the Abrahamic faiths, in fact joins an ongoing secular conversation about the fundamental nature of the human community. Likewise it joins a debate with contemporary projects that try in many respects to realize such a vision. The impulse to gather humanity around some idea, regime, system, capability, or promise that can render the world's people—so far as they can be significantly known or thought to count[1]—a single ordered community exists today in many forms: political, economic, scientific, communicative.

Nearly every such vision of global society, ancient or modern, has consisted of the proposed universalization of some existing polity or moral vision (the Babylonian Empire, the ancient Roman Republic, a Kantian ethics of duty, the British way of life) seen as a gift of wisdom to the rest of the world. Listen to John Ruskin's question, addressing the Oxford Union in 1878:

> Will you, youths of England, make your country again a royal throne of kings, a sceptered isle, for all the world a source of light, a centre of peace; mistress of learning and of the Arts, faithful guardian of great memories in the midst of ephemeral and irreverent visions; faithful servant of time-tried principles?[2]

The roles played by religious communities or ideologies in such imperial enterprises have almost always been both indispensable and ambiguous, both integrative and divisive. In nearly every such case, religious idealism has combined with economic interests and political adventurism. Sometimes religion has been at the heart of the effort. Sometimes it has been used by other integrative forces for their own purposes. Sometimes it has mitigated political violence. Sometimes it has exacerbated it. What religion may or may not offer the nascent global polities—economic, political, communicative—that struggle contemporarily to be born is a topic of high priority for this book.

Of late, the integrating imperial impulse has arisen especially in the economic realm, as mercantilism has given way to industrialization and to a "globalization" aimed at gathering the world's principal economic power sources into a single system thought capable of generating enough wealth—and hence peace and prosperity—for all. One wonders what will be the fate of the present global capitalistic experiment. This is, as we will see in the next chapter, not *only* an economic matter, involving as it does communications, education, culture, and much else. Whatever outcome one foresees, it is important for the opponents and critics of this venture to realize how much genuine, even if miscalculating, idealism has gone into it. Profit has been the main motive, of course. But many have, and still do, sincerely hold the belief that a genuine "blessing" is at hand: that the profit motive can be harnessed today to promote peace and prosperity for all on earth on a scale of inclusion unimagined by previous generations.

Whatever one may make of such an argument, we human beings know full well today that we *already* live, in many but not all dimensions of life, as a single global community. "Globalization" now names the scope of the ways things work on this planet, the ways in which human interactions are organized, the fields of information sharing and of policy deliberation. One might say that global prosperity and capacities for communication across cultures create conditions under which the many deeper life-understandings found in traditional human communities might now make their claims more successfully than before: clothing mere economics with deeper purposes. Such profounder polities, beyond mere exchange relationships, have struggled repeatedly to be born and just as repeatedly have failed to materialize or to maintain themselves for long. At some moments many of us have felt that parts of the world at least stood on the brink of achieving, out of traditional sources, deeper forms of communal imagination than those sustainable by merely governmental or economic means. Such was the hope shared by many at the inauguration of Nelson Mandela in 1995 as the choir sang the haunting national, but far more than national, anthem *God Bless Africa*.

But such inspiration, such "collective effervescence" (Émile Durkheim) has always quickly vanished. At other moments, such as the present dispiriting one only a few years later, a moment full of foreboding and despair, such goals seem not just out of reach. Indeed, pursuing them in the face of more immediate pressing needs seems the height of spiritually empty irresponsibility: what the French call *une fuite en avant*, an attempted escape from a difficult present into a high-mindedly imagined but likely unattainable future.

Perhaps it is best to write books like this one not in ecstatic moments of promise but from the depths of experienced futility, anger, and despair. At least we are now being warned every day against underestimating the power of evil in human affairs. And we are also daily warned against placing undue confidence in our own political institutions, or those of the West generally, as carriers of a promise to humankind.

Naming the Present Moment

There can be no meaningful inter-Abrahamic agenda without a situational analysis. What then is the situation as regards religious communities in the public world, and particularly in the Western world with which we are concerned? Only in recent decades have there been opportunities to think out this task with global and instantaneous means of information-gathering and communication, as well as with adequate knowledge of the actual, global, human reality in all its fullness of detail, its multiplicity of cultures, religious faiths, vital interests, and proclivities to violence. On the one hand, such detailed knowledge of the multiple expressions of the human condition relativizes all forms of high-minded generalization and enthusiasm. We know the task will require much more than waving a well-meant idealistic wand.[3] On the other hand, this sort of knowledge gives us traction: an awareness of just what it is—in all its specificity and detail—that we need to get hold of and resolve before the human race can be visibly a single community.

What of this present moment? What can be discerned about it? Of the multitude of recently articulated perspectives on our global present, each with its own tag line—"the end of history," "the clash of civilizations," "the world is flat," and so forth—my attention is caught by the simultaneity of two large shifts of cultural attitude. What may be the connections, if any, between them? What, if anything, may they have to do with the present prominence of economic considerations in the world's search for an inclusive global polity?

The first trend is a loss of confidence in the polity-sustaining power of a wide range of "modern" public institutions and political world views. The second trend, for better or worse, is a return to public prominence and influence on the part of religious and other value-bearing communities. The latter circumstance is a form of "identity politics," in which religious and other groups struggle for advantage in the vacuum left by the first-mentioned state of affairs.

But before describing these trends more carefully, it is important to understand that I do not see them necessarily as competitors in a contest for power that only one "side" can win, or as distinct life-compartments that communicate, if at all, with great difficulty. Every human being is in some way involved *both* in specific value-bearing communities *and* in the public political mechanisms, assumptions, and ideals that enable different values to coexist in the same polity. The distinction between communities that generate and maintain values and the arrangements that help such different value-worlds to live peacefully alongside one another is useful analytically. But it is a distinction *within* the whole interactive reality that is a human society. Each of us is *both* a specific value-maintainer *and* a citizen giving allegiance to the meanings maintained by the public order as a whole. Yet, as we will see, it is no easy task to describe the actual (or preferable) relationships between these elements of polity in any given case. One can see continuing shifts in the *kinds* of relationships existing between these "spheres" of life, as one moves from one culture to another, or from one epoch to the next.

Our first general observation nevertheless applies. A loss of confidence in meanings formerly maintained by public orders in the West has had profound consequences for the search for an inclusive human polity. Public values (human rights, the rule of law, etc.) that began to emerge in the seventeenth and eighteenth centuries in what later came to be called "the modern project"—a term already spoken with a certain sense of historical distance, as if we were not still living it out—now provoke more cynicism than reverence. Institutions built on such values are in consequence less able today to regulate competing religious and social identities.

Of course, this loss of confidence in public institutions and values takes different forms in different places and circumstances. It is more noticeable, at present, in the United States and less noticeable elsewhere. One must also be careful not to lump together phenomena that do not belong together. But one observes not only the "postmodern" attack on universalistic assumptions underlying democratic practices, but also the sheer deterioration and corruption, the political prevarication, the personal forms of aggrandizement, that have begun to undermine many "democratic" political institutions. Egregious illegal lobbying, private payoffs, unconstitutional information-gathering shrouded in official secrecy, legislated despoiling of the environment for private profit, all go on despite repeated pious political promises to root them out. One also sees the large-scale transfer of power from public institutions to transnational corporations run for profit. The unexpected resistance of non-Western cultures to "democratization" schemes shows, among other things, how Western democracies now look to people representing other political traditions.

Above all, we see a loss of confidence in what used to be called "public reason."[4] Public discourse deteriorates into "spin." Justifications of policy become specious. A Princeton philosopher has the appropriate word for such reasoning: "bullshit."[5] He does not hesitate to use this word as the title of his recent book. The deterioration of our public institutions and our resulting loss of trust in them are now producing the first appearing of doubt that these institutions, as carriers of democracy, *can* lead toward the world civil order that Enlightenment philosophers hoped to found.

As for the second observation, concerning the increasing "publicness" of Western religious institutions, again one must generalize with care. I emphasize "Western." This generalization looks different, if it applies at all, in, say, Muslim lands where religion has nearly always been a highly visible component of the public order. Religious publicness is thus a useful category, but one must say exactly what sort and social location of publicness one means. What I have in mind includes, but is something more than, mere frequent mention of religious matters on the evening news. It is the coming of awareness both by newsmakers and news consumers that religion, like it or not, is today having a profound impact not only on personal lives but on global events. I have in mind an extremely wide range of phenomena. There is the continued publicness of Roman Catholicism, born of its sheer size and power and public fascination with the papacy, not to speak of successful diplomatic interventions in places like Poland and Spain. There is also the rise of politicized Christian evangelicalism in the United States. Notice the way evangelicals who eschewed politics and attacked politically involved Christians while that position suited their agenda have in the last twenty years or so become political activists when they saw there were gains to be made. Formerly aloof evangelicals have become activist "postmillennial"[6] zealots. In Judaism, much now turns on attitudes, including U.S. governmental attitudes, to political decisions made by the government of Israel. And one must mention the emergence of radical Islam as a factor in policy calculations across the globe. Wahabism and other extremist tendencies seem to receive little or no public criticism from more pacific Islamic opinion, thus seeming to many in the West to speak for this entire faith.

Obviously these forms of public prominence are by no means all the same thing, either in inner assumptions or public outcomes. Long after many secularists, especially in Western Europe, concluded that religion had been permanently banished from the public realm, we see this subject on the front pages day after day: not because journalists have undergone conversions but because they increasingly realize that religious convictions, set in motion, have public impact. More often than not, the stories journalists write concern religious conflicts that threaten to impact other social institutions. "Values voters" who think in personal-conduct terms install administrations that trample some of the same values in the public realm.

We seem sometimes in danger of returning to the period of religious warfare once thought terminated by the 1648 Treaty of Westphalia, followed by the coming of Enlightenment consciousness that marginalized and privatized expressions of faith. But one can say that media tend congenitally to introduce distortions in the messages they report. A preference for recording conflict can exacerbate the actual conflicts concerned, reducing *all* to threatened schism and missing nuances representing progress toward agreement. Cynicism often marks media attitudes toward gestures and moments of reconciliation.

One has to say that the new publicness offers religious groups new opportunities for doing good in the world, but seldom is the message they transmit a fully fair representation of the message intended. Sometimes it is almost the opposite. Without publicness, one goes back to marginalization and irrelevance. With it, one has a capacity for public influence that one cannot entirely expect to control. Well-intended words and actions can be and are used by those who have an interest in distorting them, or be met with well-deserved public indifference. Publicness is indispensable for religious groups that intend to make a difference to the well-being of humankind. Yet it can be a two-edged sword needing to be wielded with great care.

The assumption has to be that these two circumstances—the unravelment of confidence in Enlightenment-based political ideas and institutions on the one hand, and the emergence of religious traditions and communities as significant "players" in public affairs on the other—are somehow connected. What is going on here? Mindless religious motivations overwhelming "reality-based" reasoning? Scheming politicians successfully using unreflective religion for their purposes? Abandonment of inclusive political symbols in favor of supportive communitarian identities? Certainly all of the above. But perhaps the interactions do not play out in exactly the ways one first thinks of. One would not be wrong to think that distrust of public political institutions triggers for some a shift of faith from secular notions of progress to seemingly irrational apocalyptic hopes and fears. Or to think that some religious bodies are taking conscious advantage of such circumstances to pursue their own institutional interests. Or to think that secular forces use religion for secular purposes and that religion uses secular forces for religious purposes. Of course, such dynamics as these take a variety of forms in different circumstances and places. Whether we speak of North America, or of Europe, of Arab lands, or of Latin America, or of the rest of the southern hemisphere, in every circumstance, the outworking of such events takes on its own historical logic and configuration.

But is any fundamental storyline discernible running through these circumstances? Astute observers have offered us several models for understanding what is going on in many of these instances. Consider what the rise of "public religion," combined ironically with the loss of the very idea of a coherent "secular" public world means to several contemporary interpreters.

It is hard, for example, to believe how recently Francis Fukuyama's book *The End of History*[7] saw both political passions and religious convictions, as well as the conflict associated with them, as having been overtaken by a world order based on technology and global economic systems and therefore shorn of the likelihood of further "history"-making conflicts. Fukuyama has since repudiated much of this position. Yet his book reminds us of the continued power of economic and technological forces that may yet engulf both political and religious forms of reflection and action.

Another older narrative, with useful lessons to teach, is still with us. This is the familiar projection by Samuel Huntington of a coming "clash" of different religiously inspired and dominated civilizations, a view that sees the "secular" institutions as unable to resist or hold the combatants apart.[8] Put this another way: for Huntington, so dominant has become the differentiating power of religious traditions in different cultures that appeals to bridges between such cultures based on shared secular political principles, or on common economic interests for that matter, will be futile. This is a view still seen by many critics as overgeneralizing in view of widely diverse kinds of evidence and, as a result, unduly neat and schematic. Yet it remains provocative. Evidence for it continues to accumulate.

But we are now beginning to hear still another, different, explanatory story: that humanity is headed for a global battle, not between religiously based cultures as such, but between, on the one hand, the "powerful particularism of religious passion and commitment," a force seen as arising similarly in many different situations and traditions of faith, and, on the other hand, the "libertarian, skeptical and cosmopolitan ideals of the Enlightenment."[9] This last-named conflict presumably runs right through the middle of each of Huntington's different "civilizations," dividing religious from secular energies in each case.

For many secular observers, this second sort of "clash" is provoking responses that seek to save Enlightenment and other forms of scientific reasoning from debilitating attack. We hear the view that religious forces are not only battling Enlightenment ideals but beginning to undermine them in principle. Some fear that we may be losing the achievements of the Enlightenment altogether in a rising tide of faith-based political activity that threatens to return us, perhaps violently, to something like the premodern world. This could threaten to be so in the Christianist politics at the moment of writing pursued in Washington. When a president of the United States, by his own assertion, relies more on divine guidance and ideology-driven convictions concerning his own messianic calling than on analysis of facts on the ground, we seem in danger of losing, at least in the political realm, much that the Enlightenment has accomplished. There are many, especially in the scientific and scholarly worlds, who think it urgent that religion be finally done away with for the sake of the future of the human race. As it stands, it is too productive of illusion, violence, and hatred to be allowed to survive. I think of books like Daniel Dennett's *Breaking the Spell*, a volume that sees religion as a fundamental danger to human well-being that must be exposed and undermined by the application of scientific reasoning.[10] The antireligious diatribe is an old literary form. But the present danger calls out new examples that together begin to look like a crusade to save human rationality from its enemies.

Many will say that an Enlightenment-style rationalization of public life has come to the West at a heavy spiritual price. But to lose Enlightenment achievements altogether to a tide of religious obscurantism and sectarian strife could plunge the world into darkness. And if the Enlightenment and modernity go down, much that we hold dear goes down with them. Hence across-the-board attacks on the "spell" of religion as responsible for superstition and violence across the globe, and tracts championing the scientific method as the basis of a new world order.

All this said, I see the *essential* problem of the modern era to lie in the inability of our connectional capacities—the organized communicative, deliberative, and necessarily *political* elements of life together—to accommodate, or even adequately respond to, the many expressions of value, of final ends, of the good, that human beings generate in families and religious communities. All this despite the essential interrelatedness of the two spheres concerned. We have lost our trust in our institutions of organization and deliberation. And we have seen competing religious values themselves become more public, and therefore aggressive or even violent in their respective claims.

Here lies the possibility of a disaster of which we will need to say more later. But there may also be the possibility of an exit from this impasse in which some social class, or force, or combination of circumstances and events, becomes the "carrier" (as Max Weber put it) of some unexpected resolution of our present troubles. Where are we likely to find such "carriers" of the next moment in human history—no doubt a moment with its own problems to deal with? Are there seeds of a just polity for humanity planted among us? Or put it another way: is there something *now* going on—whether in some corner or in plain sight—that, if we fully understood it and perceived its importance, could give us a hint of what the future will be? Or, to what trends do we hitch our hopes for a just, inclusive human polity or civil order?

To hold membership in a social group on which history has conferred the responsibility for bringing to pass history's next stage is to receive a gift of special responsibility, a gift of responsibility for playing one's inevitable historic role. Along this path of reasoning, responsibility can come to be seen as a providential gift to be cherished, protected, and acted out in confidence that one is chosen to accomplish great things.

Who, if anyone, is in such a position today? A generation ago, I would have put my trust in the Christian ecumenical movement. I am still loyal to that. But I think it must be transformed into a "next" ecumenism of Abrahamic faiths acting together. Yet many, as we have seen, perceive the carrier of the human future as the global capitalist network of trade relationships: the carrier is then the new entrepreneur. Karl Marx, of course, assigned the task of carrying the future in an awakened proletariat. Horkheimer and Adorno saw the future in the growing importance of human scientists like themselves: the analysts of society. Freud found it in the profession that could analyze persons' psyches.

One can indeed go beyond this short list of enterprises and movements that have been seen as bearing the seeds of a new pan-human polity. The scientific method and scientific community generally, the British Empire and English-speaking culture, Chinese culture bearing technological and commercial enterprise, the "language of film" said on theater trailers to be "universal," sports enterprises such as the Olympic games, the World Cup, a nascent world basketball league. Not to omit what could be the most powerful and fruitful seed of all, the Internet as instrument of both politics and culture.

It would be seen by most people as unpersuasive to identify religious communities, or some combination of them, as significant carriers of the human future. In modern times, they have either remained on the margins of public life and allowed nefarious influences (including the loss of confidence in public institutions, the diminishment of political participation) to grow unchallenged, or at most lamented with earnest wringing of hands along the sidelines, or they have interpreted their own value-bearing activities very literally, politically, and aggressively, often in an effort to gain "theocratic" control of institutions (like school boards) in the public world. Either way, they have precisely not seemed to most people to have done anything much to ensure a human future in which a global civic order, or polity, could come to be out of the creative and peaceful, orderly, interactions of ongoing communities of conviction and value.

Yet in the growing class of religiously rooted cosmopolitans one has the combination of faithful foundations and citizenship in the world of modernity that seems needed. Rabbi Jonathan Sacks and others speak of the ability to be fluent in "two languages": that of one's faith and that of the public world. Well and good, but I think we need more than the combination in each person of languages that remain different. We need a form of cosmopolitanism that is responsive to faith. And an understanding of faith responsive to cosmopolitan needs. And the combination needs to be defined and held in being by some kind of movement that perpetuates practices in which many persons can participate. And such a movement needs a level of clear social analysis and purpose that has not yet emerged. Still, let us wrestle with writing an agenda for such a movement. None of the analyses touched upon in this chapter offers much encouragement to rooted Abrahamic cosmopolitans looking for a way to mean something to modern humanity, to discharge the responsibility of speaking constructively to our world. Does there exist an analysis of the present moment that can show us a possible way forward? There is one, and I devote the next section of this chapter to expounding it, criticizing it, and teasing out its potential.

A Visionary Perspective: The Social Analysis of José Casanova

At the close of his book *Public Religions in the Modern World*, the sociologist José Casanova makes the following extraordinary statement:

> Religious traditions are now confronting the differentiated secular spheres, challenging them to face their own obscurantist, ideological and inauthentic claims. In many of these confrontations it is religion which, as often as not, appears to be on the side of human enlightenment. It would be profoundly ironic if, after all the beatings it has received from modernity, religion could somehow unintentionally help modernity save itself.[11]

Reading these words, one's first impulse is to ask what world are we talking about. Religious communities might, even unintentionally, help modernity save itself? What religious communities? What "modernity"? In what sense "save"? Already we must conjecture what Casanova means. By "modernity" we generally mean the particular historical epoch we are living through, knowing that it may now be reaching its end, under attack from "postmodernity," and metamorphosing toward whatever comes next. Surely Casanova's point is not to resist this inevitable process, saying with Goethe, "Stay, thou art so fair." Rather Casanova presumably wants modernity not to scuttle its own great achievements in the process of meeting whatever future may be in store. Modernity, we think he means, needs to be saved from the self-betrayals that have gone with its successes. It needs help in being able to act so that its promises may be less ambiguously fulfilled, made more accessible to all, than they are now. We should seek to evangelize our age by helping it make repairs where its best ideals have gone awry. This is what this sociologist thinks religious communities have, ironically enough, in some cases already done, and, taking thought, could yet do.

Casanova's assertion to this effect sums up a book-length demolition of the once widespread consensus among sociologists and others that in the "modern" world, religious organizations, activities, and beliefs would become ever weaker, more marginalized, and publicly ineffective. Casanova has produced here a denial of crucial parts[12] of the so-called "secularization hypothesis," the *grand récit* (to use a term of Fernand Braudel) or "story" of modernity favored in the last century by a seeming majority of secular scholars. At mid-twentieth century these observers believed, and many of their successors still do believe, that religion, faced by modernity, would inevitably decline in public influence, become increasingly marginalized and privatized, and eventually disappear from the public sphere altogether.

That this has not happened continues to amaze many observers. Efforts by some members of our three faiths to benefit humanity by wreaking a cleansing violence upon the "infidel" (note blessing and curse together here) are such as to lead some in the West to say, simplistically, that we must get rid of religion altogether, as if Western civilization were not in trouble quite apart from the persistence in it of religious communities. The ignorance and arrogance of some of these statements are astounding, yet so is their awareness of the fragility of the secular perspective. A quotation reported recently in the *New York Times*:

> We in the West find it incomprehensible that theological ideas still inflame the minds of men, stirring up messianic passions that can leave societies in ruin. We had assumed that this was no longer possible, that human beings had learned to separate religious questions from political ones, that political theology died in 16th century Europe. We were wrong. It is *we* who are the fragile exception.[13]

And so we who profess faith set out to help this "fragile exception" save itself by coming to understand its own nature and needs. For we need this "exception" to keep the Enlightenment critique alive and to help keep religion itself from reverting entirely to the premodern.

Casanova's analysis is designed to help by giving us case studies, admittedly only Western Christian ones,[14] in which religious communities have accomplished something like this. He shows that religious bodies, since the early 1980s if not before, began, much as we have observed, to play totally unexpected and remarkably potent political and social roles. The sociologist cites a series of developments involving Roman Catholicism in Spain, Poland, Brazil, and the United States, along with signs of a then-newly potentiated American Protestant evangelicalism.

Such groups, Casanova argues, not only began in this period to be newly effective participants in debates over public issues. They often found themselves, sometimes inadvertently, it seems, on the side of values such as democracy and human rights. The Roman Catholic Church in Poland, for example, fought for its own survival against Communism, but also—partly through its connection with the "Solidarity" movement—became a powerful democratizing influence in Polish society. In other places as well, religious institutions—often in spite of themselves—turned out to be carriers, in some sense, of human "enlightenment." Secular institutions, even those with roots in *the* Enlightenment, often did not.

In the light of these historical case studies, and in the face of a "modernity" struggling with deteriorating institutions and now increasingly given over to the destructive logics of rivalries for global dominance and the ideology of the global market, religious communities might now, in Casanova's view, turn out to be significant contributors to restoring the Enlightenment's promise of values such as freedom, human rights, and democracy to the human race.

So far, this analysis agrees generally with what I have already said about religion's new publicness. It accords as well with the widespread notion of a loss of confidence in public institutions. Talk about "obscurantist, ideological and inauthentic claims"! But what is all this about religion being "on the side of human enlightenment"? And what of the "ironic" possibility that religion might "somehow unintentionally help modernity save itself"? Casanova has moved from supporting common wisdom with detailed case studies to a fine brash hypothesis of what, given the right conditions, this might mean for the role of religion in Western society over the next hundred years.

How plausible is this hypothesis? Obviously, all Casanova's studies relate to one religion, Christianity, functioning in traditionally Christian-majority nations. Can his data also apply to the possible public roles of Judaism and Islam? An affirmative answer is not self-evident. Detailed case studies of the same sort would need to be drawn from a variety of settings of comparable cultural dominance. In the case of Judaism, such a case could only come from the State of Israel. I take up that situation briefly in chapter 8. For Islam, one could choose from a variety of possibilities, but it might be a stretch to show that Sharia law had anywhere helped "save" modernity from modernity's own self-betrayals. One has to say that an interreligious extension of Casanova's analysis is plausible mainly in Western situations where all three faiths exist under modern conditions. In those circumstances, it is plausible that cooperation among the Abrahamic faiths in public life might well enhance the Casanovian phenomenon by undercutting the grounds for saying that public witness is no more than self-interested special pleading. Jewish teachings about justice would easily meld with Christian teachings for the restoration of democratic institutions. It would remain to be seen just how Islamic teachings would do so, if only because Islam does not on the whole share the same cultural and political history.

Is Casanova's thesis in fact broadly applicable, or is it mainly a rhetorical flourish based on limited evidence by a writer relieved and happy to be on the final page of his manuscript? Suppose such a culminating hypothesis should give way to self-conscious agenda-building to help the very saving of modernity to happen. Is "saving modernity" what we want in any case? Is saving modernity a prerequisite for, or even tantamount to, founding a genuine global commonwealth or polity? One can argue, as we have seen, that humanity already has a global civilization, especially in the economic and communications arenas. Can one also say that countering the shortcomings of these achievements, supplanting their "obscurantist, ideological and inauthentic claims" with deeper human values, should bring us to the brink of the blessed inclusive polity we seek?

And why, for this purpose, should it be so important to "save modernity" rather than pursue a more direct course to the holy commonwealth? Why not build a "beloved community" of faiths acting together without taking this detour on the way to it? After all, many visionaries have long seen the "modern project" as a curse, and trying to "save" it a lost opportunity to let it die of its own self-contradictions. Yet I will argue here that, for the present moment, humanity's fate, even in majority Muslim lands, rests on modernity's fate. A collapse of modernity might well be accompanied by catastrophes that would place the continuation of human civilization as such in doubt. Jonathan Schell, in *The Fate of the Earth*, has written of no more little children, no more string quartets, no more books, no more plays, no more of anything worthwhile, if such a catastrophe engulfs us.[15]

Furthermore, we have seen that the institutions of modernity, including those oppressive institutions of economic globalization, constitute the nearest thing we now have to the comprehensive human polity we are seeking. The choice is between bringing this nascent world order down, with all the likely catastrophic consequences just mentioned and a need to start all over again, and doing what we can to "repair" it by introducing covenantal values designed to make globalization produce blessing rather than curse.

From what, after all, does modernity need to be saved? From its arrogance, from the decay of its political institutions, from the rapidly increasing differences between rich and poor, from a self-indulgent, shallow culture, from self-perpetuating hollow elitism at the top. The "best and brightest" have repeatedly shown themselves to be neither. Yet this parlous time of deeply compromised modern culture is the moment the human race must pass through on its way to whatever future awaits it. For some members of our species, the modern experiment is two hundred years old and showing signs of infirmity. For others it is an experience hardly yet assimilated. This contrast is itself a source of instability. If we do not overcome the dangers of the present time, there will *be* no human future. If we do save modernity from itself, important lessons will have been learned for making that future what it ought to be.

But in what sense might religious groups turn out to be carriers of such a project? Would all three communities of faith now be likely to see such a project as a theologically warranted responsibility? Would their traditions, even creatively interpreted, support it? Notice indeed Casanova's words "ironic" and "unintentionally." If religious communities can in fact "help modernity save itself," it will probably, this sociologist seems to think, not be because they have taken on this task as a self-conscious, thought-out responsibility. Rather, one might infer, any secular "salvation" they help bring about would likely be a byproduct of some other intention: competition for political advantage and/or cultural preference, institutional self-preservation.

Indeed, this is the predominant impression given by Casanova's case studies themselves. Certain faith communities have been at the right place at the right time for their presence to have had the effect of defending democracy or civil society against authoritarian regimes. Can such situations and events, even interpreted as Casanova does, be the basis for a future agenda? An element of conscious intentionality would need to enter in. And, as we will see, the element of intentionality in the situations described in these case studies is for the most part even more limited that Casanova's argument appears to suggest.

It is important to be clear, then, that Casanova is not *directly* supplying the agenda we seek. That is not his intention. Rather, he has offered us an analysis of a possible role for public religions in the modern world, out of which, with some critical effort, a plausible agenda might be derived. We, the members of the Abrahamic faiths, rather than Casanova or any other sociologist of religion, must be responsible for that.

A Collection of Case Studies

But this will not be easy. The way to this result lies not through naive acceptance of Casanova's theoretical vision, as if we could simply strategize on the basis of it, but by way of critical rereading of his case-study material. The great strength of Casanova's book lies in his five highly detailed, penetrating and thoughtful studies of religious leaders and communities acting in actual situations. These are exceptionally rich and illuminating. Each represents a different particular situation that for Casanova illustrates—each time in new ways—a thesis about "public religions" functioning in the "modern world."

Yet one must ask, particularly today, how one makes the move from detailed social analyses of particulars to broadly applicable conclusions of any sort. It seems that postmodernism has crept into the sociologists' and ethicists' tents, dictating an emphasis on particulars and deep suspicion of generalizations. Is this sociologist's inquiry covertly theory-laden from the start? Are his generalizations already built into his investigative method? These are questions that dog the whole sociological profession today, not to be easily dismissed or conveniently ignored.

Obviously, it would have been helpful for our purposes if this sociologist's case studies were not confined to Western, Christian, mostly Roman Catholic examples. Indeed, Poland and Spain are atypical for Europe. One wonders what sort of evidence for his thesis Casanova could have found in Germany, France, or Britain, let alone Morocco or Indonesia or Israel. Casanova's instances are surely not the only available ones of "public religion" in action. And attention to other countries would also turn up forms of modernity both more resistant to religious influence and less so than those Casanova cites. An assertion of the sort the sociologist makes at the close of his book calls for a broader, more diversified, illustrative and evidential base.

One can also think of several obvious cases that Casanova does not choose to treat: say the role of Reformation churches in fostering the downfall of several eastern European Communist regimes, or the role played by Protestant and Anglican communities in the collapse of apartheid in South Africa. Much useful information on both these subjects can be found in John de Gruchy's *Christianity and Democracy*.[16] One can also think of at least a few cases of the involvement of Jews and Muslims in modern liberation struggles. A book by the South African Muslim writer Farid Esack,[17] for example, sketches what amounts to an Islamic liberation theology out of the experience of the freedom struggle alongside Christians with whom he was in constant, productive, intellectual contact. I will treat Esack's story at length in chapter 4. Public involvement by Jewish communities is to some extent traced in the writings of Rabbi Jonathan Sacks. But the parade example is the political role of Orthodox Judaism in the modern state of Israel, an enormously complicated subject in its own right.

Casanova's book cries out for a comparative study of "public religion in the modern world" involving case studies of differing communities from all three faiths in relation to the sociopolitical worlds they inhabit. Indeed we are learning, and Casanova is now saying, after S. N. Eisenstadt, that there are different sorts of "modernities" in different parts of the world today in which the elements of "secularization," as seen from the standpoint of European sociology, are not present in at all the same ways.[18] The relation between modernity and secularization in Europe is different from what it is in the

United States, and both of these examples are different from what we find in Asia or in Africa.

European and American sociologists likewise *think* differently about their situations, taking different social patterns as normative. There may very well be situations and cultures in which the public presence of religious traditions has not receded as it has in most of Europe, and in which these traditions are in a stronger position to influence what "modernity" is taken to mean. The religious situation across the global South, where Western modernity has entered the scene by way of political and economic colonization, may tell us more about the future than European and American cases can. Indeed, Casanova himself has more recently asked, "Can there be a non-Western, non-secular, modernity…?"[19] He has not yet made such a study and can only imagine, on the basis of limited information, what sorts of data might be found. Such educated guessing is in fact at work, if only provisionally and with suitable restraints, in the arguments that follow.

Furthermore, I think that the case studies of "public religion" that Casanova does supply, despite my admiration for their acute situational analyses, do not tell the whole story that any agenda based on them would need to have told. They are, ironically, not sensitive enough to the roles played by secular forces in the contexts the sociologist describes. Notwithstanding Casanova's appropriate attention to *Solidarity*, the coming of democracy to Communist Poland was surely due to multiple other factors—culture, corruption in government, growth of the trade unions—in addition to those represented by the Roman Catholic Church. The sociologist's reporting on the remarkably influential pronouncements of the U.S. Conference of Catholic Bishops does not pay enough attention to concurrent political and social factors. Casanova's treatment of American Protestant evangelicalism, moreover, does not anticipate the extreme ideological politicization of this movement, exacerbating rather than restraining interreligious conflict, that has come to pass largely, but not entirely, since he wrote. Perhaps Casanova's modest language about religion "helping" modernity save itself implicitly recognizes this fact. Religion's role presumably was to "help" other than "religious" forces move toward democratic outcomes, not to accomplish all this by faith alone. So it would have helped to have some of the interactions between religious and secular factors more fully described.

And it seems, too, that the sorts of interactions of religious communities with public events Casanova describes may turn out to have been confined to a rather narrow, perhaps atypical, period of recent history: the mid-'80s to the mid-'90s. Could this, seen from the perspective of more than a decade later, begin to look like a small "axial period," or extremely short-lived age of positive religious social influence? Would an agenda based on such

instances be relevant now? These years saw the unusually broad influence
of events such as those just mentioned. But such ecstatic moments, by and
large, seem not to have continued. Indeed, we may now be seeing a reversion
back toward the privatization of faith. There is evidence that religious groups
are better at resistance and revolution than they are at sustaining democracy
when it is achieved. In short, we must ask whether the kind of democratically
productive religious publicness Casanova describes can be replicated today,
provided we understand it well enough, or whether these things just happened because conditions, largely beyond anyone's conscious control, were
simply right for them to happen.

Finally, it seems to me that Casanova's fine brash hypothesis at the close of
his book, to which we are paying such close attention, is not tightly enough
connected with the case studies for generalizing, let alone agenda-building,
purposes. Here again is the issue bruited first at the opening of this section.
Can any generalized results be legitimately derived from very diverse socio-
historical particulars? We cannot do without particulars, but we are hard
pressed today to know what to do *with* them. And if there is a tentative conclusion in the researcher's mind, may it not all too easily influence the choice
of case material? Sociologists cannot approach their material *tabula rasa*. All
inquiries are theory-laden and Casanova's are no exception.

We should note that Casanova's offers several preliminary formulations of
his central thesis in the body of the book. These seem (appropriately enough)
to shift from one case study to the next until they take still another, highly
speculative, form at the close. I think we must conclude that Casanova's case
studies, according due recognition to their many strengths, do not fully
support his conclusions at any point along the way, and least of all at the end.
How could they, considering the conclusion's visionary and world-historical
nature? It may well be, however, that the notion of "multiple modernities"
in some of which elements of secularization coexist with continuing public
prominence of forms of religious faith, can help us see plausibility in
Casanova's initial hypothesis.

Casanova's final statement, moreover, has a quality that resists any
attempt at empirical verification. There is no case in which one can literally
see "religion" helping modernity to "save itself." Can this stunning, world-
historical, "ironic" suggestion be derived from case material dealing in far
more down-to-earth circumstances? Can such a proposition be derived
from *any* sort of empirical evidence at all? The answer has to be that this
conclusion not only goes beyond the specific evidence Casanova gives us.
It goes beyond *any* possible array of evidence. At most, Casanova looks at
his evidence and then makes a leap of faith about what it might mean in the
long term of events. I think we can say that the evidence does not contradict

his vision. It can even be thought consistent with that vision. But the same evidence could also be interpreted in different ways: for example, by arguing that all these religious communities-in-situation were being brought along reluctantly by a prelatically perceived need to seem relevant. It could be argued that the democratic developments described could, and would, have taken place without them.

So the notion of religious communities helping to save modernity is too complex and elusive a process to see happening when one is in the midst of it or writing about it at close range. Such *might*, of course, be the conclusion of a historian like Fernand Braudel writing a half century or more later. He or she might say that when all was said and done this is what happened: in all these ways, modernity was "saved." But in the case studies offered, we can only see religious communities interacting with various circumstances, protecting their own interests in various ways, and in the process finding themselves on the side of "enlightened" social forces. They do not in themselves constitute these enlightened influences. But, in the course of events, they come to their aid, they stand at their side.

Perspectives for Agenda-Building: Enlightenment Critique

It has been important to raise questions such as these in order to head off any too-easy appropriation of Casanova for our purposes. One could think, indeed, that the foregoing seriously undercuts the usefulness of his work for the agenda setting that we seek. Yet all this is only intended to warn us to look closely at the narratives and the data, to address each new situation with the same kind of detailed thoroughness that Casanova devotes to his own examples. The question may well not be whether certain generalizations are right, but how certain generalizations are possible.

My conclusion is that what we can learn from Casanova is more methodological than it is substantive. That is, we cannot look to the Catholic Church in Poland or the U.S. Catholic Bishops' Conference for specific guidance about how religiously to rescue democratic institutions in all times and places, but we can glean certain perspectives from Casanova's project as a whole that could be useful for our own agenda-making. Instead of planning world-historical transformations, we should gather the Abrahamic communities to address specific, timely, local problems. We may hope, just as the American Roman Catholic bishops may have hoped, that what we do might play a role in something more vast. We may try to be responsible to that larger vision in all the details of our struggles, giving full attention to relevant particulars along the way, without failing to take responsibility for what is in front of our noses.

Casanova gives us an important prescription for doing this. He tells us that in order to promote modernity's well-being, religious communities need a significant ingestion of the Enlightenment *critique* of religion.

> ... only a religion which has incorporated as its own the central aspects of the Enlightenment critique of religion is in a position today to play a positive role in furthering processes of practical rationalization.[20]

What does incorporating "the central aspects of the Enlightenment criticism of religion" mean? Does this not introduce a kind of circularity into Casanova's argument? Religions are more "enlightened" than public institutions that believe themselves heirs of *the* Enlightenment *because* these religious communities, or at least some of them, have already taken on elements of an Enlightenment critique of religion whose consequences today Casanova acknowledges to be seriously flawed? What elements of Enlightenment critique does Casanova have in mind? And would he include in such an analysis Westernized forms of Islam, whose contact with the Enlightenment is very recent indeed? What might be the difference for a faith tradition between first encountering the European Enlightenment in the seventeenth century and meeting it only last week in its twenty-first-century forms?

Common wisdom sees response to "the Enlightenment criticism of religion," as leading to one or another of three broad possibilities. The first is all-out resistance to critical tendencies of any kind, as in Leo XIII's *Rerum Novarum* and Pius IX's *Syllabus of Errors*. Parallels to such retrograde responses also exist, of course, in all three Abrahamic faiths. The second response has famously been called "marrying the spirit of the age," that is, reformulating faith in terms suitable to one's present consciousness, or, better said, allowing some expression of enlightenment to control the conceptualities and terminologies of faith in order to make them acceptable in one's own time. This response also exists in liberal Christianity and in some manifestations of Reformed Judaism (e.g., Ethical Culture). It seems rarely, if ever, to be found in Islam. The third response is what can be called a "neo-orthodox" response. By using this term, I do not urge a return to Reinhold Niebuhr himself (although one could do worse), but rather a move similar to his adjusted to the conditions of the twenty-first century: an enlightened sense of historical realism enabling believers to rediscover the substance and relevance of tradition for their situation understood in existential (not necessarily existentia*list*) terms. This means saving believers from a historical literalism, enabling the rediscovery of many things long forgotten but indispensable today in the light of the promise they contain.

It sounds at first as if Casanova wants something different from any of these possibilities. He wants modern religious communities to transmit the Enlightenment at its uncorrupted best, in its pure form, by permitting their traditions to become purveyors of all that is best in such thought, while secular political carriers have distorted that thought in greed, venality, and violence. Do religious traditions taking on the Enlightenment critique thereby become "carriers" of it? Is it as if they carry with them frozen stem cells of the best of Enlightenment thought ready to thaw them and inject into the body politic at the moment of need to regrow the polity's damaged tissues?

Whether this interpretation is plausible depends, of course, on what one assumes that the Enlightenment critique consists of. There is little illumination on this point in the case studies themselves even when one is primed to look for it. Indeed, do Casanova's case studies of religious communities in public encounters show evidence of these bodies having imbibed an Enlightenment critique at all? Indeed, what would that mean? Does taking on such a critique mean demythologizing certain elements of tradition? Or does it mean dissolving particular claims into universal propositions, or substituting elements of "the spirit of the age" for historic convictions? One might suppose that absorbing an Enlightenment critique understood in these terms could turn religious groups in the direction of Unitarian or other forms of liberalism, making them *less* coherent, less devout, and probably less publicly effective too. Compare in this respect unquestionably "enlightened" Unitarian Universalists on the one hand with seemingly "premodern" Pentecostals and other evangelicals in Latin America on the other. Who makes the greater social impact? *In what sense* does "absorption of central aspects of the Enlightenment criticism of religion" make religion more publicly effective instead of eviscerating its religious content?

Such blood-thinning is not what we saw in Roman Catholicism's publicness in Poland, Spain, and Latin America. These Catholic communities did not evince anything resembling what would normally be considered an Enlightenment consciousness. Nor would one say such a thing of North American evangelical Protestantism. Hence Casanova's call for ingestion of Enlightenment criticism does *not* obviously serve to link his case studies to the conclusion that in such events modernity was being saved from its distortions of Enlightenment perspectives by religious bodies that dared, in the Kantian manner, to renounce tradition and authority and think for themselves.

So it is *not* that religious communities are here called merely to echo Enlightenment liberalism—to substitute that for their traditional doctrines and principles. It is rather that they are to accept the Enlightenment critique in such a way that they are freed from superstition and absolutism the better to grasp their own core principles and bring them to bear in the project of "helping modernity save itself." This move turns inadvertence into intentionality where this social salvational project is concerned. Fundamental doctrines and practices of religious communities—in this case the Abrahamic communities—are liberated from literalistic exclusivistic distortions and turned loose in society to do their real work.

But note that there is a second clause, not yet discussed, in Casanova's remark about appropriating Enlightenment critique. He says that absorbing this critique is for the purpose of "furthering processes of practical rationalization." These words invoke a practical interest in the way things, including society, work. They refer to the introduction of a kind of practical reasoning in which human beings take responsibility for dealing with the conditions of their lives together rather than depending only on authoritative religious teaching: taking leave of a premodern *bezauberte* world, a world of magic, for a world of known causes and effects in which one can intelligently chart one's course.

To internalize the Enlightenment critique in *this* sense is to take on the Enlightenment's sense of human responsibility for the future of humanity itself. It would be to take on a sense of the implications of our actions in history: its sense that social philosophy and social engineering could succeed where tradition had failed. Instead of retreating to religious enclaves where we wait for God to set things right, we take responsibility for intelligent interventions on history's stage. This could be the meaning of "practical rationalization." It could mean, in H. Richard Niebuhr's words, to grasp "what is going on" and to take action to try to bend events in a certain direction. Perhaps Casanova is saying that religious groups that have accepted an Enlightenment critique of themselves understand the meaning of such historically conscious responsibility-taking better than do "secular" institutions that uncritically assume themselves to be heirs of the Enlightenment promise, yet fail to deliver its promised blessings.

We are at the heart of the argument I derive from my wrestling match with Casanova. I am not at all sure that this is what Casanova means, but it is what *I* mean. Absorbing the Enlightenment critique means uncovering elements in religious tradition that support, and give direction to, such responsibility-taking. The point, which I will develop further in the following chapter, is that, instead of staging a hostile takeover of worldly responsibility from the religious authorities, as the philosophes thought they needed to do, religiously internalizing such a sense of responsibility leads to the discovery that the scriptures of all three faiths make such snatching away, or hostile takeover, of responsibility for the human community unnecessary. The scriptures teach, among other things, that such responsibility already belongs to human beings as a divine gift. This strand of thought, given eyes to see it, is present in the scriptural accounts of creation and covenant-making, as well as elsewhere in the holy books. An ingestion of Enlightenment critique refocuses our interpretative lenses: it enables us to see that the gift of responsibility is already there, and that it is tied to a promise for human life that is also already there, and does not need to be invented.

To put this in (still controversial) Christian terms, the kingdom comes when believers have made the world ready for it, and thus human beings participate significantly through the use of their minds and other capabilities to make this world right. The Asian missionary leaders meeting in Hong Kong in 1999 wondered in effect if such a conviction could be seen in "religiously plural" terms. To which question, in the introduction, I answered "yes," and called for a theological outworking of its implications.

Analyzing Present Opportunities

In the light of his case studies and of his application of Enlightenment critique, confronting a modernity struggling with deteriorating political institutions and now increasingly given over to the destructive logics of rivalries for global dominance and the ideology of the global market, religious communities may now, in Casanova's view, turn out to be significant contributors to restoring the Enlightenment's promise of values such as freedom, human rights, and democracy to the human race. Perhaps the following paragraphs show better than most what lies behind this hypothesis. Casanova writes this concerning the power of normative traditions in modern society:

> Normative traditions constitute the very condition of possibility for ethical discourse, and ... fictional "ideal speech situations" and "original positions" notwithstanding, without normative traditions neither rational public debate nor discourse ethics is likely to take place.

> ... One after another, all the modern public institutions which at first tended to exercise some of the public functions traditionally performed by religious institutions abandoned their public normative roles: academic philosophy, the specialized social sciences, the universities, the press, politicians, intellectuals. Under such circumstances one cannot but welcome the return of religion to the public square.[21]

But obviously Casanova is not thinking of the kind of "return to the public square" we have recently been witnessing across the globe, i.e., fundamentalist or very conservative groups seeking to dominate the politics of their nations or regions: evangelical extremists (not all evangelicals) in America; Wahabist Muslims in Saudi Arabia exporting their ideologies to Afghanistan, Pakistan, and Iraq; absolutist Israeli groups opposing serious peace talks with Palestinians. The list could go on. Instead, Casanova is thinking of religious groups that have imbibed enough of the Enlightenment critique of religion to be able constructively to enter the public dialogue about modernity's own self-contradictions. This is not for religious communities a matter of succumbing to some thin theological gruel in order to sound almost like everybody else. It is rather a matter of enlightened social positioning and responsibility-taking for congregations living in the fullness of faith.

To base a self-conscious theological strategy on the Casanova analysis, it is necessary to move the democratizing, humanizing effect from inadvertence to intentionality. Now that we see what happened in Poland, Spain, Brazil, and the United States, we need to ask where similar opportunities may exist in the early twenty-first-century world. Religious communities, having internalized Enlightenment critiques of their former self-understandings to the extent of seeing their traditions as validating responsible social action, may now be able to see places where they can help modernity transcend the distortions of Enlightenment values that threaten it.

But this will not happen unless traditions, such as the Abrahamic ones, Judaism, Christianity, and Islam, can act together. Only so can they overcome the suspicion of sectarian special pleading. The practice of parallel and interactive hermeneutics, i.e., reading scriptures together in relation to commonly experienced situations, can help with this. It can produce unprecedented mutual enlightenment (small "e") about one another as coactors in a uniquely shared space-time world. *The* Enlightenment generated cultural assumptions that have made such encounters possible. But taking advantage of this does not mean *substituting* Enlightenment perspectives for the religious traditions in order to make them more compatible. Rather, this activity produces enlightened attitudes *within* religious traditions as they recognize relationships within differences and differences within relationships. Such dialogue enacts a relativity-in-practice that superficially resembles the academic style of "comparative religions" but is not at all the same thing. Here actual identities are engaged, yet remain distinct. Neither conversion nor syncretism is in view. The Other becomes more deeply known, *but remains Other.* Such dialogue-in-situation generates a sense of mutual responsibility for the interpretations offered and for the public consequences of these interpretations. Fundamentalisms can sometimes be pragmatically dissolved in such situations without direct confrontation. Shared ethical perspectives can be made available to the surrounding world free of debilitating sectarian labels. Today such interfaith sharing is foundational to seeing and acting on opportunities now to be stated and discussed further in subsequent chapters. These thoughts are not explicitly Casanova's, but they spring from his work. They illustrate ways in which, as Casanova put it, "normative traditions constitute the very condition of possibility for ethical discourse."[22]

First, religious communities, acting together, can help modernity "save" itself by bringing to light its forgotten moral and religious sources. Most, if not all, programs of secular moral reasoning depend for their persuasiveness on implicit metaphors that go back to hidden religious assumptions. Without such sources, standing *incognito* behind our modern notions of the good, our glittering contemporary capabilities have little directional control. Our contemporary Charles Taylor claims, in *Sources of the Self*,[23] that modern life is full of assumptions about human rights, human dignity, and so forth, but that we are incapable of articulating the origins and root meanings of such "frameworks." It is not autonomous reasoning that leads us to such assumptions. Rather we come by them as unwitting beneficiaries of the historical and literary transmission of certain root metaphors. Many (of course not all) such sources of our ideas about our selves and our societies are found in religious traditions. To save the very fabric of our modern morality, Taylor claims, to be able to talk intelligibly about it, to be able to defend it, to be able to apply it, we need to become aware of these sources. Taylor on this point is well worth quoting.

> [Our] identity is much richer in moral sources than its condemners allow, but … this richness is rendered invisible by the impoverished philosophical language of its most zealous defenders. Modernity urgently needs to be saved from its most unconditional supporters—a predicament perhaps not without precedent in the history of culture.[24]

Religious communities that self-consciously preserve such sources by living in accord with them may in some circumstances be the only institutions around capable of reminding us who we really are. Taylor is obviously thinking of Western modernity and of moral sources maintained through a predominantly Christian cultural history. But moral sources represented by other faiths are certain to enter this picture as our culture begins increasingly to exhibit interreligious "reflexivity." Of course, not all modernities are the same. There exist modernities strongly influenced by Jewish culture (New York, Tel Aviv) and modernities that have arisen within Islamic cultures (Riyadh, Dohar, Jakarta). The terms of Charles Taylor's analysis are likely to apply across a wide range of cultural and religious situations.

Second, the public presence of religious communities working together, especially the Abrahamic ones, may help modernity better understand its militant enemies, both secular and religious. Modern culture is threatened by a dangerous ignorance of religion. The past year has seen a spate of books in England and America that identify religion as such, whether at home or in the Middle East, as the enemy of rational, "reality-based" civilization. The authors put forward arguments that they confidently believe will undermine all religious faith and destroy it. In short, they take the superiority of Enlightenment values of a certain kind as self-evident, and assume that people, once they understand, will flock to them. In fact, such attitudes only oppose fundamentalism of the religious kind with fundamentalism of the positivist scientific kind. Such naïve attitudes leave modernity exposed to both sorts of fundamentalist enemies because such a construal of the struggle fails to grasp what is really going on. It fails to grasp why the West is morally reviled by so many around the world and why the opposition is so lethally passionate. To answer such threats, modernity needs not to answer one fundamentalism with another but to reach an open, dialogical, pluralistically expressed religious consciousness that puts foundations under eroding modern values. For this it needs knowledge of its moral and metaphorical sources. It cannot have such so long as its leading thinkers assume that fundamentalism—Jewish, or Christian, or Islamic—is the only form that religion can legitimately take, or fail to understand that there are secular fundamentalists too. This is why a religious vision generated out of "parallel and interactive hermeneutics" (see chapter 5) is potentially so important. Such relationships overcome religious isolation and undermine doctrinal exclusivisms, allowing a religious or theological form of humanism to appear that can exist in many traditional expressions: Jewish, Christian, Islamic, or otherwise.[25]

And third, the gathering of religious groups into communities of constructive dialogue can, in some times and places, generate cells of "civil society" where no such thing otherwise effectively exists. Civil society, often defined as a region of public interlocution distinct from established economic and political spheres, has often proved itself to be a seedbed for the sorts of democratic assumptions needed to undergird free elections, effective parliaments, and the like. Attempts to impose these things where the cultural ground is not prepared for them have proved unsuccessful again and again. In Western Europe and North America, civil society has grown organically, only to be undermined of late by manipulative party politics and the power of giant corporations. In Eastern Europe and the Middle East, it has scarcely existed. Whether waning or struggling to be born, civil society needs the right social conditions and institutions such as coffeehouses where talk can be passionate and free. Where such conditions do not exist, religious communities acting together can now, as seldom before, begin to play this role: precisely because, in Casanova's words, they uniquely bring "normative traditions" that "constitute the very condition of possibility for ethical discourse." Knowing that they have been sources of so much sectarian violence and seeking to renounce that way of life, such groups may be particularly motivated today to form such discourse communities. In some situations, these interfaith discourses can be the only points of sustained contact among otherwise mutually alienated segments of society. Such discussions can "stand in for" otherwise missing settings for civic interaction while contributing needed moral sources to the mix. Such relationships can then prepare the ground and plant seeds for wider public involvement. They can help create conditions for the birth of democratic institutions. Such units of civil society can also become social spaces in which organized resistance to injustice and oppression can grow. Such spaces can nurture resistance, and alternatives, to political and economic tendencies from which modernity needs to be saved.

All these are ways in which we may imagine Casanova's thesis about "normative traditions" working itself out in the early twenty-first century. Yet there is always the problem of recognizing such models even when they are present amid the complexity of actual events. And actual events are bound to generate models not thought of in this paper or any other. To paraphrase a military maxim, few strategic ideas survive their first contact with the actual data. That could be the fate of these attempts to learn from Casanova's cases for our own time.

Yet is the thought that any of this might happen wholly visionary? It is too early to tell. In any case, visionary narratives have their uses. They can motivate close attention to the reality of one's situation as containing the rudiments of promise when that is not obvious to most. They can help counteract despair. It is better to approach a situation with some idea of what one is looking for, rather than with no hypothesis at all. Better even if one's starting hypothesis is later modified, as it will be, by unexpected events.

Thinking retrospectively, the French historian Fernand Braudel identified historical processes of "long duration," e.g., characteristics of "the Mediterranean world in the age of Philip II" and other similar phenomena. Here it is as if something equally portentous were being projected in advance, before the fact, as a kind of principle of orientation for future struggles. We can wrestle together as Abrahamic communities with the specific conditions of our situation and thereby generate case-study material for historians and sociologists of a future generation. Those coming after us might, or might not, conclude that our efforts were indeed part of a world-historical process in which modernity turned out to be "saved," i.e., delivered from its present travail to something like the "sunlit uplands" of which Churchill spoke at the outset of World War II. Some future writer might indeed say, "Here, at just this moment in world history, modernity began to turn the corner, above all because of what religious communities did, even if no one could have known this at the time." So we conclude for Casanova's case studies, whose future implications are yet to unfold. And so we must also think about our own.

Notes

1. It is important to see that every known vision of human unity *does* leave somebody out—the handicapped, the very poor, women, those who in principle "think otherwise." What do prevailing definitions of human "capability" make of the utterly incapable? Is their humanity to be denied?

2. John Ruskin, quoted in Robert I. Rothberg, *The Founder: Cecil Rhodes and the Pursuit of Power* (New York: Oxford University Press, 1988), 94.

3. See Julio de Santa Ana, et al., *Beyond Idealism: A New Way Forward for Ecumenical Social Ethics,* ed. Robin Gurney, Heidi Hadsell, and Lewis S. Mudge (Grand Rapids, MI: Eerdmans, 2006).

4. See John Rawls, *Political Liberalism* (New York: Columbia University Press, 1993), 212f. "A political society ... has a way of formulating its plans, of putting its ends in order of priority, and of making its decisions accordingly. The way a political society does this is its reason; its ability to do these things is also its reason; though in a different sense: it is an intellectual and moral power, rooted in the capacities of it human members."

5. Harry G. Frankfurt, *On Bullshit* (Princeton: Princeton University Press, 2005).

6. The term "postmillennial" refers to the view, in Christianity, that believers must work to prepare the world for the millennium, or second coming of Christ, by practicing evangelism and promoting justice, peace, and other virtues in the world as we know it. In contrast, the "premillennial" position teaches that all such effort is futile. Christ most come again before the world can be set right, with unbelievers subjected to eternal fire and believers "raptured" into heaven.

7. Francis Fukuyama, *The End of History and the Last Man* (New York: Free Press, 1992).

8. Samuel P. Huntington, *The Clash of Civilizations and the Remaking of World Order* (New York: Simon and Schuster, 1996).

9. See "From Culture Wars to the Global Question of Religion," an unsigned editorial in the *Respublica Newsletter* for December 2005.

10. Daniel C. Dennett, *Breaking the Spell: Religion as a Natural Phenomenon* (New York: Viking, 2006).

11. José Casanova, *Public Religions in the Modern World* (Chicago: University of Chicago Press, 1994), 234.

12. Casanova understands the "secularization hypothesis" to involve three quite different understandings: (1) secularization as the decline in religious beliefs and practices; (2) secularization as the privatization of religion; and (3) secularization as the differentiation of different secular spheres (e.g., state, economy, science) so as to "emancipate" the latter from religious

institutions and norms. These distinctions allow examination of the validity of each proposition independently, making possible the description of different patterns of secularization in different cultural situations. Ibid.

13. Mark Lilla, "The Great Separation," *New York Times Magazine*, August 19, 2007, cover.

14. I know of no analysis comparable with Casanova's that offers a study of the roles of different religions in different cultural expressions of "modernity." Keeping so many balls in the air would be a prodigious intellectual feat, but someone is bound to try it. My use of Casanova is a clear instance of the necessity of viewing matters from "somewhere" rather than "nowhere." One must constantly make allowances for the influence on the argument of one's unavoidable perspective.

15. Jonathan Schell, *The Fate of the Earth* (New York: Knopf, 1982).

16. John de Gruchy, *Christianity and Democracy* (Cambridge, UK: Cambridge University Press, 1995).

17. Farid Esack, *Qur'an, Liberation, and Pluralism: An Islamic Perspective of Interreligious Solidarity Against Oppression* (Oxford: Oneworld Publications, 1997).

18. See Casanova, "Rethinking Secularization: A Global Comparative Perspective," *The Hedgehog Review: Critical Reflections on Contemporary Culture* 8, nos. 1 and 2 (Spring and Summer 2006): 7ff.

19. Ibid., 13.

20. Casanova, *Public Religions*, 233.

21. Ibid., 205f.

22. Ibid., 205.

23. Charles Taylor, *Sources of the Self* (Cambridge, MA: Harvard University Press, 1989).

24. Ibid., xi.

25. For a different view, see the book by Lee Harris, *The Suicide of Reason: Radical Islam's Threat to the West* (New York: Basic Books, 2007).

3

The "Modern Project"

How We Got This Way and What Can Be Done about It

It is all too easy to recite the usual litany of injustices, environmental depredations, acts of violence, political prevarications, and all the other conditions that threaten our global civilization. Every one of these is a genuine ill from which modernity needs desperately, in Casanova's language, to be "saved." But there is need, before going further, to go deeper. There is need for some treatment of the underlying causes of these conditions. This chapter will do that by first sketching the ways in which the Enlightenment gave birth to a project in which human beings, in the name of autonomy, took responsibility for their own social and spiritual reinvention. It will then show how this autonomy project led to irresponsible forms of social totalization with consequences, despite our best philosophical and practical efforts, beyond our capacity for control. And finally, it will call for transcendentally responsible practices of repair and restoration in which the Abrahamic faiths could play a useful role.

The Modern Project and Its Discontents

By the "modern project,"[1] historians mean the entire historical, intellectual, industrial, political enterprise that begins with the early signs of "enlightenment" in the seventeenth century and continues today in our globalized, computerized world: a centuries-long and still current effort to adapt and enact Enlightenment insights across a wide swath of human inquiry and enterprise. An in-depth analysis of these phenomena may help gather Abrahamic communities healingly around modernity's beleaguered institutions and bewildered leaders.

The life of our civilization as we know it today is a partially decayed product of a relatively long-term and highly complex historical process. How is it that this project has produced such ambiguous and disappointing results? I argue that modernity's ills derive—not from secularity as such, as a multitude of religious writers, including several popes, have argued—but rather from this epoch's own failure to fulfill the responsibilities it took on by pursuing its characteristic projects of human autonomy, self-sufficiency, liberation, and personal fulfillment. Modernity has been irresponsible to the requirements of the world-historical venture it began when thinkers such as Locke, Kant, Hume, Adam Smith, and a host of others decided—within the Christian culture they inherited but with varying degrees of intended autonomy from it—to reinvent, on their own terms, the very nature of humanity and of human society as such.

At a certain historical juncture, the axis of cultural and scientific concern shifted from what had been laid down in the past by authority and tradition to what human beings could achieve on their own. Otherwise put, Enlightenment philosophers set out to relieve established institutions of their responsibility for human well-being and to assume it for themselves. This taking-on of responsibility for maintaining and improving the human condition on purely human terms has turned out to be at best a very mixed success.

Not that any social actor or thinker from the seventeenth century forward would have thought or said, "Now, at this moment and in this way, we human beings are taking over responsibility for the remaking of the human race on new principles." But it may nonetheless be valid to say, in the perspective of the centuries, that this is just what Immanuel Kant was doing when he set his pen to writing *What Is Enlightenment*? Or John Locke as he completed his *Second Treatise on Civil Government.* Or Adam Smith as he followed his *Treatise on the Natural Affections* with *The Wealth of Nations.* This chapter will argue that this was indeed the case, in different ways, for these writers and many others. We will see, of course, that the Enlightenment project unfolded in different ways in France, Germany, Britain, and the United States. French Enlightenment figures were mostly anticlerical, antagonistic to religion in all its forms. The British, including the Scots, were less so. At least at first they sought to combine Enlightenment insights with certain religious presuppositions. Germans and Americans, in their different ways, did the same.

But none of these articulators of the spirit of the age in which they lived may actually have thought they were taking on responsibility as human beings for what humanity's self-understanding of itself would eventually become. As this chapter will show, the Enlightenment's project of taking autonomous responsibility for what humanity would turn out to be has led to egregious forms of irresponsibility, and, of late, to consequences seemingly beyond humanity's capacities for responsible management even among the "best and brightest." Our Enlightenment forebears saw little of this. In fact, many of them were simply fascinated with understanding the way things worked, especially in ethics, economics, and society. They were fond of the notion of *homo faber*, man the maker or manufacturer, only in this case the maker of his own nature. Yet the story of these years may justly be called a story of a revolutionary kind of human responsibility-taking for what humanity would do and therefore *be*, all this after centuries of receiving, with relatively little questioning, answers to these questions from established religious and political authority.

What these philosophers accomplished was a kind of rational-evidential reconstruction of the very idea of the human-in-society, beginning usually not with a clean slate or *tabula rasa*, but with society as they experienced it. They sought to find the fundamental *logos* of social interaction in an effort to perfect it. No revolution in human thought could have been more fundamental. To the question who or what is humanity, the early moderns could answer, *we* know, because it is *we* who are at this moment making humanity become what it truly is and what it will be. We have, in effect, taken responsibility for this. The promise of whatever human beings are to become is in our hands because we have grasped how it all works. We are ready to acknowledge in response to any question bearing on the point, yes, it is we human beings who have done this, and *therefore* we bear responsibility for the outcome of our having done it.

The new sense of responsibility ramified in many interesting ways, producing significant lines of argument that continue in their own ways today. Among these, too complex to discuss here but certainly needing mention, were (1) the conviction that reality can be grasped mathematically, and therefore is subject to mechanical metaphors and to calculations of various kinds (Galileo and Descartes); (2) a principle of social-constructive rationality in which one began with some form of natural law or social assumptions based on tradition and seemingly "natural," and sought the rational reconstruction of human society by first breaking it down into its smallest units (persons, atoms) and then rearranging these more rationally (Hobbes and Rousseau); (3) a principle of personal freedom, beginning with the recognition of human rights, among them the right to pursue one's self-interest (Locke and Spinoza). And finally (4) the utilitarian calculation of the maximization of happiness as the goal of all social reconstruction (John Stuart Mill and Jeremy Bentham).[2]

Probably the most crucial presupposition behind such projects was that of human *autonomy*. Autonomy means that one finds one's authority in oneself, as opposed, say, to finding it in external or traditional sources. Human self-directedness implies responsibility in the sense that whatever we do is acknowledged to be morally *imputable* to us, making us subject to blame or to praise, to reward or punishment. The act is *my* act. I am the author of it. I am identified with it.[3]

This imputability of action to the agent, or the agent's self-identification with his/her action, is clearly one of the underlying senses of the word "responsibility," so often invoked in these pages. It is momentarily disconcerting, then, to find that this noun does not begin to be employed as we are doing until early in the nineteenth century, by which time the Enlightenment process has been underway for more than a century. H. Richard Niebuhr notes this fact at the start of his book *The Responsible Self*.[4] He speaks of the term as "a relatively late-born child," appearing in sentences such as "The great God has treated us as responsible beings."[5] He adds that the new usage gave people not merely "a new symbol with which to grasp and understand … an old idea," but also a means for articulating a fresh discovery in human self-awareness, containing "as it were, hidden references, allusions, and similes which are in the depths of our mind as we grope for understanding of ourselves and toward definition of ourselves in action."[6]

Precisely so. The socially imagined notion of autonomous human responsibility for the well-being of society actually *precedes* the appearance of language for capturing this idea in speech or in writing. By the time appropriate terminology does come into use, it reflects a whole cultural synthesis already well established in peoples' minds. They have been feeling out this idea in practice. Now they are able to talk about it. We can too, so long as we remember the complex matrix out of which the word arises: a notion of human activity bent on self-creation and willingness to be accountable for the results.

The Original Religious Setting of the Enlightenment Impulse

It is sometimes overlooked that this whole Enlightenment process of societal self-amendment began and continued for some time surrounded by more or less orthodox religious presuppositions. Carl Becker, in his book *The Heavenly City of the Eighteenth-Century Philosophers*,[7] argues persuasively that the *philosophes* lived in a medieval world of established moral assumptions that they then sought to reproduce in naturalistic terms. As someone has said, they demolished the Heavenly City of St. Augustine only to rebuild it with more up-to-date materials. For Becker, both Christians and Enlightenment revisionists "held fast to a revealed body of knowledge which provided for Christians salvation in the world to come and for the philosophers salvation in the world here and now."[8] Rejecting the Christian paradise, eighteenth-century philosophers constructed their own heavenly city. "For the love of God, they substituted love of humanity, for the vicarious atonement, the perfectibility of man through his own efforts; and for the hope of immortality in another world, the hope of living in the memory of future generations."[9]

John Locke, who lived just before the period of Becker's special interest, is the perfect example of a social philosopher whose work clearly evinces the influence of Calvinism as he takes responsibility for constructing a rational understanding of civil government. Locke is a thinker in the social contract tradition. For him, community is created by the decisions of individual human beings, who begin in a "state of nature" to order their actions toward this end. People thus take responsibility for shaping and supporting their forms of life together. Communities are not just given by revelation or custom. We freely band together to secure shared advantages not otherwise available. Preexisting communities, hence, are no longer *a priori* conditions of our humanness. Community is constructed, not piously received. Communal norms bind us only to the extent that we consent to them.

On the evidence of Locke's text, we have here a self-aware attempt to give contractual shape to certain Calvinist presuppositions. From whence come the rights and privileges exercised by human beings in the natural state? Here Locke assumes the medieval tradition of natural law, but even more a set of recognizable theological assumptions. Persons in the "state of nature," an idealized (but not primordial) community of individuals, bracketing out the elaborate class structures of seventeenth-century England, exist under, and in virtue of, God's dominion. These persons engage one another to make and maintain contracts in their shared status as creatures of God. Their status as moral actors rests on their responsibility as individuals before God. All structures of authority that persons may contract with one another to establish are also expressions of God's will.

Yet from Locke's time onward, the religious context and sometimes unspoken religious presuppositions of social contract reasoning steadily weaken, while assertions of unlimited human autonomy grow stronger. By the eighteenth century, the Lockean image of persons constituted not only by their relations as individuals to God, but also by their participation in a divinely validated network of social relations, begins to be challenged by a notion of the autonomous social actor pursuing his or her (mostly his) individual interests in the public realm. The Lockean picture is superseded by a notion that society is constituted by the ensemble of many individual actions as citizens seek rationally to satisfy their various forms of self-interest.

But there seems to be nothing in this picture to ensure social cohesion. No framework of laws and values designed to trump individual acts of will emerges until thinkers of the Scottish Enlightenment begin to speak of moral sentiments and natural affections. This is certainly not an explicitly religious, let alone a Calvinist, way of speaking. It is a general description of virtues liable to be found in any stable Protestant Christian culture, but certainly in principle replicable in other cultures, religious or otherwise. This description of the basis of social coherence appears in what is for some an unexpected place: the work of Adam Smith.

Smith's book *The Theory of Moral Sentiments*[10] seeks to find a new kind of bond among newly emerging individual, self-interested social actors. Smith finds it in the universal human need for recognition and consideration by others. Every human being, for Smith, is interested in being the object of attention and approbation. This is what generates the primary sphere of human interaction within which there arise the different forms of economic life. Economic activity itself is thus rooted in noneconomic but certainly reasonable considerations such as the need for appreciation and sympathy. This notion of a *moral* world within which economic activity is but one expression among others underlies the later development of the notion of "civil society."

Adam Smith, of course, is far better known for his book *The Wealth of Nations* and for his alchemy of the Invisible Hand, "turning the dross of rational self-interest into the gold of the public good."[11] This is, of course, the idea that the interaction of the rational self-interests of many different economic actors will lead to economic justice, providing, let us say, for the equitable distribution of grain. As stated by Smith, this seems to be a pure theory of market-driven forces and relationships: a theory that does not need moral sentiments or even recognition from others in order to work. In his effort to show how a just economy can be based on the ensemble of individual economic choices, Smith seems to have forgotten his earlier book. One may even wonder whether the Invisible Hand, in which metaphor the logic shaping this ensemble of economic choices is given a quasi-personal quality, may not actually function just because of the moral sentiments described in Smith's earlier work. Economics, in short, needs to be surrounded and undergirded by human meanings if it is to work in the real world as Smith's theory says it should.

Smith's world of natural affections and the desire for recognition is itself a form of "soft" rational construction. One can understand it as lying within the Enlightenment project of remaking human society by taking thought about how it works. But even this insight quickly begins to fade. David Hume desires to demolish the social contract tradition altogether. For Hume, consent to any set of rules for the pursuit of self-interest is not a rationally informed act, whether "hard" (as in cynically determining where one's personal advantage lies) or "soft" (as in coveting the approval or admiration of one's peers). It is nothing but surrender to inherited, irrational prescriptions. The notion of rationally based consent to such authoritatively prescribed forms of social life is a myth. What we have from Hume is a narrowing of the social territory in which reason can validly function. Inherited social conceptions may continue to function, but they cannot be made rational. It would seem to follow that it is folly for human beings to take responsibility for rational reconstruction of their social worlds. Such worlds lie outside the realm of reason. They are inherited. Reason can only function in a narrower, more theoretical, domain.

We *can* be rational in *some* spheres of life, such as the natural sciences and the calculative dimensions of economic life. A certain kind of person may pour his or her identity into such arenas, where logical considerations, like profit maximization, rule. Such persons consider themselves not responsible for the whole wide range of human phenomena that do not yield to logic, such as the realms of forgiveness, trust, solidarity, and the like. Such persons will make themselves masters of those arenas that do conform to logic. (Today we call these forms of logic "rational choice theory," "game theory," and the like). These highly focused people may gain a great deal of wealth and power, and may try to ignore, or even subdue, the seemingly illogical realms of life in favor of the logical ones they can control.

One might draw a similar inference from the work of Kant. Leaving "natural affections" aside, the author of *What Is Enlightenment?* gives us a highly individualistic and strictly logical account of moral reasoning. Kant was brought up in the context of conservative Lutheran Pietism, and it is often thought that he wished to replicate some of these values in philosophical terms. Yet neither religious tradition nor social custom has any formal authority for Kant's "metaphysics of morals." These historically contingent factors are replaced by the ideal of the self-sufficient, solitary individual governing him/herself according to the prescriptions of reason alone. The law to which we consent is the law of our own rational self-reflection, which discloses the claims of duty. Formal criteria of universality, discoverable by practical reason reflecting on the experiences of moral life, determine for us what is right. We need to be able to universalize our moral maxims. We are to treat people as ends, not as means.

A century later, the French sociologist Emile Durkheim was to make a comparable move prescinding from religion as such and endeavoring to devise its secular philosophical analogue. We must discover, he wrote in his treatise on education,

> those moral forces that men, down to the present time, have conceived
> of only under the form of religious allegories. We must disengage them
> from their symbols, so to speak, and find a way to make the child feel
> their reality without recourse to any mythological intermediary.[12]

Durkheim substituted for the morally shaping force of "religion" the almost superhuman qualities he ascribed to "society." Here the same Enlightenment impulse is present: to marginalize traditional religious language while restating its principles in humanly autonomous terms for social-rebuilding purposes.

There may still be today a temptation to borrow from, or refurbish, religious sources in this way, but we are much less confident that "society" as such can be the substitute agent for moral education. Secular society alone cannot generate the moral energy needed. It is hard to make the move from such principles to a project of shared rational reconstruction of society itself. Hume, Kant, and Durkheim notwithstanding, society has existed in all its "thickness" for thousands of years, and it continues to do so. How do people decide whether or not to consent to the social contract with which they are confronted in their historical situation? In contract theory, the *polis* is constantly recreated by our consent to it. So society is a result of the concurrence of many rational acts of will. How otherwise do we get from individual autonomy to sociality or solidarity? From whence comes the political obligation to do any such thing at all? Does the notion of duty generate the obligation to consent to a *polis*, or may it just as well produce myriad individual notions of what duty requires? One suspects that consent to any social arrangement issues from some sort of covert calculation of gains and loses, duty meaning pursuit of my own personal interpretation of obligation or responsibility, just as others may freely pursue their own life purposes. On such grounds, we come to live in a society in which pursuing such personal logics is taken as the universal law. Consent comes closer and closer to being calculation of what is best for *me*. I determine that *this* is a society in which I can pursue my personal aims while others do the same. If I recoil at this utterly individualistic view of freedom, modernity offers me the sheer heteronomy of the totalitarian state as an alternative.

Consequences for the Character of Modernity

Events and developments of many kinds separate us from the age of the *philosophes*, their predecessors and successors. But the character of modernity as we know it still owes much to them and the Western civilization they helped to bring into being. A globalizing version of the notion that autonomous aggrandizing behavior is normative for human beings began to come over the horizon with eighteenth-century colonialism and continues today as an economic version of the principles of autonomy and of universalization: precisely the value scheme behind today's planetary projection of capitalist values. It is important to see that this becomes a moral ideology that threatens to unite humankind around purely acquisitive goals, leaving out all those incapable of playing such a game, or poorly positioned to do so. The right of the autonomous rule-giver, of the one who takes responsibility for making human life what it will be, is carried over into the notion of autonomy of economic conduct in the market. In this perspective, "human rights" are often interpreted as the "right to be left alone" to pursue whatever economic schemes one wants irrespective of the impact of those schemes on other people.

We now have an ideology complete with justificatory economic arguments. We have moved from the mere fascination with figuring out how to do things efficiently—Weber's "rationalization"—to an understanding that, for many, sweeps up all human values into aggrandizing economic purposes. From what, then, does modernity-expanded-as-globalization need to be saved at this moment in time? It needs, ironically, to be saved from what has actually *become* of the "common morality" that philosophers and theologians from time immemorial have been looking for. While these wise ones bent over their manuscripts, nations seeking wealth and power, in cooperation with private economic enterprises seeking the same goals, created a global passion more powerful than any philosophically grounded universalism. The Enlightenment notion that human beings take autonomous responsibility for determining what society is to be has now produced a global project of egregious irresponsibility toward the gifts that characterize us as human beings. We need now to be saved from an ideology that disastrously distorts the benefits that economic globalization might otherwise confer.

I differ with those who sometimes write as if they saw no benefits at all in linking the world together economically. If the distribution of economic benefits were fair, which of course it is not, the capacity to exercise human rights, including the rights of women, would be greatly enhanced. The capacity for personal growth and the possibility of genuine self-determination beyond traditional limited expectations would be advanced. Developing a nation's economic capacities, for example, to the point that increasing numbers of people can develop their personal capabilities,[13] have access to news and opinion, and the possibility of expressing their own views and to build networks of opinion-exchange across the Internet is surely an educational boon to democracy. Which makes the unjust distribution of such benefits the more reprehensible.

Studies of globalizing economics have therefore left me with one overwhelming question: whether the economic activities that generate such possibilities need, for their competitive success, to be pursued with a single-mindedness that devalues, if it does not blot out, all other notions of purpose in human life. Purely economic understandings of the benefits of globalization may miss this point, so it is worth pursuing briefly. The French scholar Pierre Bourdieu[14] stresses that we are dealing not merely with an economic agenda but with a "totalizing" ideological position. He has given us a term for this perspective: "neoliberalism," a coinage still little known in the United States but now widely used elsewhere.[15]

Bourdieu uses the words "ideological" and "ideology" to mean ideas, including many with deep civilizational, spiritual, or motivational backgrounds, that have at a certain time or place been "bent out of shape" to serve the needs of peoples' political or economic interests. Ideas such as "self-reliance," "property rights," "shareholder value," or "keeping the American (or British, or French, or Iraqi) people safe," have been attached to particular partisan ends, either by the social classes whose ends they are or by politicians trying to appeal to such voters. Ideologized notions can function to justify unjust policies, indeed to mislead people and their leaders about the true meanings and consequences of the ways they are living and acting. People can be led by ideologies to forfeit their own critical capacities for naming "what is really going on."

Bourdieu (with many others) sees "the market" as having become so dominant an ideological model in this sense as to be largely beyond question for a huge preponderance of today's movers and shakers. This is the case not only for the power elites that benefit from its assumptions but for many of those injured by those assumptions as well. Here is the "truth" that Western elites seemingly now hold "to be self-evident," as if it were pure rationality in practice. So pervasive has this logic become in our time that criticism of it begins to be seen as irrational, as lying outside the boundaries of plausible discourse. We are told, in Margaret Thatcher's words, that "there is no alternative."

This logic consists mainly of cost-benefit analyses that sometimes make use of "rational choice theory." Here self-interest and profit maximization are assumed to be the only really rational (as opposed to unrealistically idealistic) human motivations. Such theory is an achievement of mathematical analysis, originally based on the work of Nobel Laureate John Nash, he of the film *A Beautiful Mind*. Far from being purely a theory of conflict, "rational choice theory" or "game theory" is also a theory of a certain kind of cooperation in which the players can be expected, in their own respective interests, to agree implicitly to certain rules. More recently, such theory has expanded in its calculations and applications to be called "mechanism design," dealing with everything from the arrangement of government bond auctions to setting up patent systems to creating new voting procedures and on and on. What we have here is in effect a new and highly mathematically sophisticated kind of social contract theory, refined to the point at which it is thought capable—through the application of complex formulas—of both regulating and predicting human actions and reactions of all sorts. The Chicago economist Gary Becker indeed won the Nobel Prize in Economics for a book extending such calculations to the understanding of all human behavior.[16]

As Jürgen Habermas has shown, such reasoning "colonizes" the life-world in ways that are often systematically and cleverly hidden. This ideology has the means, largely through capture of the media, of making itself seem quite simply true, thereby forcing the progressive disappearance of "autonomous universes of cultural production." Independent publishers and filmmakers, independent media outlets, and other cultural institutions are forced to make their way with ever-diminishing public support. The "neoliberal" ideology, as Bourdieu sees it, eventually takes over all that lies in its way, but does so in an imperceptible manner, like continental drift. Paul Treanor, a Bourdieu interpreter, has summed all this up in three short aphorisms:

> Act in conformity with market forces.

> Within this limit, act also to maximize the opportunity for others to conform to the market forces generated by your action.

> Hold no other goals.[17]

This says, in effect, that one is to keep to the spheres and objectives where rational choice, mathematical models, and the search for strategic advantage prevail. Doing so will make one powerful, wealthy, and, by definition, *ir*responsible to the people around one, their aspirations, their lives. This seems a terrible diminishment of the possibilities of the human spirit. Hold no other goals? The commercialization of all values? No wonder such a "totalizing"[18] mentality is blind to the consequences such attitudes have for most of the poor of the earth. No wonder the poor feel sidelined, marginalized, and resentful.

Furthermore, here is an impressive example of the consequences of narrowing one's conception of life to considerations capable of being dealt with rationally, in terms of profit and loss and the like. As Hume thought, broader social questions are too messy for neat minds. We inherit, and cannot change, our social conditions. The poor, we may presume, are always to be with us. But some human beings are capable of grasping financial game theory and of profiting from that skill. They will use this capability where they can, and they will grow rich on the backs of others who cannot see beyond inherited customs.

Accompanying all this is our failure to accept a sense of accountability (if only to ourselves—in the sense of acknowledging authorship) for the consequences, both immediate and long-term, of these narrow assumptions and resulting reckless actions. The Enlightenment idea of *taking* responsibility degenerates into *ir*responsibility where outcomes are concerned. And this irresponsibility ramifies in many different spheres of life. It finds expression in widespread political corruption and a resulting loss of confidence in political institutions. Uncontrolled economic competition exacerbates pollution and global warming. Economic interests with respect both to resources and markets need military protection, as do the ambitions of nations for advantage or preeminence in global trade relations. The global arms trade becomes an industry in its own right. The same ambitions fuel the proliferation of nuclear materials and the weapons that can be made from them. This list of destructive consequences, it seems, can be extended indefinitely. And it is from such consequences that modernity now needs help in saving itself.

Seeking Secular Salvations: The New Responsibility-Takers

But it is not as if secular modernity were without resources for seeking its own salvation. Besides dangerously ramifying in the ways just described, the Enlightenment tradition has generated countercurrents and counterarguments that need to be taken into account. These resistance strategies—for that is what they are—constitute a different, more therapeutic, kind of responsibility-taking. In the seventeenth and eighteenth centuries proclaiming autonomous human responsibility for social betterment meant staging hostile takeovers of prerogatives previously assigned to traditional cultures and institutions. Now the responsibility needing to be taken for the consequences of these moves is assigned to no one in the society. It does not need to be "taken over" from others, but rather "taken on" by individuals and institutions that recognize in themselves the gift of such a calling.

One is impressed by the coherence of the original Enlightenment vision and of much that has come from it. By comparison, the efforts of today's ameliorative responsibility-takers lie all over the map. Their relative ineffectiveness lies partly in their inability to find any common philosophical front. But it is worth commenting on such efforts not only because they deserve respect, but because they can help us understand what now motivates the rooted cosmopolitans among our new responsibility-takers to revisit their religious and cultural origins in search of lost wisdom.

Resistance strategies of this kind are numerous and often intellectually complex. There is room here for comment on only a few. Several of the most influential, for example those of John Rawls and Jürgen Habermas, are taken up in some detail in chapter 7, and thus not discussed here. I will comment on secular resistance strategies in four broad categories.

Critical Social Theory

Critical social theory has been in many ways a series of revisions of the work of Karl Marx, whose purpose was to emancipate capitalism from its "self-contradictions," from the economic and ideological forces that led to the sorts of domination and totalization just described. By the 1930s, Marx's own formulations began to be left behind in favor of even more subtle analyses. The theory that emerged was a form of inquiry that took society itself for its object. It exposed the structures of domination that much of modernity took for granted. To Max Horkheimer and Theodor Adorno, among the early makers of critical theory, the Enlightenment was not the liberation from religious false consciousness that it has so often been taken to be, but rather the exchange of one myth for another, leading to the disastrous instrumentalization of reason. In *Dialectic of Enlightenment*, their point is essentially that the Enlightenment developed in such a way as to contradict its own promise of freedom and prosperity for all. They want, through an immanent critique, to call the Enlightenment back to that original promise. They search for historical "carriers" (Max Weber's term) of such a return to enlightened authenticity. First, they follow Marx and find the carrier in the "proletariat." Then, giving up on the workers, they nominate their own tribe, the social and political philosophers, for this task. They set out to recapitulate, with a difference, the basic Enlightenment moves. They try to discern the fundamental *logos* of society—i.e., to discover how and on what principles it works at its best. On this basis they seek to distinguish between proper social working and its distortions. In this way they lay methodological foundations for much of the left-leaning social-scientific work of the mid-twentieth century and beyond, and particularly that of the Frankfurt School and of its representative second-generation thinker, Jürgen Habermas.

A weakness of critical theory is that it is a highly theoretical uncovering of the distortions of bourgeois society rather than a practical program for remaking the structures of modern life. It is an intellectual dismantling of capitalist reasoning rather than a foundation for restorative social therapy. It is unclear what actual social structures and practices critical theory approves. Presumably some form of democratic socialism. Horkheimer and Adorno, having handed responsibility for social salvation to members of their own academic tribe, are pessimistic, if not despairing, about the future of the modern project. An element of truth, but not the whole truth, lies here. Those who would help save modernity need to know about such analyses, but yet be anchored in something beyond them.

Reflection and Action on Human Rights

Another form of resistance to economic and political totalization can be found in the growing cross-cultural consensus on "human rights." The content of the 1948 Universal Declaration on this subject has found its way into numerous international treaties and agreements, impacting national policies and encouraging people in many places to resist the denial of such rights in any form. The work of Amnesty International—focused on the practical implementation of such convictions—is for many an expression of the global "conscience of humankind." Do we not have here a growing acceptance—on the way to some sort of "universality"—of moral claims having to do with the rights and freedoms of persons?[19]

But it is notable that social philosophers have been far less successful in agreeing about the responsibilities that go with such rights, even to the point of denying that there are any. It is true, for example, that the notion of rights can be, and often is, invoked to justify individual and group interests of every kind, without consideration for social duties owed in return. But one comes close here to the equally erroneous view that "rights" are earned, as they are in some totalitarian regimes, by obedience to prevailing social or political expectations instead of being inherent in human personhood as such. Obviously the notion that rights are only for those who earn them by conformist behavior can be exploited by those who wish to dictate the terms of fulfillment, say political loyalty to a regime or the achievement of economic power by approved means.

There is a seeming paradox here. Human rights are not a reward for obedient behavior. Yet they involve legitimate social duties and expectations. The exercise of rights invokes and enacts an inherent human dignity whose nature is to express itself responsibly: that is with integrity to the identity of the social actor and care for the integrity of others. The notion of human rights, properly understood, *confers* responsibility for consequences. This side of the rights equation has received far less attention than the former one that speaks of rights alone.

Perhaps for some of these reasons, certain intellectual trends, both modern and postmodern, have of late tended to undermine the notion that rights are universal by stressing the variability of rights languages in different situations and cultures. For many observers, moral standards retain their intelligibility and point only within the traditions that articulate them. Many, like Alasdair MacIntyre, say that we live in a situation in which many mutually unintelligible moral languages coexist, and in which even "the rights of man" is a phrase incapable of clear definition outside its culture of origin, let alone broadly accepted derivation from what we know of the human situation or the human person as such.

"Common Morality" Projects

The effort to save modernity from itself also goes on in attempts to unite the human race itself around some universal moral code that can resist economic and political tendencies to "totalization" that benefits only privileged classes. When one thinks of "common morality," one thinks of Hans Küng's several efforts, in the context of the Parliament of the World's Religions, to sketch the outlines of a "global ethic." In his books he usefully foregrounds the theme of responsibility in ways that echo the work of Hans Jonas.[20] But Küng's method focuses on the drafting of comprehensive ethical statements that leaders of world religions are asked to sign. Alternatively, he gives us albums of inspirational, but only sometimes analytic, statements of global vision from these same leaders, as well as others. Attacking the distortions of human life characteristic of modernity is clearly one of Küng's goals. He sees global moral agreements as a primary vehicle for mounting such an attack. But a weakness of his approach is that the different world religions are not here enlisted in any cultural or theological depth. Instead, high-profile persons are invited simply, by vote, to endorse a vision expressed in Western terms, in German or English prose. Religious leaders are loathe not to cooperate in such worthwhile ventures. But we hear little or nothing of the theological reasoning that takes them from their traditions to endorsement of Küng's particular vision and language. Nor does this venture seem to envision many concrete consequences apart from continued refinement of the prose and better relations among those at the top.

An exploration that uncovers many of these difficulties and others as well (without reference to Küng) in found in the highly interesting anthology, *Prospects for a Common Morality*, edited by John P. Reeder and Gene Outka.[21] Here leading social ethicists address the question of how one might articulate philosophical foundations for a common human moral world. Each essay in the book advocates a distinctive set of premises followed by a distinctive sort of argument. No two more than superficially agree. The editors' introductory efforts to map the possibilities, tracing agreements and disagreements, is a brilliant *tour de force* that wrings a certain coherence out of the volume's diverse forms of argument and expression. But in the end, the title is correct. There is no prospect (singular) for a common morality here, but only a series of "prospects" couched in diverse philosophical languages.

The fact that arguments run in different directions, of course, does not mean that they are in themselves invalid. It only means that underlying convictions that might lead to greater agreement have so far eluded us. A postmodern sensibility has its nose in the ethicists' tent. Many see the danger that moral agreement today is more likely to be maintained by power, or even by marketing, than it is by reasoning. Some philosophical moralists go so far as to say that "reason" cannot in the nature of the case reach *any* sort of consensus as to the nature of the human good. In his book *The Reasons of Love*,[22] Harry G. Frankfurt argues this case as follows:

> There is among philosophers a recurrent hope that there are certain final ends whose unconditional adoption might be shown to be in some way a requirement of reason. But this is a will-o'-the wisp. There are no necessities of logic or rationality that dictate what we are to love. What we love is shaped by the universal exigencies of human life, together with those other needs and interests that derive more particularly from the features of individual character and experience. Whether something is to be an object of our love cannot be decisively evaluated either by any *a priori* method through examination of just its inherent properties. It can be measured only against requirements that are imposed on us by other things that we love. In the end, these are determined for us by biological or other natural conditions, concerning which we have nothing much to say.[23]

So much for attempts to order human life toward the good by means of rational arguments. It would seem that neither philosophers nor social engineers, functioning *within* the modern paradigm, have the capacity to resolve that paradigm's moral contradictions. But perhaps that can be done piecemeal through communities in which we actually do act to protect persons and "things that we love."

The World of Non-Governmental Organizations

The welfare of things and persons we love is obviously a question for individuals. But these matters often also become the provinces of myriad non-governmental organizations, or NGOs. These have become increasingly numerous over the last quarter century. Those accredited to the United Nations alone in various relationships now number approximately 3,200, up from an original 40. These groups run the gamut from Bread for the World to the World Wildlife Fund, from Amnesty International to the Salvation Army, from the Carnegie Endowment to the Carter Center, from Doctors Without Borders to World Vision, and on and on. By and large they do very good work. Between 30 and 40 percent of NGOs have religious backgrounds or affiliations. Their representatives, religious or otherwise, are for the most part extraordinarily impressive people. They act, while many others theorize. The world would be drastically poorer without them.

Yet it is striking how much energy is here devoted to "single issue" concerns. It is as if resistance to global economic-political-military totalization is being carried on by persons who "have no other goals" than those of their particular focused concerns. It is as if many persons of high energy and principles are simply unable to grapple with the "big questions," or regard such grappling as a dangerous diversion when certain specific issues they see before their eyes cry out for attention. Better, they think, to make specific, even measurable, contributions to the world's well-being than to engage in probably futile theorizing about the problems of modernity as such.

Yet there may be something more behind this fragmented NGO phenomenon. It may be that we have come to a moment in the history of culture at which moral generalizations have ceased to be persuasive. It could be that coherent and comprehensive forms of resistance to totalization are not available to us. Alasdair MacIntyre has argued in a series of books that the world now speaks a multitude of incommensurable moral languages that are unable to communicate with one another. If this is so, then it would not now be possible, even if we were tempted, to organize an NGO of NGOs with common principles, let alone a coherent, communicable, global agenda. When, in 1948, the just-formed World Council of Churches took up the slogan of "the responsible society," those involved could not have known how rapidly that attractive perspective would be challenged by those of the then-emerging "third world" who saw it as merely a new expression of colonialism, "the white man's burden," all over again. They could not have known how rapidly *all* allegedly comprehensive perspectives would be challenged by postmodern emphases on the particular and the local. Today every global perspective, however well-intentioned, can be challenged as a thinly veiled agenda for domination.

So one can see NGOs as moral vehicles for principled persons who want to make a difference but also want to avoid the hubris of visions too comprehensive to be true. One can see an avoidance of things such as critical social theory, common morality visions, and even of human rights agendas without corresponding attention to responsibilities, although the latter are clearly in a special category. More than any other forms of resistance to totalization, the better NGOs have earned by their good works the right to criticize books like this one that still look for more comprehensive approaches to modernity's discontents.

A New Dimension of Ethical Relevance: Hans Jonas and Winston Davis

I would describe all four of the preceding sorts of reflection-action projects for healing modernity's ills as immanental. That is, they work within the intellectual and practical canons of the modern paradigm to find ways of setting it right. They believe, despite being highly critical of one another's principles, that the now unmanageable consequences of autonomous human responsibility-taking for reinventing society can be dealt with by now better informed and more perspicacious, but still humanly autonomous, responsibility-taking. But if the underlying issue has to do with power and with the already coopted character of the conceptual schemes we have available for regulating our common life, the question is one of generating the political will to put any one of these perspectives, or some combination of them, into effective action. The philosopher Hans Jonas does not wrestle with this question directly, but he offers perspectives that illumine the problem. I will use his work to help bring out what is at stake in empowering any of the restorative responsibility enterprises just discussed.

Jonas argues that social theory needs to account for the extraordinarily increased capacities we have now for changing the world by our deeds, for the portentous consequences of nearly every decision we make. His point, otherwise put, is that these *consequences* of Enlightenment-style responsibility-taking are such that no amount of revisionist responsibility-taking within the prevailing paradigm can heal us. It is not only that dealing with these consequences cannot be reduced to ordinary job descriptions and programs. As I would put it: these consequences are now *beyond the scope of the responsibility-taking of which human beings are ordinarily capable,* whatever social theory or program they may adopt.

In *The Imperative of Responsibility,*[24] Jonas argues that the coming of modern technology, including nuclear technology, has utterly changed the fundamental premises of moral argument. Where before the Enlightenment it was assumed that the nature of human beings, with their capacities and possibilities, was largely determined by static circumstances that narrowly circumscribed the scope of their responsibility, these simple conditions no longer hold. With the development of radically new human capabilities—to accumulate, to communicate, to dominate, to destroy—the nature of human action as such has changed. And this change calls for a different kind of ethics. It is not just that we have new subject matter for moral rumination. Rather, as Jonas says, "The qualitatively novel nature of certain of our actions has opened up a whole new dimension of ethical relevance for which there is no precedent in the standards and canons of traditional ethics."[25] There are now questions facing us for which "nobody is responsible," in the sense that nobody has these things directly in his or her job description. Ethics is now forced to look beyond the direct, immediate dealings between people and consider actions that have an unprecedented reach into the future. A new sort of moral responsibility, not one invented by human beings as a simple social construct but grounded in nature as a center of value with no less than humanity's fate for its concern, must now take center stage. Jonas's challenge must now be faced by each of the projects mentioned above that seek to resist the totalizing ideologies of globalization. These projects—the promotion of human rights, critical social theory, the mobilization of non-governmental organizations, the search for a common morality—are called by our present circumstances to embody ethics of a "new kind" or fail to generate the political will effectively to address their issues. What kind of ethics today generates from within itself what St. Augustine called the "will to will" to act on insights already in our possession but not yet released into action?

Winston Davis, a religious studies scholar conversant with Jonas's work, helps us to think out what such a "new kind" of ethics might mean. In *Taking Responsibility: Comparative Perspectives*,[26] he makes a distinction between kinds or levels or dimensions of responsibility that seem congruent with modernity's contemporary struggle for "salvation" from its failures and contradictions. First, there is *simple or routine responsibility*, meaning the sum total of our conventional, settled, duties. At this level, responsible people are dependable, reliable, trustworthy, and prudent. They are content with the givens of their situation and seek to work within those givens. Such responsible behavior is what makes the world work. It contains little evaluative or reflective component. It prizes reliability, and the trustworthiness that goes with it. I observe, however, that simple responsibility is not *that* simple. It is also the achievement of a certain kind of culture. It reflects a certain kind of confidence in the justice and effectiveness of the system within which one works. It reflects a conviction that what one does is good, despite one's inability to change the basic frame of reference of one's work. This sort of responsibility is not insignificant. The routines of homemaking fall in this category, as do the routines of industry and government. Consider the consequences if one cannot count on such functions being reliably fulfilled. Routinely responsible people can overthrow a political or economic or gender-oriented order if they become convinced that it is not contributing to their well-being. The simply responsible ones may seldom ask questions, but woe to leadership that betrays their trust. A question to put to each of our restorative perspectives is whether it fulfills this basic requirement of seeing to the social basics.

But there is a second dimension of responsibility: one that is *complex*. This is responsibility for dealing with unprecedented circumstances such as those faced by the human race today insofar as they can be dealt with managerially. Here one seeks to juggle complexly interrelated factors, such as those of global climate change, that impact human well-being. Perhaps there are more factors than human beings can simultaneously hold in mind, hence the need for mathematical models and computers. One cannot even be sure that all relevant factors are in the mix. Some supremely relevant fact may be yet to be discovered. One must take into account the relative urgency of different problems, considering what must be done now and what can wait. One must judge which simple responsibilities will continue to be supported, and which will not. One must also judge the political elements in one's situation. The "in box" test on the Foreign Service examination is designed precisely to test a candidate's capacity for complex responsibility of this kind. What messages are merely routine? Which ones merit some reflection? Which ones announce emergencies that need immediate action? In some cases, complex responsibility involves questions about how routine or simple responsibilities are best performed. How can the food supply and the streets be safe? How can electric power stay on all day in Baghdad? How can productivity and economic stability be maintained under just conditions? Again, how do the different modes of responsible resistance measure up? How do they deal with the burdens of making complex social decisions?

Without question, the practitioners of complex responsibility have a central role in addressing modernity's irresponsibility. Most of the strategies of resistance to modernity's self-destructiveness discussed earlier in this chapter are programs for the exercise of complex responsibility, in the sense of multifactored situational analysis and corrective action. This sort of responsibility goes well with the idea of "repair" (*tikkun olam*: putting the world right), or of "immanent" social criticism. An enormous amount of work can and must be done at this level, if it can be linked to a program that indeed grasps the contributing factors to modernity's ills at their source. We know many of these sources well. The skill, and courage, to devise programs to meet these problem is in short supply. And in even shorter supply is any serious social agreement on where the underlying problems are. What provides the integrating principle for handling the many particulars that go together to make a policy? In any program of resistance, it is essential to enlist the experts, the practitioners of complexity. These "experts" need not only to analyze, but also to look in two directions: toward the question of likely support from those whose responsibilities are basic, or simple, and toward those whose responsibility is related to transcendental vision of the ultimate conditions of possibility for the society itself.

Yet such responsibilities, both simple and complex, still lie mainly within the prevailing paradigm, in this case that of modernity in the Enlightenment tradition. That is, they function within the political and policy realms, within the limits of whatever people take to be "the art of the possible." But simple and complex responsibilities pursued in practice can give rise to the intuition that there may be dimensions of existence to be considered that lie outside or beyond that paradigm. These are dimensions of responsibility incapable of being articulated in cost-benefit or rational choice terms. Such a realization that something more is at stake can arise when the issue being considered has to do with the fundamental goodness, or the survival, of the "modern project" paradigm itself.

Winston Davis has a word for this further outside-the-box dimension of responsibility. He calls it *transcendental* responsibility. Given Davis's apparent meaning, I have difficulty with his choice of words. I prefer *transcending*, meaning that which "goes beyond." Transcending sorts of responsible action may well then raise transcendental questions, meaning questions about their conditions of possibility. I will soon come back to this important consideration. Meanwhile, it seems clear that, for Davis, transcending/transcendental actions are ones responding to the unprecedented complexity and portentousness of current human issues. His idea, just as it is, is important and suggestive. It is into this category that Jonas's remark about the need for "an altogether new kind of ethics" may well be thought to flow.

Davis's parade example is the manner in which the convention charged with revising the American Articles of Confederation unilaterally decided to draft a national Constitution instead, thus decisively altering their original assignment and arousing a political will that had before been dormant at best. This could be called an act of transcending responsibility because it stepped out of the Confederation mindset of interaction in certain regards of sovereign political units—Massachusetts, Pennsylvania, Virginia, and so forth—while in other regards they kept their separateness. It could be called transcending as well because it required delegates to reach out and be concerned about worlds of memories and interests other than their own. A Constitution, as opposed to a Confederation, represented a fundamental shift in the location and nature of sovereignty itself. In any case, it exceeded the limits of what people were intending at the beginning of the enterprise.

Davis sometimes seems to understand transcending responsibility as only a more challenging dimension of complex responsibility, rather than as something fundamentally different in nature. Those whose responsibilities involve high-stakes decisions among well-nigh infinitely complex factors sometimes feel that this complexity and portentousness pushes them toward something more, something infinitely qualitatively *different,* some narrative or frame of reference for making decisions that is not present in the intellectual paradigms existing society offers them. Is this sense of the *more* reality or illusion? If reality, it certainly deserves a name of its own, but also a more careful unpacking of applications and meanings.

The decisive difference between complex responsibility and the responsibility Davis calls "transcendental" is indicated by examples that Davis seems not to have integrated into his theory. These have to do with matters in relation to which we have few if any guidelines in the world as we know it. Jacques Derrida, for example, deconstructs the Enlightenment's totalizing self-certainties, declaring that "there is no responsibility without a dissident and inventive rupture with respect to tradition, authority, orthodoxy, rule, or doctrine."[27] Comparably, Thomas Keenan says that "the only responsibility worthy of the name comes with the removal of grounds, the withdrawal of the rules or the knowledge on which we might rely. It is when we do not know exactly what we should do … and when we have nowhere else to turn … that we encounter something like responsibility."[28]

One catches the sense of the transcendental in such statements, even if Derrida would not have accepted that word, with its metaphysical connotations. One also senses the Abrahamic quality of such venturing forth beyond the usual grazing grounds, the usual explanatory categories. People do act in such ways, but how is this possible? The words of Derrida and Keenan sound like evocations of solitary existential courage. There are hints here of solitary presumption—particularly in the last-mentioned quotation with its seeming claim to radical courage—that runs the risk of spiritual distortion. Taking responsibility, even in the midst of radical uncertainty, may easily become an expression of pride, or just plain dogged obsession with an idea. One brings off the revolution and then one becomes a tyrant. Such responsibility-takers can become certain that their vision is superior to all others and zealously defend the power they have achieved.[29]

Even where no calculation within the terms of established frameworks of action and meaning seems adequate, where one must simply make the risky move, there is still need for some ground of confidence in the ultimate meanings of that move. For this reason I say that decisive, identity-committing risk in the midst of indecipherable complexity can easily take on dimensions beyond the limits of mere logical-empirical explanation. Such responsibility-taking is indispensable at the point where mere management, however knowledgeable or skillful, is insufficient to address the enormity of the human situation: where decisions that demand full investment of one's personhood in all its mysterious foundations are indispensable.

Transcendental Responsibility and the Possibility of a Transformative Ethic

Do such considerations finally begin to justify the use of the word "transcendental"? This term, used philosophically as in Kant, refers to a method of inquiry into the conditions of possibility of certain kinds of knowing. (The term must be carefully distinguished from "transcendent" which Kant applied to theological or metaphysical realities lying beyond the knowing capacities of human reasoning working with the materials of sense experience.) We know that there are deeds, some already mentioned, whose moral quality and clarity exceed anything that mere reasoning about "the good" can produce. One prisoner gives his life for another in a concentration camp. French Protestants risk their lives to save Jews from the Gestapo. A man jumps off a subway platform to save another who has fallen in front of an oncoming train. What are the transcendental conditions of *this* kind of doing? We think we see in such instances a kind of responsibility-taking that is not so easily identifiable or definable in terms of the usual prudential human categories. We ask how such transcending or unusual actions are *possible* for human beings, and hence ask a transcendental question.

The French Protestants during World War II are a useful case in point. Citizens (many, but not all, of them members of the local Reformed parish under the leadership of Pastor Andre Trocmé) of the village of Le Chambon-sur-Lignon in southern France took extraordinarily risky responsibility for rescuing hundreds of Jews from the Gestapo between 1942 and 1945. When asked why they put themselves in such danger, they would typically reply that this needed no explanation. Is this not what one does under such circumstances? Well, no. It is not what most people do. It seems to be a remarkable gift, given only to some. The word used in the village for these gifted persons was apt: "les responsables."[30]

Such stories demand that we try to grasp meanings that help to explain the phenomenon by which persons sacrifice their lives for others, or, for that matter, make personal sacrifices for the good of the beleaguered body politic. Might thinkers who seek to address modernity's discontents have an interest in more rigorously asking how testifying moral actions such as these are possible? Are they to be understood as acts of the will? If so, what makes them so? Even resolutely secular social philosophers may be more open to such questions than we think. They may, of course, simply inquire empirically about radically altruistic acts as social phenomena, asking when and how such acts take place. But other theorists have recently been asking—on their own terms of course—if there are *traditions* of life still around with sufficient narrative force and coherence to provide conditions contributory to such acts of moral responsibility beyond mere competence in dealing with complexities. Inevitably, attention has been turning to religious traditions, not so much for their doctrinal content (although that could be relevant too) as for their moral witness. At a 1996 University of Santa Clara colloquy honoring John Rawls on the twenty-fifth anniversary of *A Theory of Justice*, six out of the seven speakers, in different ways spoke of their need for ethical dialogue with religiously traditioned communities.[31] They were saying, in effect, that secular social therapies should maintain their conceptual autonomy but *also* seek sustenance from deeply traditioned and ongoing forms of life.

In his latter years, the French deconstructionist Jacques Derrida was doing something much like this, mining the Hebrew and Christian scriptures, as well as the Talmud, for sources of inspiration. John Caputo writes of this work that Derrida, still professing atheism, "follows with fascination the movements of what theology calls God, observing how theology speaks, and how it finds it necessary not to speak, under the solicitation of the wholly other."[32] Derrida was even exempting certain seemingly transcendental ideas such as "forgiveness" and "justice" from deconstruction. Without giving these notions a name, he would seem to argue that some human actions are not simply explicable in any ordinary sense, but seem to rest on conditions of possibility that lie beyond reason.

One wonders, in the larger scheme of things, what all this means. Are we approaching a great reversal, even a homecoming, in the philosophical world? Are we coming to the end of a centuries-long estrangement between traditions of religious life and their autonomy-seeking philosophical progeny? We have seen, earlier in this chapter, that in the seventeenth and eighteenth centuries, visions of human society that had formerly functioned within institutionally religious frames of reference began to assert the autonomy we see so highly developed today. Like youthful offspring of not-always-wise and often quarreling parents, they decided to move out of ancestral households. They continued to bear the marks of their origins as "theologies or anti-theologies in disguise,"[33] but, as we have seen, they steered independent courses toward toleration, secularization, the marginalization of religious faith: all in the interest of social peace and well-being that had been gravely compromised by the seventeenth-century Wars of Religion.

For obvious reasons I hesitate to call these enlightened offspring of premodern parents "prodigal sons." It might seem an indication of disrespect that I do not intend. Indeed, the biblical parable needs to be considerably rewritten, especially at the end. Still, it tells an important truth. Despite their best intentions, Enlightenment reinventors of the human spent their religious patrimonies rather rapidly, discovering too late just how important specific religious teachings, liturgies, and communities had been in making former social arrangements function successfully.

In recent decades there have been signs, several of them just mentioned, that many of these offspring are disappointed by the shallowness and fragmentation of the beckoning secularities that had once seemed so attractive. Some have indicated that they would like at least to visit the homes of their parents in search of forgotten wisdom. If they were to come for a visit, they would also bring with them much knowledge and experience about worldly life gained during their years away: knowledge and experience that could transform and extend the older wisdom. These visitors would certainly have much to teach those who had remained at home about how dimly remembered virtues had fared, or failed to register, in the larger world. They would also have much to teach about moral questions unimagined only a few decades ago: questions such as those generated by the rise of economic globalization and its exacerbation of environmental risks, or proposals extending the concept of human rights to future generations, not to speak of biomedical advances raising profound ethical conundrums.

But what are these secular seekers really looking for? Are they only after ideas or images that they can use in secular forms, hoping to make Durkheim's move over again or profiting from Ricoeur's insight that "the symbol gives rise to thought"? Yes, one hears of goals like those. But many of our prodigal social philosophers also come to be confronted by the profoundly different, the unexpected. They are not much helped by religious liberals too like themselves to provide the sense of otherness, the feeling of difference, from which creatively to push off in new directions. They come looking for something more than useful ideas or ideological allies. They come looking for *testimony* to further and deeper dimensions of ethical existence, testimony to spiritual power capable of helping alter the potentially disastrous course of modern life. They come to explore the transcendental conditions of possibility for radically reparative responsibility-taking.

Do such explorations bring us closer to the "whole new dimension of ethical relevance"[34] that Jonas was looking for? A reaching-across to the Other that itself supplies the transcendental condition of possibility of the ethical relationship? We are most helped in understanding such a possibility by borrowing from the work of Emmanuel Lévinas, who is known for his radical philosophical opposition to "totalization," to metaphysical or ontological construals of reality maintained in currency by power. Lévinas wished to break through all this to the lineaments of actual human relationships through which we have glimpses of the "traces" left by "infinity," hence the title of his book, *Totality and Infinity.* In place of totalitarian demands, Levinas spoke of ethics as "first philosophy," meaning that the mutual commitments of persons to one another are more fundamental than power relationships or the forms of constrained reality-sense that they maintain. Lévinas is not speaking, in so many words, of the view that we should have "no other goals" than those of maintaining markets and political arrangements to our own advantage, by force if necessary. But he is dealing with analogous visions that wither the human spirit. He mounts a radical opposition to totalization as such, not merely ameliorative moves within already totalized systems.

The "first philosophy" that Lévinas gives us is based on the notion that each person owes a radical moral obligation to each Other person that he or she meets. We do not become moral persons by being obedient to custom or by mastering ethical arguments. We become moral persons in confronting the "face" of the Other. Lévinas's view of this obligation-to-Other has been described as all-consuming, or "exorbitant." Paul Ricoeur argues, indeed, that such a view in effect evacuates my sense of self, leaving me with no moral substance by which to respond to the Other's presence or implicit demand.[35] I need to begin with a self capable of meeting the neighbor, who then says, by his or her mere presence to my gaze, "Do not steal from me." "Do not harm me." "Do not kill me." I prefer the Ricoeurian version of Lévinas to Lévinas's own statement of his position. My antecedent capacity to respond to the neighbor is itself a gift that greets the gift of transcending demand the neighbor addresses to me.

I would put it this way: my true being is intrinsically moral in character. It is a responding or responsible being. The being I am able to claim for myself is not grounded in a solipsistic consciousness, existing in and for its own aggrandizement and having "no other goals." My true being is a being-to the Other person. And the other person's being is a being-to me. Hence the notion of responsibility arises in the very origins of selfhood. It follows that the gift of human being itself, the gift of transcendence, is given through the medium of the Other, through my responsibility to him or her. Such relationships fulfill the meaning of our having evolved from creation as conscious actors on this earth. It is intrinsic to our being human. It is for that reason that the existence of this mutually responsible relationship is the condition of possibility of all other ethical action and reflection, all that derives from it and expresses it. Here is the most philosophically precise meaning of the term "transcendental responsibility." It is the responsibility that makes all other ethical relationships conceptually conceivable and practically possible.

This notion of mutual interresponsibility also stands behind Lévinas's notion of "covenantal" community.[36] Here is the concrete frame of reference in which narratives, structures, and rules designed to honor and maintain the covenantal relationship evolve over time. Torah is one example. "New Covenant" is another. Qur'an is a third. None of these derivatives of the primordial covenantal relationship is stable in itself. Every human structure risks corruption or exploitation for the advantage of particular interests. All require the words and actions of prophets to call them back to their primordial meanings. In their struggles to maintain and ramify such responsible relationships, Abrahamic communities are called to bear testimony to the meaning of transcendental responsibility among all the other forms of responsibility-taking in the public world.

Could this be what social philosophers interested in articulating a responsibility ethic able to "take on" modernity's "discontents" are looking for? Is it what Hans Jonas was looking for? We cannot be sure. We argued, in discussing Jonas, that for any social-scientific prescription to achieve results, there needs to be a political will to make it work. And we have argued that one root of such political will lies in the shaping narratives of religious communities. In the case of the Abrahamic faiths, these are shaping narratives of covenantal obligation, in which "traces" of the Transcendent reach us through the Others to whom we are responsible. The resulting community could well generate identity-forming narratives supporting significant political will. Could that will be sufficient actually to take on the large questions that otherwise "no one is responsible for"?

Less Talk, Make It Happen!

After so long a chapter, I should no doubt be ashamed in closing to borrow the above commercial slogan of the Royal Bank of Scotland, heir to the legacy of Adam Smith. But I am not. It can take this long to make clear *what* it is that we want to see happen. Can things really work in the ways described? Only if the Abrahamic communities self-consciously try to make it so. And they today are still a long way from that. Preparing for visits by their own rooted cosmopolitans in search of spiritual wisdom would make great demands. It is not clear that Jewish, Christian, and Muslim leaders and thinkers are ready for such a challenge. For one thing, the Abrahamic witness to covenantal responsibility, such as it is today, is sectarian and competitive. Not only do these different faiths, despite their common origins, lack the sense of responsibility to one another that could generate conscious intercovenantal bonds, but they are internally divided into myriad denominations, sects, and points of view, sometimes competing violently. For another, it is not clear that the notion of mutual covenantal responsibility as a criterion of personal being, where being means being-to-the-Other, is well understood or practiced in these religious communities. And finally, it is not clear that they understand that mutual responsibility is a transcendental criterion of possibility and validity for all the rest of what we call ethics, including the ethics of responsibility for the fate of the earth. The moral validation of conduct does not come from self-cultivation, self-assertion, or achievement of power. Rather that validation comes from our fulfillment of covenantal obligations to each Other whose face we see, whose voice we hear. Each community's covenantal fabric stands for, or speaks for, the moral bonds that link us to ane another and to the entire human race.

Clearly, the principle of responsibility as being-to-Others applies not only among individuals but also among faith communities. This is why, especially today with multiple possibilities of communication and sharing, the Abrahamic faiths in particular need to find concrete ways of being responsible to one another in their therapies for modernity. They need to exercise mutual responsibility in their interpretations of sources, mutual responsibility in fashioning stable relationships, and mutual responsibility in bearing public witness. Being mutually responsible does not mean finding agreement on every point. Far from it. But it does mean taking account of the consequences for others of one's interpretations and actions. It is for this reason that the Abrahamic faiths, as a matter of integrity in their moral beings, need to ask what kinds of intercovenantal relationships can bear the weight of responsibility for mediating "blessing" to all earth's families.

What might the Abrahamic faiths need to *do* in order to communicate these gifts to humankind? Answering this crucial question calls, not for further ideational development, but for examples of actual attempts to gather the Abrahamic communities together for such purposes. The next chapter, chapter 4, seeks to do precisely this. I will offer three extended descriptions of inter-Abrahamic coalitions aimed at bearing responsibility to one another and to the troubled modern world. These examples come from different times, places, and situations. They, by their activities, generate different sorts of social space. What is more, they develop a variety of terminologies, none of which very closely resemble those used in this chapter. If they were reported as doing so, one might suspect the writer's resort to some sort of Procrustean bed. Instead, each instance is described in the language of one of its theologically literate participants. These participant-rapporteurs are Muslim, Jewish, and Christian respectively. The resulting theological-ethical accounts are as diverse as are the case studies themselves. These examples illustrate the truth that inter-Abrahamic relationships do not depend on the success of any one sort of theological argument, least of all the argument presented in these pages. The concrete social forms and products of mutually responsible testimony, by and among the Abrahamic communities, are what count.

Notes

1. The phrase "the modern project" of late has been associated with Jürgen Habermas, who, against the postmodernists, asserts that, it is much too soon to give up the idea of human universality associated with the Enlightenment and continuing today in many aspects of contemporary global civilization.

2. I am indebted for this typology to Bob Goudzwaard, "The Modern Roots of Economic Globalization," in *Beyond Idealism: A Way Ahead for Ecumenical Social Ethics*, ed. Robin Gurney, Heidi Hadsell, and Lewis Mudge (Grand Rapids: Eerdmans, 2006).

3. See Alan R. Mittleman, "The Modern Jewish Condition," *First Things* (October 1994): 30–34.

4. H. Richard Niebuhr, *The Responsible Self* (New York: Harper and Row, 1963).

5. Ibid., 47f. Niebuhr provides neither a source nor a date for this quotation.

6. Ibid., 48.

7. Carl L. Becker, *The Heavenly City of the Eighteenth-Century Philosophers* (New Haven, CT: Yale University Press, 1932).

8. Donald K. Pickens, review of Carl L. Becker, *The Heavenly City of the Eighteenth-Century Philosophers* (New Haven: Yale University Press, 1932), H-Net Review, June 2000, dpickens@unt.edu. http://www.h-net.org/reviews/showrev.cgi?path=8077962120681.

9. Trevor Colbourn, ed., *Fame and the Founding Fathers* (New York, Norton, 1974), quoted in Carl L. Becker, *The Heavenly City of the Eighteenth-Century Philosophers* (New Haven, CT: Yale University Press, 1932), 3.

10. Adam Smith, *Theory of Moral Sentiments* (Indianapolis, IN: Liberty Classics, 1982). For Smith, the power of interdependence and mutual esteem still exceeded that of interest-motivated action.

11. Adam B. Seligman, *The Idea of Civil Society* (New York: Free Press, 1992), 32.

12. Quoted in Alan Wolfe, *Whose Keeper? Social Science and Moral Obligation* (Berkeley: University of California Press, 1989), 221.

13. I am, of course, thinking here of the "capabilities" approach of the Nobel Prize-winning economist Amartya Sen, who argues that a nations GNP be measured not in purely quantitative economic terms but in relation to the human capabilities unchained and released creatively into the social world.

14. Pierre Bourdieu was a professor of the College de France and the author of books such as *The Field of Cultural Production, Homo Academicus, Invitation to Reflexive Sociology, Language and Symbolic Power*, and *The Logic of Practice*.

15. The term "neoliberalism" in this sense is less often heard in North America and, if uttered here, is likely to be misunderstood as some sort of new Rawlsianism. The minute one travels to Western Europe, or to Latin America, however, one hears the term being used, as Bourdieu does, to mean the dominance of the "market" model for all human interaction.

16. See Gary Becker, *The Economic Approach to Human Behavior* (Chicago: University of Chicago Press, 1976). A useful brief discussion of Becker can be found in Larry Rasmussen, *Moral Fragments and Moral Community* (Minneapolis: Fortress Press, 1993), 49f. As Rasmussen says, Becker is "arguing against Adam Smith's refusal to extend the logic of self-interest into noneconomic territory, together with Smith's corollary conviction that different spheres require different moralities. In this scheme individuals are all 'utility maximizers' who operate from a relatively stable set of personal preferences. Quite apart from markets, then, there is a mental process of market behavior and logic that supplies all the guidance needed for moral and other considerations necessary to the thousands of decisions we make." One may add, however, that some forms of rational choice theory, particularly in the work of John Nash, stress the advantage-maximizing properties of market cooperation. This does not, however, reduce the primacy of self-interest in the equation. Cooperation here is not altruism. It is a self-interest strategy in itself.

17. This trenchant summary is the work of Paul Treanor in his article "Neoliberalism: Origins, Theory, Definition," on the web at http://web.inter.nl.net/users/Paul Treanor/neoliberalism.html.

18. The terms "totalizing" and "totalization" have been used, particularly by such philosophers as Paul Ricoeur and Emmanuel Lévinas, to refer to conditions under which some single vision of life is given politically dominant or even metaphysical status. The title of Lévinas's book *Totality and Infinity* makes reference to the moral struggle against metaphysical totalizations of ideology maintained in force by constellations of economic, political, or military power.

19. I here follow the argument of Gene Outka and John P. Reeder in *Prospects for a Common Morality* (Princeton, NJ: Princeton University Press, 1993), 3ff.

20. See, for example, Hans Küng's book *Global Responsibility: In Search of a New World Ethic* (New York: Crossroads, 1991) and *A Global Ethic and Global Responsibilities: Two Declarations,* ed. Küng with Helmut Schmidt (London: SCM, 1998.)

21. John P. Reeder and Gene Outka, eds., *Prospects for a Common Morality* (Princeton, NJ: Princeton University Press, 1993).

22. Harry G. Frankfurt, *The Reasons of Love* (Princeton, NJ: Princeton University Press, 2004).

23. Ibid., 47f.

24. Hans Jonas, *The Imperative of Responsibility* (Chicago: University of Chicago Press, 1984).

25. Ibid., 1.

26. Winston Davis, *Taking Responsibility: Comparative Perspectives* (Charlottesville: University Press of Virginia, 2002).

27. Jacques Derrida, *The Gift of Death* (Chicago: University of Chicago Press, 1995), 27, as quoted in Davis, *Taking Responsibility,* 282.

28. Thomas Keenan, *Fables of Responsibility: Aberrations and Predicaments in Ethics and Politics* (Stanford, CA: Stanford University Press, 1997), 1–2, quoted in Davis, *Taking Responsibility,* 282.

29. Indeed the suicide bomber, by his or her own lights, almost perfectly fits the profile just sketched. A certain interpretation of a religious tradition, fueled by desperation and the belief that in *this* way one can participate in a world-historical grand narrative called Jihad, adds up to violent death for innocent people. Christians and Jews have not been exempt from Jihad-like responsibility-taking either. Think of the Crusades, or of current strategies for protecting the integrity and security of the State of Israel. This is the level of responsibility as gift, where the integrity of the person and the radical identification of personhood with deeds enters the scene. Here the gift assumes the form of being placed in a certain personal or historical situation that tests and brings out the personhood. This gift of capacity-in-situation, combined with the gift of some sort of covenantal promise that one's act is intended to anticipate, is the condition of possibility of exercising responsibility of this kind. An act of transcendental responsibility is an act made possible by the gift of such conditions.

30. On the village of Le Chambon-sur-Lignon and what happened there, see Philip Hallie, *Lest Innocent Blood Be Shed* (New York: Harper and Row, 1979).

31. The six were Ronald Dworkin, Bernard Williams, Thomas Nagel, Michael Sandel, Amy Gutmann, and Rawls himself. The speaker who did not was, ironically, the one in whom theologians have shown the most interest: Jürgen Habermas.

32. John D. Caputo, *The Prayers and Tears of Jacques Derrida: Religion without Religion* (Indianapolis: Indiana University Press, 1997), 4.

33. John Milbank, *Theology and Social Theory* (Oxford: Blackwell Publishers, 1988), 3.

34. Jonas, *Imperative of Responsibility*, 1.

35. Ricoeur conducts an extended conversation with Lévinas in the final chapters of his book *Oneself as Another* (Chicago: University of Chicago Press, 1995). Here Ricoeur argues that there is already an alterity within ourselves that responds to the "face" of the other with an impulse to obligation that, in Lévinas's rhetoric, seems unlimited. In fact, I will argue that this transcendental sense of obligation needs to work itself out in what Ricoeur elsewhere calls "just institutions" that translate the Other's imperious demands upon us into forms of life in which we can thrive.

36. By offering a philosophical rather than a traditionally religious description of the covenantal grounds for trusting, forgiving, and solidary human relationships, Lévinas offers a form of access to such covenantal ethics, open to anyone. See Merold Westphal, "Emmanuel Lévinas and the Logic of Solidarity," in the *Graduate Faculty Philosophy Journal*, published by the New School for Social Research, 20, no.2; 21, no. 1. Also the chapter by Lévinas titled "The Pact," in Sean Hand, ed., *The Levinas Reader* (Oxford: Blackwell, 1989), 211ff.

4

Parallel and Interactive Hermeneutics
Three Inter-Abrahamic Projects

There have been innumerable inter-Abrahamic projects seeking ways of wrestling responsibly with modernity's shortcomings in the midst of its undeniable achievements. Can we find theologically sophisticated analyses of such projects, written by knowledgeable participants, that will help us grasp in depth what is going on? Provided that these specifications are interpreted broadly enough, there are several instances that can serve our purposes. This chapter will analyze three of them, each taking on a different *aspect* of modernity's discontents without losing sight of the whole picture. One case is reported from the perspective of a Sunni Muslim scholar-activist; the second is instigated by the thoughtful effort of an Orthodox Jewish rabbi; the third is illumined by the thinking of a leading Methodist Christian ethicist.

Why these three in particular, of all the possibilities that could have been chosen? There are several reasons. While such activities are increasingly common, very few have enjoyed participant interpreters whose inside knowledge and quality of insight are such as to challenge and further our argument. And it helps that these commentators are Muslim, Jewish, and Christian respectively. It is important to add, of course, that none of these action-reflection interpreters finds a place in this book as an accredited representative of his faith as such. Each, in fact, is in some sense an outlier: one some distance from the opinion-norm of his own religious community. Yet it is also clear that each identifies with his community, its traditions, and its perspectives. Each would wish to lead his community in the directions indicated. Each would wish to represent his faith to the world in the terms described.

Taken together, these accounts of inter-Abrahamic projects offer a welcome variety of theological perspectives and approaches, as well as a diversity of settings. One is impressed by how different from one another these interfaith involvements have been: different in their situations, different in method, different in the materials chosen for attention, different in the kinds of social space they live in or generate. Each has had its own perceptions and purposes. We will learn most from these examples if we attend to the particular settings, methods, and objectives of each.

We should not expect at the end of this chapter to have any single theological perspective for viewing these three cases. There is no predominant and coherent inter-Abrahamic theology today, nor is there likely to be one soon. There are only different faith communities studying together and acting together. Analysis of each such instance will come from some particular viewpoint that cannot, in the nature of the case, capture all that is going on or what different participants think about it. But this fact offers the chance to compare perspectives as well as practices. Thus, in our examples, while all three faiths are involved in each situation described, the analysis provided comes from a participant representing only one of them, yet writing with knowledge of, and responsibility toward, the other two. It is this feature of mutual responsibility, with a shared sense that there is a common promise to be upheld, that seems to hold these action-reflection enterprises together.

I will, in what follows, call this a practice of "parallel and interactive hermeneutics."[1] What does that mean? The word "hermeneutics" refers to the study of what goes on in the interpretation of texts and other expressions of meaning. These three case studies are all about interpretation: interpretation of scriptures, interpretation of moral traditions, interpretation of situations. Where scripture is concerned, of course, it is important to remember that the three religious traditions, depending on whom you ask, have different views of the nature and authority of their texts. Our three interpreters do their textual reasoning in both traditional and posttraditional (or nontraditional) ways. They retain their confessional identities, with their respective understandings of what that requires, as they influence one another in responding to the situations in which they live, or have recently lived. Interpretations of sources, traditions, situations, and events come together to precipitate shared therapeutic responses to modernity. In all three cases, diverse as they are, this is what I see going on, with greater or lesser self-awareness among the actors.

Furthermore, such shared interpretative activity generates what I have called "social space." If you gather people around a concern or a cause, you create a social space of common intentions and understandings. William Schweiker calls such settings "spaces of reasons," that is, settings in which people speak a common language and understand one another because they share a certain vocabulary and a certain set of perceptions. The world of baseball with its arcane terminology is such a social space. So is the academic world, or the world of politics. Each world is defined by mutual understandings that support certain activities. Each of the movements of resistance to modernity's betrayals of its own ideals is such a "space of reasons" *constituted* by the sharing of mutually understandable symbols.

In all three cases, the objective is to gather Abrahamic communities to recognize the public responsibilities they bear. In each situation, the Abrahamic communities generate a different *kind* of social space: a political freedom movement, an academic movement developing a particular kind of reasoning, a movement that articulates the significance of certain "reflexive" characteristics of Western culture. They do this with responsibility to one another and to the surrounding human community for the consequences of their interpretations. And in doing so, without compromising or abandoning their respective identities, they are subtly influencing one another, growing toward new *ways* of believing. The task now is to attend to what is going on in each of these three Abrahamic dialogue-and-action projects.

In the first project, modernity's failure takes the form of the (now defunct) South African policy of apartheid. Here an advanced industrial economy, organized to favor the racial minority that runs it, fails to do justice to the majority of its citizens. Indeed, it enslaves them to make the economy work. This project's social space is the whole community of resistance to this unjust regime on the part of the oppressed South African majority centered on the African National Congress and other organizations. Poor Muslim communities are among those who identify with this liberation effort. This situation provokes the rise of an Islamic liberation theology paralleling the well-known Christian one. Its author, a young participant in the struggle, is the Sunni Muslim scholar Farid Esack.

In the second project, the Western world is seen to have failed to grasp the faulty nature of its reasoning processes. Presumably this failure means, among other things, having allowed such things as cost-benefit analyses and rational choice theory so to dominate human thinking processes that we "have no other goals." The results are damaging to the human spirit. Here the social resistance space is generated by the activity of a community of scripture scholars engaged in an inter-Abrahamic dialogue about "scriptural reasoning" leading to emancipatory practice. It continues toward the vision of an Abrahamic coalition for this purpose extending well beyond the original dialogue community. This initiative is reported for us by its founder and leading theorist, the Orthodox Jewish rabbi and scholar Peter Ochs.

In the third project, a pluralistic West sacrifices moral realism on the altars of radical individualism and the pursuit of power. Typical personal preoccupations entirely miss those concerns that have to do with this culture's core values, its flourishing, or its survival. Here the action space for resistance potentially includes all those persons who see this moral failure: especially those who live close to and respond "reflexively" to neighbors of other faiths. This situation is analyzed for us by a theorist who also participates in the interfaith dialogue, the Protestant Christian ethicist William Schweiker.

In each case, obviously, we must distinguish between the actual practices described, which inevitably involve many people with widely varying viewpoints, and the theological or philosophical interpretations of those practices through which we come to know of them. The implication, of course, is that not everyone involved sees what is going on in the same way, or wants to describe it in the terms our analysts are using here. And it is not, of course, as if each of these interpreters focused on only one aspect of modernity's contemporary crisis of values. It is rather that each sees the totality of modernity's betrayals of its own virtues through the prism of his own particular social location and experience.

Farid Esack: Islamic and Christian Liberation Theologies Arrayed Together in the Struggle against Apartheid

The first case is based on an interpretation by the Muslim scholar Farid Esack of the early 1990s struggle by Christians, Muslims, and Jews together against apartheid in South Africa. In this situation of resistance to a dehumanizing philosophy and practice, members of the three faiths found themselves together in a solidarity of resistance to modernity's racially based oppression. They discovered that members of faiths other than their own could be counted on for costly support in precarious moments, that these putative "unbelievers" or even "infidels" were in fact their brothers and sisters in the struggle for justice.

For Esack, the underlying, highly controversial question raised by this situation is how Muslims can be in solidarity with Christians (and some Jewish liberals) in the struggle against apartheid and still be faithful to the Qur'an. On what terms can there be solidarity with the religious Other? How can such associations be justified in Islamic terms? How can one interpret the Qur'an so as to find in it support for such mutually trusting relationships? Interfaith solidarity, Esack sees, is an intrinsic part of the South African struggle. And Christian and Jewish opponents of apartheid have similar, not to say parallel, problems. Over against traditional conservative teachings, still held by religious authorities and many others, how are justice-seeking Jews and Christians similarly to understand their scriptures in this new situation? How can theological and ideological territory be reclaimed from conservatives and proponents of religious exclusivism?

Esack notes whom the Christian interpreters in particular have been reading: Gustavo Gutierrez and Juan Luis Segundo in particular. He also notes the documents they have produced: the Belhar Confession, the Kairos Document. In effect, he sets about making comparable moves, asking himself what Qur'anic interpretation would look like in this situation when paralleled with Christian liberation theology. He looks for support in the Qur'an, and among some of its contemporary interpreters, for shared acts of resistance to apartheid by the Abrahamic faiths acting together.

Such a move represents for Esack a leap from traditional scripture interpretation to a contemporary hermeneutical awareness without the years of development this transition took, and continues to take, in Christian and Jewish circles. Esack's hermeneutic is grounded in a historical-critical consciousness not as yet over the horizon for most Muslims. Esack comes to a recognition that interpretation is an ongoing, situationally influenced process in which the text itself passes through different historical and cultural experiences in the consciousness of those who read it for sustenance and insight in ever changing contexts. He begins to use social science methods to recover the history behind Qur'anic texts: history that links these texts to contemporary circumstances. A situational hermeneutic is combined with the insight of historical-critical method that the sacred texts themselves were situational in their origins and development.

Esack deploys these insights in an argument running through his book that goes roughly as follows. We inevitably read texts through the lenses of our experience gained in some particular context. Such meaning is always tentative, never universalizable, but it is the meaning we have for our situation. According to the Qur'an, one arrives at correct beliefs through correct action. If it is right to struggle against injustice, then a Qur'anic hermeneutic of liberation is bound to emerge within such struggles. Religious doctrine is always the result of such situated intellectual labor to understand and of the resolution of disputes about such understanding. But in the case of Islam, this process over the centuries led to rigidity, and an inability to deal with otherness. Still, acceptance of the righteous and just Other remains intrinsic to the Qur'an, as many passages show. But Muslim conservativism has consistently narrowed the base for recognizing such others. And so Muslims face the hermeneutical question: what is an authentic interpretation of the Qur'anic message today? Can Qur'anic texts help *produce* meaning in new situations? Esack's answer can be compressed into two near-aphorisms: liberative praxis in solidarity with the oppressed is the initial act of understanding the Qur'an. This solidarity is *also* the initial act in understanding the religious Other.

With this perspective to guide him, Esack seeks to find grounds for an "interreligious solidarity against oppression,"[2] or, otherwise put, "a South African Qur'anic hermeneutic of religious pluralism for liberation."[3] To do so, Esack focuses on two kinds of Qur'anic word studies. The first has to do with the vocabularies of inclusion and exclusion. The Qur'an contains many texts that seem to support religious exclusivism. But the most violent of these as well as others, Esack argues, are historically contextual. They refer to the personal and social attitudes of Mohammed's opponents in Mecca and Medinah. Contrasting with this exclusion/inclusion vocabulary are certain key notions in Arabic on which Esack builds his affirmative case. Terms such as integrity, the people, the oppressed of the earth, balance and justice, struggle and praxis, divine holism and human unity. A key Arabic term is *Wilayah*, meaning comradeship or solidarity. Esack makes a case for socioeconomic, rather than doctrinal factors, in *Wilayah*. And in Qur'an 4:80, the term seems actually to refer to the *religious* other. Indeed, the meaning of "Islam," or "submission to God," is by many Islamic scholars not confined to the historical Islamic community. There is a Qur'anic connection between trusting in God and righteous deeds performed by anyone, within the Islamic community or outside. Esack wants to convert the word Islam itself from being a noun, thus subject to communal reification and the drawing of boundaries, to being a verb, descriptive of what anyone can do and be.

What is the context in Islam itself for such a hermeneutical venture? It lies almost entirely outside traditional Islamic lands, among Islamic scholars now teaching in the West. Esack finds partial support in the work of Muslim scholars who have challenged traditional Qur'anic interpretation but not with the radicality of a Gutierrez or a Segundo. Esack analyzes the work of two of these, Fazlur Rahman, formerly of the University of Chicago, and Mohammed Arkoun, formerly of the Sorbonne. As Esack sees it, Arkoun's methodology, unlike that of Rahman, is rooted in the fact of pluralism. Esack remarks of him that "he argues with impressive effect that the remarkable similarities in the theological and intellectual developments among the Abrahamic religions should be the new basis of dialogue."[4] It would be fair to say that Esack finds support in the trajectories followed by these scholars, but goes further than either of them. Esack likewise acknowledges a younger generation of South African Islamic scholars, all of them involved in one way or another in the liberation struggle: Ebrahim Moosa, Abdul Rashied Omar, Ebrahim Rasool, Sa'diyya Shaikh, and Abdulkadr Tayob. In collaboration with these thinkers, Esack wishes to open the way to more theological pluralism within Islam, as well as to Islam's ability to deal positively with pluralism outside its gates.

This writer is not without a capacity for self-criticism and appreciation for the irony (and perhaps the danger) of what he is doing. Toward the end of his book he writes:

> Pluralism itself is not without ideology, but is intrinsically related to a discourse founded and nurtured in critical scholarship, which, in turn, functions as an extension of areligious—even anti-religious—Western scholarship. This scholarship is not physically limited to the West, but is an extension of an entire cultural system which is not without hegemonic interests over the so-called underdeveloped world. Is a commitment to pluralism, even if for the downtrodden, not paradoxically also buying into neo-colonialism?[5]

Does not this insight tell us exactly why a perspective such as Esack's will have difficulty gaining acceptance not only in conservative Islamic circles, but also among all Muslims who think anything Western—let alone colonialist—is decadent and oppressive? Is parallel hermeneutics, then, *essentially* a Western idea, requiring Western thought-forms for its description and implementation? If so, is that a reason for shying away from it? Or is such an idea being implicitly acknowledged by Esack here in this quotation, a gift the West could still give to the world, if that gift could be separated from the "hegemonic interests" that threaten to accompany it?

Peter Ochs: "Scriptural Reasoning" as Therapy for Modernity's Failed Logic

The Jewish scripture scholar and philosopher Peter Ochs is the founder of an organization called the Society for Scriptural Reasoning. Here Jewish, Christian, and Islamic interpreters meet to study their respective scriptures together. Here, by the way, is a traditional Jewish practice being opened, as an act of hospitality, to others. The purpose of this new form of common study is to form pragmatic hypotheses for guiding shared action toward the "repair" of the "failed logic of modernity." This is parallel hermeneutics in a literally face-to-face form. It begins in the seminar room rather than on the front lines of resistance to dehumanizing principalities and powers, but it is intended to equip its participants to mount an "Abrahamic theo-politics" in a world gone wrong. A typical meeting of the Society will involve both papers by the members of the group and the group study of selected scriptural passages. The whole will be centered on some theme for the year or for the occasion.[6]

Clearly the different members of this group (and of its many local offshoots) entertain different interpretations of what is going on in this particular form of parallel hermeneutical process. Ochs himself, as founder and leader, has written a set of "Rules for scriptural reasoning" to which members of the group have posted their own replies.[7] Thus, once again we may distinguish the actual practice followed in this setting from interpretative commentary on the practice. We will focus here on Ochs's particular vision which, while clearly highly influential, is also uniquely his own.

For Ochs, we live in a modern world in which much has gone wrong, a world that needs *tikkun* or "repair." The Holocaust, ever present in consciousness, is evidence of the failure of modern reasoning habits. This failure has brought about untold suffering. We are still in "Egypt," in thrall to an array of false assumptions, a failed explanatory system. We approach scripture out of the actual shared experience of such suffering. But we must go beyond the alternative perspectives on scripture that modernity seemingly allows us. There is either the universalizing approach that assimilates scripture to contemporary thought-categories, or the radically antimodern approach of, say, sectarian Rabbinic orthodoxy. Ochs's practice of parallel-interactive hermeneutics is neither of these. In a postcritical posture he writes: "We come to Scripture as to the face of our Redeemer, that is the One who will repair this modernist paradigm."[8] We come to scripture with the hypothesis that it is intended to enjoin conduct, the behavior needed if the community of inquiry is to become a redeeming community.

Ochs wrote his dissertation on the American logician and semioticist Charles Sanders Peirce (1839–1914), and it is Peirce's thought that most informs his further interpretation of what is going on in communities of scriptural reasoning. There is, of course, an irony in using Peirce, one of the most modernist and American of thinkers, as a centering point for an attack on modern reason.[9] Here it is possible only to hit the high points of an extremely subtle and complex philosophical position. Clearly we are dealing here with a form of Peirce's conviction that the meanings of sentences lie in the practical maxims they tend to enforce. The product of communal scriptural reading is a communal ethic. It is shared strategies for doing. It would seem further that a parallel hermeneutics community is here likened to the Peircean community of inquiry in which working hypotheses about what we should do are subjected to the judgment of qualified observers and in which "truth" for practical purposes is the consensus reached in the community. But this consensual truth is not propositional. It cannot be "represented." It is rather that which directs pragmatic efforts to repair modernity's failed paradigm.

Ochs sees the ancient communities out of which our respective scriptures have come as likewise "communities of inquiry," likewise concerned for the "repair" of the logics of the civilizations of their time, including their own. Hence scriptural study can uncover reasonings of use to us as we try to do the same. But this must be a group study process in which individual interpretations are judged by the extent to which they appear to address the reality of our suffering, and are further tested in the consensus formation of the group.

The kind of reasoning Ochs discovers in scripture and seeks to promote in the practice of parallel hermeneutics corresponds to Peirce's notion of "abductive" inference. This is the kind of prepropositional logic that governs hypothesis-formation. Ochs's abduction is a group process, so that seeking to understand it as a form of individual reasoning is misleading. If we are trying to repair "the failed dialectical logic of modernity," deductive logic would begin with some dogma or set of definitions and try to deduce from these how we should live. Inductive logic would try to build some new system based on perceived universal truths. Abductive logic would allow the reading of scripture to correct the action-hypotheses with which we come to it and allow those corrected hypotheses to be the action-assumptions with which we come to the world we are trying to "repair," assumptions leading to more hypotheses about how we might transform it.

As Ochs says, "An abductive inquiry is to engage a community of inquirers in the activity of disclosing to one another their overlapping assumptions, and then to generate and test specific hypotheses as applied to the solution of specific problems."[10] And, again, "The bits and pieces of our individual disclosures contribute to a recognizable project only when they are pieced together into a sizable collectivity."[11] In this process, again borrowing terminology from Peirce, Ochs speaks of "A-reasonings" and "B-reasonings." "A-reasonings," simply put, are what we know are "there" in scripture as unspoken background assumptions to our collective hypothesis-formation for world-repair. We never articulate the "A-reasonings." That is, we do not attempt to turn them into maxims or doctrines, and hence do not enter divisive arguments about them. Our collective judgments move directly to the question of what is going on in the world and what we are to do about it, just as for Lévinas ethics, not metaphysics, is "first philosophy." We know the "A-reasonings" are there because we sense that some of our "B-reasonings," our daily life assumptions, have gone awry, that they keep us in Egypt. Our "B-reasonings" remain unproblematic so long as the behaviors they lead to do not fail in reality. But many of our "B-reasonings" have in fact failed. We live in a society whose behavioral logics have in so many ways betrayed their promise of blessing to all. Our ability to recognize this fact, and our discomfort at the recognition, is the evidence of the presence of scriptural "A-reasonings" that lie behind our intuition that something better than modernity as we know it is possible for human beings. These unspoken reasons implicitly guide our step-by-step pragmatic moves, or are somehow present *in* our moves, so long as we do not try to say explicitly what they are.

For Ochs, the three Abrahamic traditions will contribute to the repair of a world gone awry if they approach their scriptures together with perspectives like these. Joining the three faiths together in such an enterprise does not let us articulate "A-reasonings" any more than scriptural study does within the particular faiths. It may, however, let us test certain hypotheses in the form of patterns of common action. Hypotheses are together entertained about what has gone wrong and what shared behavior on our part would be redemptive. Such behavior is tried out, step by step. In this process we discover aspects of our particular traditions that seem to speak to our condition and are therefore to be foregrounded in what we do.

All this means that correcting our behavior toward one another is the aim of our thinking. In this process, we make, in effect, a covenant with one another to act toward one another in truthful ways. And this truth-engendering way of acting is also enjoined in the content of what we read as interpreters in parallel and interactive relationships. Torah and Sermon on the Mount and Qur'an instruct us to behave in truth-engendering ways. Our relationships to one another here constitute our truth. By interpreting accordingly the signs we meet in our common world, we enter into a certain kind of ethical or behavioral logic called "scriptural reasoning."

Ochs envisions a whole series of interpreting communities conceived on principles like these. Many such local efforts exist already. But Ochs also envisions a broader "Abrahamic Theo-Politics" that "subverts the dichotomous logics of modernity."[12] "Certain Muslim, Christian and Jewish scholars/religious leaders will proclaim this politics as the tripartite work of God in response to the dominant political crisis of the contemporary West."[13] And such theopolitical action need not be limited to leaders. Ochs envisions clerical and congregational meetings carrying out successful programs of Abrahamic study. He concludes that "such sessions may generate innovative models for efforts of peacemaking that emerge from out of the indigenous religious traditions of Muslim, Jewish and Christian people who are currently, or potentially, engaged in various forms of political conflict."[14]

William Schweiker: "Hermeneutical Realism"—Battling Modern Humanity's Individualist Self-Cultivation and Lust for Power

William Schweiker presents us with a different sort of model. Unlike Esack and Ochs, Schweiker does not base his work on the experience of any single sort of Abrahamic dialogue undertaken with the intent of helping to repair modernity's malfunctions. Rather he sees much of modern culture as a space, or "space of reasons," in which parallel-interactive hermeneutical practices of a different, but very recognizable, kind go on. In religiously pluralistic situations we interact daily with persons of many cultures and faiths other than our own. As all concerned seek to articulate their distinct identities, we interpret the language and behavior of others just as they interpret ours. Schweiker calls this character of our common life "reflexivity." He seeks to bring this reality to a kind of conceptual consciousness that can help us see its significance as a backdrop for addressing the moral dilemmas of this present age.

Here we are dealing with "practices" and attitudes that suffuse the common life of large swaths of Western culture. The fact that in many sectors of contemporary society adherents of different religious cultures live closely side by side and influence one another constitutes a practice of sorts: only one that is not yet as intentional or self-conscious as the parallel yet interactive hermeneutical practices previously discussed. This parallelism is as much a fact of our time as is the hostility of different religiously founded cultures to one another recorded by Samuel Huntington. Potentially it is more important. Insofar as every religious culture is itself a hermeneutical process in action, where ancient texts are interpreted and reinterpreted to serve modern needs, we can view many parts of the world as places where these interpretative, adaptive processes are significantly interacting. Jews, Christians, Muslims, and others are simultaneously interpreting their traditions by the way they live them, and they are doing so in ways that show various forms of mutual influence. Such parallel and interactive hermeneutical processes, mixed with secular inputs, generate the cosmopolitan, differentiated societies we know today.

All these influences are at work in Schweiker's calls "spaces of reasons"[15] or social contexts in which signs and symbols operate that provide human motivation and meaning. These spaces may be whole cultures or they may be specific religious communities. The implication is that every culture supports, and is dependent upon, a complex of situated reasoning processes that lie behind whatever is taken to be meaningful or rational in the culture concerned. The reasoning that typically goes on in these spaces will determine whether the culture is morally healthy or not. As Schweiker puts it, we have responsibility for being "agents for creative reflexivity between cultures, rather than agents aiding the devolution of the world into a clash of civilizations."[16]

For Schweiker, what goes on today in these "spaces" is decidedly flawed. He draws a picture of the rejection of "moral realism" in modern cultures, in favor of the view that what values we have are human constructs. The problem, as he sees it, is that neither divine command ethics in any form, or the belief that there are moral norms written into the nature of things, is easy to sustain in our situation. Over against moral realism in either of these forms, the modern world has posited the freedom of self-determination. One appreciates and supports such freedom, but one also sees that the emphasis on human freedom puts a premium on the acquisition and exercise of power. This eventually creates an unjust, unequal society in which power is exercised unfairly for private gain by a wealthy elite.

In sum, the human capacity for self-determining action has become the measure of all things. Schweiker calls this an "overhumanization" of our reasoning processes. Paradoxically, as Vaclav Havel has said, such overhumanization has the effect of dehumanizing us. By making our own proclivities and capacities our sole horizon of value, we reduce ourselves to being simply conniving power-seekers. The result is troubled cultures, in which we know that something is wrong, but are not sure what to do about it. The challenge is to find ways of helping the presence of parallel and interactive hermeneutical processes of the world religions in our midst to come to life in ways by which a sense of realism with respect to moral convictions might become accessible once more to human beings.

Schweiker's response to this challenge is highly suggestive, but at the same time elusive. It is embodied in his concept of "hermeneutical realism."[17] In the philosophy of science, a hermeneutical realism addresses the stark alternative between believing that our hypotheses access reality by direct correspondence, and believing that hypotheses are purely working constructs supported by whatever is the current scientific culture. A hermeneutical realism for science offers a third possibility: that we gain access to reality through the interpretation of the *signs* of itself conveyed in the form of its ascertainable properties. In Schweiker, "hermeneutical realism" means that we encounter the Source of value in the world only in the variety of experiences and ways of speaking of the Divine available through diverse texts, communities, and traditions.

We best understand this notion of hermeneutical access to reality through an analysis of what it means to be an agent; to act, and to take responsibility for what one does. Taking such responsibility means traveling a meaningful path through the signs of the world in a manner that bespeaks integrity in one's identity. For this reason, the experience of being a moral agent in itself offers a unique form of access to the final power with whom we have to do. In hermeneutical realism the signs and symbols through which we pass are found to match, to articulate, this experience of agency. We know the reality of the world through the experience of being an actor in it. We need symbols and the ability to interpret them in order to articulate what that knowing-through-acting means.

Sometimes, as actors in the world, we encounter situations or moments of what Schweiker calls "axiological surprise," where values are enacted that function as windows to a source of moral authority beyond our own self-determining wills. Each reader can supply his or her examples. Schweiker speaks poignantly of "the last lingering touch of a dying parent" that bespeaks the transmission of both responsibility and promise to the next generation.

But in a reflexive, multicultural world, the symbols by which we interpret the meaning of our acting will lack coherence unless the living religious traditions find ways of entering into one another's reasoning spaces. Otherwise one has only a struggle for preeminence, an effort in which the power-seeking morality that supplants moral realism is adopted by the religious communities themselves in a search for cultural influence. The point at which Schweiker begins to show how these different hermeneutical processes can meet creatively in the public square comes out in his account of what goes on in comparative ethics. Reflexivity among religious traditions is the fact at hand. Comparative religious ethics is an interpretation of how such traditions can self-consciously relate to one another.

Every social interaction in a religiously reflexive society involves rudimentary comparative ethics: in the sense that we try almost instinctively to understand what pattern of symbolic mediation of reality motivates the other person. In a power-oriented society, this understanding is usually deployed to get the better of the Other. Anyone negotiating financial deals on a cross-cultural basis will confirm this. But comparative religious ethics can also be pursued in order to knit the fabric of symbolism among the faiths reflexively present to one another in our time. Comparative religious ethics then becomes a form of consciously pursued parallel and interactive hermeneutics.

Schweiker rejects two theories on the bases of which such comparative ethical inquiry is often pursued: first, the notion of universal deep structures of moral awareness and, second, the notion that we could devise what Jeffery Stout calls a "moral esperanto."[18] Rather Schweiker argues in effect that we assess the other's performative utterances or behaviors by recapitulating them in our own frames of reference, while the Other is doing the same thing with what he or she perceives about our own actions, our own performative self-presentations, in the world.

Schweiker early on associated this form of understanding with the classical notion of "mimesis," but of late has preferred performative language. Here we have two reciprocal hermeneutical operations aimed at mutual understanding among persons of different religions and cultures. How does such a process of mutual understanding turn outward and begin to influence what happens in the public space of reasons?

Schweiker's answer to this question lies in his notion of "theological humanism." Such humanism is intended to thwart the depredations of "overhumanization" by which human beings have unwittingly diminished themselves by their self-assertion, engulfing all life in anthropocentric conceit. It also is intended to thwart a systematic antihumanism by which the world loses its human dimension. Schweiker asks, "What religious meanings can be introduced into the reflexive flow of open societies that will bend those processes toward prizing human dignity and yet transforming overhumanization in the direction of what will represent and enhance the integrity of all life?"[19] To make this possible, theologies must begin with the ethical claim of the Other, "to see faith traditions as ways of life rather than primarily systems of belief and doctrine."[20] Recognition of the ethical claim of the Other leads to openings in social experience to the divine. Such "lateral transcendence" is always saturated with the reality of God. Responsibility with and for others manifests "life's porousness to the divine." Theological humanism must show that "in the dynamics of the societies within which we actually exist, people already live, move, and have their being in God, precisely because they bear responsibility for the integrity of life with fellow human beings."[21]

Schweiker has helped to organize several formal opportunities for inter-Abrahamic conversation on such matters. One of the most recent of these, in 2003, was a set of lectures and discussions at the University of Chicago Divinity School titled *Humanity Before God: Contemporary Faces of Jewish, Christian and Islamic Ethics.*[22] The purpose was "to examine anew the shared ways in which the three monotheistic faiths in the Abrahamic tradition conceive the idea of humanity before God and how each contributes to contemporary understandings of fundamental claims about the inalienable worth of human life."[23]

Do These Case Studies Exhibit Significant Shared Insights?

Having sketched the work of Esack, Ochs, and Schweiker, we must ask the question whether these three case studies belong together in the first place. Or are we dealing here with apples, oranges, and persimmons? There is need to recapitulate the messages implied in the different situations and terminologies of Esack, Ochs, and Schweiker in some common terminology without losing the concreteness of each circumstance and each response. In our present postmodern atmosphere, with its emphasis on difference and particularity, this is difficult to accomplish with confidence. I think I know better than to try to find some universally present "essence" of parallel hermeneutical practice across these diverse situations and among the different ways they are interpreted.

At most, I can find only some sort of Wittgensteinian "family resemblance" tying these case studies together. Certain characteristics overlap to a degree from one case to another, but few if any are to be found in all three. Thus I think, not of identical elements but of affinities or regions of overlap and resemblance. This approach no doubt drives logicians and lexicographers with neat minds to distraction. Donald Mackinnon, expounding Bishop Butler, used to say, "A thing is what it is, and not some other thing." But that *is* "essentialism," and not the way we must think in our diverse, fragmented, pluralized postmodern world.

Perhaps we are dealing with something like Robert Schreiter's "global theological flows" in which certain leading categories of thought emerge from time to time out of the background noise of global intercommunication among diverse situations and cultures.[24] We can then say of a leading category, like Schweiker's "hermeneutical realism," that it *resembles* something else: something perhaps in another world of discourse and called by a different name. But does saying this sort of thing give us genuinely new knowledge? I argue that it does. Perhaps it brings us to the edge of affirming once more (say, in Ricoeurian terms or in those of Lakoff and Johnson[25]) the metaphorical basis of thought. Similar symbols and metaphors embedded in the literatures of many cultures can "give rise to" quite diversely expressed ways of thinking.[26]

The expression introduced at the start of this chapter, "a parallel-interactive hermeneutics of responsibility" is useful at this point. No thinker studied actually uses this term. Yet, on reflection, I believe this descriptive label illuminates what has been going on in these cases and points ahead to the argument to come. This much can be said now. A parallel-interactive hermeneutic of responsibility is a practice of which each of our three case studies is an instance. To use *this* template for interpreting what three examples have in common is to locate their commonality in a certain kind of together-doing that constitutes an interpretation of what it means to grasp the nature of the opportunity to help modernity save itself (i.e., finding our own ways of appropriating Casanova's conjecture). It also involves an interpretation of what it means, in any given setting, actually to take on together the responsibility for helping to do this. So devising a parallel and interactive hermeneutic of responsibility means seeing our situation, our sources, and our sense of what it might mean to help "save" modernity as incorporated into some kind of consistent story. As we interpret, so we act. As we act, so we interpret.

Having resolved to join communities that seize the Casanovian opportunity, our three participant-interpreters describe what is involved in such a story. They do so in three very different settings—a liberation movement, a project to explore the character of scriptural reasoning, an academic analysis of ethics in the contemporary West. Despite these differences of setting, the analyses of our participant-interpreters methodologically overlap. They do so in arenas of activity common to all three: situational interpretation of sources, mutual interpretation of moral traditions, and the interpretation of public policies and institutions. These arenas of overlap need elaboration because they help us see more of what the three projects in this chapter have in common and where they may lead.

Interpreting Sources: What Does Covenantal Inquiry Disclose?

First, it is plain that emerging from such situational interpretation and analysis are some radically new perspectives and practices in scripture interpretation, some of which are elicited by the parallel and interactive context itself. These have to do with breaking out of confessional and hermeneutical solipsism. Read naively, the scriptures of the three faiths are full of seemingly contradictory commands, meek obedience to which prevents us from acknowledging the contradictions and resolving them toward mature responsibility toward the underlying message. Failure to grasp that scripture seeks to take us out of ourselves is a form of hermeneutical irresponsibility. By contrast, there is in each of our cases an effort to use the scriptures of the different faiths to propel the imagination beyond the bounds of traditional, often self-protective, communities of interpretation. I infer that this enlargement of the hermeneutical platform is made possible in part by the insights of historical-critical method, as used by Esack in particular. But the move to responsible interpretation—meaning by that responsibility to one another and for the consequences of interpretation—goes well beyond that. It betokens a move from isolated hermeneutical irresponsibility to genuine responsibility toward the gifts and tasks that are evident in the text. Parallel and interactive approaches to scripture help to disclose these gifts.

It used to be thought sufficient for scripture interpreters to work mainly within their own religious or confessional traditions. There were (and still are) plenty of opportunities for dialogue with difference within those traditional contexts. But today, with the dawn of various forms of global consciousness and the phenomenon of what Schweiker calls "reflexivity," some gatherings of hermeneutists need to be multireligious in nature. This is true especially where the traditions concerned overlap textually in various ways.

Here Esack takes the lead in one way and Ochs does so in another. Esack's attempt to supersede centuries of traditional Qur'anic interpretation to build an Islamic liberation theology is a notable and courageous departure from virtually the entire history of Qur'anic interpretation: a departure seemingly only possible for Islamic scholars working outside traditional Islamic lands.

The very possibility of Esack's having done this rests on his having brought his work into methodological parallelism with that of certain Western Christian scholars, both in the historical-critical and the liberation veins. Is this not, in Schweiker's terms, a case of "mimesis," or performative parallelism, meaning the appropriation in one's own terms of the perspectives, signs, and symbols of the Other, in this case those of the methods generated by Christian biblical scholars and liberation theologians?[27] These notions may function as conceptual frames of reference for explicating how parallel-interactive hermeneutics wrests us out of hermeneutical solipsism into responsibility toward what goes on in our world.

For Ochs, any gathering of diverse scriptural interpreters for such a purpose functions like the company of the qualified observers in C. S. Peirce. Many interpretations are entertained in a community of shared reading, and the community judges which ones speak most effectively to what is collectively perceived to have gone wrong in the human condition. For this to happen, there must be some shared justification in the minds of the group for leaving aside, at least temporarily, what the scriptures in question have been traditionally been thought to mean in their religious communities of origin. The line of argument to this end, expressed in different ways by Ochs and Esack, is that scripture itself is the product of communities of inquiry and action similar to the one in which they are now engaged. In the case of Ochs, he is helped in this direction by his "postcritical" stance in which he is able to read the tradition for what it says in the present moment (as he believes earlier generations of interpreters also did). Esack, paradoxically perhaps, is liberated from traditional interpretation within the Islamic community by his use of the historical-critical method, which uncovers the situated historical origins of key Qur'anic passages, and is learned in the parallel hermeneutical situation.

Interpreting Moral Reasoning: What Does Covenantal Responsibility Require?

The need to distinguish between adequate and inadequate "reasonings" in the construction of humanity as a community of responsible integrity is present in the thought of both Schweiker and Ochs. It is also clearly implied, though differently expressed, in Esack. Each of these three parallel and interactive projects implies some vision of moral responsibility to one another. Helping to save modernity from itself requires the pursuit of human transformation toward such mutual moral obligation. We need in each case an interpretation of this pursuit that fosters common recognition of those signs in the "wilderness of the world" that mark a path toward human fulfillment. The different moral traditions of the Abrahamic faiths, pursued in parallel, foster this kind of recognition.

Esack, Ochs. and Schweiker, each interpreting a different inter-Abrahamic project, offer us distinctive understandings of the ways in which we should identify such signs, and hence arrive at different plottings of what in the end must be a common path. Each of these understandings constitutes a particular hermeneutic of responsibility, appropriate to the kind of project each author describes.

The Ochsian company of qualified scripture interpreters reasons "abductively" from a sense that some of the practical B-reasonings that govern daily life have gone wrong (say in focusing only on self-development). They need to express a shared hypothesis about how we ought to live. This shared hypothesis is not propositional, but rather practical, in form. The A-reasonings (having to do with the promise as such?) that are sensed to lie behind it are not directly accessible. What comes out of the abductive argument *toward* human fulfillment (i.e., reasoning from the intuited properties of something to its reality, or from signs along the way to confidence in the reality of the destination) is a pattern of acting in relation to one another and to our broken world guided by signs that give us confidence. We can share with others a relationship to this pattern of acting without presuming to share any single common representation of it.

Am I then justified in saying that abductive argument stands very close to what is implied in Schweiker's central notion of "hermeneutical realism"? In hermeneutical realism do we not reach toward a reality by participating in the signs and symbols of it: by opening ourselves to what they say about live options and possibilities? And may not Schweiker's notion of "mimesis" in the practice of comparative ethics—through which we appropriate in our own terms the signs and symbols of the Other— function as a conceptual frame of reference for explicating what goes on in parallel-interactive hermeneutics along the path toward human fulfillment? In my view, Ochs's redeemed "reasonings" are what need to go on in Schweiker's "spaces of reasons" to constitute the very fabric of human life beyond moral solipsism.

A new humanity built upon the integrity of communicative reasoning seeking the road toward the promise can only be a journey of Abrahamic covenantal responsibility toward one another and toward a future for humankind. We move from the signs and symbols of a hypothesized form of life to the conviction that we *can* live together in the manner described, that the possibility is realizable. I believe that such a mode of argument enables us to move from the figures of the sacred found in our texts to hypotheses about what it would mean to act so as to encounter God's presence at the junctures of ethical challenge in the common human world.

Interpreting the Public World: What Can Covenantal Witness Make Possible?

In all three projects there is a perceived need for moving from common scripture reading and shared moral reasoning to new kinds of human thinking for generating and maintaining social being through time. At stake in all three cases is a sense of the integrity, or lack of it, of discourse and argument within the ongoing human community as such, not just of Muslim, Jewish, or Christian humanity. Such integrity is a form of responsibility to the scriptural promise. Distortions of this integrity demand new kinds of society building and sustaining reasonings.

Our three writers agree in seeing that something has gone terribly wrong with the way modern humanity, for the most part, thinks about and justifies its actions. Casanova's hypothesis that modernity needs somehow to be "saved" is amply affirmed in all three cases, if not in Casanova's language or conceptuality. But each writer focuses on a different manifestation of this modern failure. Esack's Muslim liberation theology, and his personal participation in the South African freedom struggle, makes humanity itself (as opposed to an Islamic vision for humanity) the primary category. Ochsian "B Reasonings," i.e., practical calculations of how to get things done, are not intrinsically distorted. But they are vulnerable to various forms of errancy, as when Eichmann rearranges otherwise practical German railroad schedules for purposes of the Holocaust. Such errant uses of practical reasoning occur when people take for granted that every human action as an expression of self-interest in a struggle for power: precisely the consequence of "antirealism" in ethics as analyzed by Schweiker.

Can we provisionally connect these different manifestations to a single underlying theme? Not in any simple way. In modern cultures it seems self-evident to far too many people that normative human aspiration should have to do either with self-development or with the drive for personal power and possessions. Missing from this equation is much sense of public responsibility for being agents for the human good, seeking, for example, to help protect the earth from environmental disaster. What we consider personally fulfilling is too often detached from any sense of responsibility for the larger social consequences. We will do anything we think is needed to protect our self-esteem and our comforts, including the oppression of an underclass that has us outnumbered four to one. This is the sort of situation that Esack confronted with his Islamic liberation theology. This may be part of what Ochs thinks is wrong with our typical moral reasoning processes.

Our three writers in effect ask themselves what it means to "take responsibility" for confronting such egregious flaws in the cultures of modernity. What might it mean responsibly to walk together through such a world? Where might one find and diagnose specific symptoms of the modern world's irresponsibility toward the moral quality of its life and toward its expectations for the future? Where might one find signs of successful treatments of the conditions underlying such symptoms? How might we join ourselves to such therapies? Taking responsibility toward such issues means acknowledging our participation in modernity's self-destructive story and trying to use our different traditions for telling new stories. Such differently sourced, but energetically shared, story discerning and story living is one form of what I mean by a parallel and interactive hermeneutics of responsibility.

Where May All This Lead?

What is the directional yield of these three case studies and of our attempts to tease out family resemblances among them? Do these projects have anything more robust in common than occasionally comparable conceptualities and methods? I think they do. All three projects, different from one another as they are, represent ways in which their participants have moved from unquestioning religious obedience to worldly responsibility, from commonplace religious rootedness to cosmopolitan concern. Esack, Ochs, and Schweiker each interprets for us an inter-Abrahamic project that refuses to accept traditional cultural roles for these faiths. Each challenges traditional assumptions concerning scripture interpretation. Each searches for markers on the way toward a just human future. These examples show that it is possible for Abrahamic groups to respond in very different ways to the kind of challenge represented in Casanova's conjecture: to take responsibility for helping modernity "save" itself. Projects such as these, even if their results are not immediate or spectacular, are certainly gifts to the larger human community.

Part II, consisting of chapters 5, 6, and 7, seeks to generalize the overlapping characteristics of our case studies into ideal-typical models of practices that can be pursued in any inter-Abrahamic situation. Thus we now turn to three versions of parallel and interactive hermeneutics: the first concerned with actual scripture interpretation (chapter 5), the next concerned with the shared interpretation of covenantal norms or virtues in a modern context that incompletely understands them (chapter 6), and the third concerned with the shared interpretation of principles of justice and the social contract as broadly received in the Western public world (chapter 7).

Notes

1. Given the esoteric reputation of "hermeneutics" as an academic subject, it is important to see what practical questions are really involved, and to see that adequate hermeneutical understanding is a signal form of responsibility. I use the word "parallel" to stress the fact that the different faiths concerned maintain their distinctiveness in such conversations along the way. Each continues to understand the common project in terms of its own history and presuppositions. Yet they proceed alongside one another and are perforce influenced by one another. Hence their interpretations of themselves in situation are also "interactive." But such mutual influence is not meant to, and typically does not, produce syncretistic results. Walking the common way does not lead to a common faith. Influence by one faith on another is generally processed in the language and perspective of the faith that receives such influence. The result is three faiths that have each grown more generous toward one another, always on their own terms, not some amalgamated faith in the making. The notion of a hermeneutics of Abrahamic responsibility is thus a way of describing interfaith relationships in a variety of ways and settings. Mutual communication in the light of the promise to and in Abraham goes on when we sit together to do scriptural interpretation. It also goes on when we explore the connections among our different understandings of virtuous action. It also goes on when we, together, seek to bring our sense of the promise to the public sphere, thus encouraging the coming of a good society, a covenantally ordered society. In each of these hermeneutical spheres, I try to express in Christian terms certain (not all) things I am learning from my Jewish and Muslim colleagues, and they try to do the same. We are honest with one another about difficulties and apparent dead ends.

Here parallel and interactive hermeneutical responsibility takes on a mode reminiscent of H. Richard Niebuhr's notion of response in *The Responsible Self* (New York: Harper and Row, 1963). I only recently saw the connection of parallel-interactive hermeneutics with Niebuhr's notion of "answering." Hermeneutical interaction is a form of answering, and "fitting" response depends on what we believe the Other is trying to say by his or her words and actions. Such response needs to be responsible. We need to be concerned for the consequences of certain kinds of responding. The model of diplomatic negotiation suggests itself. Irresponsible reacting (not really responding) fuels the cycle of violence and revenge. A suicide bombing leads to the bulldozing of houses, which leads to more suicide bombing. Attack followed by revenge leads to another attack. This is irresponsible responding. In some measure it is the deliberate failure to understand. What is adequate, or "fitting," in any situation depends not only on mutual understanding but on the ultimate context in which we place the hermeneutical enterprise. Hence the notion of "responsibility to the promise" of Genesis 12:3 and other such passages.

2. Farid Esack, *Qur'an, Liberation, and Pluralism: An Islamic Perspective of Interreligious Solidarity Against Oppression* (Oxford: Oneworld Publications, 1997), 14.

3. Ibid., 12.

4. Ibid., 78. See Mohammad Arkoun, *The Concept of Revelation: From the People of the Book to the Societies of the Book* (Claremont, CA: Claremont Graduate School, 1987).

5. Esack, *Qur'an, Liberation, and Pluralism*, 260.

6. Full information on the SSR, including papers given at meetings since 2002, is available online at http://etext.lib.virginia.edu/journals/jsrforum/.

7. Peter Ochs, "The Rules of Scriptural Reasoning," in *Journal of Scriptural Reasoning* no. 1 (May 2002), (an electronic journal available at the website above).

8. Ochs, *Rules*, 10.

9. My attention was called to this point by William Schweiker in private correspondence.

10. Ochs, *Rules*, 11.

11. Ibid.

12. Peter Ochs, "Abrahamic Theo-Politics: A Jewish View," in *The Blackwell Companion to Political Theology*, ed. Peter Scott and William T. Cavanaugh (Hoboken, NJ: Wiley-Blackwell, 2003).

13. Ibid.

14. Ibid.

15. See William Schweiker, "Religious Conviction and the Intellectual's Responsibility," *Criterion* (Autumn 2003): 12.

16. Ibid., 18.

17. "Hermeneutical realism" in Schweiker bears a certain resemblance to "symbolic realism" in the thought of Robert Bellah.

18. Jeffery Stout, *After Babel: The Languages of Morals and Their Discontents* (Boston: Beacon Press, 1988), 5, 6, 72, 74, 105, 166, 193, 286.

19. William Schweiker, lecture in Prague, Czech Republic, Summer 2003, 20–21.

20. Ibid., 21.

21. Ibid., 13.

22. See William Schweiker, Michael A. Johnson, and Kevin Jung, eds., *Humanity Before God: Contemporary Faces of Jewish, Christian and Islamic Ethics* (Minneapolis: Augsburg Fortress, 2006).

23. Ibid., 1.

24. See Robert Schreiter, *The New Catholicity: Theology Between the Global and the Local* (Maryknoll, NY: Orbis Books, 1997).

25. George Lakoff and Mark Johnson, *Metaphors We Live By* (Chicago: University of Chicago Press, 1980).

26. See Paul Ricoeur, *The Symbolism of Evil* (Boston: Beacon Press, 1967), 19.

27. "Mimesis" was originally the topic of William Schweiker's dissertation.

Part II

Dimensions of
Inter-Abrahamic Discourse

5

Reading Scriptures Together
Obedience and Responsibility in the Abraham Narratives

Retrieved from amidst the debris shoveled away in the aftermath of the September 11, 2001, destruction of the World Trade Center in New York was a suitcase that seems to have belonged to Mr. Muhammad Atta. In it, or clinging to its shreds, were discovered two documents. The first gives us five pages of religious justification for the September 11 "action." Issued "in the name of God, of myself, and of my family," it scripts a kind of sacred drama in which the technological might of the United States is overcome by simple tools: a bag, a cloth, a knife, a handgun. The object is religious "slaughter," (the Arabic word *dhabaha*) described in terms that call to mind Abraham's preparation to "slaughter" (not merely "kill") Isaac in Genesis 22. The attack on the towers is "the intended sacrifice of God." The second document is Atta's will. This makes the reference to Abraham explicit. Besides much else, Atta exhorts his family and other readers to "do what Ibrahim ... told his son [Ishmael] to do, to die as a good Muslim."[1]

Here, then, we have another instance of contemporary hermeneutical practice. One might find a least a few similar instances in Jewish and Christian circles. It is a literal rendering of what the interpreter infers that obedience requires of him. This is not to say that Atta's interpretation speaks for all Muslims, any more than comparable words speak for all Christians or Jews. Manifestly they do not. But what, short of an Enlightenment consciousness that relativizes all such texts, is to restrain such interpretations from being made and put into practice? Is there a way, with positive and peaceful intent, to "read the ancient texts in ways that matter,"[2] that is in ways that take them seriously but not lethally? My response is to challenge Jews, Christians, and Muslims to read their texts together so that destructive and exclusivist interpretations are canceled out: not by wholesale Enlightenment-style dismissal of the very idea of scripture, and not by allegorization or selective philosophical translation, but first of all through a building of mutual responsibility leading to forgiveness, trust, and solidarity (see chapter 6) among the interpreters—that is, across religious lines. This chapter on the Abraham narratives sets out to help this happen.

It is well to remember that what follows models a kind of practice. In no way is it intended as an exhaustive, or even adequate, review of opinions over the centuries on the Abrahamic texts. To do that would take many volumes. Rather I offer notes on what might go on if Jews, Christians, and Muslims were to sit down together with the texts before them and compare interpretations in the light of "what is going on" in their respective worlds. In fact, this sort of thing is already happening in many places. Some of these are mentioned in chapters 1 and 4. The present account, however, is not based on an actual dialogue. Instead, it offers elements for a conversation that might take place, aware that any actual inter-Abrahamic discourse would inevitably be different from this one, if only because living, breathing Jews and Muslims were across the table from this Christian writer.

Some Opening Orientations

The three "religions of the Book" are, of course, much more than variant forms of Abrahamism.[3] I have called them, no doubt vastly oversimplifying, Mosaic Abrahamism, Messianic Abrahamism, and Islamic Abrahamism. But these Abrahamisms, as my three adjectives inadequately suggest, have each gone through vast ramifications from their points of origin, and in that process interpreted and reinterpreted their founding narratives. Studying the Abraham stories together, with some of these later ramifications in mind, could be the beginning of a process of mutual exorcism of the tendency to interpret them as justifying violence against one another in the name of God.

Where to begin? My initial suggestion would be the story of Abram's call from Ur to Haran to Canaan, followed by the initial promise to Abram of nationhood, greatness, and blessing to come. We are, of course, beginning in the middle of a story. The first eleven chapters of Genesis have taken us from the creation and Garden of Eden narratives; to Cain and Abel; to the flood, Noah's Ark, and the rainbow covenant with "every living creature;" to Babylon's abortive attempt to unify humankind by imperial means; to Terah's migration with Abram and Lot from Ur of the Chaldees to Haran in the land of Canaan. We join this account at Genesis 12:1–3:

> Now the Lord said to Abram, "Go from your country and your kindred and your father's house to the land I will show you. I will make of you a great nation, and I will bless you, and make your name great, so that you will be a blessing. I will bless those who bless you, and the one who curses you I will curse; and in you all the families of the earth shall be blessed."

Having heard these words, Abram keeps moving. He journeys westward from Haran by way of Shechem and the oak of Moreh, proceeding to a stopping place between Bethel and Ai. Here Abram, before moving on toward the Negeb, is promised *this* land, presently occupied by Canaanites, for his descendants (Gen 12:7). In his pilgrimage, he has been called to take on a new sort of trans-Bedouin responsibility, a role in the fulfillment of God's promise of a universal blessing for humankind. Abram's subsequent confidence in YHWH's promise of myriad descendants through which his calling will be fulfilled is "reckoned it to him as righteousness" (Gen 15:6). There are significant echoes of much of this, as we will see, in the New Testament, and later in the Qur'an. As for the former, see Peter's sermon in Acts 3, and the argument of Galatians 3, where Paul recalls the promise to Abraham as the basis of his own ministry to the gentiles and his understanding of salvation by grace alone received in faith. As for the latter, see numerous Qur'anic references to Abraham and his righteous obedience, for example Sura 37:108, in which Abraham is promised his reward for his submission to Allah, before he has done any righteous work. In the Qur'an, of course, the descent from Abraham is through the line of Ishmael, the son of Hagar, rather than through Isaac, the son of Sarah.

No doubt the foreseen blessing to "all the families of the earth" is understood differently in Judaism, Christianity, and Islam. Yet the Abrahamic covenant is a foundation for all three faiths, even if ramified in seemingly incompatible ways. But can some version of resistance to sectarian moral totalization and discovery of a responsibility ethic be seen as characteristic of the "Abraham community" in whatever form it may have existed? There is a school of scripture interpretation that sees early, pre-Jewish Israel precisely as a community of covenantal resistance to the imperial life assumptions of the ancient Near Eastern empires—Sumeria, Babylon, Egypt. This early Israelite community is seen as simultaneously engaged in creating a new frame of reference for life that, later redacted and crystallized, underlies Torah, Gospel, and Qur'an alike.[4] These traditions in particular give a certain interfaith coherence to this material. Abraham himself is neither Jewish nor Christian nor Muslim. He is prior to these distinctions, and prior to, or at least apart from, the great dynastic struggles of the ancient Near East. This can be important for our subsequent argument about religious resistance to what Emmanuel Lévinas calls the "totalization" of forces at work in modernity.

But now, before going further, there is a second Abrahamic text to be considered. The famous passage, Genesis 22:1–19, concerning "the binding of Isaac" (known to Jews as the *Akedah*) must be read concurrently with Genesis 12:1–3 because the "binding" passage represents itself as an account of the test of faithfulness to which God puts Abraham regarding his worthiness to be the instrument of the divine promise to "all the families of the earth." This narrative describes God commanding Abraham to take his only son Isaac and offer him as a burnt offering on a mountain three days' journey away. We read of Abraham's cutting the wood, saddling the ass, placing the wood on Isaac's back, and setting forth. We read of the pair reaching Mount Moriah, of Isaac asking his father where is the sacrificial lamb, being told that the Lord will provide, and finally of Abraham's binding Isaac himself upon the altar. Just as Abraham raises his knife for the "slaughter," an angel speaks:

> Do not lay your hand on the lad or do anything to him; for now I know that you fear God, seeing that you have not withheld your son, your only son, from me. (Gen 22:12)

Abraham then espies a ram, caught by its horns in a thicket. Abraham takes the ram and offers it as a burnt offering instead of his son. God's response is, in effect, a renewal of the covenant promise of blessing to Israel and the nations in Genesis 12:1–3:

> By myself I have sworn, says the LORD, because you have done this, and have not withheld your son, your only son, I will indeed bless you … and by your descendants shall all the nations of the earth bless themselves, because you have obeyed my voice. (Gen 22:16–18)

Commentary on these verses of Genesis has been endless over the centuries, no doubt because they seem to represent a moral conundrum: God commanding Abraham to sacrifice his only son Isaac who is, so to speak, the genetic bridge toward fulfillment of God's promise of future blessing, only at the last moment to provide a ram to be sacrificed instead. Any attempt to unravel all this in a few sentences would be the height of presumption. Is the divine command only part of a dream? In what sense is this a true test of faithful obedience? On this subject we will have much more to say as we begin to look at what the different Abrahamic traditions have made of questions such as these.

The problem of appropriating even these two Abrahamic passages for today is complex. One thing we learn from others who have previously tried to do so is that a purposeful dialogue among serious persons on this subject can itself quickly degenerate into mutual recrimination rather than mutual illumination.[5] The most significant conflict-hazard lies not in differences of interpretation as such, but in the ways these differences can be interpreted and exploited for political, ideological, or emotional purposes. Apart from the simplistic idealism that just ignores the rocks along the path, the most prominent hazard of late has been the misuse of the stories of Abraham and his descendants to justify different modern interpretations of God's gift of the land of Palestine, whether to Jews or to Muslim Arabs or to both.[6]

Whatever views on such matters we may entertain, we will do well to avoid this mode of argumentation at first. All three faiths have authentic, if different, connections with the Abrahamic covenant. The manner of their descent from the Patriarch "according to the flesh," a factor that could have implications for land tenure, is not the issue. Islam honors Abraham as one who behaved righteously, as one who "submitted" to God. Jews and Christians will be wise in this kind of dialogue at least to try on, if only provisionally, the mode of "submission" to the texts before them.

Our task is to conduct a parallel and interactive hermeneutical inquiry into the three versions of the Abrahamic tradition that not only takes account of such hazards and others like them, but also aims at resistance to totalization and seeks the construction of frameworks for abundant life. Such an approach by modern scholars has already been described in chapter 4. I presuppose that Jews, Christians, Muslims—together with the "secular" partners in struggle whose solidarity they solicit—should all continue to interpret their sources, their historic traditions of shared life, with the fullest independence and integrity, but also begin to do so as if walking next to one another along a common path. This journey should not be undertaken for the purpose of devising a doctrinal or symbolic merger, or for seeking to construct a "common belief system." We are too attitudinally postmodern to want to do any of that. But along this path we could ask whether the notion of a covenant of resistance to totalization, a covenant of mind-renewal toward a more just social framework, could be seen as supported, however variously, by the Abrahamic traditions from which we come. As we ask this question in our own various ways, we ask it in the knowledge that others alongside us are asking it in their ways too.

I have already defended my use of the word "parallel." I believe that the already identified differences and difficulties among the traditions amply justify that term. And I have also insisted there on the terms "interactive" and "reflexive," indicating that interpretations conducted in parallel also influence each other. But why also that perhaps over-technical scholarly word "hermeneutics"?[7] Is this practice not simply a matter of reading scriptures together? And, if so, why should it not simply be called that? Indeed, that is what it is called in many places where it is being tried.[8] And that is the way it needs to begin. But the word "hermeneutics" recognizes something else about such parallel practice. It recognizes that what is being compared are not merely scriptures as such but "readings" of scriptures. We each come to scripture with our own "hermeneutic," or way of reading it. This may reflect the dominant "reading" practiced in our particular religious tradition—a Jewish reading, a Christian reading, and Islamic reading (or Methodist, or Roman Catholic, or Reform, or Conservative, or Orthodox, or Sunni, or Shiite)—or it may reflect a school of thought—Barthian, Tillichian, Bultmannian, or whatever. The examples could be multiplied. Any sort of reading/interpreting *enacts* some hermeneutic, or point of view, about the text, and it is texts-with-interpretations that are being compared. Now of course we hope that parallel practice helps us redirect our hermeneutical imaginations in two ways. First, we interpret in the simultaneous knowledge of how others are interpreting. And, second, we ask if our own texts say anything different to us in the light of that knowledge of others' interpretations.

A program of "parallel hermeneutics" pursued in such depth further recognizes that *within* each tradition of life and faith there is what William Schweiker calls a "hermeneutical realism" at work.[9] I take this to mean that symbolism located within a certain identity-determining context lends authority to moral assumptions and precepts for those who inhabit it. Finding one's identity within a given community lends a quality of self-evidence or apparent apodicticity to that community's expectations. That quality of specific, contextual moral awareness needs to be carefully preserved. It is precious in an age such as ours. It is the territory in which the sense of moral obedience to divine command functions effectively.

But we also do our interpreting in a world of pluralism both inside specific religious traditions and beyond them. We are now unprecedently living in a common social space-time, a world of currently competing and overlapping identities. As William Schweiker again has written, our world is one in which "cultures or civilizations act back upon themselves with respect to information coming from other cultures and civilizations."[10] Schweiker calls upon the word "reflexivity" to describe this global phenomenon of continuous mutual adjustment of religions and cultures to one another. We are able to observe and reflect critically upon the ways we respond to the roles of others in contexts we find significant. We can critically appropriate the meanings we find in their presence. We must try to make those reflections as inwardly searching and as outwardly constructive as possible. In short, however different from each other we may be, we bear hermeneutical responsibilities toward one another: to hear accurately and to reply fairly. We are responsible also for the practical consequences of our interpretative work in the worlds we share.

Religiously uncommitted interpreters of common human experience, such as secular NGOs, also need to participate in this parallel/interactive hermeneutical process. Many of these activists reflect former or ancestral religious commitments in their work. They can tell us much about the journey of such originally religious ideas through the forms and expressions common in the public world. "Social contract" thinking, for example, often embodies ideas of religious origin. The paths such ideas have taken "outside" religious communities can be very instructive to those who are now trying to make sense of them "inside." Awareness of the many "worldly" transcriptions of covenantal narratives can help religiously committed communities to position themselves more imaginatively in society. They can try to discern where their own narratives are, or are not, resonant with what can be said or heard meaningfully at any given time in the public world. This point will be illustrated at some length in chapter 7.

Most important of all, such worldly resonances can also function as bridges *among* the different religious traditions. We can see, in a commonly shared world, the consequences of what we do and believe. We can see what has been made of our covenantal traditions by thinkers and actors who know these traditions but stand personally apart from active participation in them. These many considerations may or may not arise in any given experience of dialogue. But they need to be in the backs of our minds as we meet.

Jewish, Christian, and Islamic Interpretations of the Abram/Abraham Narratives

We now begin to explore our three Abrahamic traditions in whatever depth is possible under the circumstances of our conversation. Doing this serially, of course, as one must in written communication, is no substitute for actual meeting and sharing results with our counterparts of other faiths and traditions.

It is important to realize too that these narratives, as they come to us, are already embedded in ongoing hermeneutical processes. Religiously motivated scribes have already been at work in shaping the earliest versions of the Genesis stories that we can detect by critical methods. And we quickly agree that what we find is "far from offering a tranquil scene of hospitality played out beneath the generous canopy of the Abrahamic."[11] Indeed, "the Abrahamic family tree is a tangled thicket, sprawling, impossibly overdetermined."[12]

The detail into which this inquiry now takes us may strike some as tedious. But something like this is needed to put flesh on the idea of a parallel, yet interactive, hermeneutics of the Abrahamic covenantal narratives in the three faiths. What follows, indeed, offers only a superficial impression of the complexity of these relationships, and of the multiplicity of lines of interpretation in each faith. Each religious community—Jewish, Christian, or Muslim—has *within* it more than one hermeneutical tradition. And now we are advocating studies of these traditions in parallel *across* the lines of the faiths themselves. The word "parallel" is well justified by the *differences* we find and must freely acknowledge to be there: not to speak of misunderstandings and difficulties that are bound to arise. But the relationships among these hermeneutical traditions also justify calling out to one another across these differences while holding on to our identities, sharing insights while holding one another in profound respect.[13]

Jewish Interpretations

The Genesis Abrahamic narratives tell of events represented as having taken place long before there was such an entity as "Judaism." Still, these chapters, as they were successively edited from earlier narratives by generations of scribes, form part of Jewish sacred scripture. The passages in question *both* reflect ancient Near Eastern Bedouin religion and society before the dawn of "Judaism" *and* bear marks of having been shaped from earlier tales for subsequent religious purposes. Scripture scholars have labored for centuries to disentangle these elements without reaching wholly agreed results. Here we need only be aware that the distinction between original tales and religious redactions exists in every faith community, and proceed with caution accordingly. It is also the case that these Abraham passages, interpreted somewhat differently, form part of Christian scripture and are present, as it were "by reference," to numerous texts in the Qur'an. Thus we return to them, with new perspectives, in the paragraphs on Christian and Islamic perspectives that follow.

Early Israelite scribal editing of the Abrahamic and subsequent patriarchal stories (which may, according to some scholars, have originated independently of one another) has created the familiar narrative chronology of the book of Genesis. Jews (as opposed to Christians and Muslims, who found it necessary to argue in different ways for the connection) regard themselves as the original and natural heirs of this story. They read it straightforwardly. Isaac, whose birth is taken as a sign of the covenant promise, is the favored son of Abraham and Sarah (rather than Ishmael, the son of Abraham and Hagar, the actual firstborn, of whom we will hear more). Jacob is born to the favored one Isaac, and becomes the father of the founders of the traditional "Twelve Tribes," including Joseph. The narrative leads on to the descent into Egypt and the coming of Moses. The scribally edited narrative is read as continuous: in its simple, natural sense.

Little attention seems to be paid in Jewish interpretation to the sorts of implications we have found in Genesis 12:3, especially in the closing line which says that in Abraham's descendants "all the families of the earth will bless themselves (or will be blessed)." The latter word implies not merely static well-being, but a gift of responsibility to a divine promise.

These verses of course can be, and have been, read in more imperial ways than we have done. They can be read to mean that the future greatness of Israel, enhanced by YHWH's differential curses and blessings, will set up a sheep-and-goats situation. The difficulty centers on the words "I will bless those who bless you, and the one who curses you I will curse" (Gen 12:3). This exclusivistic language is not repeated in any of the subsequent reiterations of the Genesis promise of blessing. Is that because the ancient scribes saw such words as an embarrassment? But then why not edit them or erase them? Modern interpreters sometimes omit the words in public readings. Their meaning seems to be that some nations will recognize the power of the God of Israel in YHWH's evident favor and protection, and will gather to Jerusalem to share such blessings, so learning the wisdom of Torah. Other nations will not. Is there condemnation, and not merely differentiation, meant here? The thought that Israel might be the instrument of such universal blessing in some other way, for example by being the Servant of the Lord as claimed in Isaiah 42:1–4, 49:6, and elsewhere, is more often found in Christian interpretations than in Jewish sources.

We have seen that there is already in the ideas of being blessed and blessing others a sense of responsibility that follows as a gift issuing from obedience. This needs to be held in mind as we come to the story in Genesis 22 of the "binding of Isaac." In Jewish tradition the *Akedah* (for so this narrative is called) becomes the test of faithfulness to which Abraham is put with regard to the covenant of Genesis 12:1–3. That passage in fact is paralleled at the close of the *Akedah* narrative. The moral problematic here is plain to every reader, even if attempts to resolve that thicket of difficulties are themselves nearly as numerous as "the grains of sand on the seashore." There exists a long tradition of rabbinic wrestling with this passage: wrestling that turns (as we would put it) on the question of the relation between religious duty (to follow God's command to perform the sacrifice) and general ethics, particularly the Decalogic command "thou shalt not kill." Here a the dialectic between obedience discourses and responsibility discourses emerges in our texts and in the interpretations given them.

Traditions often repeated in various forms in the rabbinic literature hold that Abraham completed the sacrifice and that afterward Isaac was miraculously revived. Or that Abraham killed his son and burned him to ashes: the ashes remaining as stored-up merit and basis of atonement for Israel in all generations.[14] Ibn Ezra, in his commentary on Genesis 22:19, quotes a similar opinion that Abraham actually did kill Isaac, and the latter was later resurrected from the dead. Ibn Ezra rejects this view as completely contrary to the biblical text. Shalom Spiegel has demonstrated, however, that such views enjoyed a wide circulation and occasionally found expression in medieval writings.[15] One may speculate that some responses of this type may have come in response to medieval Christian teaching.

It seems fair to say that no single treatment of the Abraham narrative, or of the *Akedah* as part of it, has become canonical for Jews. Or, to put it otherwise, it is not thought necessary to resolve the moral meaning of *this* passage in order to establish or clarify the role of Abraham as a patriarch of the faith, or even to establish the basic character of Jewish ethics. Such questions apparently remain open to commentary as long as rabbis and others wish to argue about it, which means indefinitely. It is enough to say that the patriarch "believed God and it was reckoned to him as righteousness," (at least as the narrative is now constructed) well before the question of the sacrifice of Isaac arose. Hence the reality of Abraham's belief and obedience does not turn, for Jews, centrally on the *Akedah*. Nevertheless it is celebrated in Jewish tradition. The ram's horn or *shofar*, sounded at Rosh Hashanah, is traditionally thought to go back to this ancient account.

Less attention is paid by Jews (and Christians) to the stories of Ishmael, the actual firstborn son of Abraham through Sarah's maid Hagar (Gen 16:1-6). But this account is important for our purposes because it is taken by all three faiths to account for the origin of the Arabs, from whose stock later arose the founders of Islam. Ishmael is circumcised at thirteen (accounting for the Islamic custom in this regard), given Abraham's blessing, promised fertility and numerous offspring. He will be father of a great nation, in fact, of twelve chieftains. Sarah, having meanwhile borne Isaac (who is circumcised at eight days, accounting for the Jewish custom), asks Abraham to cast out Ishmael and Hagar. God, over Abraham's protest, enjoins him to do as Sarah says. God will make a great nation of Ishmael's descendants also, for he too is of Abraham's seed. Genesis 21:1-21 then tells the story of Ishmael and Hagar in the desert. They depart to the wilderness of Paran, close to the borders of Egypt. Twelve sons of Ishmael, presumably the forebears of Arab tribes, are listed in Genesis 25:12-18.

We learn no more than this about Ishmael and Hagar from the *Tanakh*. But the *Book of Jubilees*, written sometime between 135 and 105 BCE, repeats some of this information, and adds more. This account has Abraham summon Ishmael and his twelve sons, with Isaac and his two, commanding them all to continue to keep the rite of circumcision, and to avoid fornication, uncleanness, and intermarriage with the Canaanites. Abraham, who has already been extraordinarily generous with Isaac, now also gives gifts to Ishmael and to his sons, sending them away from Isaac's lands. Ishmael and his sons, and also the sons of Keturah and their sons, go together and settle between Paran and the borders of Babylon, "in all the land that is toward the East facing the desert." These tribes mingle with each other and come to be called Arabs or Ishmaelites (*Jubilees* 20:11–13).

These passages appear over the years to have been oddly satisfactory to Jews, Arabs, and later to Arab Muslims, alike. The texts in question have established a widely acknowledged genealogy of the Arabs as descendants of Israel, together with circumcision at age thirteen, and even the strange claim to descent from Sarah, hence "Saracens." To Jews, the texts account comfortably for the origin of the Arabs, giving them honor, but not the degree of honor afforded the sons of Isaac. To Arabs, and later Muslim Arabs, these same passages constitute an "Abrahamic" claim to territories as far West as today's Palestine, as far East as today's Iraq. All this was soon enough translated into real territorial debates. Rabbis, long after the alleged fact, imagined lawsuits to have been brought against the Jews, before no less a personage than Alexander the Great, by Phoenicians, Egyptians, Ishmaelites, and Ketureans claiming scripturally grounded rights to different parts of the land.

Certain medieval Jewish (and Christian) interpretations of Genesis 22 come close to making it a prooftext for resurrection, taking the "binding of Isaac" as somehow a productive sacrifice for the well-being of the people. In some representations from the Middle Ages, Isaac bears an uncanny resemblance to Jesus.[16] And some Christian typology makes a cross from the wood on Jesus/Isaac's back. So, as if in echo, some medieval *midrashim* imagine Isaac himself carrying the cross. And others suggest that the ram was also called Isaac! The latter "Isaac" dies, but the other Isaac is spared. The death, or almost death, of Isaac is thought to produce sustained life through divine forgiveness. Because of the *Akedah*, we read, reports of Israel's sin will go in one of God's ears and out the other. We read even of resurrection: "By the merit (or blood/ash) of Isaac who offered himself upon the altar, the Holy One, blessed be he, will in the future resurrect the dead."[17]

Wrestling of a less fantastic kind with the meaning of the *Akedah* has gone on in Judaism to the present day. On the one hand, this account, difficult as it is to justify ethically, runs centrally through the life and ritual of Judaism, particularly that of Rosh Hashanah. On the other hand, there appears to be no "orthodox" interpretation of the story on which the structure of Jewish faith must rest, without which all would collapse into confusion. Indeed to suggest the notion of "orthodoxy" in Judaism is to suggest strict observance of the moral commandments, the ritual and dietary laws, not "correctness" in scriptural interpretation as such, much less in doctrine understood as a network of propositions. Where doctrine is concerned, Jewish orthodoxy lies in the practice of endless rabbinic (and certainly now lay) argument. This fact will soon become important to our case.

I will offer one example of post-Enlightenment, indeed contemporary, rabbinic commentary on the *Akedah*. This is a sermon for the second day of Rosh Hashanah, 1998, by Rabbi Philip Borenstein.[18] Typically, the rabbi goes through a series of interpretations found in the literature. We should all be willing to do whatever God asks of us, even if it seems abominable. Or be prepared like Isaac to sacrifice yourself for God. But other views, the rabbi says, see this narrative as a polemic against child sacrifice, thought to be not unknown among the early Israelites. Hence, even if it sounds to you like God is asking you to sacrifice your child, don't do it. God doesn't want that! Or perhaps this whole story, considering its intergenerational aspects, is one of family dysfunction. In the end, Borenstein has to strip the *Akedah* of its literal elements and take it as an allegory about a symbolic father and a symbolic son. This helps us see, he argues, that the modern challenge is not what Abraham faced, one of obeying God's word too strictly. It is, rather, "the challenge of stepping back from the world long enough to decide for ourselves what is right."[19] Once more, the command to obey gives rise to the demand for responsibility.

It remains to be seen what insights may emerge when traditions of Jewish interpretation of the Abrahamic covenant are placed alongside Christian and the Islamic interpretations of the same, under conditions in which all participants acknowledge a moral obligation to one another of mutual forgiveness, solidarity, and trust: the very virtues we will examine in chapter 6.

Christian Interpretations

The entire Genesis story, obviously including the Abraham narratives, is likewise canonical for Christians. Yet Christians have traditionally read it differently: as an "old" covenant or testament in contrast to a "new." Christian iconography occasionally shows Isaac bearing the load of wood like Jesus bearing the cross. Yet Jesus is the one actually sacrificed, hence the "lamb of God." Yet among the many specific New Testament references to the Abrahamic covenant, the *Akedah* or "binding of Isaac," as we will see, is mentioned only in relatively late works, Hebrews, and the letter of James. Apart from these instances, the notion of Abraham's righteousness is made to rest, not on his willingness to sacrifice his son at God's behest, but rather on his acceptance of the original divine call in Genesis 12:1–3 and parallel passages. It is Abraham's faith in the promise of an heir (Isaac) and innumerable descendants that is "reckoned … to him as righteousness" (Gen 15:6). As for Ishmael and his story, he apparently figures in the New Testament, yet without being named, only in Galatians 4 where Paul makes an allegory of slavery and freedom based on the stories of Hagar and Sarah and their respective sons. Early Christianity appears to take little interest in the history of the Arabs who were one day to become Muslims.

Abraham becomes a central New Testament figure first through the writings of Paul, who makes of him a type for the notion of salvation by faith alone. The entirety of Romans 4 is an argument that just as Abraham was justified by faith, in the fact that he "believed God" (Gen 15:6) that he would be the father of many nations and that this justification took place before, and not after Abraham was circumcised, clearly refers to the original promise of Genesis 12:1–3. This is Paul's basis for arguing for the admission of the Gentiles to the early Christian community without requiring circumcision. In no way does this argument rest on Abraham's faithfulness in the "binding of Isaac."

An argument similar to that of Romans 4 occurs in Galatians 3:1–29. Much of this chapter turns on the ideas of promise and promise keeping, of which more later. Again making the point that the Gentiles may enter the covenant by faith, without need for circumcision, Paul writes in Galatians 3:6–9:

> Thus Abraham "believed God, and it was reckoned to him as righteousness." So you see that it is men of faith who are the sons of Abraham. And the scripture, foreseeing that God would justify the Gentiles by faith, preached the gospel beforehand to Abraham, saying, "In you shall all the nations be blessed." So then, those who are men of faith are blessed with Abraham who had faith.

The same point, in essence, is reflected at several points in later New Testament writings. Matthew 1:1, besides tracing Jesus's genealogy to Abraham (omitting, of course, any mention of Hagar or Ishmael) may be reflecting Paul's thought when Matthew has John the Baptist say to his fellow Jews, "Do not presume to say to yourselves 'We have Abraham as our father.… God is able from these stones to raise up children to Abraham'"

(Matt 3:9). Could "these stones" possibly be a distant reference to the altar on which Abraham was about to sacrifice Isaac in Genesis 22? This is a possible, but not a common Christian interpretation of the passage, which is generally thought to refer to the notion that God makes children of Abraham "by faith," just as Paul says. But the possibility in Matthew 3:9 of a reference to the *Akedah* is worth considering. If such a reference is intended, however, it is strange that Matthew, considering the significance of the point, does not make more of it.

Or does he not? Matthew records the story of the Sadducees' question to Jesus concerning a woman successively married to each of seven brothers who die one by one. Whose wife will she be in the resurrection? Jesus' reply is that in the resurrection they will neither be married nor given in marriage. But then Jesus goes on to say,

> And as for the resurrection of the dead, have you not read what was said to you by God, "I am the God of Abraham, and the God of Isaac, and the God of Jacob"? He is not God of the dead, but of the living. (Matt 22:31–32)

Luke fascinatingly portrays Abraham preaching social justice in the story of the rich man Dives and the beggar Lazarus (Luke 16:19–31). Both die. But while Lazarus finds himself "in Abraham's bosom," Dives goes to the place of torment by eternal fire. Dives shouts across the gulf, entreating Abraham to return from the dead to warn his five (presumably equally avaricious) brothers to mend their ways. Abraham refuses. "If they do not hear Moses and the prophets, neither will they be convinced if some one should rise from the dead" (Luke 16:31).

Abraham most significantly plays a key role at Acts 3:25–26. The reference occurs in Peter's sermon in Solomon's Portico of the Jerusalem temple, not long after the day of Pentecost.[20] But of course the account itself, as written, is probably quite late. Peter tells the crowd, "You are the sons of the prophets and of the covenant which God gave to your fathers, saying to Abraham. 'And in your posterity shall all the families of the earth be blessed'" (Acts 3:25). Here we have a direct quotation of the Septuagint version of the closing words of Genesis 12:3. Here the Greek verb is clearly passive. The possibility of a reflexive meaning seems not to be present. These words are placed by Luke (as probable author of the Book of Acts) in such a way as to be a frontispiece to Paul's Gentile mission journeys to the "ends of the earth."

As I have said, the *Akedah* finds mention in the New Testament only after the main lines of argument in Paul, Matthew, and Luke are well established without any mention of it. But the letter of James, arguing that "faith without works is barren," writes,

> Was not Abraham our father justified by works when he offered his son Isaac upon the altar? You see that faith was active along with his works, and faith was completed by works, and the scripture was fulfilled which says "Abraham believed God and it was reckoned to him as righteousness"; and he was called the friend of God. (Jas 2:21–23)

The final New Testament passage needing attention is the treatise on faith in Hebrews 11 in which a series of "men of old" (*sic*, verse 2, despite the inclusion of Sarah), Abraham prominently included, are celebrated for what they did "by faith." Here *both* Abraham's risky going forth from Ur of the Chaldees *and* his readiness to sacrifice Isaac on Mount Moriah are offered as instances of the faith that is "the assurance of things hoped for, the conviction of things not seen" (v. 1). First, Abraham's going forth from home:

> By faith Abraham obeyed when he was called to go out to a place which we was to receive as an inheritance; and he went out, not knowing where he was to go. By faith he sojourned in the land of promise, as in a foreign land, living in tents with Isaac and Jacob, heirs with him of the same promise. For he looked forward to the city which has foundations, whose builder and maker is God. By faith Sarah herself received power to conceive, even when she was past the age, since she considered him faithful who had promised. (Heb 11:8–11)

And then, a few verses later, we read of Abraham's willingness to sacrifice Isaac:

> By faith, Abraham, when he was tested, offered up Isaac, and he who had received the promises was ready to offer up his only son, of whom it was said, "Through Isaac all your descendants be named." He considered that God was able to raise men even from the dead; hence, figuratively speaking, he did receive him back. (Heb 11:17–19)

I have cited enough evidence in these passages to justify having called Christianity "a messianic form of Abrahamism." Yet the question of how the "new covenant" relates to the old has been contentious down the centuries. Here again the letter to the Hebrews, very likely written at a time when the Christian and Jewish communities were beginning to feel the mutual tensions that led them afterward to become distinct, gives us the most explicit information about at least one view of the matter in New Testament times. For the writer to the Hebrews there are at least two covenants, in Moses and in Christ, the second superseding the first. The letter quotes at length from the famed "new covenant" passage of Jeremiah 31.

> The days will come, says the Lord, when I will establish a new covenant with the house of Israel and with the house of Judah; not like the covenant I made with their fathers on the day when I took them by the hand to lead them out of the land of Egypt; for they did not continue in my covenant, and so I paid no heed to them, says the Lord. This is the covenant I will make with the house of Israel after those days, says the Lord: I will put my laws into their minds, and write them on their hearts, and I will be their God, and they shall be my people. (Heb 8:8–10)

One has to say that something like this has been the prevailing view of Christian circles from early times. The covenant with Israel is superseded, hence the term "new" testament as opposed to "old," and hence the more modern term "supersessionism." The "new" covenant is "not like" the "old" in all sorts of particulars. Jesus Christ is the new "high priest" who has opened the Holy of Holies, and so forth.

But, with deference to scripture scholars of both faiths, I note that in these passages the superseded covenant is the Mosaic covenant, the one that produced all the moral laws and ritual commandments, not the covenant with Abraham and Sarah, which the author of Hebrews has told us was entirely a matter of "faith." My inference is that in these passages from the letter to the Hebrews, the Abrahamic covenant as such is *not* said to be superseded, and hence, by faith, is still alive and valid. The Abrahamic argument is therefore essentially an antisupersessionist argument: one on the basis of which Judaism and Christianity may well explore whether they are not members of a single covenant people after all.

Paul's "ingrafting" metaphor of Romans 9–11, speaking of an olive tree as a figure for Israel, is central to his understanding of this issue. He writes to the Gentiles,

> But if some of the branches were broken off, and you, a wild olive shoot, were grafted in their place to share the richness of the olive tree, do not boast over the branches. If you do boast, remember that it is not you that support the root, but the root that supports you. (Rom 11:17–18)

And the original Israelites are far from lost. As they see the ingathering of the Gentiles, they will return, "for God has the power to graft them in again."

For if you have been cut off from what is by nature a wild olive tree, and grafted, contrary to nature, into a cultivated olive tree, how much more will these natural branches be grafted back into their own olive tree. (Rom 11:24)

Paul, as against the writer to the Hebrews, supports the idea of a single Abrahamic covenant in which Moses and all the other leaders of Israel have played their role, and in which the people later called "Christians" likewise have a role to play. It is on this basis, with these assumptions, that parallel hermeneutical discourse can best go on between Jews and Christians.[21]

Islamic Interpretations

The Abraham stories, considering the fullness with which they are told in Jewish and Christian scriptures, are only partly present in the Qur'an. The Qur'anic literary dependence on these stories is unmistakable, but many of the original details are not repeated, some are changed, and some are elaborately embroidered. Some of the original Abraham material seems to be present only "by reference." That is, certain Qur'anic passages only make full sense if the reader knows the original stories supplied only in part in the Qur'anic text. Yet it is probably true to say that Muslims are not interested—as Jews and Christians are—in arguing their spiritual descent from the Hebrew book of Genesis. The evidence shows that the Qur'an knows Genesis and uses it, but provides its own account of the origins of the Abrahamic covenant. The orthodox Muslim tradition, of course recognizes none of this, claiming that the Prophet dictated the whole under divine inspiration.

Sura 6:74–89 describes Abraham remonstrating with his father Azar for idolatrously "associating" other gods with the One True God. Abraham refuses to worship the heavenly divinities worshipped by his father. Neither star, nor moon, nor sun is worthy of such worship. They all rise *and* set. "I am through," Abraham says to his people, "with those you associate with God" (6:78). Abraham believes in the true God, not in beings associated with him. All this is *within* God's knowledge. Allah here gives Abraham an argument he can use. Allah exalts Abraham, Isaac, Jacob, Moses, Aaron, Jesus, and many others, favoring them above all other people, showing them the right path and expecting faithfulness in return. These are the people to whom Allah gave the Book, the Law, the prophethood. If they reject these things, Allah will give them to a people who will not deny them. God guides those among his creatures whom he will. It is vain to associate other divinities with him.

This "covenant of Allah," broadly understood as just outlined, is mentioned many times in the Qur'an.[22] This covenant offers Allah's favor and protection in return for "submission" (the meaning of the Arabic word *Islam*). Submission includes the duty to spread the faith. Covenants (in the plural) are thought to have been concluded with a whole series of prophets. Abraham among them (Sura 2:124), who submitted to the responsibility of keeping and propagating the faith. The Qur'an then refers to communal forms of covenanting among those who have accepted the covenant of Allah.

Sura 2:30–145 is a lengthy treatise on the fate of "the People of the Book," a term which here means Jews and Christians only. The narratives of Genesis and Exodus are taken to be records of Allah's dealings with the patriarchs, with Moses and Aaron, and others. Allah makes covenant with the Children of Israel, but in time these and their descendants disobey and fall away, making necessary the coming of a new prophet, Muhammad. One passage is of particular interest:

> O Children of Israel, remember the grace I bestowed on you, and remember that I preferred you to all other nations.... And when Abraham was tried by his Lord with certain commandments which he fulfilled, [Allah] said: "I am making you a spiritual exemplar to mankind." Abraham said, "And what about my posterity?" [Allah] replied, "My covenant does not apply to the evil-doers."

> And [remember] when we made the house a place of residence for mankind and a haven [saying]: "Make of Abraham's maquam [stand] a place for prayer." We enjoined Abraham and Isma'il [saying] "Purify my house for those who circle it, for those who retreat there for meditation, and for those who kneel and prostrate themselves." (Sura 2:121–24)

The "house" in question is no doubt the Kaa'ba in Mecca. Abraham (as well, in other passages, as Ishmael) is pictured as having been in the Muslim holy city. Indeed, he is pictured in this and other passages as, in effect, the first Muslim. We read of Abraham's prayer: "Make us submitters, a people submissive to you" (*ummah musilmah*, 2:127). Hence is established the Islamic religion of Abraham, the chosen one. Abraham further prays: "I submit (*aslamtu*) to the Lord of all the worlds" (2:130). Abraham then proceeds to assign this legacy to his sons. They answer, "We shall worship your god and the God of your fathers, of Abraham and Ishmael and Isaac, the one and only God, and to him we are submitters" (*muslimuna*, 2:132). Against the possibility of their thereby becoming Jews or Christians, they say, "No, we follow the religion of Abraham, the upright, who was not an idolater" (2:134).

As might be expected, passages such as this generated controversy. According to the *Life* of the prophet, Jews said Abraham was nothing but a Jew, and Christians said he was nothing but a Christian. So Allah proclaimed (Qur'an 3:55–58), "O People of the Scripture, why argue about Abraham when the Torah and the Gospel were not revealed until after him? Have you no sense?" The *Life* explains that Abraham was neither a Jew nor a Christian, but an upright man who surrendered to God and was not of the idolaters. "Lo, those of mankind who have the best claim to Abraham are those who followed him, and this Prophet and those who believe [with him], and God is the protecting friend of the believers" (*Life*, 383–84).

What of the "test" to which Abraham was put according to Genesis 22, the story of the *Akedah*, called by Jews the "binding of Isaac"? The Qur'anic counterpart to the Genesis passage is found in Sura 37:100 and following. But it immediately departs from the Genesis account by offering a dialogue between Abraham and his son, who, asked what he thinks about the matter, consents to being the sacrificial victim.

Then, when he attained the age of consorting with him, [Abraham] said, "My son, I have seen in sleep that I am slaughtering you. See what you think." He said, "My father, do what you are commanded; you will find me, Allah willing, one of the steadfast." (37:102)

Here, at once, the command to Abraham to sacrifice his son is connected with a dream, which may or may not, for Muslims, lessen its apodictic character. The son's consent in any case changes the moral character of the story from what it is in Genesis, where no consent, or even foreknowledge of what is to take place, is mentioned. Here, in the Qur'an, the son himself prays to be one of the steadfast. The story continues:

Then, when they both submitted, and he flung him down upon his brow;

And We [i.e., Allah] called out to him: "O Abraham,

You have believed the vision. Thus we rewarded the beneficent.

This, indeed, is the manifest calamity."

And We ransomed him with a large sacrifice.

And We left with him for later generations:

"Peace be upon Abraham."

Thus, We reward the beneficent.

He is indeed one of Our believing servants.

And we announced to him the good news of Isaac as a prophet, one of the righteous.

And We blessed him, and blessed Isaac; and of their progeny some are beneficent and some are wronging themselves manifestly. (37:103–13)

The proper name "Isaac" appears for the first time only in verse 112, indicating the close tie this narrative has with the earlier account in the Hebrew scriptures. We would have expected the name "Ishmael," the son of Abraham by Hagar, whom the Qur'an elsewhere sees as the carrier of the covenant promise to Islam. In fact, many Islamic scholars go out of their way to correct this apparent mistake, arguing that the near sacrifice must have taken place before Isaac's birth. In any case, Abraham's "son" here once again receives a "blessing" clearly implying not only the favor of Allah but also the gift of a responsibility to be "beneficent" to others, that is, convey-ing the blessing to them with its consequences for good. The text clearly acknowledges that some of the "progeny" will take on this responsibility of "beneficence" (perhaps understood as reaching all earth's families?) and others will not, instead "wronging themselves manifestly." These words "wronging themselves" suggest an echo of the idea that blessing confers an identity and a destiny that the one blessed nevertheless has the freedom to refuse: that alongside the implied obedience there is also freedom to interpret "blessing" in other, less generous, indeed irresponsible, ways.

Returning to the Qur'anic narrative, notice the use of the verb "submit," the central notion and literal translation of the word *Islam*. And note that the son does not assume the position on his side normally associated with animal sacrifices (and depicted in Jewish and Christian iconography) but is flung down upon his brow, taking the Muslim posture for prayer. Furthermore, whereas in Genesis it is said that "Abraham believed God," referring to the patriarch's acceptance of the covenant promise in Genesis 12:1–3, here Abraham believes "the vision." This terminology apparently refers only to the content of the dream. He believes what he is told in this dream, rather than the divine promise taken as a whole. Moreover, no reference to a ram caught in a thicket appears. The sacrifice needed to "ransom" Isaac is apparently, somehow, performed by Allah rather than by Abraham. And, in contrast to the Genesis account, Isaac's own righteousness and believing servanthood become prominent parts of the story.

What are we to make of this? Nothing is apparently said of this being a "test" of Abraham's overall faithfulness in performing his role in relation to a covenant promise. Abraham actually consults his son before taking action. He says to him, "See what you think." The story is an instance of the righteousness of "submission" rather than a dramatic episode in a covenant narrative. Islamic interpretation of this account relates the "sacrifice" to resurrection only in that it locates its account in a Sura about the righteous who will obtain paradise. But the beloved son is not allowed to die, even partially, as in some of the more fanciful Jewish *midrashim*. The account "makes little or nothing of sacrificial logic whereby life is made dependent on redemptive power of death."[23] Maybe "a tiny bit of the son's blood seeps into Islam, but nothing redemptive comes of it."[24]

Perhaps we are to read the verses that follow (Sura 37:114ff) as meaning that Abraham's progeny are somehow empowered by this almost sacrificial act. Allah may be saying to Abraham and Isaac that because they have done this, he will bless them and scatter their sacrificially fertilized seed throughout the world. If this is the case, the Qur'anic account may stand closer to the Parable of the Sower than to the practice of blood sacrifice. Abraham and his son are not then sanctified by sacrificial death as such. They are simply part of a long chain of "submission" (*Islam*) that stretches from Noah to Moses, Aaron, Elijah, Lot, Jonah, and so forth, eventually to Jesus.[25]

The notion of a line of righteous persons who, long before the time of Muhammad, "submitted" to Allah in a covenant relationship, inviting others to covenant around them, suggests that Islam lacks any clear notion parallel to what in Christian parlance has been called "supersessionism." Nowhere in the Qur'an, in any case, do we read of a "new covenant," one "not like" the covenant made with the patriarchs (Jer 31:31–32; Heb 8:8–9). Rather Allah calls righteous persons to faith, who in turn call others to faith, throughout history. Some of these persons remain faithful. Others do not. The call to Muhammad follows centuries of widespread unfaithfulness to promises Allah has already made. But that call does not fundamentally change the terms of the covenant except to make its nature more manifest through the Qur'an, the "clarifying Book" (Sura 37:117).

It follows that the Qur'an sees faithful persons of the past, both Jews and Christians, as having stood in covenantal relationship with Allah. Whether this is so also for Jews and Christians living after the Prophet's time, after the appearance of the "clarifying Book," is another question. Sura 3 contains a lengthy and positive reflection on the Hebrew prophets, Mary and Jesus. Sura 3:64 suggests a compatibility, at least in principle, among the Abrahamic monotheisms. But a more exclusivist and even incipiently supersessionist interpretation of Islam is found in Sura 3:19, 3:85, and 61:9. One has to say that "clarifying" the covenant is not the same as replacing it. There are openings here for dialogue about what these and other similar passages can be taken to mean today.

Hermeneutics for "Rooted Cosmopolitans"

In her book *The Human Condition*, the philosopher Hannah Arendt, a rooted cosmopolitan if one ever lived, gives us a reading of scripture obviously informed by Enlightenment critique, with results illuminating for the Abrahamic passages just treated. She is concerned throughout to show that a worldly or common-human-experience side of what originates as response to scripturally warranted authority can take on humanly communicable meanings. Her name for the particular meaning at hand well describes Abram's covenant-fostering work among the Canaanite tribes: "the power of stabilization inherent in the faculty of making promises." Of this promise-making faculty Arendt writes,

> . . . we may see its discoverer in Abraham, the man from Ur, whose whole story, as the Bible tells it, shows such a passionate drive toward making covenants that it is as though he departed from his country for no other reason than to try out the power of mutual promise in the wilderness of the world, until God himself made a covenant with him.[26]

Theological critics will say that Arendt's restatement of the Abrahamic tradition leaves God's *prior* promising initiative out of the picture, in favor of a kind of merit-based adoptionism, thereby fundamentally distorting the message. But perhaps we may infer that God's covenantal intention is indeed theologically prior, but that Abraham—or anyone—must live into the earthly meanings of that covenantal possibility, and the moral conundrums associated with their finitude and incompleteness, before the promise behind, and ahead of, human promise-keeping can be fully articulated as God's. Is this what Arendt is telling us? I think her interpretation of Abraham is open to such a construal. Again and again she is saying that our capacity as human beings to grasp and act on certain fundamental ideas—forgiveness, trust, solidarity—arises from the originary presence of such ideas as commanded in scripture. For Arendt, once such possibilities of human understanding and behavior are in circulation, we may need to be reminded of their scriptural origin, but apparently we no longer need to honor scriptural authority as such, as this is understood by continuing religious communities.

But for the present writer, a just society needs the continued presence of faith communities that do recognize the authority of scriptural commands that underlie the exercise of publicly sharable gifts of responsibility. Otherwise people's understanding of the responsibility-*gift* will deteriorate into hubristic, competitive, self-aggrandizing responsibility-*taking* with eventually catastrophic social consequences. The gift received becomes the gift usurped. Jewish, Christian, and Islamic communities, loyal to their origins and scriptural warrants, are necessary components of the *polis* if a shared witness to the original power and purpose of responsibility-*giving* in creation and covenant is to remain alive.

Put this another way: Given this continued witness to the source of the gift concerned, we can see that Arendt is translating the Abrahamic covenant narrative from confessional terms available only to traditional believers into philosophical language accessible to cosmopolitans who wish to communicate these meanings pragmatically to others. She has in effect paralleled a characteristic idea of Paul Ricoeur: that philosophy *begins* when we provisionally adopt "the motivations and intentions of the believing soul," but then *proceeds* as that provisionally adopted symbolic language "gives rise to thought." Ricoeur argues that all philosophical reflection rests in this way upon some original "gift" of sense provided by "the fullness of language": narrative, parable, metaphor.[27]

In the case of Abraham, both the original covenantal language and its philosophical—that is to say, public—yield have to do with the basis of human polity as such, the "blessing" of "all the families of the earth" (Gen. 12:3). The possibility of "stability" in Arendt's terms (read *moral-social framework*) in the "the wilderness of the world" (read *the present human situation*) lies in an ability, understood theologically as a covenantal gift, to make and keep promises to one another. This ability to make and keep promises is for Arendt the basis for all human social institutions. It is the payoff in terms of common human experience of what the scriptures understand in confessional terms. It is thus understandable both to persons committed to it in terms of their faith-traditions and to persons without such commitments.

As I have already claimed, this "cosmopolitan" translation of covenanting as social promise-keeping has a potential bridging function among the Abrahamic faiths' understandings of obedience. Whatever their differences (and they are many), these faiths live today in interconnected social worlds and have to deal with myriad similar conundrums of political and social relationships. They are seeing their own covenanting traditions, transformed into terms of common human experience, being acted out in the world around them. Promise-keeping, something they know well, turns out to be fundamental to the stability of all social institutions.[28] Given the continued presence of scripture-based communities on the human scene, it is possible to restate and act out the divine gift of responsibility in terms accessible to all. Maintaining this three-faith presence, we do not permit the meaning of responsibility to promise to deteriorate into abstraction or exploitation, or be subject to the shifting meanings of words in "the wilderness of the world."

A way of protecting the divine initiative behind the responsibility-*gift*, while maintaining the cosmopolitan, accessible, human quality of our interpreting, is to try to ground our understanding of the gift in a thicker reading of the Abrahamic materials than the one offered by Arendt. We need a reading that brings out, once again, the manner in which worldly responsibility is dialectically grounded in obedience. Words of Walter Brueggemann, excerpted earlier from his essay "Law as Response to Thou," effectively introduce this deeper reading. They help us discern the obedience/responsibility dialectic in a wider variety of Abram-Abraham passages. Brueggemann writes:

> Abraham and his family after him are a *responding community* that takes responsibility for a world . . . this first utterance in Genesis 12, is defined by the demand of YHWH that Israel be a vehicle and an instrument for assuring the well-being, security, joy, and dignity of all nations . . . . Israel has responsibility for the health of the world. It is a responsibility, given in the same breath, given in this initial utterance of generosity.[29]

Obedience to "the demand of YHWH" confers on Israel "a responsibility, given in the same breath, given in this initial utterance of generosity." This is the gift of responsibility to be discerned, in various ways, at the origin of each of the three Abrahamic faiths. One might say that taking on such responsibility is *included* in the scope of appropriate human response to the divine command. We are imperiously summoned to do those things that make us free in relation to the promise of "blessing" extended to all human beings. And here, in this vision extended and developed as the following chapters seek to do, lies the theological possibility that the three Abrahamic faiths can come to compatible interpretations of the gifts of worldly responsibility they have received, maintaining their own traditional understandings of the divine authority that has given them such a gift. The exercise of God's gift of responsibility to the promise of blessing to all is the appropriate depth response to God's summons. It leads to worldly sorts of actions understandable within common, that is to say cosmopolitan, human experience.

Let us see how this is so. What happens after Genesis 12:3 seems at first a descent from a portentous conversation with YHWH himself to the pragmatic world of petty tribal rivalries. For most of the next five Genesis chapters we have a series of narratives of Abram's adventures among the "kings" and tribes already settled in Canaan, as well as a dangerous trip to Egypt. These narratives precede the narrative in which Abram becomes Abraham (Gen. 17:5), "the father of a multitude of nations," leaving the impression that, at least for the compilers of the "last" text, the text we have before us, these accounts of Abraham's dealings with his neighbors are important for understanding the nature of the universal "blessing" that is the heart of the promise to which Abram-Abraham and his descendants are called to be responsible.

On the one hand, these chapters tell a story of occupation by Mesopotamian *habiru* or "wanderers," interlopers in territory already occupied by a score of tribes with prior claims. On the other hand, they also give us the story of Abram the reconciler and covenant-maker, who brings to these tribes examples of fair dealing and thoughtful reconciliation of conflicting claims. Abram's covenant-fostering activities invoke an extraordinary recognition from the king-priest of an indigenous Canaanite religious community. Melchizedek, "king of Salem" (Jerusalem) and "Priest of God Most High" (El-Shaddai), speaks words to the invader remarkable in the circumstances: "Blessed be Abram by God Most High, maker of heaven and earth." Besides functioning as a foundation-narrative for the central role of Jerusalem in Israelite history, this narrative shows a recognition of blessedness across a significant difference of faith-identity, based on recognition of Abraham's honesty and wisdom in matters of common human experience, namely the experience of semi-nomad tribes jockeying for comparative advantage. Abram, in effect, helps found covenantal relationships among some of these tribes. This gives them a measure of shared stability and security commonly found in those times only under the protection of great empires: Sumeria, Babylon, Egypt.

In short, before the promise of blessing to humankind in Genesis 12:1–3 is confirmed and Abram becomes Abraham the "father of many nations," the patriarch has already brought a measure of blessing to the warring tribes already situated in Canaan. The story has a certain realism. Abram's efforts are not wholly successful. We read of kidnapping, trickery, violence, and death. But Abram, at least as depicted in this narrative, seems to assume that the gift of the *promise* of eschatological blessing to all is also a gift of responsibility for him to try, stumblingly, to bring something like this about, in his own time and place, in his adopted Canaanite neighborhood. The contrast with the violence of Israel's later reoccupation of Canaan depicted in the books of Joshua and Judges is striking.

Through these early chapters of Genesis one sees a dialectic between an *ethic of literal obedience* to what is taken as divine command and an *ethic of responsibility to divine promise* on the stage of history. Sometimes these two moral modes are nearly juxtaposed. In Genesis 2:16 we read: "… the Lord God commanded the man … 'of the tree of the knowledge of good and evil you shall not eat.'" In Genesis 2:19 we find something different: "So out of the ground God formed every beast of the field and every bird of the air and brought them to the man to see what he would call them, and whatever the man called every living creature, that was its name." Obedience in some matters, responsibility in others, and in some cases a move from obedience to responsibility in the same matter: all are to be found intertwined in these Genesis texts.

Let me briefly illustrate how such a perspective might work in the case of the "binding of Isaac," the *Akedah*, which Genesis 22 makes an integral part of the narrative of Abraham's call. The *Akedah* story seems at first to stand on both sides of the obedience/responsibility dialectic. On the one hand, it is the parade instance of a divine demand for obedience overriding all other considerations. But on the other hand, YHWH, at the last moment, stays Abraham's hand and provides the ram caught in the thicket precisely as a gift that returns to Abraham an opportunity to exercise his own capacity for responsibility *to* the promise of a covenantal future of blessing for humankind, by letting Isaac live.

Comparing the Jewish, Christian, and Islamic accounts of the *Akedah* narrative sketched above, there is ample evidence that the scribes of old were already struggling with the evident difficulties in this account. Some scholars conjecture that the original Abraham story told of an actual human sacrifice, that being a custom in ancient pre-Israelite society.[30] If that is the case, the Genesis narrative as it comes to us has already taken the step of making this an "almost" sacrifice rather than a real one. And, as we have seen, the Christian narratives of Abraham's faithfulness avoid mentioning Genesis 22 at all until late in the first century at the earliest. The Qur'an begins to dissolve the seeming arbitrariness of the command still further by having it occur in a "dream" and be subject to a *discussion* between Abraham and his son. In a sense the son becomes, in the Qur'an, the *truly* obedient one. It is he, not Abraham, who speaks the Islamic language of "submission." Hence what we have in the Qur'an comes close to being "voluntary" martyrdom, rather than arbitrary child-sacrifice. But of course we know today about such voluntary martyrdoms. Such coerced, or very strongly encouraged, voluntarism comes close to being ritual sacrifice nonetheless. But in all three accounts it becomes plain that God does not want the sacrifice of the son. Presumably God never did want this.

That this passage could actually have to do with a former religious sanction of child sacrifice, and may have been read as such by Muhammad Atta, makes it the more imperative to reconsider it here. I do so with something of the "fear and trembling," the sleeplessness that Søren Kierkegaard said he felt, in writing his book of that title on this very subject. There have been many interpretations down the years, but fortunately few if any of these have been seen as impacting the core convictions of the faiths concerned.

The point that emerges for cosmopolitans today from the *Akedah* story is that Abraham's freedom is the product of his obedience. He is, paradoxically, ordered to be free after he has demonstrated that he is obedient to command in the first place. Abraham *chooses* to be obedient, and in turn is commanded to be free, to see the alternative, the ram caught in the bush, and take it. The command to be free can only be *heard* by he who is already obedient. Freedom is a form of obedience we discover when we are obedient to the One who *gives* us such freedom. It is not something we simply take over in the name of ideological autonomy. Freedom is given in the form of a gift of responsibility. I "submit" and find a deeper freedom to take responsibility in obedience. My free responsibility is a form of obedience that I must recognize as a gift that comes only to those who first freely choose to submit, and in doing so discover the real depth of responsibility that freedom gives.

Freedom without the sense of responsibility to an identity-*giving* calling can be a kind of vertigo. Responsibility as something purely rootless and normless can be a burden that can break me if I do not obediently receive the gift of responsibility to a promise of blessing. I need confidence that conscientious living by the sense of this gift renders me able truly to act in freedom. My confidence in my own judgment rests on a sure sense of my identity as recipient of a gift of blessing.

Understandably, the elements of this dialectic have tended over the centuries to come apart. A primary interpretative emphasis on obedience to command tends the reader toward fundamentalism and exclusivism, and therefore to personal *ir*responsibility. God's word says it, and therefore we must believe it and do it. Such a perspective also leads eventually toward the elaborate legal casuistry we find in the rabbinic and similar Islamic writings, designed to wring flexibility out of absolutism. There is indeed much basis for a divine command ethic in the early chapters of Genesis. Following Karl Barth, in no way do I intend to denigrate this reality or leave it aside. The very *possibility* of human responsibility is grounded in the divine command.

But this gift of responsibility must be responsibly received. So doing leads us to take seriously those passages in which the command requires human beings to take responsibility for what they do, in short to *interpret* the command to bring out its meaning in relation to actual historical experience. This leads us toward a more searching hermeneutic of our own times, and toward the possibility of interfaith cooperation in fulfilling obligations to humankind living in those same times. Just as the civil rights movement of the 1960s and 1970s saw something new in the Exodus, we can see something new in Genesis 12 and Genesis 22.[31]

Such interpretation is open to the possibility of a religiously plural sense of God's rule to which the different faith traditions contribute because they are able to see the gift of responsibility given in creation and fulfillment as now indicating their responsibility likewise to interpret the gift in new ways. Again, I am far from saying that the ethic of obedience (or "submission," as in Islam) must be left entirely aside. The truth lies in a dialectic. An ethic of *obedience* gives authority precisely to those texts that confer the gift of *responsibility* for crafting new responses, in this case interfaith responses, to God's promises.

Compare this interpretation of the gift of responsibility to Abraham with Søren Kierkegaard's just-mentioned treatment of the *Akedah* in *Fear and Trembling*. Instead of being a radical, existential, confrontation with God that stands above all universalizable moral positions of the Hegelian or Kantian type, hence modeling the stand of the solitary believer, the "knight of faith," I argue that the confrontation in the *Akedah*, when the full text is read, turns radical personal obedience into a charter of responsibility for the blessing of others. It locates the roots of blessing differently from those provided by the Kantian model. Rather than saying that we children of the Enlightenment are blessed by our achievement of universally applicable ethical principles, we realize that such principles come to us not through our argumentative ingenuity but through obedience toward the final Power with whom we have to do. Our responsibility for the well-being of our fellow human beings is a gift issuing from our submission to a Power not conceptualizable in our self-generated moral categories.

But, be this interpretation what it may, I have consistently argued that such submission, leading to responsibility, should not be expected to yield a common, and independent, religious "Abrahamism," of which Judaism, Christianity, and Islam should be seen as no more than variant developments. One is, admittedly, tempted to go in that direction. It is indeed tempting to exploit the fact that Abraham is represented in scripture as pre-Mosaic, pre-Torah, pre- all other developments. But while Abraham's times are agreed by all three faiths to have been before there was a Moses or a Torah (or a Jesus or a Muhammad), what we know of him is nonetheless dependent on his story having been described in the source materials later edited into Torah. Abraham himself is not "Jewish" but pre-Jewish, yet the narratives concerning him emerge exclusively in the scriptures of developing Israel. Christian and Islamic versions of the story are substantially dependent, no matter how much altered or embroidered along the way, on that source.

I am arguing, then, not for a syncretistic, independent Abrahamism but for the possibility that a sharing of hermeneutics of the Abrahamic traditions could bring about changes in the way each tradition of interpretation understands itself. The Jewish, Christian, and Islamic versions of Abrahamism will not soon meld into one, but they can come to be seen respectively as less stiffly self-sufficient. Just for each faith to see that there are other ways of reading what is sacred to them, and that these ways have occasionally influenced one another in the past, means that each faith's reading today will be different from what it might otherwise have been.

Different in what way? Different in that, for the first time, these different readings of the Abraham story are going on in what is increasingly acknowledged to be a common human condition. This means that groups of Jews, Christians, and Muslims reading together come to their own and one another's texts with overlapping apprehensions of what is happening on this planet, gained from the same global media, the same shared experiences. Each fresh reading in each such group of readers becomes a new stage in the hermeneutical history of each of the traditions involved.

These conditions allow us to think dialectically in a manner compatible with scripture but distinctly modern as well. One may say of the *Akedah* (a story that obviously will not soon go away) that, with several other Genesis episodes, it points to a fascinating moral paradox. It turns out *not* to be God's will that Abraham should sacrifice Isaac, *not* God's will that Abraham should do something contradictory to the very substance of the promise of universal blessing, and yet for Abraham to have judged this to be so at the start of the narrative and not to have set out on the journey to Mount Moriah, depending in effect on his innate moral judgment as equivalent to God's, would have been—in terms of this narrative—an act of unfaithfulness. Abraham at first submits both his own judgment (whatever that may have been) *and* the seeming logic of the covenant promise (as he understood it) to God's superior and unaccountable wisdom. Thus he places his human moral judgment and logic within a larger logic. He submits his human moral logic to God's will only to have his own human logic, in that very moment of submission, divinely confirmed. God provides an alternative. Abraham chooses it.

Does this say, then, that, human moral logic is forever indemnified because God will save us from our mistakes *if* only we can see in time the alternatives God provides? Is Abraham's undoubted initial reluctance to set forth toward the mountain of sacrifice now a sufficient basis for human morality because that reluctance is in the end divinely confirmed? No, it means that human moral responsibility must always function within obedience to a promise whose nature is to contradict any disobedient pretensions that our human logic may have to self-sufficiency or finality. Human judgment is simultaneously sound *and* limited or chastened. It must both think for itself and submit to God's will. But such judgment must never presume, even in that submission, that it perfectly replicates the will of God. The "way out" that God provides is a way out of destructive and fanatical forms of piety. There is little more dangerous in our world than the illusion that God commands that we use our God-given wits to commit irrational, destructive acts when we have been given the moral intelligence to do otherwise.

Tradition as Ongoing Argument

What is the yield of all this argumentation? In one sense, I have been only been doing some of the homework needed before speaking authentically about hermeneutical parallelism. Much more could certainly be done, but this is a starting point: enough, one hopes, to encourage members of the different faiths to try reading their scriptures together, exploring the different hermeneutical perspectives in play. Of course these readers will not entirely agree about what they find. Each version of the Abraham story—Jewish, Christian, and Islamic—in itself founds a massive tradition of interpretation, each composed of many subhermeneutics representing different tendencies, times, and places.

One would think that all this might sow confusion rather than clarity. Simply reading certain passages together to compare what they seem to say directly in the moment may be simpler. And that, indeed, is what is done in many of the contemporary "reading scripture together" initiatives described in chapter 1.[32] Yet to be aware of the interpretative traditions that lie behind every reading is important. Such awareness, among other things, can give us some idea of where many readings come from and where they may possibly lead.

One thing above all emerges from each of the sketches of the Abrahamic tradition just given—whether traditional or cosmopolitan. It is that each of these traditions already bears witness throughout to a lively internal *argument*. Each age of humankind provokes a new stage of that argument. One might even say that each tradition *consists* of an argument that begins in principle with the very first page and continues to this day. The traditions seem to some degree aware of this fact. Perhaps it is plainest in the Jewish rabbinic tradition of argumentative scripture interpretation that never ends. But Jesus engages in debate with his interlocutors, and at one point says to his disciples, "Why do you not decide for yourselves what is right?" (Luke 12:57). And the Qur'an enjoys ripostes like "Do you have no sense?" (Sura 3:58) and "See what you think" (Sura 37:102). While particular passages inevitably seem thoroughly apodictic and self-certain in their intention, other passages can nearly always be found that speak of the same things in other, even seemingly contradictory, ways. This means, I think, that interpreters of the Abrahamic traditions through the centuries have consistently recognized their responsibility for creatively determining what obedience to God's laws means in each situation. The call to membership in each faith community implies a call to obedience to its moral laws. This lays upon us the spiritual gift of responsibility to be part of the community of interpreters through the centuries, including the present century, in which the traditions begin to interact with one another.

All this becomes especially evident in the light of modern critical scriptural scholarship. One has to acknowledge that such academic inquiry into scripture is further advanced in some religious communities than it is in others. The very idea of setting Abrahamic commentaries side by side, as I have just sought to do, no doubt reflects a certain Enlightenment sensibility that not all will share. But the important point is this: once this is done, the different scriptures themselves function to convince those whose scriptures they are that we are not only dealing with differences and tensions and arguments among the Abrahamic faiths in their different expressions, but also with differences of opinion *inside* schools of interpretation that have long thought of themselves as self-consistent. It then becomes easier to see one's own viewpoint not as offering a single settled view of the world, but as a problematic sustained over centuries, within which one must work creatively to gain any sort of intellectual or spiritual foothold.

To realize the extent to which each tradition is *already* a centuries-long argument about its own meaning is to feel freer to join in the same creative argumentation today. Only now, and probably for the first time (there may have been some instances in Spain in the Middle Ages), the argument goes on inside each of the Abrahamic faiths with participation by the other faiths. This, as we have seen, makes a significant difference. The practice of parallel and interactive hermeneutics calls for responsibility to one another for what is said and responsibility for the consequences of certain interpretations in the world at large. An exclusivistic, potentially violent interpretation of scripture has consequences for which we are *responsible*. It is no longer good enough just to say that scripture commands this or that and therefore we will do it. We are free and must identify ourselves with our deeds, if only because others with similar commitments are watching. This fact creates a new hermeneutical situation precisely by calling all participants to stand provisionally outside their own traditions of faith to see the view from elsewhere. Such new hermeneutical positioning can encourage important new things to be thought and said. Interpretation in the twenty-first century, among other things, needs to address the gift of transcendental responsibility (chapter 3) for humanity's future, for the planet's future. It is not only that we learn new things about ourselves from one another, although that is indispensable. It is also that together we can think our thoughts in a new, liberating, hermeneutical context.

Forms of "enlightened" moral sensitivity are helping us to be aware of the unfolding of distinctively scriptural ethical logics. Studying the different Abrahamic hermeneutics in parallel helps us grasp the various logics that are being worked out *within* the scriptural narratives themselves.[33] It is easy for post-Enlightenment readers to assume that earlier ages held essentially heteronomous attitudes: that they were unquestioning, especially where revelation was concerned. It is easy for us to assume that we contemporaries are the only real questioners, and that scripture must come before the bar of the modern intellect and give an account of itself. But perhaps we need first to enter the complex questioning and answering that lies inside scripture, and especially so when we are reading different scriptures in parallel. Yvonne Sherwood has challenging words to say about this. Her paragraph is nuanced, intricate, and bears close reading:

> Could it be that the pre-Enlightenment condition of being Jewish, being Christian, being Muslim before all choice leads to more active and audacious acts of interpreting, deciding and choosing in complex relation to the texts and vocabularies in which one lives, moves, and has one's being—for when the vocabularies and texts of God and Abraham simply *are*, they cannot be feared to vanish or diminish in the face of critique. Instead of simply ushering us into a new era of autonomy and choice, might it be that modernity, by leading us to choose our place as "religious" or "non-religious," and identify with (protect?) that choice thereafter, also—at least potentially—*replaces* these little acts of micro-choosing and micro-critique with one vast act of macro-choosing?[34]

Sherwood seems to be telling us that, in an enlightened world, religious traditions are so insecure that opting for them leaves us fearful of interpreting them in new ways lest we undermine the radical choice we have made. "Little acts of micro-choosing and micro-critique" were possible, she thinks, when faith traditions, seen whole, were so politically and culturally dominant that they could not be shaken by ingenious revisionists. But now, she seems to say, with faith itself continually under attack, we cannot engage in this sort of creative scriptural reasoning without risking the weakening of the traditions themselves, or perhaps encouraging their inadvertent assimilation to the "spirit of the age." Indeed it is possible that claiming to find new meanings *in* scripture is sometimes only a disguised way of importing the modern influences that suit us. But the "hermeneutical circle" is, after all a circle that can become a spiral upward or, better, outward. We cannot read without presuppositions. But our presuppositions, exposed to scripture, can emerge radically changed.

Furthermore, pre-Enlightenment interpretative moves were not always so "micro" as Sherwood claims. Innovative scriptural reasoning inside secure traditions sometimes brought about major upheavals. Think of Martin Luther commenting on the Epistle to the Romans and touching off the Protestant Reformation. Are we to read Sherwood as saying that no courageous acts of reinterpretation within traditions are possible today because modernity has rendered potential reinterpreters too insecure in their faith to try rethinking that faith? Is one "vast act of macro-choosing" the only possibility? Either we choose modernity or we choose tradition, and that is it? Perhaps the problem is not so much that tradition dissolves at the first hint of reinterpretation but rather that it fragments. There are *too many* new interpretations with too little sense of common direction. So, do we conclude that an interpretation, like the one in this book, that seeks to challenge the Abrahamic traditions to face today's interfaith challenges and thereby help heal modernity's self-betrayals, is doomed from the start because it weakens the force of each person's macro-decision for faith itself? Or is such reinterpretation doomed because it will inevitably call forth ripostes from those who want to make other sorts of hermeneutical moves, or to make the same moves differently?

This chapter has sought to find ways to enter into the processes of scripture's internal argumentation, to follow the twists and turns of "scriptural reasoning," in such a way as to find there the *potential* of those ancient internal arguments to be carried forward to today in ways that speak to us. I call the continuation of ancient scriptural reasoning with a new intercommunally responsible moral logic ("parallel and interactive hermeneutics") our way of inheriting for today the gift of responsibility to an ancient promise. The term "gift of responsibility" points to our need to exercise our finite but indispensable human judgment while realizing that this capacity is itself a work of grace within us. The word "promise" speaks of the larger covenantal context in which we are called to do this. To live, as human beings, in responsibility to a covenant promise means, as I will show in chapter 9, that we can practice a *covenantal* sort of "humanism." If humanism in the Enlightenment sense is a claim to autonomy exercised consistently with our moral duty, as Kant claimed, then a "covenantal" or "Abrahamic" humanism is in play when our moral judgment, wise as it may be, is recognized as a blessing or grace at work in us that both undergirds our autonomy *and* can overrule it. We, like

Abraham, can only know this when our judgment is confirmed by events as corresponding to God's promise, not to the promise we see in our own plans and possibilities, however much involved with our *idea* of God these may be. And confirmation that this is so may be long in coming. A theological or covenantal humanism says that our obedience must be linked with a grasp of the *logic* of the inter-Abrahamic promise. We are called to affirm our all-too-human moral reason and, in the same moment, to be willing in God's name to relativize it. We are not to equate our human voice with God's voice, but at the same time we are not irrationally to distrust it.

For now, we can only see this far. The issue is not one of choosing between Enlightenment autonomy and pre-Enlightenment heteronomy. It is rather a matter of allowing the Enlightenment, both in its achievements and in its shortcomings, to alert us to the importance of our traditions of responsible reflection and scriptural argumentation. What Christians call "doctrinal" propositions (and Jews and Muslims will debate with Christians as to what these are and what they mean, and all can learn from George Lindbeck's book *The Nature of Doctrine*[35]) are only temporary fixations, for certain times and places within the stream of ongoing arguments. My proposition is that understanding these continuing debates can be more productive for our time than tying ourselves to the fixations.

Contemporary ways of thought have thus enabled us to find new things in ancient texts. I believe that the most important discovery at this point in our argument is this: YHWH, or God or Allah, tells Abraham that his descendants will inherit a responsibility to the world in fulfillment of which they will need to use their full capacities for a generous kind of moral reasoning. Recall Walter Brueggemann's words. Yahweh *demands* "that Israel be a vehicle and an instrument for assuring the well-being, security, joy, and dignity of all nations . . . . Israel has responsibility for the health of the world. It is a responsibility, given in the same breath, given in this initial utterance of generosity."[36]

If this is so for Israel, then it is true too for Christianity and Islam. Abraham's covenantal ethic of blessing and promise-keeping, articulated in terms of common human experience, is the nub of what can, and should, become a full-fledged responsibility ethic. And such a responsibility ethic, as chapter 6 will attempt to show, calls equally for the covenantal virtues of forgiveness, trust, and solidarity. To carry forward the thesis of this book I will need to show how such "covenantal virtues" are both presupposed and further enacted when the three Abrahamic faiths begin to practice the generous calling of mutual "moral hospitality" and begin to live out the consequences of such hospitality in the world.

Notes

1. This greatly compressed account is informed by an article by Yvonne Sherwood of the University of Glasgow, "Binding-Unbinding: Divided Responses of Judaism, Christianity, and Islam to the 'Sacrifice' of Abraham's Beloved Son," *The Journal of the American Academy of Religion* 72, no. 4 (December 2004): 821ff.

2. Ibid., 825.

3. In actual fact, "religions of the Book" was a phrase used by early Muslims to refer to Judaism and Christianity. The employment of this expression for all three faiths is appropriate enough, but a much more recent usage.

4. See Henri Frankfort, *Before Philosophy: The Intellectual Adventure of Ancient Man* (Baltimore: Penguin Books, 1974) and George Mendenhall, *The Tenth Generation: The Origins of the Biblical Tradition* (Baltimore: Johns Hopkins University Press, 1973). Of course, it is clear that we know of "early Israel," if such an entity ever existed in history, only through texts redacted in the later period of the Israelite kings, priests, and prophets by persons with commitments variously reflecting the theopolitics of their own times and situations. How, then, do we distinguish early Israelite material from subsequently framed narratives that either tell the patriarchal stories or subsequently interpret them for their own ulterior purposes? My point is not that we can make such a distinction with any confidence today, but rather that the Abrahamic narratives in principle do not belong to any one set of redactors or interpreters. In principle what underlies these narratives belongs to all and passes judgment upon all. Whatever redaction may have taken place was likely for the purpose of accommodating the narratives to a royal ideology, and therefore unlikely to have introduced these critical features.

5. I have experienced this kind of outcome at least twice firsthand: once in a 1995 seminar (which I chaired) involving representatives of the three faiths and sponsored by the Center for Hermeneutical Studies of the University of California at Berkeley and the Graduate Theological Union, with notably careful preparation and internationally known speakers, and again at a thoughtfully conceived meeting in 2004 between social ethicists teaching in Presbyterian theological institutions and representatives of Jewish organizations in the Chicago metropolitan area. The lesson seems to be that good intentions are not always enough. Language even slightly carelessly considered can set off strong emotional outbursts from normally sophisticated and cosmopolitan academics.

6. The notion that Islam is descended from Abraham and Hagar by way of Ishmael is not present in the Hebrew Bible as such (written long before Islam began to exist) but is rather an interpretation of these texts. For Muslims, they lead back to Abraham (Hagar, interestingly, is not mentioned in the Qur'an) and a claim to Abrahamic territory. Some Jews and Christians see the descent through Hagar and Ishmael as giving Muslims at best a tainted or secondary relationship with Abraham, an honorable status perhaps, but without any scripturally based claim to territory.

7. I am assuming that "hermeneutics" here is the plural of the singular word "hermeneutic," which means *a* given way of interpreting: Shiite, Bultmannian, rabbinic, whatever it may be. So, in using the word "parallel hermeneutics," I am speaking of many encounters of texts with different types of interpretation conducted, so to speak, within earshot of one another and

with a certain sense of mutual responsibility. Confusion arises owing to the fact that the word "hermeneutics" also has a singular sense, referring to the field of study of what goes on when texts or textlike objects are interpreted.

8. The stunningly successful program preceding the inauguration of Iain Torrance as president of Princeton Theological Seminary in March 2005 was titled simply "reading scriptures together." Speakers were David Ford, an Anglican Christian, Peter Ochs, an Orthodox Jewish Rabbi, and Aref Ali Nayed, an Islamic scholar from Cambridge University, UK.

9. William Schweiker, "Religious Convictions and the Intellectual's Responsibility," in *Criterion* (Autumn 2003): 5.

10. Ibid., 13.

11. Sherwood, "Binding-Unbinding," 825.

12. Ibid., 832.

13. For these accounts of Jewish, Christian, and Islamic interpretations of the Abraham narratives, I have drawn on F. E. Peters, *Judaism, Christianity and Islam: Volume I: From Covenant to Community* (Princeton, NJ: Princeton University Press, 1990). I have also drawn for particular perspectives on Sherwood, "Binding-Unbinding." Scriptural texts are quoted from the Revised Standard Version of the Bible, and from *The Qur'an: A Modern English Version*, trans. Majid Fakhry (Reading, UK: Garnet Publishing, 1997).

14. *The Torah: A Modern Commentary* (Cincinnati, OH: Union of American Hebrew Congregations, 1981), 151n5, quoted at http://www.jewsforjesus.org/special//hh/rh_akedah.html.

15. *Encyclopedia Judaica* (New York: Macmillan, 2006), 2:482, quoted ibid.

16. I owe this paragraph's references to medieval *midrashim* to Sherwood, "Binding-Unbinding," 837.

17. Ibid.

18. Rabbi Philip Borenstein, *Sermon for the Second Day of Rosh Hashana, 1998*, http://www.rjca.org/5759rh2akedah.html.

19. Ibid.

20. See C. H. Dodd, *The Apostolic Preaching and Its Developments* (Grand Rapids, MI: Baker Books, 1982), *passim*.

21. Contemporary Christian leaders and thinkers have increasingly preferred the nonsupersessionist position in relations with Judaism. An official deliverance of the Presbyterian Church, USA, dated 1992, has made this especially clear by preferring Paul's "ingrafting" metaphor of Romans 9–11 to questionable inferences drawn from either Jeremiah 31 or Hebrews 8 as the basis for its understanding that the Abrahamic covenant remains valid.

22. Sura 3:76, 187; Sura 5:7; Sura 16:91; Sura 57:8.

23. Sherwood, "Binding-Unbinding," 389.

24. Ibid.

25. Ibid., 389f.

26. Hannah Arendt, *The Human Condition* (Chicago: University of Chicago Press, 1978), 219.

27. Paul Ricoeur, *The Symbolism of Evil* (Boston: Beacon Press, 1967), 19.

28. I use the word "institutions" in the two senses described by Robert Bellah: institutions as organized structures (e.g. the Roman Catholic Church or the British Parliament, or the United

Nations), and institutions as established patterns of behavior (e.g. marriage, or churchgoing, or shopping, or apartheid). Institutions in the first sense typically provide frameworks for the support of institutions in the second sense. See Bellah, et al., *The Good Society* (New York: Alfred A. Knopf, 1991).

29. Walter Brueggemann, "Law as Response to Thou," in Winston Davis, ed., *Taking Responsibility: Comparative Perspectives* (Charlottesville, VA: University of Virginia Press, 2001), 91. Italics in the original.

30. There may be reason to doubt this thesis of pre-Israelite nomad child sacrifice. So-called "foundation sacrifices," connected with erecting permanent structures, seemingly were practiced by city-dwellers, not nomads. And if child sacrifice had been a custom in Abraham's tribe, why did he need to conceal his true intent as he set forth to Mount Moriah?

31. I am adapting here an insight of my mentor Paul Ricoeur, who taught that the meaning of a passage lies not only in the conscious intention of its author, but also in the history of the interpretation of that passage. We live today in a new era of the history of interpretation. See Paul Ricoeur, *Essays on Biblical Interpretation*, Lewis S. Mudge, ed. (Philadelphia: Fortress Press, 1980), 16ff.

32. Something like this apprehension of meaning "in the moment" seems to be involved in readings done from a postmodern perspective, as recommended by Peter Ochs for the Society for Scriptural Reasoning. This certainly is the impression the present writer received in taking part in some of the Society's annual sessions at the American Academy of Religion.

33. The idea of "scriptural reasoning" has been worked out in detail and with persuasive force by Peter Ochs. See chapter 4.

34. Sherwood, "Binding-Unbinding," 856.

35. George A. Lindbeck, *The Nature of Doctrine: Religion and Theology in a Postliberal Age* (Philadelphia: The Westminster Press, 1984).

36. Brueggemann, "Law as Response to Thou," 91.

6

Communities of Covenantal Virtue

Forgiveness, Trust, Solidarity

It is time now to ask what sort of interfaith community, if any, is growing among those who take part in parallel and interactive hermeneutics. At the very least, one has something useful: a dialogue group that promotes mutual understanding among the faiths. But it can make a difference what category of self-understanding the group adopts, and hence what associations and objectives it takes on. Such a group can organize itself as a program element in some larger enterprise (e.g., a "Parliament of the World's Religions") or as a seminar in a theological school (either one belonging to one of the faiths, or one including many faiths), or as a seminar in an academic graduate department of religious studies, or as an interfaith scripture study project sponsored by local congregations, or as part of an organized intellectual project (e.g., Peter Ochs's "Society for Scriptural Reasoning"), or even as an "Abrahamic Family Reunion" (a term used by the Strategic Planning Workshop of the Esalen Institute). In each case, the discourse borrows some particular institutional self-understanding from the array of possibilities available in modern Western society. And in each case, that borrowing shapes the methods and objectives of the enterprise. Apart from one or another such model of "the art of association," without some such supportive social location, it is hard to imagine inter-Abrahamic dialogues even getting started.

These are the sorts of social locations typically available as rooted cosmopolitans begin their work—before theological questions arise. Yet at some point in the process, the realization dawns that these models of discourse are no more than provisional frameworks for the deeper task of describing in more searching terms what is taking place in these conversations. We ask, Does there exist a *theological* expression for what is going on among us?

Do dialogue groups of this sort, as they begin to reflect on what it *means* that they are reading Abrahamic texts together, have potential for becoming in some sense *covenantal communities* reflecting the values of the texts they read? Can there emerge a link between the material studied and the evolving character of the group doing the studying?" I believe that the answer is yes.

Thinking about What We Are Doing

We need to find our place—portentous or merely evanescent—in the long history of the interpretation of sacred texts. It is important here to have a sense of proportion, as well as a sense of possibility. Literatures of scripture interpretation in Judaism, Christianity, and Islam are voluminous over time. Not only is there a far wider range of scriptural texts to be considered than we have seen up to now. It is also important to remember that each faith has its own long and complex history of scriptural exegesis, with many historical periods, many centers of scholarship, many schools of thought. In Judaism there is Mishna and Gemara, Halakhah and Haggadah, the whole Talmudic tradition of endless textual, moral, and legal argumentation. In Christianity there is the long process of establishing the canon itself, followed more or less in historical order by the hermeneutical work of the church fathers East and West, the bishops, the monks, the reformers, the counterreformers, and professorial hermeneuts from the eighteenth century onward. In Islam one has a similar complex history of scriptural interpretation including the Sharia, or legal code for Islamic states. These schools of interpretation have for the most part dealt with other faiths as alien, as not part of the process of determining the meaning of indigenous faith, not supposing there could come a time when traditions might be interpreted together. Yet, even here there are exceptions. Genuine inter-Abrahamic encounters have happened, and have even been established as customary, in such places as medieval Andalusia, the Ottoman Empire, twentieth-century South Africa, and no doubt elsewhere.

The point of this recital is to say that the parallel hermeneutical encounters now going on across the globe may come to be seen as only the latest phase in long, hitherto mostly mutually isolated, histories of interpretation As we meet today, we are at best invited only into the anterooms[1] of these ancient hermeneutical traditions. We are given tourist-appropriate hints of what took place inside. Each modern dialoguer should sit at table and imagine behind him or her a vast *hinterland* of many generations of interpreters in his or her own faith and in the other faiths, interpreters who have lived lives of devotion and have struggled with many challenges. The only appropriate reaction for the modern dialoguer is silently to ask, What am I, with my limited knowledge, doing here? What right have I to speak? And then he or she should speak out, both lovingly and boldly, thereby carrying a long tradition into its next, interreligious, stage.

This new hermeneutical possibility is, as we have seen, accompanied by the emergence of a new sort of hermeneutical community. We are still struggling with the question of describing this community theologically. Social realities, we are told, are marked by the prevalence of certain kinds of relationships, by the persuasiveness of certain kinds of discourse. They may or may not have visible institutional form. I have described the values underlying the discourse-community presupposed in chapter 5 as requiring expressions toward one another of transcendental responsibility, responsibility beyond routine. We reach out beyond tribal or confessional boundaries to hear one another truly and to interpret one another fairly. And we take responsibility, again beyond usual identity boundaries, for the consequences of the interpretations we propose. In short, by being involved in such conversations, the participants make certain implicit promises to each other to maintain their relationships however great may be the strains of discovered difference. It is this characteristic that may elevate the practices of parallel and interactive hermeneutics from being institutional exercises of one sort or another to being discourse communities with *covenantal* qualities.

I hesitate to propose this word "covenantal." It may seem to claim too much. But this chapter comes, at the close of its argument, to a guarded, but affirmative embrace of the term. I am far from claiming that the mere existence of groups reading Abrahamic texts together has the power to bring whole faiths together in some world-historical transformation. Even less do I mean that this hermeneutical process founds some distinctive new faith community alongside the existing ones. Yet the question of what such communal interpretative practices are and where they may lead needs to be answered somehow.

To claim covenantal character for such scriptural reasoning spaces is, of course, not something that can be justified solely on the basis of studying ancient texts. It must also be a work of outright theological construction for an unprecedented human situation. There are at least two problems here. The first has to do with the nature of the sources, themselves. The second has to do with the nature of the process of interpreting them.

There are, first, many who doubt that a move to call dialogue groups covenantal lacks sufficiently coherent or widely recognized foundations. To call a novel relationship covenantal, even as a work of modern theological imagination, could be to ignore the checkered character, for some, of the roots and memories that this word implies. The question is fairly clear for Jews, less clear for Christians, and least clear of all for Muslims. The picture is confused by the variety of situations and attitudes that have shaped the meaning of this word. While it is central for Jews, only some Christians (despite the term "New Testament" or "new covenant") think it important. And while present repeatedly in the Qur'an, the word "covenant" is not as constitutive or tradition-forming for Islam as it is for the other two faiths. My own Reformed or Presbyterian tribe makes more of this idea than most other Christian groups do. I am no doubt influenced in offering it by having this background. But in the present argument, the notion of "covenant" does not take the form it did for John Calvin, the Puritans, and others. Shorn of such historical particularity, perhaps it can sound less like an imposition, and more like an invitation.

But even if the sources are coherent enough, the sort of contemporary theological construction proposed may be thought by some to constitute an illicit interpretative leap. I would answer that the histories of interpretation just described have been marked by many innovations well beyond the horizons of the original scriptural authors. The legitimacy of such creative interpretation is indeed questioned today by scholars for whom "authorial intention" is the sole basis for saying what a passage means. But, of course, authorial intention is often available only from the very passage under interpretation, so that it is a leap on our part in any case to say we know what that intention was. Far better, I think, the insight of Paul Ricoeur that there is no theoretical limit to the succession of new interpretations in new situations a text may receive. The meaning of a written text for Ricoeur lies in "the direction of thought opened up by the text" in every new situation in which it finds readers. I believe that the reading of ancient Abrahamic texts in three faith communities today legitimately opens up new directions of thought. That is what I am trying to do in calling the dialogue communities themselves "covenantal" in character when no previous interpreter has done so.[2]

One begins to justify the adjective "covenantal" today in the light of the notion of transcendental mutual responsibility beyond routine relationships. What is "covenantal" is that which is found in shared responsibility to a promise that defines one's faith. In this case, the promise is that of blessing to all the earth's families. Loyalty to such a promise by definition reaches out beyond routine occupational duties and ancient tribal lines to express responsibility transcendentally, as giving conceptual coherence to an unprecedented, inclusive field of human discourse. Parallel and interactive Abrahamic hermeneutics have the power to generate spaces of reasons potentially having this world-embracing character. It is not that they will do so in and of themselves. They will do so as their participants glimpse the possibility and muster the political will. Such responsibility-links can define close-knit communities of common love and labor. But they can also define networks of common concern that extend over vast distances and varied circumstances.

Secular thinkers have had much to say today about the ways dialogue (or "communicative action") both requires and fosters assumptions about such interacting networks of responsibility. The German philosopher Jürgen Habermas has given us the phrase "speech act immanent obligation" to describe the mutual responsibility required for any successful dialogue.[3] But Habermas thinks all of this works, and *must* work, apart from traditional moral norms. Indeed his whole purpose is to replace the latter with a "discourse ethic" operating inside a "communicative action" theory. The demand to take responsibility for backing up what we say with evidence and argument is a requirement of human discourse itself. It is "immanent," as Habermas likes to say, in the speech-act. But in my present argument "speech acts" are interpretative in character. I want to graft sets of scripturally articulated assumptions into Habermasian thinking. We are responsible to one another for our interpretations because we are responsible to a covenantal promise of universal blessing. Habermas does not give us an analysis of the discourse situation in which a transcendental responsibility to the Other for such speech-act obligation is also the subject matter of the dialogue. In parallel and interactive hermeneutics of the Abrahamic texts, we are being made aware of the mutual ties among interpreters needed for adequately understanding such texts and articulating their message in provisional forms of shared life.

But the word "covenantal" alone may be too abstract to make the solid connections among continents of faith we need to make. The word may be useful only after it is given new, richer meanings. Moreover, that enrichment cannot be confined to scriptural or "religious" language. Robust, covenantal connections need to be expressible in the languages of today, in terminologies that reflect ancient scriptural language but that measure up to the expectations of rooted cosmopolitans with "infinite capacities for taking planes" (an expression once current among World Council of Churches staff members) to the far corners of earth. I propose in the rest of this chapter to meet these demands for concreteness by exploring three virtues that could be called expressions or carriers of covenanting with respect to issues that any such community will encounter. These acted-out virtues are (1) giving and receiving *forgiveness*, (2) fostering conditions of *trust*, and (3) acting in *solidarity*. Notice the gerunds, the verbal nouns—giving, receiving, fostering, acting—the robust expressions of virtues-acted-out. We are talking not merely about words, but about patterns of action that characterize covenantal relationships. Why these particular "virtues"? Others could have been chosen. But these have to do with the very substance of covenantal relationships among different faiths. Faiths in dialogue must deal with the mutual violence and destruction of the past: hence "forgiveness." They must address the questions of ties that bind them together: hence "trust." And they must consider what it is in the public realm they stand for: hence "solidarity." By studying the patterns of relationship and activity conveyed by these action-expressions, we are studying covenanting not merely in principle but in its concreteness. Hence the discussion to come helps to make the case for using covenantal terminology in this book, and especially in the last chapter, whose theme is "covenantal humanism."

It helps, of course, to insist on the adjectival form "covenantal" rather than on the substantive term "covenant" as such. I do not claim the existence of a "new" covenant among us superseding the older ones, as if we were positing some new divine initiative validating our deepening relationships. But what we do together can be called covenantal in senses derived from our existing covenantal *callings*. And the best way to get at the nature of relationships deemed covenantal by derivation is by investigating their shared content. The purpose of what follows is to do that by exploring the meaning of these three enacted virtues that can be called covenantal by implication.

Notice one other thing. We begin, as do most of the inter-Abrahamic dialogues themselves, with modern or cosmopolitan terminologies for what we do. We begin by presupposing the common modern definitions of words like forgiveness, trust, and solidarity that make our initial meetings possible. But the further we look at these cosmopolitan resources, the more clear it becomes that these words, as commonly defined, are not adequate for describing in depth what we are doing. Pursuit of the deeper meanings to which such words should be windows in each case runs into what philosophers call *aporias*, or conceptual blockages beyond which we cannot coherently proceed. The scriptural worlds of meaning to which these expressions are supposed to point do not easily join hands with the modern expressions, nor do the modern expressions readily access the scriptural meanings. So Abrahamic communities, seeking to define themselves covenantally as arenas of forgiveness, trust, and solidarity, suddenly find themselves with a vocation: of reconnecting their modern terminologies so far as possible with scriptural originals and at the same time constructively fashioning new acted applications for both to meet the modern need.

But this is no simple matter. The scriptural terminologies do not begin to have the inter-Abrahamic possibilities of modernity in view. They cannot simply be translated to make the connection. Scriptural language needs now to be taken up into new modes of covenantal thought that cannot have been imagined in earlier times. We are dealing, after all, not only with words, but with patterns of activity, with gerunds: forgiving, trusting, acting in solidarity. The inter-Abrahamic communities *themselves*, through their activities, need to come to embody the covenantal virtues in new meanings in such a way as to build bridges between the worlds of our roots and the worlds of our current cosmopolis.

So we will proceed now to explore these three covenantal patterns of activity that we claim to be of the essence of the community of shared inter-Abrahamic interpretation. They constitute different activity-patterns in the fabric of sharing in the gifts of responsibility. They do so *both* by constructively interpreting ancient scriptural models *and* by being of the essence of the kind of "discourse ethic" (Habermas) necessarily embodied in the interpretative process as such. Forthcoming sections of this chapter are devoted to analysis of each pattern of covenantal activity. These analyses share a recognizable common pattern, with variations appropriate to the subject matter. In each case we begin with the notions concerned in common human experience, where dialogues among rooted cosmopolitans nearly always begin. There follows for each a discussion of the ways in which such virtues, expressed as action-statements accessible to contemporary cosmopolitan consciousness, fail to capture in depth what is going on in dialogues of this kind. Forgiveness, trust, and solidarity are deeper notions in this context than they are in ordinary cosmopolitan parlance.

We cannot do without these common words because our own self-understandings are located, in part, in the cosmopolitan worlds they inhabit. But inside our multirooted dialogues we find them inadequate. There, we are experiencing deeper understandings than these words in their ordinary meaning appear able to bear. These felt limitations of meaning and reference, we will see in each case, are confirmed by philosophers who have studied such words and how they work. The word "forgiveness" as it functions in our culture does not permit us to get to the bottom of what we sense this word should really mean. Trying to define it and apply it, our intellects lose their way. Our best efforts to act out the meaning of this word fall well short of the profundity to which we know it points. It does not say enough "to forgive," says Jacques Derrida, because in principle only victims can forgive, and the victims of our worst deeds are dead. The ordinary word "trust" does not say enough, says Adam Seligman, because in practice it is used only to mean irrational risk-taking or confidence in the efficacy of audits and security cameras. The word "solidarity" may say *too much*, implies Paul Ricoeur criticizing Emmanuel Lévinas, because it can be understood to drain away our responsible identification with our own acts, leaving us held "hostage" to the demands of the Other whom we seek to serve.

The conclusion we reach is that the covenantal reality is in the world not because its essence can be captured unequivocally in words but because there is in the world a community that acts it out, or embodies it. The attempt to define the covenantal purely in terms of its forgiving, trusting, and solidarity *qualities* founders on the limitations of such ideas and words. One lives the covenantal virtues by living and acting within the covenantal community, which *represents* in each particular time or space the potential covenantal quality of the human community as a whole. Willful estrangement from that community is forgiven when, at a price, we are restored to it. One is trusted by being taken accountably into its inmost deliberations and being given responsibility for its actions. One expresses solidarity with it and with its allies by identifying publicly with its aims and its promises.

These points are developed in some detail for each covenantal virtue in the pages that follow. But this is not done in the kind of lockstep that would suppress the different histories of the words in question, or their different contemporary usages. The chapter ends with a preliminary exploration of the relation between the covenantal community and the larger human community of whose promised blessing the covenant is a visible sign.

Giving and Receiving Forgiveness

The first of the three "covenantal" virtues that communities of Abrahamic scripture interpretation need—in order to create conditions for their own continuing existence—is a capacity for giving and receiving forgiveness. Among us there is much to forgive. Deep resentment still festers among many for violent episodes both centuries ago and as recent as last week. Memories of these things are deliberately stoked for today's political reasons. Violent acts and harsh words are hard to forget, especially when rehearsed in elementary school and burned into peoples' consciousness through propaganda. Projects of conquest and domination, scriptural dismissals of one anothers' rights to exist, systematic theological justifications of violence: all these things remain alive in the memories of many.

In the case of the Abrahamic faiths, one must hold in mind the enormity of some of the specific historical atrocities. The Muslim cultural and military conquest of the Mediterranean world, the Crusades, the Inquisition, the Holocaust, Palestinian suicide attacks against the Israeli occupation, Israeli military responses, the destruction of the World Trade Center, violence in the Balkans and in Northern Ireland, and so much more, all energized by belligerent interpretations of faith by perpetrators on different sides of such conflicts. We ask, indeed, how parallel and interactive hermeneutical work among Abrahamic faiths can even have been begun without some sort of prior, mutually forgiving acts.

Yet in fact beginnings have been made, as we have seen. One reason that has been possible is no doubt that "rooted cosmopolitans," children of the

Enlightenment with continuing religious affiliations as they are, are largely emancipated, personally and culturally, from the atavistic worlds of mutual hatred in which violent acts receive their justification. Yet hermeneutical relationships that hope eventually to bring whole traditions with them cannot ignore such things. Violence crops up in the texts that are studied. Cosmopolitans sometimes surprise themselves with moments of anger against one another that go back to very deep early layers of socialization in their original faith communities.

The key thing, I think, is to recognize that the issue of forgiveness gets serious when we talk about forgiving the unforgivable, when we talk about forgiving hurts that can *never* be made whole because people have lost their lives: the Holocaust, the squandering of fifty-eight thousand American and untold numbers of Vietnamese lives for nothing by men who *knew* the war was fruitless, the murder of Archbishop Romero by forces we helped to fund. Forgiving the unforgivable. Only the victims can forgive, and they are dead. Can *we* forgive on their behalf? The idea verges on blasphemy: *we* have not suffered as they have. Forgiveness of the unforgivable cannot be our doing. It can only be, as we will see, the work of God in opening the doors of contemporary history to covenantal community of a new kind.

The giving and receiving of forgiveness is obviously the opposite of harboring resentment and taking revenge. Revenge seems to be by far the more frequently chosen way of "settling" disputes among human beings today. Only revenge never settles anything. Instead it re-energizes the cycle of violence. Revenge is sought in return and violence escalates. Religious communities seem as prone to revenge thinking as any other kinds of communities. Even to them, forgiveness often seems a weak response that may restrain acts of retaliation but leaves victims vulnerable to being further exploited by persons to whom being forgiven means little but the opportunity to go on taking advantage.

For any form of inter-Abrahamic discourse to go deeper than mere palaver for its own sake, the participants need to find some form of release from such burdens. This release granted in and by forgiveness applies both to the offender and the offended, the violent party and the victimized party. It applies where both parties are both violent and victimized. Forgiveness is the bearer of the gift of release and of new possibilities. We are delivered by this gift from resentment into new relationships of responsibility toward one another. Such forgiven and therefore responsible relationships are the foundation of our capacity to speak through both actions and words to one another and to humankind.

But why take on the burden and spiritual complexity of calling for forgiving at all? Why not just depend on forgetting? In some cases, forgetting seems to work for practical purposes just as well as a release from the past, particularly where events can be, or are allowed to be forgotten. Maybe it sometimes works better. Forgetting, if it can be achieved, may not be so fraught with strong feelings as all that must be undergone to achieve real forgiveness. Indeed, in the common use of the word, forgiveness may mean no more than a will to forgetting. Nigel Biggar, a wise observer, has studied in detail the processes of peacemaking that have followed conflict in such places as Northern Ireland, Bosnia, Guatemala, and elsewhere. He sees forgetting as almost always an evasion of the issue. Victims do not forget even if others do. Grievances without redress tend to fester, infecting future generations. The resulting hatred and mistrust constitute "an unstable mixture that, under certain conditions, is liable to explode and to rupture the half-forgetful present with the unfinished business of the past."[4]

At some point in the inter-Abrahamic dialogue, the question of forgiveness is bound to arise. One asks, given the overlapping of traditions and the possibility of building covenantal bridges between them—possibilities that have always been there waiting for the right conditions—how relations among the Abrahamic faiths can possibly have gone so wrong, with such destructive human consequences, over so many centuries. A provisional forgetting in order to get started, all that forgiveness sometimes means in today's cosmopolitan situations, may actually create conditions for facing the forgiveness question with less risk of waking up past mutual recriminations. But in many cases we seem *unable* to forget. In the north of Ireland, in Kosovo, in Israel-Palestine, a hundred other places, politicians, seeking their own interests, make sure we remember, sometimes over centuries. All too often the *remembering* of hurt, or of victory over one's enemies, is encouraged and arranged through organized public events. Forgiving is not intended to blot out such memories. It is intended to *redeem*, to transform, memory. Merely attempting to blot out memory lets *us* off too easily and the induced amnesia may not last. Where there is hurt, memory often *cannot* be blotted out. Instead, it festers. The sting has to be extracted. The West finds it easier to forget or put memories into desuetude,[5] while more traditional religious cultures hold memories of slight much longer. The more we inquire into deep traditions and the ways they have been interpreted, the more forgiveness we need. The more violence and death in our histories, the deeper mutual forgiveness we need.

Indeed we know that however reluctant we may be, especially as sophisticated cosmopolitans, to ask or to give forgiveness, our survival as a species may depend on our learning to do so. So forgiveness becomes more and more important. The judgment as to what is needed becomes more and more urgent. Putting things behind us may or may not be possible depending on the culture. Holding grudges may be taught by certain cultures. Most difficult is the feeling that we have in some way been betrayed. Can we build deep relationships, even among intellectuals, without some sort of forgiveness? Should we want to do this? Or does the attempt just open Pandora's Box? Can time heal all?

At some point we human beings must face the question not merely of putting the past behind us but of fleeing from what the past has done to us. That requires forgiving and being forgiven, not merely forgetting. As Hannah Arendt observes, the keeping of promises—the very heart of covenantal responsibility—is humanly impossible without forgiveness. "Without being forgiven," she writes, "released from the consequences of what we have done, our capacity to act would, as it were, be confined to one single deed from which we could never recover."[6] But, in the end, we cannot forgive ourselves, nor can we receive transforming forgiveness from other poor sinners. Here Arendt, the Jewish writer, reaches out toward the tradition as preserved by Christians for the model she needs. The notion of "forgiveness" in ordinary secular language, she claims, owes everything to its original use in religious language, going back, in fact, to the words and actions of Jesus. She writes:

The discoverer of the role of forgiveness in human affairs was Jesus of Nazareth. The fact that he made this discovery in a religious context and articulated it in religious language is no reason to take it any less seriously in a strictly secular sense.[7]

By evoking "Jesus of Nazareth," Arendt in no way takes on board what Christians have believed doctrinally about this religious teacher. She refers to the "Jesus" who belongs in different ways to all three Abrahamic traditions. And in doing so, she makes an important point. The forgiveness founded by Jesus is useful to us today "in a strictly secular sense." If inter-Abrahamic discourse at a certain point discloses that the question of forgiveness is unavoidable and also that conditions have come to exist in which that question can genuinely be raised without risk of reopening rather than closing old wounds, we must begin with the common "secular," cosmopolitan, meaning of the word, with "the role of forgiveness in human affairs," before, I think necessarily, beginning to draw on the different spiritual wisdoms of the three faiths underlying it.

I have argued, indeed, that the passage of originally religious ideas through secular contexts like Arendt's can teach us a great deal about the intrinsic power of those ideas, perhaps giving them more immediacy for us than studies of ancient texts, however necessary, can quickly deliver. We are not losers for beginning by looking at our commonly understood worldly derivatives of differing scriptural traditions in order then to reconnect our shared current experience with those sources, indeed to see much more clearly the pressing need for doing so. For the truth concerning Arendt's "secular" insights about the persistence of sin and the need for forgiveness "in human affairs" is that societies cannot go forward on their own for long without falling into self-destructive violence. She appreciates the depth of the common human problem of sin and forgiveness without offering us any reason to believe that human beings in their own power can solve it. This is a judgment we must hold in mind, because the difficulties in thinking out what forgiveness really means are far more formidable than we may think.

Let us begin by following Arendt's advice. What do current, cosmopolitan notions of forgiveness look like, how do they operate, in the contemporary world we share? There are what I will call "given" institutions and words in our vocabularies with which we try to approximate the idea of forgiveness in the public world. There are judges and prosecuting attorneys and school principals and rabbis, pastors and imams, all of whom are socially empowered to exercise the discretion not to hold a miscreant's misdeeds against him or her. There are words like acquittal, expungement from the record, pardon, or "second chance." Most of the time, when we speak "forgiveness," we mean something closer to one of these socially given, possible moves. Somehow the word "forgiveness" itself is avoided, unless in deliberately religious rhetoric, for it has a quality which exempts it from being merely a social given. "Forgiveness" implies a "gift" from beyond our institutions and customs, an observation that will become important later in this chapter.

The topic of forgiveness has also spawned a fairly extensive contemporary literature that, in various ways, seeks to underline our social need for something like forgiveness, not just something like pardon, in the times in which we live. Many writings point to the experience of the Truth and Reconciliation Commission headed by Archbishop Tutu in South Africa as evidence of the power of forgiveness, even if evidence for the social effectiveness of the TRC is more ambiguous than some would like to believe. Meanwhile, the idea of forgiveness, however understood, is being picked up by psychologists, sociologists, political philosophers, and historians today. They are beginning to think it "works." Yet, as followers of Durkheim are beginning to learn, if you take a "workable" idea out of the religious traditions in which it arose, you will likely lose much of its original context, fullness, and power. So it is in this case.

We are not talking about the secular opportunities for "conflict resolution" however useful. Valuable indeed, just to find a way of "getting along," and that is all that families often do. Deep resentments remain. In the South African case, it has been emphasized by commentators that the Truth and Reconciliation Commission (one of the many varying examples, in different

lands, of this mode of resolution of an atrocity-filled past) resulted from a
hard-fought legal compromise between prosecutions Nuremberg-style and
a blanket legal erasure of the record of past events. The TRC was a brilliant
construct out of available South African legal givens. But I maintain that the
particular compromise reached would not have been possible unless the con-
testants were functioning in a religiously shaped cultural space that offered
the notions of forgiveness and reconciliation also as gifts: possibilities for the
commitment of lives, spaces into which to move, spaces in which a secular
but profound legal alternative could be constructed. A space of forgiveness
in the religious sense helped politicians build a space of amnesty in the legal
sense. The fact that these are related ideas but not the same illustrates the
opening to something further which amnesty-space was able to afford.[8]

A similar transfer of "forgiveness" as a theme from religious to secular
contexts has been the subject of a number of other recent writings, from
which hermeneuts and theological ethicists can in turn learn.[9] The key
point again is that one does not have to buy into specific religious beliefs,
e.g., atonement in the Jewish or Christian sense, to be able to enter the
spaces maintained by believing practice in order to replicate its content in
nonbelieving terms. A signal example is the book *Forgiveness and Mercy* by
Jeffrie G. Murphy and Jean Hampton,[10] in which these meanings are self-
consciously transferred from theological settings into legal philosophy.
Comparable arguments beginning from a legal or diplomatic perspective
and moving to a theological one are made in Donald Shriver's *An Ethic for
Enemies*.[11] In this work Shriver studies the making of peace treaties and finds
there examples of forgiveness carried into effective action, despite the fact
that the word itself is rarely used.

In a class by itself is Geiko Müller-Fahrenholz's powerful little book *The
Art of Forgiveness*.[12] Here the question turns largely on the impact of the
Holocaust on the next generation of Germans and on the survivors and their
children. The opening lines speak volumes:

How dare I, as a German, talk about forgiveness? From a Christian
scriptural point of view, forgiveness combines remission of the guilt of
the perpetrators, and healing the scars of the victims. And forgiveness
likewise concerns those whose relations to atrocity are only indirect, as
in the case of the present generation of Germans. Without forgiveness
they cannot wholly escape their nation's past. Yet forgiveness of the
past is no substitute for justice-seeking today. The two are inseparably
linked. But, for our purposes, the key sentence of this book reads,
"Those who want to go forward together need to walk through their
histories together."[13]

The depth of this account teaches us that the need is not merely to offer conflict-resolution advice of possible religious origin to religious cosmopolitans, but rather to help them be moved by, and in turn to move, their ancient traditions of faith. At this level things become much more difficult, not merely because hatreds die hard but because the formerly religious ideas of forgiveness seemingly available to us seem in principle inadequate to the need for resolving deep-seated religious enmities that seem to persist as long as the religious communities in question do. But if, finding modern notions too shallow, we search the Abrahamic scriptures for more profound insight, we find that our ancient forgiveness traditions are almost entirely focused on repentance of personal wrongdoing by individuals and remission by authorities of the penalties and exclusions that accompany whatever it is that these perpetrators have done. Asked to bring ancient resources to this discussion, neither Jews[14] nor Christians[15] nor Muslims[16] are likely to find much that applies to the sins of whole religious communities against one another. These ancient codes operate within communities deemed fully capable of value judgments concerning personal conduct, virtually without outside reference.

But what happens when forgiveness is needed for whole religious cultures, for acts of violence against others, acts considered at the time to have been religious duties for those who carried them out? At the world level, there are few religious authorities in a position sufficiently representative to offer any such thing. The only authority who comes close is the Pope. One must give John Paul II credit for having tried hard to ask Jews, Muslims and others for forgiveness for atrocities done, not by the Roman Catholic Church as such but by its "sons and daughters," a significant limitation. I am not aware that there have been more than symbolic responses in the sense of receiving the Pope in synagogues and mosques, significant moves in themselves to be sure. But is there not a presumption in "taking responsibility" for bestowing forgiveness on others for what we regard as their sins, especially when we are not in the position of having been victims who bore in our own bodies the consequences? How magnanimous of us to place others in a position that they may well not have desired to be in at all. Better to ask forgiveness for our own sins.

But is the central issue to grasp what is the case when forgiveness is not the task of religious authorities at all, but the prerogative solely of the victims of religious authority? Indeed, only this last case, forgiveness of perpetrators by their victims, may begin to get to the heart of the matter. Toward the end of his life, the French philosopher Jacques Derrida took up some of these underlying issues in ways that may help us. Derrida both sought to give forgiveness a central role in his thought and indicated its problematic character so long as it remains a purely secular institutional construct. This great deconstructionist writer and professed atheist, a Jew by birth, brought up in a Muslim country, passionately interested in St. Augustine, toward the end of his life was mining the Hebrew and Christian Scriptures, as well as the Talmud, for sources of philosophical inspiration. John Caputo writes of Derrida that, still professing atheism, he "follows with fascination the movements of what theology calls God, observing how theology speaks, and how it finds it necessary not to speak, under the solicitation of the wholly other."[17] This work, combined with many other considerations, led Derrida to begin to exempt certain ideas from his life-consuming program of deconstructing metaphysical concepts. The first three exempt ideas seem to have been "justice," "forgiveness," and "gift."

At a philosophical colloquy in 1999,[18] I asked Derrida what one would call an idea thus exempted from deconstruction. Would one call it a "transcendental" idea, that is, a notion presiding over the conditions of possibility of some "space of reasons" (like mathematics, for example), whose existence in the world is self-evident, but whose grounds of coherence need to be accounted for? Derrida grinned and replied with a poke to my stomach, "*You* could call it that!" I, the theologian, was granted a permission that the philosopher denied himself on principle! Forgiveness for me is a transcendental idea presiding, in the Kantian sense, over a space of mutual responsibility and shared responsibility to promise. The notion of "forgiveness," like the other two "exempt" notions, holds open reasoning spaces in which people may act. Hence it is a transcendental idea that helps give coherence to what we mean by covenantal community.

But the worldly reality to which this coherent lived space of reasoning refers is elusive indeed. At the meeting just described, Derrida dwelt for nearly two hours and more on this theme, arguing that forgiveness reaches its true dimension only in the face of the unforgivable, e.g., the Holocaust, that only the victim can truly forgive and the victim is usually dead,[19] that hence forgiveness is in human terms "impossible." Here is the way Derrida put it:

> This may be one of the reason, certainly not the only one, why forgiveness is often asked of God. Of God not because he alone would be capable of forgiveness, of a power-to-forgive otherwise inaccessible to man, but because, in the absence of the singularity of a victim who is sometimes no longer there to receive the request or to grant forgiveness, or in the absence of the criminal or the sinner, God is the only name, the name of an absolute and namable singularity as such. Of the absolute substitute. Of the absolute witness, the absolute *superstes*, the absolute surviving witness.[20]

He goes on:

Thus forgiveness, if it is possible, if there is such a thing, is not possible, it does not exist as possible, it only exists by exempting itself from the law of the possible, by impossibilizing itself, so to speak, and in the infinite endurance of the im-possible as impossible; and this is what it would have in common with the gift; but besides the fact that this enjoins us to try to think the possible and the impossible otherwise, the very history of what one calls the possible and "power" in our culture and in culture as philosophy or as knowledge, we must ask ourselves, breaking the symmetry or the analogy between gift and forgiveness, if the urgency of an im-possible forgiveness is not first what the enduring and non-conscious experience of the im-possible gives to be forgiven, as if forgiveness, far from being a modification or a secondary complication or a complication that arises out of the gift, were in truth its first and final truth.[21]

But without forgiveness, human society cannot continue. What, then, can these words possibly mean? "God . . . is the name of an absolute and unnamed singularity as such." Forgiveness of the unforgivable is impossible, yet urgent. It is a gift in that gift's first and final use. A gift of responsibility through which forgiveness can somehow be communicated in human terms? Derrida does not say exactly this, but he suggests it. Does it follow then that only God can forgive the betrayal or refusal of this gift of the possibility of forgiveness? And, if so, how do we enter into relationships with this "God"? Do we do so through relationships to human communities that use the language of "God"? No, we see ourselves commanded to be free in the exercise of transcendental responsibility—responsibility beyond job description, beyond routine—for what happens on earth.

Derrida, who here so clearly "follows the movements of the believing soul" and if anything makes them more profound, remained to his death a self-stated unbeliever. Originally scriptural notions of forgiveness have, in this philosopher's thought, passed through an intensely secular experience, that is, an experience detached from explicitly articulated belief in God. But far from being weakened, the insight has been ramified in such a way as to place new demands on today's scripture interpreters. The result, if faithfully pursued and realized, could be a deepened religious understanding of forgiveness that Christian, Jewish, and Muslim communities can proceed to assimilate, and then enact in various forms of public space, thereby offering moral hospitality to nonbelievers for the deepening and further-ranging of an articulated possibility, or space of reasons in which to move, already available in the world through its expressions in the Abrahamic traditions.

But I want to say more. These Abrahamic traditions, so interpreted, grant access to the terms and conditions of a still larger covenantal community of all humankind. Not forgetting a single act, not forgetting a single victim, but vowing to receive the gift of a new covenantal reality: to membership in which we are admitted by the God we all worship, acting together to draw as many of our people in through our traditions newly interpreted. Not just an analysis of forgiveness, but an analysis of the deeper meaning to which Abrahamic dialogues can come: themselves to represent a new interpretation, a new constructive interpretation of what it can mean today to be children of earth's covenantally blessed families. To be drawn into such a relationship is forgiveness.

What we see in examining the ancient materials is that forgiveness begins by being an element in the legal expressions of the nature of membership in good standing of some particular religious community. In Torah and its intricate Talmudic interpretations, in Sharia and its applications, even in the Christian Sermon on the Mount understood as new Torah, where the disciples are given the power of "binding and loosing." In every case forgiveness is restoration to the community, and to the responsibilities of membership in it. There is little or no guidance in any of the scriptures and their traditions of interpretation for forgiving whole religious communities for their attitudes and actions toward other such communities. The question does not arise. But now it does.

Forgiveness as absolution of one whole community by another can be imagined, but it does not work across the board today in practical terms, for reasons given. Forgiveness at the level we must deal with now is restoration to a new covenantal community representing in principle all of humankind, a community of which inter-Abrahamic relations are a sign, and perhaps a forecast. Sins by Christians against Jews or Muslims are thus redefined as sins against humanity. And who can forgive sins against humanity but humanity itself somehow speaking with one voice? And, although yet divided, we are given a gift of responsibility not to Torah or Sharia but to human fulfillment as represented in Torah, Sermon on the Mount, and Sharia. And, for this purpose, the ancient covenantal rules, however expressed, will need to be reinterpreted. These law codes now cease to be the codes of religious tribes in isolation. The tribes now "stand in for" and represent something larger in granting forgiveness as restoration. Not forgetting any moment of the past, the Abrahamic communities respond to the gift by gifting one another with responsibility to a larger promise and insisting to one another that they fulfill that responsibility. Religious duty now becomes inclusive, and it is the task of each religious community to use its laws and structures to support that larger understanding of responsibility. Much in each of the traditions anticipates this universal human reading of religious duty. This becomes the hermeneutical principle for reading the laws of particular faiths as regional introductions to laws of restoration to responsibility in the life of the human whole. In this sense religious laws become vehicles of gift and vehicles of restoration of those who have spurned such gifts.

All this means more than merely "forgetting" a violent past. More than silencing the drums of those whose interest lies in keeping old conflicts alive. It means taking up the institutions and ideas of the past, some of which have been expressed violently against others, and giving them something greater to be ideas and institutions of. Imagining matters in this way will mean that some formerly religious duties will fall into disuse, and others will be lifted up. Hospitality to the stranger will trump the execution of prisoners of war. Social righteousness will trump ritual rules. We thus arrive at a principle of hermeneutical selectivity for the further interpretation of our existing laws of sin and forgiveness. It will no longer be a matter of saving our own particular communities from ritual pollution and shame, but saving the human race from real, actual pollution and shame.

The gift of responsibility to the promise here becomes the gift of a new, comprehensive sense of the community in question, the comprehensive human patchwork of many differences to which the promise has been given. Giving and receiving forgiveness is granting and receiving restoration to that community of promise. The space of forgiveness in this case is the new community itself. The very existence of this community of promise, immanent in and ahead of the existing Jewish, Christian, Muslim, and other communities, is the means by which God's gift of forgiveness for the resumption of each one's responsibility to promise is given. And it is a justification for calling this new community of humankind "covenantal" in character.

Fostering Conditions of Trust

If we are to live and work together in a community deserving to be called "covenantal," we need not only to forgive and be forgiven, but also to trust and be trusted. Forgiveness and trust are obviously not the same. We may, through giving and receiving forgiveness, have freed ourselves from the weight of the past, but still not be quite ready to trust more than superficially those across the table from us. They remain strange, members of a different tribe. We have not yet penetrated the mysteries that attend their differences from us.

Yet our discourses cannot go on unless there is reason for each participant to trust in the probity of words and actions representing the Other. We need confidence that what is said is to be believed, that it is free of any sort of obfuscation or dissimulation. Abrahamic dialogue makes no sense, and there is no use in asking what it means that it is going on, unless the dialogue is of such a character to elicit on all sides this sort of confidence in one anothers' trustworthiness. This fact underlines the ethical character of parallel and interactive hermeneutics. It restates what I mean by saying that in such dialogue we are responsible to one another for our ways of saying what we hold to be true, and responsible to those around us for the consequences of our interpretations of tradition. All this calls us to address the question of "conditions of trust."

But parallel and interactive hermeneutical work typically begins, and even makes considerable progress, without much conscious attention to such conditions. Perhaps, where trust is thus unreflective but yet acted out, the results are reassuring. But perhaps they are less so as time passes. We begin to wonder: Do these others really share our basic assumptions about sacred texts? Can we be sure that the words they use mean the same things to them as they do to us? Trust is indispensable to our dialogue, but yet there is the possibility that, as our conversation goes on, our condition of mutual trust may diminish, or even be undermined, by what we hear, and by how we are heard.

It turns out that most inter-Abrahamic discourse among religious cosmopolitans tends to begin and continue for some time on the basis of trust among relative strangers as it is understood in the surrounding culture. This pragmatic sort of confidence in the Other suffices for many routine relationships. Most people can be trusted to perform the basic responsibilities of their occupations, selling us groceries and airline tickets, filling our gas tanks and giving us traffic tickets. They can also be trusted with complex responsibilities, exercising contextual judgments of all kinds for our benefit. We are not yet basing the trust we feel toward one another on the character of the Abrahamic community we are trying to form. We do trust one another at many levels from the start,[22] but our trust is not yet covenantally grounded. For that, we must take leave of our cosmopolitanism and penetrate to root meanings of the word that its modern usages do not bear.

It does not take much reflection to realize that in Western societies levels of trust just below the surface remain stubbornly tribal. We trust members of our families and our own ethic groups. There are generational trust networks. Teenagers and parents have their respective communities in which they can speak freely. There is honor among thieves. It is striking how much mistrust exists in Western societies beyond intratribal and/or simple routine relationships. Politicians are mistrusted by people, corporations by customers, and so forth. We come to the point of realizing that we understand little of what we are doing when we trust. Are we making judgments about others' personal character on the basis of scanty evidence? Or are we relying on what sociologists call "system confidence," meaning that our institutions are designed to minimize cheating through regular audits and the use of surveillance cameras and other sorts of social oversight technology.

So we are conducting inter-Abrahamic discourses that require mutual trust while resting our trust not on theological but on very fragile public foundations. We may well ask whether, instead of depending on these shaky foundations, Abrahamic dialogues might find their own grounds for mutual trust and also thereby contribute something extremely important to the world around us. Sociologists echo the obvious: that the factor of trust in human relationships underlies the very possibility of any sort of cohesive society, whether religious or civil. But evidence for an atrophy of trust in Western cultures, if not in others as well, is already apparent in the sorts of instances just mentioned. An ample sociological literature confirms our unscientific judgments, not to speak of numerous studies of this subject in political and economic theory. Among more recent writers, both Robert Putnam[23] and Francis Fukuyama,[24] in their different ways, find trust to be an indispensable ingredient in the "social capital" needed to make contemporary societies work. Putnam finds a strong factor of trust (especially in the political realm) in the stable, relatively law-abiding communities of northern, as opposed to southern, Italy. Fukuyama studies the positive economic consequences of trust as social solidarity, or practice of the "art of association," in certain countries such as Germany and Japan, as opposed to the United States with its looser social structures. Add to these two penetrating studies by Adam Seligman,[25] the first identifying trust as the key ingredient within a broader treatment of civil society and the second focusing entirely on "the problem of trust" as such.

The works mentioned supply rich empirical data and illuminating conceptual analysis. But they offer little of a constructive nature. Seligman, in particular, after two volumes of philosophical effort to give trust a rational, secular basis, seems close to despair. He believes that without trust we lose "the very terms of rationality," a catastrophe that could land us in a "more brutal and Hobbesian" world.[26]

The notion of "trust," as we have already seen, is notoriously hard to define. What trust "is" depends on the conditions, shared assumptions, and institutions—in short the social "givens"—that make it possible. These vary enormously from time to time and from place to place: infant and responsive parent; investor and responsible accountant; pacts of all kinds that are expected to be kept. Indeed, "trust" becomes tangible only in actions. An act of trust makes sense only if someone else—over whom I have no control—can be counted on to respond as I expect.

My reasons for entertaining such an expectation may be of various kinds: past experience, knowledge of the person concerned, traditions of the organization of which we both serve, cultural assumptions about the nature of human integrity, or even calculation of how the other person will see his or her interest in the matter concerned. Whatever my reasoning, my action is either an instance of trusting behavior, or it is not

All this indicates why I speak of "conditions (circumstances, narratives, dispositions) of trust" rather than "trust" alone. In our world, such conditions may or may not exist. But at least we are able to talk about what they are, or could be, in any given case. Analysis of "conditions" takes our study beyond dictionary definitions of a word into the historical and social circumstances of the sorts of mutually expectant actions I have described.

Characteristic early modern notions of the conditions of trust tie them closely to social contract doctrines. Several of these, in turn, drew at one time on (mostly Christian) versions of the covenant tradition. Readers will recognize some of the following as focusing on the implications for trusting relationships of material already presented in chapter 3. In the work of John Locke, for example, the social bond is moored in a providential (remarkably Calvinistic) narrative of each individual's accountability lived out under God's watchful benevolence. In Locke's view, the worldly reasoning that constitutes society arises from a "law of nature" (strikingly different from Rousseau's later vision of the "noble savage") in which individual persons—pictured as already property-holders—stand responsibly before God and voluntarily take leave of their "natural" state to form a commonwealth reflecting the fundamental principles of a primordially God-given order or framework. If persons were to be trusted, Locke thought, it was because all—the trusters and the trusted alike—were assumed to stand accountably, that is, responsibly, in such relationships. Rights, privileges, freedom, equality, a complex set of social "givens," all follow. Human affairs and the reason that governs them are thus validated in implicitly covenantal terms.

But by the late eighteenth century, Scottish Enlightenment thinkers such as Adam Ferguson and Adam Smith began to avoid references to the Deity in their theories of society, and to couch these theories increasingly in economic terms. The individual was thought to be constituted in his or her individuality through the very act of exchange with others. Yet the world of exchange still functions within relations of "moral affections" and "natural sympathy." Interpersonal bonds surround and mitigate the raw operations of rational self-interest. The world is still seen in a general way as ruled by divine providence, but such factors less and less enter into social explanations.

But soon we begin to see an outright disengagement of this trusting moral sense from any direct theological linkage.[27] The thinker who undermined the former fragile syntheses was David Hume. Hume separated interest-based exchange relations from grounding in any prior type of relationship, theological or otherwise. He argued, in effect, that society-engendering agreements to work together are simply based on the desire for efficient resource use. Here, as I have already argued, are the foundations for a new social world of rationally adjudicated, jostling individual interests.

We have today, in effect, generalized Hume's notion into a conception of individuals as morally autonomous actors whose activities, whatever they may be, alone constitute the marketplace, the political realm, and a multitude of accompanying institutions. The problem of social coherence then becomes one of grasping the conditions of trust among such agents. We may have confidence that institutions simply based on adventitious networks of human activities work tolerably well. But, under such conditions, trust can be nothing more than confidence in the predictability of one anothers' "reciprocal behavior," because the economic or political rationality of such behavior is in principle transparent.

But such a conception of society, and of our reasons to be confident in its workings, suffices only up to a point. As modernity advances, institutions themselves begin to become differentiated and insecure. Social roles come to be more fluid. As individuals come to play multiple roles in different aspects of their lives, an element of risk begins to enter the picture. At a certain point, one cannot count on mere institutional expectations in taking actions that anticipate predictable responses. Increasingly, we mean by the word "trust" an inner disposition to risk initiatives that confidence in institutions as such cannot justify: the honesty of a business partner, the decency of a contractor. Trust, as opposed to mere institutional confidence, begins to be focused on a notion of the intrinsic integrity—the trustworthiness—of the enlightened and principled individual.[28] Social institutions increasingly depend on people being willing to take such risks: risks that cannot themselves be institutionalized. Actions that are risky because they rest on some sort of transinstitutional, transcultural confidence in the Other's response can be seen as involving what we have called "transcendental responsibility."

Inevitably, and especially as postmodernity dawns with its deconstruction of reliable frameworks of social meaning, this demand for transcendental confidence in the Other[29] often turns out to ask too much of us. We find diminishing agreement concerning the nature and content of the moral personhood on which institutions depend. The neighbor cannot he comprehended today within any set of putatively universal social concepts. The neighbor is now genuinely Other: unfathomable in his or her alien freedom. We may gradually cease to produce the kind of individuals who trust and are trustworthy because of who they are, and begin to produce persons having largely group-based identities with very little sense of individuality, persons with no disposition to trust individuals of other groups at all, and indeed see, not the personal risk of trusting in dealing with others, but rather the danger these others pose because they are members of another group not to be trusted at all. Society today is becoming a sphere of systemic ethnic or religious distrust of others. These others are seen to pose potential dangers just because their inner lives and motives are anything but transparent.

So we proceed to limit the dangers posed by such opaque otherness by subjecting public behavior to a plethora of rules and regulations in many arenas of life: for the stock market, for academic behavior, and even for relationships between the sexes. Regulation enhances what sociologists call "system confidence." But this is not the same thing as trust. It is, rather, confidence based on rules and audits and surveillance and well-publicized investigations of alleged wrongdoing. As people inevitably look for ways to get around the rules and controls, we are burdened with endless questions of interpretation. What, exactly, constitutes securities fraud, plagiarism, or "date rape"? It may, and often does, take thousands of pages of legislation to answer such questions.

Rational choice theory then claims to come to the rescue. It develops in directions designed to help economic and political players turn the rules to their advantage, assuming that others can be "trusted" to be doing the same. Human interactions thus come in our time to be understood in terms of game theory. Social thinking becomes the calculus of how a relentless pursuit of private interests, even in highly regulated environments, will lead ourselves and our competitors to behave.

Such a situation is ultimately unstable because it leads either to tyranny by those who win the power game or to an anarchy of competing interests.[30] Either way, genuine human potential in the form of social capital is substantially diminished. There is no "invisible hand" at work here. Our present economic nexus will not even be sustainable unless there are new associational relationships capable of moderating purely economic forces. In the end, an absence of trust, however defined, between persons, institutions, and social groups means that instead of building relationships based on mutual confidence, we constantly have to use our wits to defend ourselves against competitors who will take advantage of us if they can. This absorbs attention and energy to the point that society cannot be openly democratic and cannot proceed to build truly participatory institutions.

This is the point that we have reached in the West today, as chapter 3 seeks to show. We have little trust in fellow human beings, and often even less in democratic institutions. The question, then, as before, is whether the ancient traditions and narratives of trust in the three traditions can be invoked to illumine and generate in fact the conditions of trust today's dialogue communities need for their authenticity. Dialogue on this subject will, as before, lead the participants to bring forth their wares. What scriptural and traditional visions of trust in one anothers' truthfulness and responsibility might the different Abrahamic faiths bring to the table? That will depend on the particular people present and the particular human situation involved. So, as for "forgiveness," so also for "trust," it is not appropriate (or even possible) to offer the Jewish contribution, or the Christian or the Islamic contribution. Rather, with notes on likely sources, we sketch the sorts of elements of tradition Jews,[31] Christians,[32] and Muslims[33] might contribute to the conversation, knowing that their roles in any actual discourse will be different.

The conditions of trust needed are not merely those that support trusting relations between particular human beings. The conditions needed are such as make possible trust among whole faith communities, whole traditions of life. In examining the ancient texts, we find, as in the case of forgiveness, much that refers to trusting and trustworthiness among individuals and even among tribes or theological factions. But the ancient writers do not have trust among different distinctive religious cultures in view. One reads of diplomatic arrangements involving trust in keeping agreements between Jewish and Gentile Christians (Acts 15:6–21, the "Council of Jerusalem") and of similar pacts from time to time between Shi'ites and Sunnis. Arrangements for civil life together among the three faiths as such are also known to history, as in medieval Andalusia and during the Ottoman Empire. But the latter are not so much based on conceptions of mutual trust as such but rather on enlightened legislation written and enforced by the hegemonic power on the scene. In both the cases mentioned, that power was Islamic. One may compare today arrangements among Hindu and Muslim religious cultures in India before 1947 under the British Empire, and even internal arrangements for Christians, Muslims, and different varieties of Jews maintained by the present State of Israel. We thus have historic examples of interfaith peacekeeping sponsored by authorities of each of the Abrahamic faiths. There is little or nothing in any of these instances that speaks to the question of symmetrical trusting relationships among entire, disparate religious cultures: Judaism, Christianity, and Islam entered upon with free mutual intentionality.

Until today, the need for such a relationship had not arisen. But such a need has emerged today, precisely at a moment when civic understandings of trust have so deteriorated that no power, not even that of the "Christian" West, can be the wise hegemon: no one can provide more than a temporary model or framework for such a thing. Interfaith groups can operate with secular understandings of trust such as they are (that is, they can incorporate, have constitutions and bylaws, seek charitable tax exemptions, and the like), but ties more indigenous to faith itself are needed. Hence the question of interfaith trust remains for the religious traditions themselves to work out in unprecedented conditions. The idea and the reality need to grow organically out of the experiences of small groups, in which the notion of covenant receives, once again, a wholly new expression for a new time. One may find inspiration in the ancient texts so long as one realizes that they do not address the modern question. But one cannot construct a modern intercovenantal framework for trust by quoting scriptural or traditional materials from here and there, fitting them together as in a diplomatic jigsaw puzzle. A contemporary realization of covenantal trust will rest, rather, on mutual recognition that each faith is the channel of a gift of responsibility to a promise to humankind as a whole. Trusting my Muslim or Jewish friend is trusting the promise to humankind as it is represented in each of them.

We need some new sort of covenantal community, learning from ancient models but now pointing to an inclusivity in which humanity itself is the "in-group," one in which the "tribe" is the human race itself. It follows that the answer I give to the question of conditions for trust is analogous to the answer given to the question of forgiveness. The answer lies in the character of the dialogue group itself: whether it can come to be an anticipation, or a representation, of the human race itself as community of the Promise. We can trust one another in such a society because each member is understood to have the same gift of responsibility to the promise of blessing for all.

Another way to say this joins hands with our previous argument. We trust one another because we understand ourselves to be entrusted with responsibility to the promise of blessing. We are trustworthy not because of ascertainable character traits, but because we have *been* entrusted with a covenantal vocation. This sense of *being* entrusted with a gift of responsibility is of the essence of the community that we are trying to define.

Yet this inner sense of gift does not mean that the whole secular argument about conditions of trust can be abandoned, as if it belonged only to an unredeemed world. On the contrary, trust of the practical kind that holds civil society together is what makes it possible for communities of inter-Abrahamic discourse to begin and be sustained in the first place. We depend on peaceful civil institutions as givens that allow such conversations to happen. Such givens are not in place everywhere on earth. Where they are present, they need to be honored and protected. And the theological sense of being entrusted with something more than mere civic responsibility—a conviction arising within the dialogue itself—in turn by its social presence can help deepen those existing, or "given," civil relationships. The presence in

the civil order of communities recognizing a gift of transcendental responsibility for forgiving and trusting beyond routine can help spread the power of
the promise, by functioning for now as carriers of the stablilizing power of a
deeper trustworthiness (or "promise-keeping" as Hannah Arendt would put
it), as we wait for the promise to be fulfilled.

But is this a plausible vocational description for any imaginable grouping
of human beings of different faiths, whose composition can only be representative of some of the nearby human "tribes," but hardly of the whole? Perhaps
only the actual whole of humanity can be, as it were, a model or instantiation
of itself. The lived reality is then the symbol and the lived symbol is the reality. Particular dialogue communities may then be understood to have some
directional or pointing capacities. They may represent the human whole by
having a certain quality of life together rather than being literally representative of humanity with all its immense variety. Perhaps a global network of
such communities, each embodying trust for its own cultural context, while
transforming it, can come closer to achieving the needed representation.

Acting in Solidarity

When Abrahamic faith communities set out to explore one another's
traditions, they learn not only to give and receive forgiveness and maintain
conditions of mutual trust. They also prepare the way for acting together in
both communal and public expressions of solidarity. This is to say that they
may come to the point of taking common positions on social issues or of
defending each other against prejudice or political oppression. Or they may
act in solidarity with social movements with whose values and objectives
they agree.

I borrow the heretofore largely social-political term "solidarity" to refer
to this stage of interfaith development. This choice of words may or may not
prove to be a happy one. It could prove problematic if it fails adequately to
connect with the kinds of mutual theological confidence in the presence of
continuing difference on which my argument has been based. While the terms
"forgiveness" and "trust" both go back to recognizable scriptural expressions
and narratives (even though the scriptural materials for the most part do not
have in view the modern-world questions being addressed), "solidarity" is a
word whose appropriateness in modern parallel-interactive interpretations
of Abrahamic traditions has yet to be established. The term seems first to
appear in European languages in the late eighteenth century, and there bears
mainly other-than-theological meanings. Nowhere, to my knowledge, does
it appear in any vernacular translation of Hebrew, Christian, or Islamic scripture. To use this secular word to describe a form of interfaith relationship

otherwise grounded in such profoundly scriptural ideas as forgiveness and trust is a move needing thoughtful defense.

Yet unquestionably some such word is needed to describe relationships that already exist. Inter-Abrahamic ties have in many places already reached a point at which the three faiths begin to share not only acts of forgiveness and conditions of trust but also substantial worldly commitments. Jewish, Christian, and Muslim congregations can self-consciously come to stand for the same civic virtues. They can form coalitions for various practical purposes. They can come to be committed to support one another in adversity. If one faith comes under public opprobrium or attack (say because its adherents are, or were, citizens of a nation thought to have terrorist intentions, or to be illegally occupying another nation), congregations of the other two faiths can come to that community's aid. If a common civic project is in view, the three faiths can join in it together. Peter Ochs catches some of these possibilities with calls for an Abrahamic "coalition," meaning a practical collaboration of the three faiths for largely public purposes. I think that "solidarity" is a richer expression, the carrier of deeper implications, and by that token also the carrier of more interesting conceptual challenges to make the needed theological connections.

Certainly examples of solidaristic behavior are very numerous among myriad instances of inter-Abrahamic relationships in today's world, instances of which have been offered in chapter 1. Indeed, "solidarity" might well have been offered as the first of our three protocovenantal relationships rather than as the third. Mutual commitments to common goals may well give rise to questions of forgiveness and trust, rather than the other way around. It is significant, in any case, that a modern expression, rather than a scriptural one, seems needed to describe a kind of relationship that eventually engages, or builds upon, interfaith ties that rest at the same time on shared interpretation of ancient texts.

The Oxford English Dictionary defines "solidarity" as "the fact or quality, on the part of communities, etc., of being perfectly united or at one in some respect, especially in interests, sympathies, or aspirations."[34] This word seems to have come into the English language in the early nineteenth century from the late-eighteenth-century French term *solidarité*, whose history, as we will see below, has left its mark on contemporary usages.

There is, of course, a precedent for the French term in classical Latin: the term *solidum* (whose literal meaning is "the full amount"). I am in a state of *solidum* with a person if I agree to guarantee his or her repayment of a loan. I bind my own integrity to that of that other person. I stand alongside that other person in such a way as to protect him or her from the debt collectors should he or she default. I promise to come if necessary to that person's assistance, and that person now has an obligation to me to do everything possible to see that this necessity does not arise. These assumptions create a very concrete relationship between us.[35] Given this pedigree, the noun "solidarity" may easily be extended to refer to such a state of affairs obtained among groups or communities. We stand alongside one another in a manner that involves our own integrity and an expectation of integrity from our comrades, over against some sort of threat or challenge, some alien, potentially totalizing, power.

The French usages that underlie, and continue after, the adoption of the term into English *may* go back to the revolutionaries of the late 1780s.[36] But certainly the term is in use among those involved in the uprisings of 1848 and of the Paris Commune of 1870–71. Such usages in every case express a solidarity of resistance to entrenched power. It quickly spreads to European anarchists or radical socialists of all kinds whose objectives were to bring down established orders in the name of new social principles, often defined only as other than the prevailing ones.[37] Solidarity in this sense referred to the binding together of militant groups with common identities and common causes.[38]

But by the late nineteenth century in France, solidarity has also come to refer to a decidedly *un*revolutionary political theory of society. It has become a form of social contract doctrine in which people recognize their personal and collective dependence on one another in a network of taken-for-granted social support. Here solidarity is a social "given," not subject to question, not given to crusades. Common social identity now becomes the primary value, as well as being a collective form of wealth (one form of what we today would call "social capital") that is in everyone's interest to uphold and preserve.

Society, with its fabric of solidarity, is considered in effect to have been always there, yet always subject to negotiation through which it gradually evolves. Societies organized on this principle provide what amounts to a collectively funded insurance (like the Latin *solidum*) against the consequences that may befall individuals. There is a known level of risk that this will happen, and solidaristic societies take that into account. In this form of solidaristic doctrine, society is not founded on the basis of some principle external to it—say "natural law." Society is just there, a "given," the context into which one is born. It therefore legitimates itself. It is in each person's interest to live by it and uphold it.

In the twentieth and twenty-first centuries, as communications improve and societies become more mobile, we see a somewhat new phenomenon. A sense of community against a common adversary or around a common cause can be combined with a wide range of views on other points. Coalitions develop among otherwise highly diverse groups that come together where their interests or aspirations intersect. A common enemy can invoke the sense of solidarity among those who share *that* position whatever other analyses-of-situation and purposes these persons and groups may entertain. Solidarity in the face of a common enemy can also transcend sharp differences of opinion as regards ideology and tactics. The parade instance is, of course, the "Solidarity" movement in Poland that brought together quite diverse popular and ecclesiastical forces to bring down a Communist government and make Lech Walesa president of the Republic.

But despite the powerful Polish example, we also see situations today in which little sense of solidarity exists at all, where by rights there ought to be at least some such awareness. This is often because the connections between different objectives and causes are ignored in favor of "single issue" politics. People work on environmental matters through the question of air pollution but not of water rights. Debate concerning the issue of torture becomes disconnected from the wider question of state-sponsored violence. Solidarity, if the word is to be used at all, becomes focused on smaller and smaller groups of the very like-minded. And even when larger coalitions are formed, they are generally based on evanescent and short-lived agreements. The experience of participation is often more strategic, and even calculating, than it is solidary. There may be no more than a temporary realization of commonality among persons of diverse identities, momentarily bound together by their similar reactions to striking public events or causes. Experience of this sort often has little to do with commonly held philosophical doctrines.[39]

It is notable in our day, especially in the West, that groups of persons who, objectively seen, do have common interests and common adversaries, let us say in the economic realm, often cannot grasp that commonality because the ideology of individual economic calculation and striving blocks the awareness of it. Such strivers feel no sense of solidarity with others in the same boat when by all rights they should. If I may be shamelessly partisan for a moment, it seems clear that southern "poor whites" in America who vote Republican do so against their own economic and political best interests: interests that successful political propaganda and their own misperceptions have prevented them from seeing.

The checkered history of this word may make it seem even less available for describing a covenantal virtue than we first thought. But some of the usages described evoke scriptural anticipations of the interfaith ties growing today: situations in which no equivalent of the word "solidarity" appears but in which the fundamental idea is assuredly present.

Abrahamic communities, because they need the word (or one like it) to describe a very common form of relationship between them have resources that can permit them to give this word a distinctly scriptural usage. Solidarity may be ready to gather together religious meanings that make of it a covenantal virtue that only becomes salient for us with the events of our time.

Let us mention some of the resources that Jews, Christians, and Muslims might bring forward to support the idea of mutual solidarity that they are already acting out. I stress that the following sketches serve illustrative purposes only. What materials members of the three faiths might actually call upon in such a conversation would in every case depend on the circumstances and the persons concerned.

No single Hebrew word invites an English translation as "solidarity," yet many scriptural narratives express the idea. The Adam and Eve narratives (Gen 2:4b–24), as well as the Noachian covenant account (Gen 7–9), both indicate a presumption of solidarity among all human beings. We are told that man and woman become "one flesh" (Gen 2:24). We hear the words "let all flesh bless his holy name" (Ps 145:21), or "all flesh shall see the salvation of our God" (Luke 3:6), or "I will pour out my spirit on all flesh" (Joel 2:28; see Acts 2:17–21).

Or consider the "covenant renewal" ceremony in Joshua 24. The message in this and related passages is that the tribes of Israel are being drawn from relative isolation into an amphictyonic solidarity (i.e., an intertribal league) around the worship of YHWH, a solidarity over against the idolatrous worship of the Canaanites and the political and metaphysical totalizations of the ancient Near Eastern empires and their gods. Of course, the word "solidarity" itself is not present in the text. It is rather a term we choose to use to grasp and communicate a social reality that the different Abrahamic scriptures describe.

An issue of solidarity arises in the narrative of Joseph and his brothers, just as does the issue of forgiveness. On the one hand, the brothers display little solidarity with their brother Joseph, leaving him to be captured by the Egyptians. On the other hand, even after years as a high official in Pharaoh's courts, Joseph recognizes by several acts his solidarity with them. The question of common Israelite identity among the "tribes" represented by these brothers arises again and again, to be expressed and then betrayed by the kings that emerge, turning solidarity in common covenantal identity into mere political allegiance to the sovereign (Saul, David, Solomon, and their successors) on the part of petty tribal chieftains and their people. The allegiance soon fractures into northern and southern Hebrew kingdoms.

Today the ancient tribes no longer effectively exist, a development aided by the disappearance of the ten "lost" tribes. But they are effectively replaced by different manifestations of "Jewish" identity (*Ioudaioi* in the Greek after the tribe of Judah). One finds today not only Orthodox, Conservative, and

Reform Judaism, but also Sephardic and Ashkenazic Judaism, "secular" and "religious" Judaism, Israeli and diaspora Judaism, and so forth, with a complex array of many smaller groupings. The actual word "solidarity" comes into Jewish parlance today as a way of focusing the question whether Jews the world over experience a sense of identity with or obligation toward one another across such differences. Raising the possibility of "solidarity" among Abrahamic faiths today may seem an irony in face of the open question whether "solidarity" is the right word for current inter-Jewish, inter-Christian, or inter-Islamic relationships. Our approach to the latter question of solidarity could have an impact on our approach to the former.

Christians addressing the summons to solidarity-in-situation with the Other will draw on resources shared with Jews and on resources uniquely their own. Again, solidarity within one's own community of faith and solidarity with Abrahamic others are two different things. The question is how the first kind of solidarity, if it exists, can be converted by employing Abrahamic principles of responsibility to promise to bring into being solidarity of the broader interfaith kind. Fortunately the Christian scriptures contain few, if any, obstacles against situation-shaped relationships of solidarity over, say, justice issues with other communities of faith. Apparently exclusivist passages, e.g., "No one comes to the Father, but by me," or "I am the way, the truth, and the life" (John 14:6), do not preclude practical relationships of solidarity with Others whose interests overlap with one's own, without requiring particular doctrinal deliverances regarding those other religious commitments.

The term "flesh" (or *sarx*) is borrowed by Christians from Hebrew scripture to expresses the idea of a solidarity with all human beings, yet not necessarily as redeemed human beings. Likewise, the term *soma* or "body" speaks of solidarity in "the body of Christ" (*soma tou Christou*), but also has meanings that express the idea of the human condition (i.e., Paul's expression "this body of death" in Rom 7:24) outside the faith.

The English word solidarity does not occur in translations of the New Testament any more than it does in the other Abrahamic scriptures. It is far too newly coined for that, as we have seen above. Terms that suggest the idea may be *koinonia* or "communion," or the notion that God through Jesus Christ has entered into solidarity with humankind in "the form of a servant," or, to use a later term, is *homoousios* (i.e., "of one substance") with us in respect of his humanity, as expressed in the Chalcedonian Definition of CE 451. None of these usages has in view the question of solidarity among different families of Abrahamic faith. Rather they are tied into Christian doctrinal formulations that tend to block the emergence of any such usage today. *Koinonia* has doctrinal implications in the area of ecclesiology, and *homoousios* has implications in the realm of Christology that virtually preclude applications that could undermine basic Christian identity assumptions: something we are saying such relationships should not encourage or require.

Yet the Christian notion that God has placed Godself in solidarity not only with Christian believers but with the whole human race opens the door, as it does in Judaism, to a theological move from solidarity *ad intra* (i.e., within the particular faith community), to solidarity also *ad extra* (i.e., toward the human race as a whole). As Karl Barth said, God has determined Godself for us human beings in such a way that "the electing God and the elected man coincide,"[40] further elaborating this idea in his small book *The Humanity of God*.[41] Just as do Jews, Christians need to explore the relationships between their own internal divisions that can undermine intrafaith solidarity even for practical purposes, and their capacity to articulate what sorts of solidarity between themselves and other faiths can be theologically articulated and defended in today's world.

Again, the kinds of solidaristic consciousness Muslims can bring to our spaces of meeting and spaces of reasons will depend on what sort of Muslims they are, on who are the Christians and Jews they are interacting with, and above all on the character of the issues is that bring the three faiths together. As before, what follows is illustrative of possibilities. It does not describe or prescribe for any particular meeting between the faiths, but tells us what possibilities are likely to be present as the traditions interact. An Islamic notion of solidarity across lines of different faith commitment may possibly be provisionally derived from the frequent usage of the Arabic term *wilayah*, roughly "comradeship" that may or may not include those of other faiths. Inclusion stands over against apparent Qur'anic prohibitions (e.g., Sura 5:51) of any such relationships.[42] Yet the meaning of this term, as seen by generations of exegetes, is very fluid, moving from formal agreements to personal bonds, and sometimes referring to trust in God. Terms such as "alliance," "comradeship," "collaboration," even "affectionate closeness" appear as contemporary translations of this word. The modern term "solidarity" seems suitable for translating *wilayah* only in certain contexts and circumstances. In most contexts the relationship in question is at most intertribal. A further step, a "new thing" as Hannah Arendt would say, is needed to see the term *wilayah* as appropriate for describing interreligious forms of solidarity. Perhaps such an extended usage of the term would be illustrative of what I have called "transcendental" or "Abrahamic" responsibility; reaching beyond the normally expected categories when extraordinary conditions require one to do so. For a contemporary circumstance, one finds a contemporary word to translate the Arabic term indicating the new sphere of meaning now found in it, hence "solidarity" as calling for an interfaith tie.

Extraordinary conditions mentioned in the Qur'an include especially those in which the different faiths recognize in one another a common piety, or ethic, or interest (not doctrinal agreement), or face a common adversary, or share a common struggle for justice, or perceive that such an alliance is necessary for their survival. Farid Esack (whose views we have discussed at length in chapter 4) found such extraordinary conditions in the South African apartheid society of the 1980s and early 1990s. Today's global circumstances are not exactly like those of that or any other time, but they are extraordinary enough to justify an extension of Islamic intertribal or intergroup "solidarity" (so far as that exists between, say, Shi'ites and Sunnis) to "solidarity" with Christians and Jews against the oppressive consequences of the Enlightenment's failure to bring its promised secular blessings to all human beings.

Hence the meanings Arabic-speaking Muslims may find in the word *wilayah* will depend on circumstances, interlocutors, and perceived challenges. An Abrahamic hermeneutic, or interpretative practice according to an Abrahamic principle, can free all the participants, Jews Christians and Muslims alike, to acknowledge that interpretation can validly bring out new things, that obedience can become disobedience when it literally follows words meant for other times and places, and that the promises on which all three faiths are based are addressed not merely to them but to all of humankind through them.

But the more deeply we try to invest modern interfaith understandings of "solidarity" with ancient meanings, the more urgently certain barriers to the transparency of this idea (what philosophers call *aporias*) begin to come to our attention. The more we apply it to interfaith situations, the more questions arise about what it means for those who practice it. And out of this questioning could come more clarity about the link between today's forms of practical cooperation and primordial covenantal identities we are seeking.

The question is whether calling practical cooperation "covenantal" in character necessarily drains meaning away from original internal covenantal ties variously expressed in our three faiths, seeming to call for a transfer of fundamental religious identity from ancestral faiths to new relationships. Perhaps it is safer to avoid saying that coalitions around particular social causes have covenantal character of their own, even where synagogues, churches, and mosques live side-by-side and pursue parallel-interactive hermeneutics. Rather than deciding this question one way or the other, I prefer a both-and perspective.

It may help to clarify how one could think in this manner by supplying a very brief philosophical interlude. The *aporia* or stumbling block in thinking about solidarity lies in question of whether pursuit of solidarity requires me to merge my will, or, even more, my identity with that of the Other. Is solidarity with the poor equivalent to a commitment to see the world exclusively through their eyes, and no longer through my own? Does the Other make such a demand on me, that I abandon my own identity in face of the Other's need? The Jewish philosopher Emmanuel Lévinas seems to suggest that there is no limit to the ethical demand on me in the face of the Other in need. In solidarity, do my own will and intellect disappear?[43] It was this implication in Lévinas that Paul Ricoeur attacked in his book *Oneself as Another*.[44] Ricoeur answered no, because it is "I" who continually joins my will to the other's aspiration. In doing so, I am still the author of what I do. I identify myself with my acts. In solidarity with my neighbor, I remain responsible to my own identity. I tie myself to my words and deeds, thus taking responsibility for them. Where solidarity is concerned, my words and deeds are ones in which I join my will to the will of the Other, and thereby affirm my identity in relation to a world seen through his or her eyes. So it is my responsible self that maintains the solidaristic identification with the Other. I affirm myself in my self-expression in this way, and hence my self does not disappear in this transaction. I responsibly allow the Other to fill out the content of my selfhood. I am thereby identifying myself with my actions still more fully, for these actions occur out there in a world of many signs and meanings, and my words and actions, once uttered or performed, take on meanings of their own in which they may be, and usually are, creatively enriched beyond own my too-limited notions of my original intent. The world then gives back to me—transformed—that with which I identify myself in responsibility. In declaring solidarity, I still help determine where and how in the world this restoration of my identity through transformative encounter with difference occurs. I am still the one who wills and sustains the act of solidarity.

I believe that such reflections by Lévinas and Ricoeur on the interpersonal dimension of solidarity can also be extended to illumine solidaristic relationships by whole religious bodies toward other faith communities. We come to see the world through the eyes of others without needing to submerge our own identities. Our identities come back to us not alienated but enriched and deepened. Such insights, I think, justify our speaking of such relationships as not merely coalitional, but also covenantal. We begin to enter through the doors of our particular traditions into the larger covenantal context of blessing to all the earth's families.

It seems fair to say that, understood in purely secular terms, the notion of solidarity has by now lost much of its capacity to hold together the many ways persons organize their resistance to totalizing forces in the world. For there to be coherent communities of solidarity today, different lived narratives of resistance to totalization need to intersect in something other than philosophical analyses or strategic expedients. Perhaps this can happen in the interaction of covenantal communities such as the "religions of the Book" whose narratives contain sources out of which notions of solidarity originally arise, and which may yet transform its meaning in the contemporary world. The religions of the book, meeting around their parallel interpretations of the public world, may find ways of linking today's forces of resistance to totalization in solidarities that reanimate and embody their underlying covenantal traditions. They would then be translating the "gift" of God's promise keeping to them as distinct peoples into a common "gift" to humankind. They would be seeking to articulate concretely God's prevenient will to solidarity with the human race.[45]

Such a notion, I believe, lies behind the phrase "covenantal solidarity," used today in Christian ecumenical circles to refer to a form of solidarity with a "vertical" as well as "horizontal" dimension. This notion has many implications. One is that one group, emulating God's reaching out, projects its identity to identify with another group's cause, to stand with them, to share their suffering, to rejoice in their success. The idea of a "preferential option for the poor," adopted in 1968 by the Second General Conference of Latin American Bishops at Medellín, Columbia, is a declaration of this form of solidarity.

Here something quite new is at work. The term "solidarity" is increasingly used now in this new perspective to express the idea of one community's total support of, and self-implication in, the burdens and aspirations of another. One community invests its grace-given capacity for promise keeping in an act of identification with the other in need. This "investment" is not an act of calculation but an act of communion. The return on it, as for the act of forgiveness or the act of trust, is not subject to calculation. Through my community of faith, I invest my being and hope in the being and hope of another community. I imaginatively stand in that other's place. I associate my story of hope for fulfillment with that other community's different story of hope for fulfillment. I enter that other community's Abrahamic story. But this can also mean letting the other stand in for me. It means letting the struggling ones represent me also in their struggle.

Such solidarity often involves a move toward a place materially weaker but spiritually stronger than one's own. The gift is not merely given; it turns out to move more strongly in return. To be in solidarity is to receive a gift of responsibility to and for the other person or community. Without loss of my own identity, it is to receive the promise once again through the struggles of the Other. To be in covenantal solidarity is to gather around, and share the blessings of, those in whose struggles the God of Abraham is perceived to be keeping God's promises in the world.

The Givens and the Gift: Transition to the Public World

We have now explored the semantic worlds of three kinds of relational virtues both presupposed and fostered by the practice of parallel and interactive hermeneutics among the Abrahamic traditions. It is hard to imagine this sort of interpretative sharing apart from certain spoken or unspoken implications: that forgiveness of past wrongs is being given and received, that effort is being made to build conditions of mutual trust, and that such relationships may lead to both personal and public acts of solidarity. To the extent that each of these virtues involves taking transcendental responsibility, responsibility beyond routine expectations, we may describe them as covenantal in character.

It is important to grasp that studied here are not simply words and their definitions, but whole semantic worlds governed by verbal nouns or gerunds: giving and receiving forgiveness, fostering conditions of trust, acting in solidarity. One can imagine countless ways in which such relationships have been acted out in the past, and may be acted out in the future. The words themselves serve as markers for the relationships sought, but the fullness of meaning in each case lies in the sorts of actions concerned and in their historical contexts. Forgiveness, for example, is clothed with particular meaning by being painfully offered and received after the Nazi period in Germany, or in the wake of apartheid in the South Africa of the 1990s. Trust, for example, finds a fullness of meaning when considered as an element in the integrity of diplomatic or financial transactions designed to make peace in the Middle East. Solidarity takes on thicker meaning in a shipyard workers' strike in Poland, or in refusal to cross a picket line in Detroit. In each case the virtue named has a large historical-cultural footprint. We are dealing not merely with language as such but with whole spheres of action in different human contexts.

Projections of such relational virtues in the cosmopolitan, or nontheological, language sphere are important to our argument. We have seen that forgiveness, trust, and solidarity in their ordinary "secular meanings," however limited these meanings may be, are what make it possible for representatives of different faiths to meet in the first place, before they begin to plumb the deeper meanings of their relationships. Such "ordinary" expectations of civility, the expectation that we will not humiliate one another, are gifts the modern world gives to religious communities that seek to meet one another. Being recipients of such gifts of peaceful expectations, we then hope to generate gifts that give something back without returning modernity to barbarism. Before trying to give relational virtues covenantal meaning, Abrahamic actors need to be sure that they are living up to the best of existing cosmopolitan standards, that they appreciate what the modern world, with all its deficiencies, has achieved. That achievement has been named by one thinker the expectation of "decency."[46]

What goes beyond "decency" in our relationships can be described today only in the languages of covenantal communities that one way or another speak of a gift of responsibility to an all-embracing promise to humankind. To be rooted in such a gift of responsibility lends worldly life an elusive but real quality of "how much more" (Matt 6:30 as rendered by Paul Ricoeur) for which modernity has no adequately funded words. Perhaps this more manifests itself in moments of what William Schweiker calls "axiological surprise." Or in what Lévinas calls "traces" of the divine. Such surprising traces of something "more" might consist of action springing from the unspoken covenantal narrative of promise to each human being and each human family, together with the conviction that believers may be the instruments of such a surmise in the lives of others, who thereby may come to see their lives as more promising than they had before been able to imagine. Such would be a different quality of human interaction that might call for such words as "goodness," or "righteousness," were such terms available for public use in our time. Through such a quality of action, words like forgiveness, trust, and solidarity could find the covenantal meanings that lie beyond, or on the other side of, the aporetic limitations of reasoning about these subjects in modernity.

We can still be modest, yet incipiently theological, by saying something like "decency with a difference," meaning this as a kind of linguistic marker for the presence of what we have called "transcendental responsibility," the responsibility that goes beyond any possible job description toward taking responsibility for the implications of what modern human beings, for good or ill, are now able to do, in the world and to the world, by the decisions they make.

But are we equipped to make such portentous decisions? Our central point has been that the action-languages of which we are secularly capable, and hence the relational acts that mark our worldly lives and make parallel hermeneutics initially possible—if separated from the original covenantal narratives of scripture—are not able to deliver the full depths of meaning that human decisions and actions at this level need in order to be truly responsible to the promise. Some lesser, more pragmatically graspable, relationship is found as a substitute for the deeper relationship. We speak of forgiveness but are able to offer only artful forgetting or legal amnesty. We speak of trust, but are able only to take security measures against violations of trust. We speak of solidarity but are able only to deliver coalitions with appropriate bylaws and goals.

The role of the Abrahamic communities in a world of this kind could be to make present acted parables of these words' deeper, fuller meanings, thereby offering resources for rendering the world's words and relationships more meaningful and deeply rooted. It is as if we were to speak of the given meaning-spheres of modern society on which we depend for stability and sense, and were to intuit these givens as supplemented by gifts of acted reference to the promise they point to. It is the calling of human institutions spiritually transformed by the gift of transcendental responsibility to promise, to help transform whole spheres of meaning in which human beings think and act.[47]

To put this another way, I am saying that publicly understandable expressions of forgiveness, trust, solidarity, and other virtues are not in themselves covenantal until they rest not merely on cultural and linguistic "givens" or artifacts, but on "gifts" mediated through believing faith communities, their scriptures, their hermeneutical processes, their symbols, their actions, and their relationships. Such communities have the opportunity to live so as to harvest the fruits of Derrida's exemption of the notion of "gift" from deconstruction. They may do so by acts of *generosity* that break through the aporetic obstacles that used to block the very conceptualizability of "a gift outright" as object of thought. Covenantal faith communities help make plausible to humanity the restoration of "gift" and "giftedness" as transcendental ideas governing worlds of possible concrete particulars, just as we have shown they can do for notions like "justice" and "forgiveness." These communities are called to live out forms of life that move into and hold open Derrida's reconstituted philosophical spaces, spaces that permit our reception and enactment of gifts of responsibility *given* by a covenanting God, not merely "given" as ways of speaking already in the dictionary, handed down like mental furniture from generation to generation.

Such impact, I am certain, is real, but difficult to discern, or explain, in monolinguistic terms. It helps, however, to see the covenantal dimension as expressed in accepting and living out the Abrahamic gift of responsibility to the promise of final, universal blessing. Ordinary human interactions gain covenantal quality by their associations with the Abrahamic stories, and the Abrahamic stories gain worldly traction by their association with expressions of common human experience. It is appropriate to name the transactions of meaning and activity involved—both among the traditions as such and between the traditions and the larger human world—by using the adjective "covenantal." This covenantal responsibility is to the whole body politic of humanity. The covenant completes its meaning by being a gift of blessing not only to those who explicitly receive the covenantal promise, but a gift of blessing to others through them. The question at the end of this chapter then is how this gift of the covenantal community of forgiveness, trust, and critical solidarity with others in the body politic is to be understood. Mediating to all the gift of promise arising at the core of the Abrahamic faiths requires serious thought about how this mediation is to be done in practical terms.

What, in short, are the politics of giving this gift? One can think of many ways in which such an intention to do this can be misunderstood. For example, the theocratic misunderstanding: taking responsibility to rule, to control others "for their own good." Or the privatistic misunderstanding, that we impact society by making better individuals, people who are more ethical, and so forth. Or the cultural domination misunderstanding, that religious communities, in a majority position to do so, have a vocation to influence public media, school systems, public monuments. Rather the appropriate strategy is a matter of generating and maintaining a "spaces" of covenantal reasoning in the larger spaces of "civil society." Remember that virtues rooted in covenantal responsibility are all composed of elements of common human experience. But they need to be lived out in communities of rooted cosmopolitans that can bring them into lived touch with the original scriptural narratives. This is not a matter of getting people to speak their religious languages in public. It is rather a matter of forming covenantal communities within civil society that can act out rooted responsibility narratives within the configurations and plots of common human experience. It is a matter of acting responsibility narratives couched in ordinary terms that exhibit a deeper meaning and wider range by what they say and do. They in fact give and receive forgiveness, create conditions of trust, and maintain solidarity with others who travel the same way. It is through sharing covenantally grounded forgiveness, trust, and solidarity with the larger human community that the Abrahamic faiths can help modernity save itself from its own self-distortions. These faiths can together, in these terms, generate new spaces of reasons within the different sectors of human interactivity that constitute civil society. Among the many social-political-institutional givens of society on which all depend, Abrahamic communities—together with other faiths and secular initiatives—can bring forth the gifts of the spirit that help make them work and resist the distortions of dishonesty, greed, and power seeking that ever threaten to undermine them. Chapter 7, which comes next, will have more to say about this notion of "civil society" as a public sphere, and how covenantal Abrahamic communities can understand themselves in relation to it.

Notes

1. I once had a memorable experience of being significantly invited into an anteroom, but no further. On a mission to Rome for the Chicago Cluster of Theological Schools to speak to Father Pedro Arrupe, then Superior General of the Jesuit Order, to express dismay at, and try to reverse, his decision to close the Jesuit School of Theology in our city, I found myself led into a spartan ground floor anteroom to which Father Arrupe presently came down from his upper sanctum (which I had looked forward to seeing) to cordially greet me. What could this mean? An act of humble submission on his part to a supposed Protestant preference for plainness? Or an unmistakable signal saying "outsider"? Such are the sorts of equivocal messages we often receive in entering the anterooms of other communities of our own faith, and even more those of other faiths.

2. See Paul Ricoeur, *Interpretation Theory: Discourse and the Surplus of Meaning* (Fort Worth, TX: Texas Christian University Press, 1976), 92.

3. See Jürgen Habermas, *The Theory of Communicative Action: Reason and the Rationalization of Society*, trans. Thomas McCarthy (Boston: Beacon Press, 1984), 319ff.

4. See Nigel Biggar, ed., *Burying the Past: Making Peace and Doing Justice After Civil Conflict* (Washington, DC: Georgetown University Press, 2001), 8.

5. "Desuetude" literally means a discontinuation of use or practice, something different from mere "forgetting" and perhaps more applicable to the challenge of putting violent interpretations of faith "out of our minds." One hears this term occasionally in Roman Catholic circles, where it refers to doctrines and practices that remain "on the books" but have fallen, in many cases happily, into disuse.

6. Hannah Arendt, *The Human Condition* (Chicago: University of Chicago Press, 1958), 215.

7. Ibid., 214.

8. The difficulties and recriminations accompanying the release of the Commission's Report do nothing to diminish the power of this *idea* as a social possibility for South Africa and elsewhere.

9. Donald W. Shriver Jr., *An Ethic for Enemies* (New York: Oxford University Press, 1995).

10. Jeffrie G. Murphy and Jean Hampton, *Forgiveness and Mercy* (Cambridge, UK: Cambridge University Press, 1988).

11. Shriver, *Ethic*.

12. Geiko Muller-Fahrenholz, *The Art of Forgiveness, Theological Reflections on Healing and Reconciliation* (Geneva: WCC Publications, 1997).

13. Ibid., viii.

14. Jews in any given dialogical relationship might make reference to the story of Joseph's forgiveness of his brothers (Genesis 27–50), and perhaps even to the interpretation of these chapters by Thomas Mann in his three-volume novel of that name. We may say that this act of forgiveness needed as form of responsibility to the promise embodied in the amphictyonic integrity of that band of brothers to whose descendants comes the question of whom they will serve and who cannot serve the promise wholeheartedly unless the sting of the ancient

betrayal (for Thomas Mann, sending Joseph into the underworld, no less) is withdrawn. The question is one of who authentically inherits Abraham's blessing. Have Joseph's brothers abdicated that inheritance? Can Joseph's forgiveness give it back to them? Or Jews might enter such an Abrahamic discourse with reference to rabbinic teaching on repentance and forgiveness. Their tradition is not of one mind concerning the steps by which one comes to repentance (*teshuva*) and thence to the possibility of forgiveness given and received. One must recognize one's sins as sins, feel remorse, desist from sin, make restitution, and finally come to the point of ritual and personal confession. Only the offending party can thereby set right the wrong of sin. Only the offended party can forgo the debt of the sin. There are two Hebrew words for forgiveness: *mechila* and *selicha*. The first means only that the offended person foregoes the offender's debt, relinquishes his or her claims. The second term for forgiveness goes much further: it is an act of the heart implying empathy for the sinner and mercy toward him or her. And then, of course, there is the forgiveness as "atonement" (*kapparah*) or "purification" (*tahora*). Such forgiveness can be granted only by God. But little or nothing in this material refers to the collective guilt of religious communities toward other religious communities.

15. Similarly there are abundant resources that Christians might choose to bring to shared discourse. They might make reference to the many instances in the synoptic Gospels in which forgiveness for debt becomes a theme against the background of the ruinous debt culture of Palestine in Roman times. See, for example, many passages relating to forgiveness of debts in the Jubilee Year (Lev 25:1–17) as well as the line of the Lord's Prayer, "Forgive us our debts as we forgive our debtors." The New Testament Greek word translated "forgiveness" or "remission" is *aphesis*, often used to refer to the Jubilee provision for remission of debt. Later the notion of forgiveness, or absolution, is embodied in the whole complex of materials Christians call "atonement," i.e., the question of what it takes, what it costs, to make things right with God. Ultimately the Christian tradition has attributed such atonement to the sacrificial death of Jesus, affirmed in its meaning by the resurrection. Forgiveness is costly. But these materials do not address collective debts between whole religious communities.

16. We may likewise conjecture what Muslims would choose to bring to the dialogue. Many Qur'anic terms seem to express aspects of the field of meanings covered by the English word "forgiveness." Frequent among these is the Arabic term *'afw*, used to speak of God's forgiveness of human beings and even forgiveness of the Prophet himself. "Most forgiving," or "compassionate," Arabic *'afuw*, is indeed one of the names of Allah cited at the head of each Qur'anic sura. Sura 7:25 describes Allah as always forgiving those who repent and turn toward him. Human beings are constantly reminded to behave in the way that God does. In the Qur'anic version of the Adam and Eve story, Allah forgives the couple in such a way that no "original sin" remains for their descendants. Adam and Eve become positive examples. Adam, the forgiven one, indeed becomes vicegerent of Allah on earth. Sura 42 speaks of the benefit of giving forgiveness over seeking revenge. In fact, offering forgiveness when one is in a position to take revenge is seen in this sura as a virtue superior even to prayer (one of the "pillars" of Islam) and almsgiving. Disputes are to be resolved before the next time of prayer. For forgiveness to be a condition of the possibility of prayer gives this practice an essential role in Islam. Forgiveness is essentially a change of heart, of attitude, toward one who has done one wrong. It does not necessarily mean remission of the punishment for wrongdoing. Again, the

need for forgiveness of whole religious cultures for violent deeds done in confidence that they are religious duties is seemingly not present in the Qur'an.

17. John D. Caputo, *The Prayers and Tears of Jacques Derrida: Religion without Religion* (Indianapolis: Indiana University Press, 1997), 4.

18. "Religion and Postmodernism 2: Questioning God," a symposium held at Villanova University, Pennsylvania, October 14–16, 1999.

19. Jacques Derrida, "To Forgive: The Unforgivable and Imprescriptible," in *Questioning God*, ed. John D. Caputo, Mark Dooley, Michael J. Scranton (Bloomington: University of Indiana Press, 1999), 34.

20. Ibid. 46.

21. Ibid. 48.

22. An example of this initial, civic level of trust: one prominent (and very learned) participant in the inter-Abrahamic dialogue in Oakland, California, is a graduate engineer for the water company whom we all must trust to maintain the sufficiency and purity of our supply. We trust others for similar practical reasons without thinking very deeply about doing so.

23. Robert Putnam, *Making Democracy Work: Civic Traditions in Modern Italy* (Princeton, NJ: Princeton University Press, 1993).

24. Francis Fukuyama, *Trust: Social Virtues and the Creation of Prosperity* (New York: Free Press, 1995).

25. Adam Seligman, *The Idea of Civil Society* (New York: Free Press, 1992) and *The Problem of Trust* (Princeton, NJ: Princeton University Press, 1997).

26. Seligman, *Problem of Trust*, 175. He writes, "We may well query if the loss or transformation of trust as a mechanism of social interaction (public and private both) is not part of a broader transformation which will see a transformation of the very terms of rationality, perhaps in the direction of a *wiederbezauberte* world. Whether, as I suspect, an enchanted world is also a more brutal and Hobbesian one is an empirical question, the answer to which may not be long in coming."

27. Seligman, *Idea of Civil Society*, 30.

28. See N. Luhmann, "Familiarity, Confidence, Trust: Problems and Perspectives," in *Trust: Making and Breaking of Cooperative Relations*, ed. Diego Gambetta (Oxford: Basil Blackwell. 1988), 102.

29. By transcendental confidence in the Other, I mean understanding my confidence as presiding over a coherent sphere of meaning into which empirical data can be drawn but which empirical information alone cannot support. When I trust the Other, I take him or her into this transcendental sphere of meaning held in being by my confidence that such a relational sphere exists and reflects a higher sense I am free to call "covenantal." My confidence that this is so must, in turn, rest on warrants beyond my knowledge of the trusted individual's history or character. It must rest on what I believe to be true about the world, created and redeemed.

30. I have in mind Kenneth Arrow's insight that there is an essential inconsistency in public reasoning unless all are of one mind, which means submission to the will of a "dictator." See Kenneth Arrow, *Social Choice and Individual Values*, Cowles Foundation Monograph series, 2nd ed. (New Haven, CT: Yale University Press, 1970). I infer then that a world reduced

to "rational choice" principles will be either an inconclusive competition among "preferences," or some interest will corner the market and be able largely to determine the direction of common life. I am indebted for the Arrow reference to Dr. Austin Hoggatt, professor emeritus in the Haas School of Business at the University of California, Berkeley.

31. Jews may well first bring to this conversation their conviction that the Lord alone is worthy of trust. Three such passages occur in the Psalms: "Trust in the Lord, and do good; so you will dwell in the land, and enjoy security" (Ps 37:3). To trust and do good implies we need to do our share. This means to trust God and be trustworthy. "I trust in the steadfast love of God for ever and ever" (Ps 52:8); "In God I trust without a fear. What can man do to me?" (Ps 56:11). Clear in all three passages is the sense of protection from external enemies. Isaiah picks up some of the same sense of apprehension: "Behold, God is my salvation; I will trust and will not be afraid" (Isa 12:2). Conversely we are warned not to put trust in anything less than God. "Woe to those who go down to Egypt for help and rely on horses, who trust in chariots because they are many and in horsemen because they are very strong" (Isa 31:1). Or, "Behold you trust in deceptive words to no avail" (Jer 7:8).

The vocabulary of Hebrew is exceptionally rich in words that convey the notion of trust in its various overtones. The word "trust" appears 134 times in the King James translation of Torah, but several different Hebrew words stand behind the English, each associated with something that can be sensed, and each having its own nuance of meaning. One starts with *emunah*, which ordinarily means faith or belief. But trust in God and God's promises is a form of faith, and also has an element of "belief." Note the related form *aman* in Psalm 78:22: "Because they had no faith in God, and did not trust his saving power." Here the word means to be "firm" or "sure." This is the verbal form of the word "amen," meaning "I stand firm on this prayer." Note the Hebrew for "In God we trust": *Ani ma' amin bashem.*

Among other terms: *batach* meaning to trust or be confident, *betach* (feminine form *bitchah*) meaning to place confidence in or be secure and safe, or have the feeling of trust. *Chasah* has the meaning "to lean on" someone or something. See Psalm 18:2: "The Lord is my rock, and my fortress, and my deliverer, my God, my rock in whom I take refuge." Note also *betach* in Psalm 56:4, where it means "to cling." And *yachal* in Isaiah 51:5: "and for my arm they hope," where the image is holding to God's arm for support. All such standing firm (and the other meanings) make the person "trustworthy." What then is entrusted to those who "trust" God? "Trust in a faithless man in time of trouble is like a bad tooth or a foot that slips" (Prov 25:19).

32. Christians, of course, are heirs to the entire Hebrew tradition and depend upon it for basic orientation. In addition, one finds the notion of trust powerfully expressed in several of the Gospel parables, notably those in which a master entrusts portions of his estate to servants for investment while he is away from home (e.g., Matt 25:14–30). The master "entrusts" (*paredōken*) them with his property, giving them responsibility, but yet no specific instructions, for caring for it. The parable seems to be saying that the trustworthiness of those who serve the Lord consists not in playing it safe but in taking risks commensurate with the way they see promise in the situation the master has placed them in.

Paul's theology expresses this notion of a gift of responsibility differently. Here the operative Greek constructions extract ranges of meaning from the noun *pistis,* meaning not only faith or belief, but also trust in God's faithfulness to God's promises. In Romans 4:3 (paraphrasing Genesis 15:6) we read, "Abraham believed (*episteusen*) God. and it was reckoned to him as righteousness." This "reckoning-as-righteousness" is not our due, but rather a gift. We are to "trust (*pisteuonti*) him who justifies the ungodly" (Rom 4:5). We can then say that we are entrusted (i.e., reckoned righteous: forgiven our past sins, gifted with freedom, sent into the world) with life on these terms, provided we receive the responsibility for the gift it is. Romans 1:17 describes this trustworthiness "revealed through faith for faith" (*ek pisteōs eis pistin*) as a "righteousness" that comes to us in faith. Galatians 5:22 speaks of "faithfulness" (*pistis*) interpretable as incorporating the sense of trustworthiness because it is now appears in a list of virtues seen as fruits of the Spirit. In 2 Timothy 4:7, Paul argues for the trustworthiness of his witness by saying, among other things, that he has "kept the faith" (*tēn pistin tetērēka*).

33. In Islam, trust means primarily belief in another's integrity or reliability. In the Qur'an, the two terms most typically translated as "trust" are *tawakkul* and *amana*. The first is derived from an Arabic root meaning "to give oneself over to," or "to rely or depend upon," or "to have confidence in." *Tawakkul* means primarily trusting oneself to God. If one trusts a fellow human being, that is because one expects that the other likewise trusts him or herself to God, and is thus trustworthy. One trusts God that one is not deceived in taking the risk of trusting another. The second Qur'anic term translated to mean "trust," *amana*, a variant on the Hebrew *emunah*, literally means something *given* "in trust," with the expectation that "it will be cared for diligently and carefully by the trustee." We might wish to say that what is given in trust could clearly include what we are calling here a "gift of responsibility" to humankind, but neither the Qur'an nor the Hebrew or Christian scriptures offers much justification for taking this step The step required is a new one.

34. "Solidarity," Oxford English Dictionary (Oxford University Press).

35. I owe this classical example to Julio de Santa Ana.

36. See Francois Edwald, "Solidarité." in the *Dictionnaire d'ethique et de philosophie morale*, ed. Monique Sperber, 3rd ed. (Paris: Presses Universitaires de France, 2001), 1513–20.

37. A rudimentary Internet search under the headings "solidarity" and "revolutionary solidarity" gives this impression very strongly. These terms seem almost to have been taken over by groups, mostly very small, that call themselves "anarchist" or use language to that effect. The sense of unequal struggle against tyrannical regimes sets these groups looking for allies that can be trusted.

38. Such an awareness of common cause and possibility continued into the twentieth century. It lay behind the independent trade union federation among Polish shipyard workers—formed in September 1980, and taking "Solidarity" as its name—under the leadership of Lech Walesa and supported by the Roman Catholic Church. Forced underground for a time by government repression, "Solidarity" grew in power until it achieved recognition in 1989 as a party eligible to compete in the Polish general elections. This led to a "Solidarity"-led coalition government in 1990.

39. The decline in contemporary thought of Marxist philosophy as a coherent and current system may have something to do with this. The thought of Karl Marx is of course as inherently coherent as it ever was. What I mean is that we seldom today take it on board as a whole. Certain Marxist ideas, e.g., his theory of ideology with its implications for the sociology of knowledge, are alive today at least in intellectual circles. Other Marxist ideas, e.g., "the dictatorship of the proletariat," are not.

40. See Karl Barth, *Church Dogmatics* (Edinburgh: T and T Clark, 1938), 2:2, 63.

41. Karl Barth, *The Humanity of God* (Richmond, VA: John Knox Press, 1960).

42. I am indebted in this discussion of the meaning of *waliyah* to the information and insights of Farid Esack, *Qur'an, Liberation, and Pluralism: An Islamic Perspective of Interreligious Solidarity against Oppression* (Oxford: Oneworld Publications, 1997), 180ff.

43. See Emmanuel Lévinas, "Ethics as First Philosophy," in *The Levinas Reader,* ed. Sean Hand (Oxford: Blackwell, 1989), especially pages 82–84. Lévinas writes of responsibility to the neighbor, "It is the responsibility of a hostage which can be carried to the point of being substituted for the other person and demands an infinite subjection of subjectivity" (84). See also Emmanuel Lévinas, *Totality and Infinity: An Essay on Exteriority,* trans. Alphonso Lingis, (Pittsburgh: Duquesne University Press, 1969), section III.B: "Ethics and the Face."

44. Paul Ricoeur, *Oneself as Another,* trans., Kathleen Blamey (Chicago: University of Chicago Press, 1992), 188–89.

45. I am aware that the notion of "God's will to solidarity with the human race" is Christian in origin, even if it is not an "orthodox" or traditional formulation. Is there any echo in Judaism or Islam?

46. "A decent society," writes Avishai Margalit, "is one whose institutions do not humiliate people." See Avishai Margalit, *The Decent Society,* trans. Naomi Goldblum (Cambridge, MA: Harvard University Press, 1996), 1. To speak of "decency" is to hesitate before pronouncing such words as "goodness" or "righteousness." These tend to embarrass us, perhaps by seeming to set the bar too high for today's human beings. Decency, as in the expression, "He/she is a very decent human being" says a great deal in itself, especially in a world such as this one, unable to speak of any more profound recognition. But even to reach the point of decency is in many cases a significant achievement in itself. We should see that we go this far at least before attempting theological moves that take us beyond today's common human experience.

47. It is evident by now that we have here an understanding of the virtues that avoids the medieval (and still influential) distinction between the classical (indeed Platonic) worldly virtues, such as prudence, temperance, justice, and courage or fortitude, sometimes augmented by Stoic patience, wisdom, and self-control, and the "theological virtues" of faith, hope, and love. The Aristotelian-Thomist hierarchical ladder of being (*analogia entis*) from lower to higher levels, as applied to ethics, no longer speaks to our condition. *All* virtues, including the most pragmatically cautious, are capable of being "theological" to the extent that they both plumb and carry covenantal meanings. They are "theological," that is, so long as they speak of Abrahamic responsibility to the Promise of blessing to the nations. They remain meaningful, yet worldly, to the extent that they do not.

7

Political Philosophy for an Abrahamic Public Presence

I have tried throughout this book to describe how today's Jews, Christians, and Muslims, like Abraham of old, can see themselves as bearers of a gift of responsibility to the human race. The chapter just concluded sought to see how these faiths, holding fast to this gift of responsibility to promise, can come to forgive past wrongs, to trust one another, and to live in solidarity across cultural and religious differences. I have argued that fostering such relationships generates groups with covenantal characteristics. Such inter-Abrahamic gatherings can speak healingly to modernity's broken self-understandings. They can bring gifts of transcendental responsibility to everyday social givens, helping to empower the latter more adequately to curb the irresponsible use of contemporary human capabilities—scientific, economic, industrial, military—that threaten modern civilization. They can contribute righteousness to routine job descriptions. Such covenantal discourse communities need therefore to position themselves politically in order to be able to make such contributions to the societies around them. And to do that, they need an understanding of certain political-philosophical ideas, notably "civil society" and the "social contract."

The present chapter tracks this public positioning of Abrahamic communities in terms of such ideas about the public world, with attention to their practical consequences. I will try here to show how these faiths can gather around the project of generating and maintaining a civil society for the purposes of fostering critical discourse about the social contracts that constitute society itself, and hence the very expression of the human at any given time or place. Such social contracts, pursued together by Abrahamic responsibility-bearers, need deliberately to resist the dominance, outside its proper sphere, of the sort of "game theory," "rational choice theory," or "social mechanism design" that has reduced interhuman relationships so largely to various forms of cost-benefit calculations.

The Abrahamic Faiths in Public Interaction

But let us be realistic. Imagine three faiths interacting in the most difficult circumstances possible, in Israel-Palestine or elsewhere in the Middle East. Can democratic civil society and open discourse about social contracts appear under such conditions? That is a question much in the news at the time of this writing. The present U.S. administration has declared something like this to be a goal of its imperial interventions in that part of the world. The *New York Times* columnist Thomas Friedman tells us repeatedly that Islam, in particular, needs to come to terms with democratic institutions and with the modern world generally,[1] or, as we would put it with José Casanova, begin to internalize the Enlightenment critique of religion, just as some (but not all) sectors of Western Christianity and Judaism have already done.

As far as I can tell, Friedman accepts the proposition that this is to be accomplished in the same way as it has been in the West: by inducing religion to accept the sort of marginalization and privatization that gradually followed upon the 1648 Peace of Westphalia ending the European "wars of religion." The consequent secularization process as we know it, including the "separation of church and state," has been premised on the assumption that if one lets religious interests too much into the public world they will inevitably fall into conflict with one another, creating what the American founders called "factions." These tear the body politic apart. I have already argued that religious wars both hot and cold are only partly generated out of various sorts of theological exclusivism. Such wars also occur when religious communities allow themselves to be used by political and economic interests to mask, or legitimate, purposes that are not religious at all.

Much of the argument of this book has been designed to help religious communities resist this kind of cooptation. One of the advantages of looking at the coming of democratic processes to places like Palestine, Iraq, Afghanistan, or Indonesia is that we can see how such processes work, or fail to work, under conditions other than those of eighteenth-century North America. I say "democratic processes" rather than "democracy" as such because Americans (and others) are too prone to identify the latter with their own particular democratic systems, and see democratization as a matter of exporting those systems more or less intact. Democratic processes can be conceived and coordinated in many different ways corresponding to different cultures. And we also see something in many lands, including some in Western Europe, that North America has not seen until recently: the rise of avowedly religious political parties that bring such "factions" squarely and openly into the public arena where they can be co-opted by various political and economic interests.

The upshot of all this interaction between religious communities and struggling democratic processes across the globe could turn out to be only a confirmation of the wisdom of the American Constitution makers of 1789, namely that one can have a genuinely open civil society only by making it constitutionally "secular." But I am arguing in this book that such "secularity" often masks the cynical misuse of religion by power interests: misuse that confirms religion's sometimes deserved reputation for factionalism and violence. I am arguing that religious communities can and must inoculate themselves against such misuse. For they may, as Casanova says, turn out to be the genuine carriers of enlightened values that the secular world has since distorted or lost.[2] They may be able to carry such values into society in the communal and narrative forms in which these values were first embodied, before being "naturalized" by eighteenth-century *philosophes* and their political followers. Religious communities could now find themselves the principal carriers of socially enlightened values: values that stand against political and economic exploiters and rationalizers.

So it is crucial in a world such as this that the role of religious communities in the public world be looked at once again. Especially so if the argument of this book is persuasive, namely that the Abrahamic faiths, they at least, can come to a new sort of self-consciousness about themselves and their public roles. That possibility, as I have shown, needs to rest on a reappropriation of the sort of covenantal responsibility-bearing found in the Abrahamic texts (as explored in chapter 5), and in learning to practice the covenantal virtues of forgiveness, trust, and solidarity among the responsibility-bearers (as described in chapter 6). By no means will all Jews, all Christians, or all Muslims come to see their faiths in this manner. I am speaking of a vanguard of "rooted cosmopolitans" in each faith: the responsible ones able to live in covenant with one another across religious boundaries as they play significant roles in the cultures of modernity.

Faiths Meeting One Another in "Civil Society"

The first task, of course, is to generate and maintain the kind of "social space" in which public relationships among the three faiths, with secular allies, can be carried on. Such spaces of discourse—whether coffee houses, universities, political associations, or otherwise—find their home in what political philosophers have called "civil society." Civil society is not the name of a particular institution or social location. Rather it is the dynamic enactment of free and potent interchange among the inhabitants of a place, citizens in the legal sense or otherwise. It is the acting-out of an assumption that society should be inclusively participatory, that it is, in essence, a shared discursive activity. Such activity begins to thrive in certain institutions close to the people—marketplaces as nodes of information exchange—and ramified into institutions that function on a larger scale—organized town meetings, newspapers, magazines, political talk shows, and the like. Without such activities and institutions, the shared cultural values and ethics of the people cannot gain expression, and democratic processes cannot thrive.

Yet civil society, where it exists, is largely the product of certain historical and cultural forces that have not existed everywhere. It has been mainly, but of course not exclusively, a Western European and North American phenomenon. The lack of it in other places helps explain why Western democratic concepts have had such great difficulty taking hold in parts of Eastern Europe, the Arab world, and elsewhere: not to suppose, of course, that they somehow "should" have done so. And, even where civil society has emerged, it remains an exceedingly fragile accomplishment. Its distinctive sort of social space is constantly being challenged by forces external to it, mostly governmental and economic. Jürgen Habermas calls such incursions "colonization" by interests inimical to the open exchange of perspectives that civil society is intended to foster.

As opposed to the regions of society dominated by government or the market, civil society is the natural social location in which religious communities can bear their moral witness to greatest effect. They should learn to make the most of this, to consider it their duty to do so. And civil society is also the place in which the question of the social contract or contracts by which we live can become thematic, and thus subject to strenuous questioning. The whole purpose of discerning a new public vision for the "religions of the Book" derived from their ancient Abrahamic sources, is to equip these faith communities to play such a social role, and hence to be bearers of "enlightened" values in ways intrinsic to their own distinctive natures and histories.

Let me put this another way. Perhaps the most important reason for introducing the question of civil society is that here lie the greatest possibilities for religious communities, working together, to confront the need to update their traditional moral self-understandings, to meet the conditions of modernity. John Kelsay writes of the work of Sohail Hashmi that for him,

"Civil society stands for a sphere within which the virtue of tolerance allows a free and democratic exchange between Muslims speaking with one another and, in the typical case, with Jews and Christians as well."[3]

A practice of civil society has historically been fundamental to the development of democratic institutions. But let us be realistic: the Abrahamic faiths in different times and places vary greatly in how far they have been exposed to this idea, or involved in realizing its implications where they live. Furthermore, the reality of civil society and the presence of systematic reflection about it are two different things. Western Protestants in particular (less so Roman Catholics and Eastern Orthodox) have been deeply implicated in civil society developments from the seventeenth century onward, yet may not, for the most part, have consciously connected these developments with their faith. Still, philosophers with Christian connections like John Locke and others made important contributions to systematic thought on the subject. Yet a paradox gradually emerged in the ways this thought developed. Civil society theory provided materials for the idea of "citizenship" as such. But Enlightenment thinking—for example in the work of the French *philosophes* Immanuel Kant and others—quickly set about universalizing this notion of "citizenship," to become citizenship in the human race itself. As it developed, the latter grand idea had little apparent use for notions of small-scale neighborhood participation in political discourse despite its original debts to those homely ideas.[4] Forgiveness, trust, and even solidarity are virtues that belong primarily in face-to-face human relationships. Yet they are also factually indispensable as foundations for broader, even global realizations of human commonality. But how do such small-scale relational virtues carry over into formulations of the idea that we are also citizens of the world? Here we have the familiar paradox of the "rooted cosmopolitans" in a different form: moral roots in some particular focused arena of life together, say in Kwame Appiah's ancestral village in Ghana, as the basis for citizenship in the still-abstract notion of a global humanity.

What experience with the idea of civil society does one find in Judaism? Again, we maintain the distinction between the actual social reality and the work of theorizing about it. Something like civil society has been part of the Jewish self-understanding for centuries, from the antiestablishment ferment generated by the prophets to the habits of ongoing argument modeled by the rabbis to life in the Warsaw ghetto. While Jews were marginalized in the West during the years of the emergence of civil society practice and thought among Christians, they subsequently came to play central roles in civil discourse as public intellectuals both among themselves and in the population at large. One thinks of the broad agenda-setting roles of Jewish intellectual communities in New York City and a host of European capitals. One must say that the reality of civil society has been significantly maintained by Jews to the benefit of all.

At the level of theorizing, Jewish scholars have also made preeminent contributions. Possibly the best contemporary overview of the subject can be found in Adam Seligman's *The Idea of Civil Society*[5] in which one can find a brilliant account of the development of the idea in the Christian West as well as case studies of civil society in Budapest, Jerusalem, and Los Angeles. An exhaustive theoretical account drawing heavily on the work of Jürgen Habermas (on whom see below) is provided by Jean Cohen and Andrew Arato in *Civil Society and Political Theory*.[6] Of late two Jewish scholars in particular, Michael Sandel and Michael Walzer, have been among the leading theoreticians of the civil society vision. The latter scholar has worked extensively on Jewish legal resources of value to the modern world. This chapter will draw substantially on Walzer's work in its conclusion.

As for Islam, the material on this subject is both rich and controversial. One has the impression that a remarkable flowering of something very like the later Western ideas of civil society occurred at different moments during the long period of Islamic hegemony in Andalusia, southern Spain, between the seventh and the fifteenth centuries. Here Jews and Christians also participated in a remarkable cultural synthesis that encouraged public discussion, within limits, and helped invent institutions needed to support it. The story of Al-Andalus has been told with not a little romanticism as a model for today's world. Yet this medieval picture is clouded also with contradictions, pogroms, and the like. Likewise, in much of modern Islam, one encounters cultures seemingly not well acquainted with the notion of civil society and not culturally prepared to encourage it. Islam in Turkey and in Indonesia comes closer to the ideal than Islam in most of the Arab lands.

Significant numbers of Muslim scholars have recently been giving attention to the roots of this matter in Islam, among them the Canadian scholar Amyn B. Sajoo, who in 2000 and 2001 led a project on Civil Society in the Muslim World at the Institute of Ismaili Studies in London.[7] While many have argued that civil society is "a western dream ... that does not translate into Islamic terms,"[8] members of the London project argue that something like civil society has existed and exists scattered in a variety of Islamic contexts across the globe. The conditions under which this political vision is cultivated are not exclusive to the West alone. Sajoo writes, "The respective Arabic and Persian terms for civil society, *mujtama' al-madani* and *jame'eyh madani* have long invoked the sense of institutions organized along civil lines (*madani* being derived from *medina* or 'city')."[9] Forms of "civic Islam," meaning non-state-controlled citizen action, are for Sajoo directly relevant to civil society discussion and found in a variety of Muslim cultures.

Sohail Hashmi[10] has still more recently taken up this question. Among many other observations, he notes the importance for this subject of the earliest Islamic society in the full sense of that term, created in Medinah under the Prophet himself after his immigration from Mecca in 622. Hashmi sees this early community as foundational for Islamic ethics. Its basis was a series of contractual agreements concluded by Muhammad with the tribes native to Medinah. "Thus the basis of the first Islamic civil society was literally a social contract. The so-called Constitution of Medinah spelled out the mutual rights and obligations of all members of the Muslim society. It did not obliterate tribal identities. It superseded this tribalism with the *ummah*, the community of the faithful."[11]

Hashmi goes on to tell us of the position of Jews and Christians under this Constitution. The Jews at least are an *umma* alongside the Muslim *umma*, with autonomy in their own internal affairs. This arrangement seems to have reflected not only the Jews' economic importance to the city, but also "the Qur'an's view of the Jews and Christians as potential participants in the God-oriented community that it charges the Muslims with constructing. The Qur'an repeatedly emphasizes the similarities and not the differences that unite all 'peoples of the book' in a community of the faithful."[12]

Far more evidence of this sort could be adduced for all three Abrahamic faiths. The conclusion one reaches is that these faiths abundantly possess historical resources that could justify their making connections with contemporary civil society discourse. They even have resources to support the idea of their constituting civil-society communities *together*, perhaps inviting participation in their riches by persons not members of any faith. They also possess means for directly engaging the political-philosophical discourses of modernity, possibly to help restore values that modernity has lost.

Framing the Question Conceptually

It is important to focus now on the question of how such shared participation by Abrahamic cosmopolitans in contemporary social discourses can, or should, be conceptually framed. How might contemporary political philosophy accommodate such an idea? It may help to clarify what I am urging here with the proposals of contemporary social contract theorists, such as John Rawls and Jürgen Habermas.[13] These thinkers work by proposing alternative secular social models: models *for* the way we should relate to one another rather than simply models *of* the way we actually do relate. In such models-for, the actual meeting of religious traditions for addressing public issues occupies a secondary place. Rawls sees such encounter as reflecting only a rather sedentary "overlap" of "reasonable comprehensive doctrines" in support of an independently conceived theory of justice as fairness. Habermas does something analogous with his notion of a "discourse ethic" enacting the philosopher's ideas of the basic characteristics of "communicative rationality" and the "ideal speech situation." Within such independently derived but culturally shared understandings of the nature of moral discourse, different groups are invited continuously to adjudicate their various interests.

John Rawls on Frameworks of Justice

I have chosen to frame our issue initially in Rawlsian terms. I could have done otherwise. There is, on the surface at least, everything wrong with having chosen Rawls. He was, after all, an American social philosopher writing from a privileged social location, the Harvard Faculty of Arts and Sciences. The use of his work might be thought to fall under the stricture mentioned above, namely the danger of seeing the question as one of exporting one's own particular form of democratic consciousness, rather than observing what (if any) democratic processes, in what combination and with what forms of cultural embeddedness, obtain in any particular part of the world. But Rawls was an analyst of the concept of justice as such. He worked with ideas, such as giving priority to the least advantaged, that attracted not a few liberationists in his time. It may not be too much to say that Rawls remains one of the two philosophers (Jürgen Habermas is the other) in terms of whose thought much work by others on religious communities in civil society has been done.[14] Above all, Rawls was—in my view at least—the twentieth century's most important social contract theorist, who illumined the terms on which citizens of democratic societies in effect agree to live together.

I intend to use Rawls's conception of the relation between social justice and the contributions of "reasonable comprehensive doctrines" (among which he includes certain, but not all, religious communities) as a kind of baseline for setting up the question before us. We will find that Rawls's work is highly suggestive for this purpose, but that it needs to be supplemented for our purposes, partly by reference to Habermas and finally by reference to Michael Walzer.

Of Rawls's widespread influence there can be little doubt. With the publication of *A Theory of Justice*[15] in 1971, this philosopher became the principal *theorist* (rather than originator, of course) of the consensus which in one form or another has dominated most Western polities since the horrors of the seventeenth-century wars of religion set in motion a social marginalization of traditional religions in favor of secular public rationality in the service of nationalistic faiths. I think it is fair to say that something like this sort of consensus—despite its obvious Western origin—is being presupposed in many of the movements toward modernization, secularization, and the adaptation-to-context of democratic processes in different parts of the globe. I call this consensus, borrowing from our friends in astrophysics, the "standard model." It goes more or less as follows:

(1) Certain basic and universal moral beliefs are required by the structure of human reason independently of any particular visions of the good or specific religious convictions.

(2) Autonomously reasoned out, these convictions provide a public order that protects particular religious or other visions of the good, giving them room to flourish so long as they do not intrude their special pleading into the realm of public discourse.

(3) Religious groups are free, within their own communities, to *interpret* this independently derived, autonomous vision of society in terms of their own larger conceptions of human existence, and thus *support* the commonly held conception of the public sphere even if they are prohibited from publicly articulating their theological reasons for doing so.[16]

Rawls has probably been more responsible than anyone else in our time for rearticulating the fulcrum concept at work in this "standard model": the nearly unanimously received opinion among contemporary "liberal" political philosophers that practical questions of justice in society at large need to be separated from final questions of the "good" for human beings that cannot be dealt with in the public realm. As is well known, Rawls sought in *Theory* to articulate a set of social principles to this end derived from human reasoning processes alone, apart from communal moral traditions or specific constellations of self-interest. He did this by hypothetically placing a group of discussants in what he calls the "original position" behind a "veil of ignorance" that prevents them from knowing who they are and what are their "interests" in the real world, the better to reason out what a just society would be like. This experiment yielded what amounted to a social contract consisting of just a few basic principles: freedom consistent with similar freedom for others, free access to careers open to merit, only the degree of inequality in social rewards needed to benefit the whole of society and especially its poorest citizens. The watchword was "justice as fairness." The content of this contract was deliberately "thin." It was basic to Rawls's position that theories of the good, of what human flourishing should consist of, are not matters for public debate.

In response to criticism, Rawls has since given more attention to political relationships, at least as he believes they should ideally be constituted, hence the title *Political Liberalism*.[17] This is some distance from being a plunge into actual political realities, but it is a step toward the real world from *A Theory of Justice*. It is here that Rawls seeks to illumine the character of "public reason," by which he means the processes by which just societies reach practical decisions. Rawls writes:

> A political society … has a way of formulating its plans, of putting its ends in an order of priority and of making its decisions accordingly. The way a political society does this is its reason; its ability to do these things is also its reason, though in a different sense: it is an intellectual and moral power, rooted in the capacities of its human members.[18]

Rawls further develops (i.e., from the first book to the second) his idea of an "overlapping consensus" among "reasonable comprehensive doctrines" in support of "justice as fairness." Reasonable comprehensive doctrines are coherent conceptions of the good for human beings embodied in broad teachings about the underlying nature of things to which groups of citizens give their allegiance. As examples, Rawls offers the doctrines of Kant's moralism, or of Mill's utilitarianism, or of the unitarianism of William Ellery Channing. The last named is the closest Rawls comes to mentioning an identifiably *theological* position, although one thinks he would include any that he felt to be inherently "reasonable." What does "reasonable" mean? In this context it apparently means a disposition not to behave in ways that challenge the established liberal order of things. Some doctrines are not "reasonable." Rawls mentions those of Nietzsche and of Ignatius Loyola! It is not clear what he would have said of the Abrahamic faiths, or other world religions. Such lived "doctrines" seem not to have been within his purview. But perhaps, if challenged, he would have said that faiths such as these could be, and sometimes were, even if not very often, propounded in "reasonable" forms. It is another question whether we should wish to lodge this book's category of religiously cosmopolitan "responsibility-bearers" comfortably within Rawls's scheme of things.

The notion of "overlapping consensus" is yoked with Rawls's concept of "reflective equilibrium," by which he means the constant testing of the results achieved in the "original position" behind the veil of ignorance against a society's "considered judgments" concerning justice in particular cases. In one sense this is a matter of society's "uptake" of theory into practice. Definitions of justice for Rawls need to be continually adjusted to match the practical testing that goes on in this "uptake." Presumably the justice principle is taken up into the "overlapping consensus" formed in the confluence of "reasonable comprehensive doctrines." This whole, essentially political, process of achieving reflective equilibrium between moral theory philosophically understood and considered moral judgments reached in the actual life of society flows into Rawls's idea of "public reason."[19]

For religious groups willing to see themselves in terms of Rawlsian reasonableness, then, the philosopher sketches out a modest, respectable role in contemporary society. But he does more. He sketches a scene in which comprehensive doctrines share an "overlapping consensus" in their support of the liberal order, and presumably in support of the sort of public reasoning characteristic of that order. One has to say, however, that it is not clear what an "overlapping consensus" in Rawlsian terms is or means. If such a "consensus" has content, is the content drawn from different sections of different bodies of doctrine judged, somehow, by someone, to be homologous, or congruent, with one another? Are various aspects of the different bodies of conviction concerned thought by some neutral observer to share some identifiable property and therefore singled out to participate in the substance of the consensus? Or is this consensus somehow consciously worked out in an appropriate forum? We are not told.

In view of questions like these, it is not surprising that Rawls says little to make us think that his "overlapping consensus" gives public reasoning any significant *content* beyond what is already generated by the "intellectual and moral power" that citizens of a liberal society are presumed to possess. On the contrary, one gathers that the "overlapping consensus" would not exist were there not already a process of public reasoning based on "justice as fairness" to elicit it and give it a supportive role. Certainly the proponents of comprehensive doctrines have not consciously agreed to make a common front in support of a given social vision. It is "justice as fairness" that draws them together and serves as the sole content of the "overlap."

But is this all? Rawls makes clear that the "overlap" is not a mere *modus vivendi* or negotiated truce among antagonists. Support at least, if not the provision of content for public reasoning reflecting the "justice" project, presumably comes from deep within the various comprehensive doctrines' systems of self-understanding. Presumably they are serious and principled in giving their assent. Perhaps they even support Rawls's own theory in particular. Still, the impression remains that comprehensive doctrines are not thought to contribute substantively to the *content* of the notion of "justice as fairness." They merely endorse, in their own ways and without apparent collusion, the same set of principles for a justice-seeking public reason that has its own autonomous reasons for being.

In fact, religious communities represent a wide range of the cultures and interests that need to be involved in any effective "overlap." Rawls's theory would be more persuasive if he had been more aware of the question of *how* religious bodies represent the cultures and interests they do. First, if they have been listening, religious bodies have begun to have more than the usual sense of the new forms of ethical consciousness our age demands, possessing, as they do, traditions capable of resonating with such requirements. And, second, it is therefore possible that such representation will be more effectively "enlightened" than more purely interest-based advocacy, say, by trade unions. Religious groups *may* clothe the interests and ambitions of their peoples with a kind of critical-cultural legitimacy instead of the usual arbitrary claims to turf. They *may* thereby present their peoples' claims in what Ronald Dworkin calls their "best light."

This observation connects with an often-forgotten aspect of John Rawls's version of the social contract. In arriving at the sheaf of disinterested agreements constituting the so-called "original position," the direct pressing of conflicting interest claims is disallowed. The actors behind the "veil of ignorance" represent what these claims would be like if they were articulated at their moral best, that is, without being self-serving. It would be naive to suppose that having religious communities as presenters of group claims could actually reproduce such an admittedly idealized situation. Yet religious communities could help member groups present their claims in a manner less dependent on competing interests and more enlightened by knowledge of dimensions of justice beyond those invoked in their own cases. Could something like this be what José Casanova meant by saying that, in comparison with secularism's "obscurantist, ideological, and inauthentic claims … it is religion which, as often as not, appears to be on the side of human enlightenment"?[20] The contracting or covenanting process through which religious communities help (as Casanova says) to "save modernity" generates a new kind of social space, a place for new kinds of spiritual-cultural resonance, a place in which a genuinely unprecedented reaching out not only to *the* Other but to all Others may come to pass. Thus the kind of social contracting that begins with the practice of a "parallel hermeneutics" of traditions continues into the actual practice of public affairs.

Such reasoning displays the potential of Rawls's theory at its best. But religious communities may very well not be ready to take part in the "overlapping consensus" on Rawls's terms. The reasoning leading to such participation among proponents of different doctrines would be as various as the doctrines themselves. For some, support of the liberal order would rest on a strong sense of basic affinity between the Rawlsian formula and their own visions of life. For others, support would be largely a matter of practical self-interest. Many would find themselves somewhere in between. These differences could be significant in trying to work on what an "overlap" might mean if it were to take account of the actual substance of different visions of life, including theological visions. But such a "consensus" of diverse communally maintained visions of life presumably would not exist at all were there not a thin but politically dominant secular social contract already in existence to attract such agreement.

My argument that the so-called "overlapping consensus" displays little awareness of what religious communities are actually thinking seems consistent with this position. Entering the "overlapping consensus" turns out to be like going behind the "veil of ignorance" in the first place. The persons behind the veil reach their own consensus of the principles of justice by calculating probabilities of weal and woe (seemingly in terms of personal self-interest) without knowing what "reasonable comprehensive doctrines" if any, they hold in the real world. This notion of a bloodless primordial "overlap" may be plausible to Rawls only because his notion of the range of possible reasonable doctrines is so narrow. To move only from Kant to Mill to William Ellery Channing is to cover a rather restricted spectrum of admittedly dead white authors. It is to miss virtually all of what makes *politics* so interesting: forceful competing personalities, deep antagonisms between left and right, attempts to make peace between organized (and sometimes armed) interests, and the like.

Given that Rawls began to admit, by 1985 if not earlier, that his justice theory was not the conceptually autonomous construct he originally thought it to be, but rather articulates "the way we live," one is surprised that he does not see that reasonable comprehensive doctrines, which certainly constitute aspects of "the way we live," might have some impact on public reason. For Rawls to acknowledge this point, of course, would mean to sacrifice the "thinness" of his notion of the public world, vitiating the distinction between justice as a public principle and visions of the good life as communal or traditional principles, such as those represented in the Abrahamic faiths, the distinction on which his entire theory is based.

Jürgen Habermas on Discourse Ethics

To a degree, Rawls's shortcomings for our purposes are mitigated in the work of Jürgen Habermas. Habermas's project in itself has strong ethical overtones. The "theory of communicative action" is intended as a theory of social justice achieved through communication among different views and traditions. These, as Habermas sees them, are bound to be culturally variable. But a search for justice is the indispensable ground floor of any moral project involving different faith traditions. Habermas pursues this search by means of an inquiry into the logic of human communication as such. Moving in

the Kantian frame of reference that prescribes the logical universalizabil-
ity of one's maxims of conduct as the primary criterion of moral behavior,
Habermas asks what universal conditions we presuppose in the very act of
communicating with others. These fundamental conditions of communication become the basis for a universal, if "thin," ethic for the modern world.

Briefly stated, Habermas posits a "speech-act immanent obligation"
in every act of communication whereby the communicator takes on, and
expects from others, an accountability for justifying what has been said,
what we in this book have called mutual hermeneutical responsibility. Such
a view of communication in turn presupposes an "ideal speech situation" in
which all can participate free of restraint or any sort of ideological disadvan-
tage, and the assumption that one's own communications are unconstrained,
candid, and truthful. But it is Habermas's assumption that the resulting ethic
is incompatible with all forms of "traditional ethics," that is, "with any ethical
system which keeps 'a dogmatized core of basic convictions' away from the
demand for justification."[21] I agree, furthermore, with Stephen White,[22] that
such an ethic is rather minimal in the sense that it does not provide much
basis for "sorting out types of ethical positions as more or less rationally justifiable," and that it is based not on a universally applicable concept of communicative action, but only on a distinctively modern notion of argumentation
shared by only a portion of the human beings alive today.[23]

Habermas writes as if all qualified participants in the human dialogue will
in the long run recognize "the better argument." What does this assertion
really mean? I think it is a way of saying, with Hegel, that ultimately "the real
is the rational and the rational is the real," even if we cannot prove, except
by way of a kind of pragmatic "as if," that it is so. Habermas is building an
interpretation of what Hegel called "objective spirit," as it were, from below.[24]
The fact that he does so procedurally, rather than ontologically, does not
blind us to what is, in Kantian terms, "postulated" by the very fact of entering
a moral argument in a field of communicative action. Needed to complete
the logic of this field of discourse is something like a notion that all human
beings, given sufficiently extended conversation, will find themselves within
a single field of rationality in which "the better argument" will be evident to
all discussants.[25]

If Habermas is right, we need some sense of what "the better argument"
would be like. Recent attempts to understand the nature of practical moral
reasoning (see chapter 3) do not reassure us that agreement will come at the
end of a dialogical process, even if that is envisioned as indefinitely prolonged.
The current field of debate has settled into an argument between the "objectivists" on the one hand and the "relativists" or "tribalists," on the other. In
the first camp, there is the position of Rawls, who is an antitraditionalist,

neo-Enlightenment figure, who seeks to eliminate the element of personal interest in argumentation by postulating the formation of moral principles behind a "veil of ignorance." Rawls illustrates one option: try to grasp principles that lie beyond all particular cultural locations, all special interests. But it has become clear since *A Theory of Justice* that these principles are not as universal as Rawls once thought. They represent only what seems right for educated women and men of the West in the late twentieth century.[26]

In the opposite camp, there is Alasdair MacIntyre, who is trying to repristinate a clear tradition of moral argument (the Aristotelian) in terms that would make it communicable in the contemporary intellectual marketplace.[27] MacIntyre illustrates the other option: take a particular tradition of discourse and find a way to state its essence in terms that can be widely shared in the modern world. But it is not clear that this attempt succeeds either. Richard Bernstein's critique of MacIntyre suggests not only that the moral tradition of the Aristotelian virtues is less coherent than the Catholic scholar alleges, but also that his derivation of basic virtues from the practical needs of realms of "practice" involves a *non sequitur*.[28] Can one translate the pragmatic essence of a moral tradition into language that will pass muster in a world of "communicative action" without also defending the "biological metaphysics" or other fundamental assertions of the tradition's classical texts? Can such a defense possibly succeed in the public world with which we are concerned? One way to evade the clash of objectivists and relativists may be by recourse to two of Hans Georg Gadamer's central convictions: that the meaning of interpretation lies in application of our inherited meanings to pragmatic concerns and that such application leads us to a process of practical reasoning or *phronesis*.[29] A contemporary definition of the latter term runs as follows: "Phronesis is the historically implicated, communally nurtured ability to make good sense of relatively singular contexts in ways appropriate to their relative singularity."[30] This is as good a description of the actual character of reasoning in the public sphere involving different faith traditions as any I know. It says that, quite apart from the theories of either "objectivists" or "tribalists," we settle public questions by piecemeal argument in ways appropriate to the kind of question we are dealing with and the specific situation we have to face. Political, legal, economic, educational, and other kinds of questions need attention in the vocabularies and conceptualities native to those disciplines. But they are translated into the public realm in highly practical ways, on the basis of some sort of minimal general agreement among people about what "makes sense." While special interests and ideologies always enter the debate, in the end we are very pragmatic about what we do. If we want broad support, we have to confine ourselves to a sense-making that is communicable at press conferences and on the evening news.

It would seem that the closer one comes to actual rough-and-tumble politics, the less well a liberal-minded rationalism either describes what is going on or prescribes medicine for our political ailments. Our political actions are in fact interpretations of the stories on which we have been brought up and the doctrines we hold. Hence hermeneutical insights may need to be "grafted" (Ricoeur's phrase) into Rawls's and Habermas's respective problematics. The public world may better resemble a high-temperature struggle toward temporary "fusions of horizons" (Gadamer) than a field for the exercise of cool calculative capacities. What is coherent and even persuasive as a rational-liberal moral philosophy does not fit into the realm of practical political horse-trading. An aggressive interplay of forces, not calmly detached reasoning, makes the public world what it is. "Justice as fairness" does not sit serenely on a pedestal once the theory behind it has achieved clarification. A lived "conflict of interpretations" (Ricoeur) of moral formations of all kinds yields the field in which we seek to do justice.

Shortcomings of Rawlsian and Habermasian Theory in a Fragmented World

It has been worth our while to dwell for a few pages on Rawls and Habermas, if only because they have been the West's most persuasive philosophical exponents of the meaning of public reason in the liberal democratic context of many communities of meaning, religious and otherwise. They represent the enlightened political ideal of "modernity" at its best. They brilliantly expose, at least in theory, many of the considerations involved in the dialectic between confessional or community-based perspectives, what Rawls calls "reasonable comprehensive doctrines" and Habermas calls "lifeworlds" (as opposed to "systems") and a philosophy of public reasoning concerning justice issues. All future work on such matters must take account of their categories and insights. But neither philosopher's work describes the actual social reality of liberal democracy in the world today. Rather they give us idealizations of what it ought to be. We have seen in chapter 3 that the reality is quite different. The enlightened liberal ideal of democratic society has deteriorated. What Rawls called "public reason" has become detached from its cultural and religious sources. It has turned to condoning reasoning based on greed and the acquisition of power: cost-benefit calculation designed only to prevail in a competitive world. Such a version of "modernity," José Casanova has argued, needs to be saved from itself by religious communities that are carriers of a deeper sort of enlightenment. If the Abrahamic faiths and other religious communities are to gather around the project of encouraging more deeply enlightened democratic processes in many different cultures— including those who have never before experienced such processes—and if they are to do this in such a way as to benefit human beings of all faiths (or of no faith at all), then they must do so, so far as possible, out of their own resources without reference to a philosophical argument that idealizes justice but does not contend for it in the political rough-and-tumble. The problem, in short, lies in the gap between any ideal social conceptuality, whether Rawlsian or Habermasian, and the actual political-social reality of what pass as democratic processes in many parts of the world. Much that is presupposed in these high-minded theories is simply no longer the case, if it ever was. One cannot take for granted a willingness of competing economic or political interests to gather—even in their wildest imaginations—behind a "veil of ignorance" or assume "speech-act immanent obligations" to think out what justice might require of them.

There are writers who believe, in fact, that the whole effort—by Rawls, Habermas, and many others, some of whom have been named—to construct an ideal theory of society has come to nothing. Alasdair MacIntyre[31] has told us, for example, that we live in many incommensurable moral worlds. These universes of discourse evince their own internal forms of coherence as "arguments" sustained over time in which others cannot easily participate. Tristram Engelhardt goes further.[32] Writing from a postmodern perspective, he sees Western society as a world of "moral strangers," individuals who find coherent moral discourse among themselves impossible. Distinctive moral communities do exist here and there, but none has the potential for integrating our fragmented public world. The modern liberal project in its various Kantian, utilitarian, or Rawlsian forms is thus for Engelhardt a failure. Unlike MacIntyre, who hopes that an Aristotelian coherence may triumph over Nietzschian nihilism, Engelhardt concludes that Nietzsche accurately foresees our fate. Under such conditions, issues can only be resolved by "peaceable negotiations" of an *ad hoc* type, characterized by free and informed consent among individuals and rights of privacy in relation to the state. The result is a permissive sort of bioethics, a form of secular humanism, notably open to market mechanisms that offer a form of "pure procedural justice." Here is an utterly minimal framework for the practical cooperation of individuals whose lives are constructed around purely instrumental goals as they pursue "the goods and pleasures of this world." There is no basis here for resistance to economic or other forms of injustice: no possibility, in Casanova's terms, of rescuing modernity from itself.

We live indeed in a pragmatic, possibly even Rortyan, social space where many views jostle, where we lash our ruminations together by means of a sort of *bricolage*. I maintain that what makes sense in such a sociality is precisely what citizens of many persuasions in actual fact find "fitting." It is what comports with the overlapping possibilities of many forms of moral imagination or spaces of moral possibility. It is not that MacIntyre is wrong in holding that we live in many different moral worlds, and employ many different sorts of moral discourse. But these worlds are not "incommensurable." Out of those different moral universes we nonetheless create pragmatically overlapping spaces of moral imagination without assuming that we all reason the same way. Thus we can agree to a point what we will support in the commonly shared social world. We can agree, to some extent, to merge our public spaces of reasoning. So much the better if social policy does *not* claim to be based in some closed but supposedly universal system of secular reasoning that we are all asked to support.

In short, one cannot take for granted the relevance of *any* political philosophy of the Rawlsian or Habermasian type when it comes to trying to reconstruct a just world. One must begin with the supposition that we are utter strangers to one another; that we cannot comprehend what Rawls asks us to do in discussing justice together behind the "veil of ignorance" because we have virtually no categories in common. As the coherence of Western modernity diminishes and as experimentation in democratic processes goes on in cultures with little or no previous experience in any case with Western Enlightenment-type categories, or violent revulsion against them, the problem becomes one of constructing peaceable, reasonably liberal orders of society out of the whole cloth of competing ancient religious traditions.

Let us suppose that Engelhardt's account is at least descriptively accurate. Let us suppose that this is our condition: one to which Rawlsian or Habermasian arguments cannot effectively speak. Yet Engelhardt still speaks of the possibility of "peaceable negotiation." There must remain, then, *some* tattered traditions of discourse, at least, in this fragmented, instrumentalist society that permits such peaceable negotiation to take place. It is useful to confront Engelhardt's picture with William O'Neill's reconstruction of just such a notion of discourse grounded in a conception of human rights embedded in community-sustaining language. In his article, appropriately titled "Babel's Children: Reconstructing the Common Good,"[33] O'Neill works this out in somewhat Habermasian terms.[34] A common good is enacted in a discourse community in which "the practice of rational claim-making presumes the mutual respect of practically rational agents,"[35] in which human rights "derive their backing from the principle of mutual respect,"[36] and thus "serve as warrants in our 'reasoned speech,'"[37] and in which there is a correlation between the "said" and the "shown" in the justification of rights.[38] O'Neill concludes, "Interpreted discursively, the common good signifies the regime of basic rights presupposed in reasoned speech within and across our narrative traditions."[39]

O'Neill's approach combines an appeal to the putative universality of the human capacity for reasoned speech with an openness to specificity that invites the participation of traditioned communities. Those who either defend or deny such practices of rational-claim making "appeal, implicitly to a universal audience for vindication."[40] But such "rights rhetoric does not so much suppress our native tongues in a grand metanarrative as ensure that all may speak. The universal maxim of respect for the 'concrete other' bids us attend to its *particular* narrative embodiment."[41] Otherwise said, the traditions of particular communities, Abrahamic communities, for example, are needed to clothe with specificity the abstract rhetoric of rights language. The presence of such communities, in which practices assure some correlation between the "said" and the "shown," is therefore indispensable to the ongoing enactment of the public good as O'Neill understands it. One may reason about rights, but there are no rights historically deployed apart from communally lived narratives that embody them.

O'Neill's way of dealing with the post-Rawlsian situation here described is helpful for at least two reasons. First, he presupposes a general human capacity for "reasoned speech" (thus recalling Rawls's proposals about "public reason") without specifying any single, culturally given pattern of reasoning. If the reasoning in question has to do with "human rights," at least we are dealing with a topic broadly discussed in many different ways across cultures, in accordance with Robert Schreiter's notion of "global theological flows."[42] One does not need to impose a particular "theory of justice" upon all possible situations to make this recognition possible. Second, O'Neill invokes, much in the style of Emmanuel Lévinas, the demand for respect for the concrete Other: again a demand that knows no single cultural location. And if the Other confronts us with a demand, we must attend to the communal narratives that make him or her the person he or she is. Between myself and him- or herself, there is need for what I have called a parallel, yet interactive, hermeneutics of traditions (see chapters 4 and following). Rights language *per se* may be abstract, but it is hermeneutically grounded in the mutual respect due when persons meet, and especially when these persons represent different life-narratives, different cultural formations, that encounter one another in the meeting.

I can say this differently. My parallel/interactive hermeneutical description of the meeting of religious traditions in the public world aims to be independent of any theory of society reached under conditions of idealized rationality in the scholar's study (i.e., all interests represented behind Rawls's "veil of ignorance" by morally perfected versions of themselves). Instead of a passive, rather blurry, "overlap" of traditions judged "reasonable" if they support the philosopher's theory, I want to see independent, tradition-based interpretations of the public world going on in a manner actively responsible to the embodied religious narratives that meet one another in this way. I want to see actual covenanting, followed by contracting, among value-laden communities as a source of public values. I think of a very down-to-earth political process in which many different cultures try to reach ways of living together that untidily embody practical compromises that can grow into just social relationships.

"Thick" and "Thin": The Perspective of Michael Walzer

A helpful model of such down-to-earth relating among value-laden communities can be found in the writings of another, in this case Jewish, political philosopher, Michael Walzer, first in his *Spheres of Justice* and then particularly in his small volume *Thick and Thin*.[43] Walzer's vision sees "maximal" moral identities, precisely such as those of religious or other specific cultural groups, as primary in the constituting of the larger society. Holders of "thick" moral codes—such as those of Judaism, Christianity, or Islam and their many variants—interact with one another so as to produce "thin" agreements for specific circumstances representing society as a whole. These "thin" public agreements build upon, crystallize for particular times and places, the pragmatic meetings of different worlds of moral imagination. And in turn they constitute the building blocks of more covenantal, more just social contracts in the public world fostered by the kind of interactions among "thick" traditions that I have described as "parallel hermeneutics." There is no appeal here in Walzer to common "liberal" theory (e.g., that of Rawls or Habermas) of what "the" social contract *ought* to be like. Rather Walzer describes a process of dialogue by which one group appeals to the experiences or sympathies of the other, thereby building a solidarity of responsible trust between them. As Mark Douglas has written, "So understood, one group's appeal to another group's moral sense is not an act of derivation, but one of imagination."[44]

Here is the value of the mutual moral imagination fostered by parallel hermeneutics. How do we imagine such acts of imagination taking place? In a considerable variety of ways, depending on circumstances. Certain metaphors for such a process are helpful. One may think of Abrahamic traditions and secular initiatives discovering, or pursuing, a certain "resonance" between their visions of life and public policies: a recognition that, however unfamiliar may be the public languages in use, they are tuned to nearby wave lengths.

To hear such resonances, we need discernment of the ways covenantal impulses have worked themselves out in the complexities of social history: as described for example in chapter 6, dealing with giving and receiving forgiveness, fostering trust, and living in solidarity. These verbal expressions, we remember, are ways of denominating certain kinds and qualities of human interaction that express what Abrahamic religious covenants are about: by restating them so far as possible in terms of common human experience. These mutual hermeneutical explorations may function to bridge the gap between Abrahamic covenantal traditions by articulating the quality of relationships they together hope to foster in the world of public institutions. They refer to qualities of human interaction in society in which the keepers of the Abrahamic traditions may be able to recognize a certain degree of congruence with their own experiences of moral formation, thus generating public spaces in which the traditions can meet.

In this perspective, *the* social contract has evolved from being a hypothetical construct by political philosophers to explain society's very existence (as it is in Locke or Rousseau, Rawls or Habermas) to become a set of imaginatively shared assumptions about the ways we live together, the ways we are "minded" to relate to one another. Being "so minded," we are eventually able to enter into specific legislative agreements that regulate the contracts we enter into in everyday life. Insights such as these prod us to revise our effective social contract so that the now dominant totalizing ideological trends are no longer supported, no longer taken for granted.

One could then ask of a proposed piece of legislation whether it evinces the "covenantal virtues" developed in chapter 6: that is, (1) whether it reflects readiness for forgiveness and reconciliation; (2) whether it is offered in such a way as to engender conditions of trust; and (3) whether it is conceived in solidarity with the interests of those least able to defend themselves. In short, we can, as faiths acting together, ask whether this legislation represents a stance of responsibility for the future of the community in question, and ultimately of the covenantal promise of blessing offered the human race in Genesis 12:3.

Such questions could make possible certain directional decisions, certain common agreements about the character of possible next steps. These could, in turn, lead to something resembling what J. H. Oldham,[45] and after him John Bennett,[46] called "middle axioms," that is, agreements that in particular places and situations one's first principles should be expressed in terms of more focused, but not yet contextually detailed, policies or orientations. These could, again in turn, help guide specific actions: drafting a particular piece of legislation, supporting a particular initiative, voting for a particular bill. Such particular actions in themselves would be regarded by Walzer as "thin," focused on very specific matters, specific small steps along the way toward the goal of an intercovenantal society.

Presumably a succession of many such at-first-minimal steps gradually produces a public political tradition. This in time grows "thick" in its own right, generating institutions, laws, customs, public culture, all the products of parallel actions authorized by the many more maximal cultures of their origin. In Walzer's terms, thickness interacts with thickness (tribe meets tribe) and works out limited practical agreements that both express mutual obligations and expectations and face common threats. Such pacts in turn help generate the social capital needed to deal politically with questions related to the future of humanity as such, not just the survival of particular groups in competition with one another.[47]

Perhaps there is need to make an agreement over land use, water rights, intergroup marriage, or some other vital interest. The resulting arrangement—perhaps a treaty or legal precedent—will be very specific (Walzer will call it "thin") in comparison with the cultures on either side of the agreement. But it will need to draw, at least indirectly, on those factors in the cultures of the parties concerned that offer promise that the terms are understood and that the bargain will be kept. Each side finds in the other sufficient grounds for expecting support of the common agreement. Each discovers elements within its own culture that offer analogies for comprehending the terms of the treaty and reasons for observing it. Each ideally finds parables of its own "truth" in the other's songs and stories. Covenant breaking is then seen by both to violate who they *are*, to undermine their very identities.

I suggest that such elements of social contract, in their original "thin" forms, based on perhaps minimal intercultural overlaps, function subsequently as "armatures" on which thicker cultural flesh may form. In practical terms, of course, it is not always which comes first, the armature or the clay. Neither comes into being *de novo*. Always there are predecessor armatures and predecessor embodiments. People may first need a minimal framework of justice before they begin to lay on the human form. Or they may already have a "thicker" set of relationships whose underlying framework they need, for one reason or another, to discover. Either way, the analogy from sculpture seems to me apt: you build up the human shape in layers upon the thin, minimal framework, or you ask what lies behind the figuration of life you already have. If you live for a while with a "thin" agreement. you begin to supplement it with other sorts of relationships. At the very least, the agreement needs to be commonly interpreted, founding a shared legal culture, grounded in a shared moral" framework." Confidence raised by forgiving, trust-building, and solidaristic behavior at one point spawns confidence at other points.

Indeed, I believe that the dialectic between the framework and the flesh illumines how common cultures emerge and gain stability where before there was only plurality. Around each formal or informal pact, a new shared culture extending to other matters arises. To the extent that the core agreement fosters some form of life together, analogous stories may come to be shared. The fact that a dominating culture is likely itself the product of many previous accords between disparate groups does not change the basic equation. If new groups are encouraged to join, there is still the need for covenantal acts of mutual imagination. But then, of course, disparities of power need to be recognized and taken into account. Each group needs to find its own reasons for taking the risky responsibility of reaching out to establish such relationships in the culture of the other (at least as manifest in the negotiation if not through deeper knowledge) for confidence that the agreement is fair and will be kept.[48] One can imagine that such primordial relationships among the Canaanite kingdoms of the second millennium BCE are what Abraham sought to establish through his culture-sensitive interventions described in Genesis 15–19.

At some point along this way, the communities engaged in articulating thin, and eventually thickening, agreements out of exercises in mutual moral imagination may or may not find it useful to draw on the work of political philosophers such as Rawls or Habermas. My point is that neither such political philosophies, nor the distinctively Western political institutions their theories seek to illuminate, can serve as the sole ground for arranging meetings among disparate religions or cultures. Acts of mutual moral imagination are needed first. The need for academic theorizing or a borrowing of specific institutions like "democratic" elections always should follow on the establishment of reciprocal moral imagination to the point that questions begin to be asked indigenously, from within growing mutuality about capturing and preserving growing mutuality by the use of ideas and institutions adapted from other sources. This borrowing needs to be initiated from *within* the space of mutual moral imagination among religious cultures, not imposed on those spaces of discourse by Western zealots anxious to spread their own versions of "democratic ideals" across the globe. The questions are always *what* democratic ideas and institutions can help stabilize accomplished interreligious understandings and *how* such ideas can be adapted to the specific situations involved. Perhaps the work of Rawls or Habermas or their successors, the work of religious scholars or political institutions, such as legislatures or courts or cabinet structures, will prove useful as situationally adapted to the forms of civil society already generated out of more primordial practices of moral hospitality and interreligious moral imagination. Such practices are precisely those involved in what I have called "parallel and interactive hermeneutics."

The chapter that follows puts these perspectives to the sternest practical test one can imagine: that of illuminating what is at stake in the conflict among the Abrahamic faiths in today's Israel-Palestine. I will try to lay out the practical matters in dispute as best I can and inquire how the different religious traditions construe their situations in relation to these struggles. I will look at processes of international diplomacy in the Middle East, both as the competitive pursuit of a variety of different national strategic interests and as the attempt to hammer out workable structures of justice for all concerned. I will look at the three religious communities living in the midst of all this and ask if they have the potential for forming a single, yet complexly textured, civil society capable of articulating the meaning of the "blessing," many of them yearn to live out together on behalf of the promise to all earth's families.

Notes

1. Thomas Friedman has made this point in numerous Op-Ed columns in the *New York Times,* as well as in several books. See chapter 1, note 3.

2. See chapter 2 for a detailed treatment of Casanova's argument.

3. John Kelsay, ed., in *The Annual of the Society of Christian Ethics* (Washington, DC: Georgetown University Press, 1998), 161ff.

4. I am indebted to Adam B. Seligman, *The Idea of Civil Society* (New York: Free Press, 1992), 145ff., for this insight and others in this chapter.

5. Ibid.

6. Jean L. Cohen and Andrew Arato, *Civil Society and Political Theory* (Cambridge, MA: MIT Press, 1992).

7. Amyn Sajoo has edited the results of this study into a volume titled *Civil Society in the Muslim World: Contemporary Perspectives* (New York: St. Martin's Press, 2002). Chapters by nine other writers are also included in the volume, among them an essay "Locating Civil Society in Islamic Contexts" by the eminent scholar Mohammed Arkoun, professor emeritus at the Sorbonne, Gifford Lecturer, and Chair of Islamic Studies at the U.S. Library of Congress.

8. Sherif Mardin, "Civil Society and Islam," in *Civil Society: Theory, History, Comparison,* ed. J. A. Hall (Cambridge, MA : Polity Press, 1995), 278, quoted in Sajoo, *Civil Society,* 1.

9. Sajoo, *Civil Society,* 15.

10. Sohail H. Hashmi, "Cultivating a Liberal Islamic Ethos: Building an Islamic Civil Society," *The Journal of the Society of Christian Ethics* 27, no. 1 (Spring/Summer 2007): 3–16.

11. Ibid., 7

12. Ibid., 8.

13. See John Rawls, *A Theory of Justice* (Cambridge, MA: Harvard University Press, 1971) and Jürgen Habermas, *Theory of Communicative Action: Reason and the Rationalization of Society,* trans. Thomas McCarthy (Boston: Beacon Press, 1984).

14. My own teacher, Paul Ricoeur, who commented extensively on Rawls, would habitually confront nearly every question on which he wrote by first tracing it through the thought of classical thinkers: most often Aristotle, Kant, Hegel, Husserl, or Heidegger. With my treatment of Rawls, I am doing much the same thing. We will then see where this process leads us.

15. Rawls, *Theory of Justice.*

16. This account of the "standard model" is derived, with certain amendments, from John P. Reeder and Gene Outka, eds., *Prospects for a Common Morality* (Princeton, NJ: Princeton University Press, 1991), 5.

17. John Rawls, *Political Liberalism* (New York: Columbia University Press, 1993).

18. Rawls, *Liberalism*, 212f.

19. The referenced revisions and extensions of the original Rawlsian theory are found in a series of journal articles now collected and edited by Samuel Freeman as *John Rawls: Collected Papers* (Cambridge, MA: Harvard University Press, 1999). These papers further illuminate the background of *Political Liberalism*.

20. José Casanova, *Public Religions in the Modern World* (Chicago: University of Chicago Press, 1994), 234.

21. See Stephen K. White, *The Recent Work of Jürgen Habermas: Reason, Justice, and Modernity* (Cambridge: Cambridge University Press, 1988), 54.

22. Ibid., 55, *et passim*.

23. It is worth noting, as well, that Habermas heavily depends on the psychological theory of moral development worked out by Piaget and Kohlberg, and specifically on the assumption that Kohlberg's sixth level of moral development, the "universal ethical principle orientation," is implicit in the idea of communicative action and exhibits the moral potential of the modern world at its best. See Lawrence Kohlberg, "From Is to Ought," in *Cognitive Development and Epistemology*, ed. Theodore Mischel (New York: Academic Press, 1971).

24. I do not mean that Habermas self-consciously bases his thinking on Hegel, but only that here, as in so many other places in German thought, the legacy of Hegel's formulations lies just beneath the surface. Compare Holub's remark about Gadamer: "The fusing of horizons actually takes place, Gadamer maintains, but it means that the historical horizon is projected and then canceled or eliminated as a separate entity. In an almost Hegelian manner it seems that understanding is historical consciousness becoming aware of itself" (Holub, *Habermas*, 59). Is not the theory of communicative action also an instance of "historical consciousness becoming aware of itself"? Is it not itself a form of rationalizing reflection upon the fusion of horizons?

25. It is important to grasp what is at stake here. Habermas's emphasis on rational consensus is only another version, as Rorty has observed, of the assumption "that all contributions to a given discourse are commensurable." For Rorty, "hermeneutics" (as he uses this expression) is "largely a struggle against this assumption." Richard Rorty, *Philosophy and the Mirror of Nature* (Princeton, NJ: Princeton University Press, 1979), 316, quoted in Richard Bernstein, *Philosophical Profiles* (Philadelphia: University of Pennsylvania Press, 1986), 79–80.

26. See Rawls's own comments in "Kantian Constructivism in Moral Theory," *The Journal of Philosophy* (September 1980): 77. He modifies the universalistic claims of *A Theory of Justice*, remarking that his theory is directly applicable only to "a democratic society under modern circumstances" (518).

27. See Alasdair MacIntyre, *After Virtue* (Notre Dame, IN: Notre Dame University Press, 1981).

28. See Bernstein, *Philosophical Profiles*, 124.

29. See Hans Georg Gadamer, *Truth and Method* (New York: Seabury, 1975), 20ff., 278ff., 376ff., 490. Gadamer connects practical reasoning with the *sensus communis* or sense that

founds human community. *Phronesis* is knowledge that "is directed toward the concrete situation" (21). It is "a determination of moral being which cannot exist without the totality of the 'ethical virtues,' which in turn cannot exist without it" (22).

30. Charles W. Allen, "The Primacy of *Phronesis*, A Proposal for Avoiding Frustrating Tendencies in Our Conceptions of Rationality," *The Journal of Religion* 69 (July 1989): 359ff.

31. MacIntyre, *After Virtue*.

32. Tristram Engelhardt, *Bioethics and Secular Humanism: The Search for a Common Morality*, as described by Arne Rasmusson, *The Church as Polis* (Notre Dame, IN: University of Notre Dame Press, 1995), 273ff.

33. William O'Neill, SJ, "Babel's Children: Reconstructing the Common Good," in *The Annual of the Society of Christian Ethics, 1998*.

34. One may add that such enacting and protecting of human rights as they pertain to a discourse community will always require some sort of legal system. Indeed it has been said that in contemporary America the language of law is familiar in some degree to everyone. It is the great exception to the general fragmentation of our discourse. Most of us know the rules for suing one another! Not without reason has Ronald Dworkin been called America's most important *social* philosopher.

35. *The Annual*, 164.

36. Ibid., 166.

37. Ibid.

38. Ibid., 167.

39. Ibid., 169.

40. Ibid.

41. Ibid., 170.

42. Robert Schreiter, *The New Catholicity: Theology between the Global and the Local* (Maryknoll, NY: Orbis Books, 1997).

43. Michael Walzer, *Thick and Thin: Moral Argument at Home and Abroad* (Notre Dame, IN: University of Notre Dame Press, 1994).

44. Words of Mark Douglas from *Thinking Again about the Reformed Tradition and Public Life*, drafted by Mark Douglas, Lewis Mudge, and James Watkins on behalf of the Consultation on Public Leadership group representing Presbyterian Church-Related Seminaries, October 10, 2001. This report suggests that Walzer's position has some interesting implications. I follow Douglas in drawing out two of them. First, if Walzer is understood to mean that thin moral propositions are persuasive—and therefore useful—only *because* they arise out of thick ones, "it follows that only those accounts that are sufficiently thick to cope with the moral complexity of the world—that is to say, quite thick accounts indeed—can give birth to helpful thin accounts." The thick moral accounts supplied by specific cultural groups thus deserve a place in public discourse: at least in discourse about the thin agreements based imaginatively upon them. "It follows," Douglas continues, "that the range of arguments that may be admitted into public conversation is considerably larger than the classic liberal tradition has allowed."

45. See W. A. Visser 't Hooft and J. H. Oldham, *The Church and Its Function in Society* (London: George Allen and Unwin, 1937), 209f., quoted in Michael Kinnamon and Brian E. Cope, *Ecumenical Movement: An Anthology of Key Texts and Voices* (Grand Rapids, MI: Eerdmans, 1997), 277. "It is not the function of the clergy to tell the laity how to function

in public affairs, but to confront them with the Christian demand and to encourage them to discover its application for themselves. Hence between purely general statements of the ethical demands of the Gospel and the decisions that have to be made in concrete situations there is need for what may be described as middle axioms. It is these that give relevance and point to the Christian ethic. They are an attempt to define the directions in which, in a particular state of society, Christian faith must express itself. They are not binding for all time, but are provisional definitions of the kind of behavior required of Christians at a given period and in given circumstances."

46. John Bennett in *Christian Ethics and Social Policy* (New York: Scriber's, 1946) effectively uses J. H. Oldham's "middle axiom" idea. I have used some of Bennett's examples: the need for international collaboration in UN, the need for balance between free enterprise and government control of the economy, the removal of racial segregation in church and society. "Middle axioms" lie strategically between unchanging principles such as the Christian love commandment and the particular legislation you support.

47. Is Walzer, like Lévinas, here offering us insights from his own Jewish tradition in a neutral philosophical form, thereby inviting us to accept that tradition's "moral hospitality" without incurring specific religious commitments? One might conjecture so. Walzer is now at work on a multivolume edition of the political and social wisdom of Judaism. This work will offer readers—Jewish and non-Jewish, religious and nonreligious—access to this store of wisdom.

48. Narratives constitutive of long-established and dominant communities (the Horatio Alger myth, for example) will often valorize certain sorts of economic behavior, which may or may not be in the interest of the weaker parties.

Part III

For All the Families of the Earth

8

Civil Society and Social Contracts in Israel-Palestine

No situation could present a more searching test of the cogency of what I have argued in these pages, yet be more important to the well-being of all earth's families, than that of contemporary Israel-Palestine. A case from Africa or Indonesia would no doubt be simpler and less burdened with global ramifications. But Israel-Palestine is the case whose resolution could also make a global difference. If it were to be justly settled, it could open the way for deeper relations between Jews, Christians, and Muslims everywhere. While it remains unresolved, those relationships often remain tentative and precarious, vulnerable to the latest news bulletins from the region.

The choice of such a topic for this book, however briefly considered, calls for serious recognition of its difficulties. There is a sense in which one must earn the right to have opinions on this matter by having been there, on the ground, to appreciate the depth of Israeli and Palestinian feelings and convictions. Even statespersons and diplomats schooled in every outward detail of the conflict must know that the mentalities involved on each side are largely impenetrable for all who have not grown up with them. The bloodshed, the horror, the anger, the sheer complexity of everything, are, in the end, indescribable to those living at a safe distance. Thus to use any such case study merely to advance the argument pursued in this book could suggest that the writer does not fully grasp the tragic reality he is dealing with. Yet the Israeli-Palestinian impasse is sorely in need of any fresh perspectives that can possibly be brought to bear, so long as these are offered with deepest respect to those struggling with its enormous complexity on the scene.

There is also a sense in which, despite all these difficulties, I *owe* the reader this particular case analysis. It complements the case studies offered earlier: those from José Casanova's *Public Religions in the Modern World* (chapter 2) and those based on the reports of Farid Esack, Peter Ochs, and William Schweiker (chapter 4). Recalling Casanova helps us see that historical origins and outcomes are often but dimly grasped by actors at any given time. The Israel-Palestine matter is in fact part of a much longer Braudelian *grand récit*, already four thousand years in the making. This broader view helps me as a Christian writer to acknowledge something else. Nearly two thousand years of persecution of Jews by my people have helped make necessary the Zionist project, setting the stage for what is now happening in the Middle East. We Christians have a responsibility here that demands attention before this book reaches its close.

Some day observers will suddenly realize the present Israel-Palestine impasse has reached its denouement and already given way, for better or worse, to a substantially different historical moment. Then we will ask ourselves what made the difference. Diplomacy? Sheer exhaustion? Or, as I think, a gradual flowering of inter-Abrahamic forms of civil society in both territories? Discourses designed first of all to deepen interreligious understanding can turn out to have unexpected political consequences. Their existence, noted a decade or more later, *could* turn out, alongside other forces, to have helped moved affairs to a favorable tipping point. One cannot literally see such things happening from a position down among the day-to-day events in question. But one can intuit a certain desirable direction of events and try to help them move that way.

Public Discourses in the Israel-Palestine Conflict

Most speaking and writing on the Israel-Palestine question begins and ends with issues described in largely strategic political, military, and economic terms. This is understandable, given the sorts of issues involved. I will not try to describe all this in detail, but merely indicate the range of interrelated topics. The issue is land and its borders (and with it, air and water and crops and roads and checkpoints and all the rest in all their possible permutations). The issue is Jewish West Bank settlements and territories apparently reserved for more settlements in the future. The issue is the status and residential geography of East Jerusalem. The issue is the "right of return" and what religious majorities and minorities will look like next year or a generation from now, and where they will be located. The issue is the existence and routing of "security fence" or "the wall." The issue is the current lack of contiguity of Palestinian territory. The issue is the attempted regulation of all these matters by threat of reprisals for grievances: suicide attacks on one side and high-technology military responses on the other. The issue is the apparent role of Iran and Syria in supporting organizations such as Hezbollah and Hamas. The issue is the role of ongoing political, military, and diplomatic involvement by powers such as Britain and the United States. And there is much more.

All this detail surrounds the overwhelming fact of "occupation." For many Palestinians, the occupation began in 1948 with the United Nations authorization of a State of Israel on what was then, and still is, considered Palestinian soil. For many others, the "occupation" began with the military expansion of this state, in response to attack, beyond its originally authorized borders. For still others the main problem is the Israeli settlements on the West Bank, the "security fence," the checkpoints, the humiliation, the bulldozing of Palestinian homes, and so forth.

These and other issues have proved intractable above all because the different actors live in terms of different metanarratives, giving different meanings to these circumstances: stories within which supposed "facts" are described very differently, and some "facts" conveniently appear or disappear from the different recitals as political needs require. These narratives emerge from powerful feelings. On the one side, deeply motivated resentment of the occupation, almost of the Nietzschean variety[1] that shapes one's very soul. On the other side, a desperate instinct to survive in the face of yet one more threat to Jewish existence in the millennia-long history of such threats

And one must not forget the secular perspectives that dominate the news of contemporary Israeli-Palestinian politics: from politicians and military leaders on both sides to the views of secular Jewish communities in Tel Aviv to European and American diplomats, business people, and intelligence officers—all rely implicitly on situational narratives couched in modern terms. These run from the peacemaking power of secularity to the manifest destiny of U.S. power in the region as a whole. Such ideal-typical accounts generally draw their lessons from what has happened in the territory concerned over the last sixty years or so, with all the connected political, economic, and military ramifications, rather than from ancient sources.

The appearance of the matter is that many people are largely imprisoned in different ethnic, political, and religious construals of events that in varying degrees are grafted, not always openly, into religious eschatologies. Current happenings, as they occur, are fitted into such prophetic or apocalyptic narratives in order to make them seem to make sense. Events, actions, episodes that do not fit are likely to be ignored. Thus to the "outside" (but never altogether unbiased) observer, Palestinian accounts of Israeli military actions seem seldom to mention Palestinian suicide bombings. The latter seem so justified by the situation as a whole as not to count when the horrors of Israeli counterattacks are being described. Likewise for Israelis telling of Palestinian suicide or rocket attacks, the story tends to be constructed as if it were occurring in a vacuum, without mention of provocation from the Israeli side. Nothing called "occupation" seems to figure in the typical Israeli narrative. It does not fit into the storyline and therefore is inaudible to Israeli storytellers and hearers, not to speak of U.S. administrations that have consistently sided with the Israeli perspective. Realities known to both sides are called by different names. What to Palestinians is "the wall" is to Israelis the "security fence." Above all, there is the factor of the Holocaust, which figures in every narrative either by emphasis or by denial. For some, it is the justification for Israel's existence as a state. For others, if credited at all, it is an irrelevancy in face of current Israeli oppression and injustice.

The politically situated tellers of all these different stories seem to have little motivation for overcoming their differences. It is either (for the Israelis) "We are strong and have powerful allies: why should we compromise?" Or (for the Palestinians) "We are weak and divided: we cannot afford to compromise." Where essentially nonnegotiable symbols, or symbolically powerful facts on the ground, encounter one another, violence is the frequent result, directed by Palestinians against Israelis, or by Israelis against Palestinians.

Above all, and suffusing almost all these perspectival narratives, is the sense that some atrocities cannot be forgiven, some persons and peoples cannot be trusted, some forms of human solidarity are beyond imagination. In short, "covenantal" virtues are unable to unite the conflicting perspectives. Such feelings have elsewhere been described as constituting a "wall" in peoples' minds, more powerful than the physical wall, over reciprocal accusations of guilt answered by reciprocal affirmations of moral justification. Each side refuses to consider the possibility of forgiveness, or trust, or of solidarity until the other side first acknowledges its wrongdoing.

Combustible combinations of these narratives combined with the sorts of recriminations just noted generate reciprocal mimeses of violence. Certain narratives feed off one another, producing action-reaction effects. Suicide bombings provoke air strikes. Rockets provoke invasions. René Girard's theory of the mimesis of violence seems well borne out by these facts. Irreconcilable perspectives like these cannot both be lived out peacefully at the same time in the same geographic space.

Diplomacy and Its Limitations

Into this time and space the diplomats come, whisked from airport VIP lounges to luxury resorts, seldom setting foot on the lands at issue. These emissaries from afar, working with political authorities, seek to devise "roadmaps" that could bring peace. Such professional diplomats are likely to recommend a focus on larger political frameworks, albeit conceived and administered with some sense of distributive justice, designed to keep people from each other's throats. The question is whether externally conceived frameworks are possible that can also be perceived to be just by most of those who live under them. Diplomatic solutions involving various forms of partition are popular today precisely because they appear not to need inquiry into the true nature of historic religious identities. Religion is sometimes treated as if it did not exist, or as if its violence-generating nature could be neutralized with security fences without addressing the inner sources of violent religious zeal.

One can understand from all this how one or another form of outside impetus is often needed to move the different parties out of their deeply entrenched positions for long enough to hear and understand one another, and to move from this point to some form of practical accommodation. Indeed the State of Israel itself is the product of a long series of international diplomatic moves, from the Balfour Declaration of 1917 to the UN Resolution of 1947 to widespread and rapid recognition of the new state on May 14, 1948, including *de facto* recognition by the United States, it is said, eleven minutes after the proclamation was promulgated in Tel Aviv. International diplomatic moves have been needed to end and settle the results of each of the wars between Israel and its neighbors, beginning a few months after the original proclamation and continuing (at the time of this writing) to the 2007 action against Hezbollah in Lebanon.

This kind of diplomatic action does not, for the most part, take into account the different identity-stories that are so fundamental to different aspects of the Israel-Palestine situation. Such action rather gives the combatants a narrative framework for suspending hostilities that they cannot devise on their own. The terms involved are to some degree enforced either by UN resolutions, or threatened sanctions (U.S. aid might come with new strings) or international public opinion, or all three.

But what sort of new narrative framework is thus introduced? Western diplomacy is often (but not always) practiced on the analogy of the "rational choice theory" or "zero-sum game" characteristic of neo-liberal economics. Here the "land" is treated as a commodity or as a possession, for these are the only categories available for such purposes in typical Western thought patterns. The object of diplomatic negotiation is, then, to analyze one's own options and those of competing profit maximizers to devise strategies by which to come out with the most marbles (see chapter 3). One remains committed to this kind of diplomacy only so long as one considers it to be to one's potential advantage to stay in the game. One plays diplomatically or politically in this "continuation of warfare by other means" (Clausewitz) always ready to use stalling tactics, until the moment at which one's national or partisan interest is no longer perceived as served by continuing the negotiation. Episodes in the diplomacy regarding Israel/Palestine suggest the influence of such strategic thinking from time to time. The very episodic character of these negotiations suggests it. A favorable configuration of national interests, a perception of possibilities for gain, domestic political advantages and/or the possibility of partisan "spin" back home, seem to trigger diplomatic offensives that most participants can enter with the expectation of gain, but with the knowledge that it is more likely in any given situation that some will gain and others will lose. And, in the latter case, the losers do not keep their agreements for long. They quickly withdraw their investment in the "Camp David Accords," "Oslo Process," or "Annapolis Initiative," or whatever it may be. Changing conditions and rational-choice reasoning explain why few parties remain invested in the effort for as long as it might take to ensure a lasting success. Successful diplomatic outcomes are often achieved only with great skill, effort, and persistence. They are much to be preferred in every case to a continuation of hostilities. But one cannot overlook the fact that the periods of peace achieved are often relatively short. Diplomatic efforts seldom reach deeply into the cultures involved or respond to the narratives that motivate conduct.

And it needs to be stressed that diplomats arriving from the U.S. State Department, European chancelleries, the UN, and so forth represent cultures with narrative embodiments of their own. Diplomatic efforts from these sources represent efforts to overcome or reconcile existing parochial narratives by replacing them with larger and presumably more powerful narratives, narratives tied to superpower versions of democracy, industrial might, military power, and scientific progress. Hence diplomatic mediation by Western powers is often much more than the application of useful, ideologically neutral negotiating techniques. It is that, of course. But it is also the importation onto the scene of what the diplomats see as more workable master narratives of international deliberation and cooperation that are not beholden in principle to either Israeli or Palestinian stories. Yet, as events have often proved, a Western diplomatic story can sometimes be harnessed to either an Israeli story or a Palestinian one, giving one or the other enhanced negotiating power.

Western diplomatic efforts, one must not forget, represent the capabilities of cultures regarded by many Muslims as morally corrupt to the core. What is still more important is the fact that Western, and particularly U.S. diplomacy, is very often an extension of those nations' imperial interests and intentions. This, of course, is not a connection invented first in America. British diplomacy—the Balfour Declaration of 1917, Britain's handling of the end of its Palestine mandate granted by the League of Nations in 1920 and extending to 1948—was all wrapped up with the projection of

British power, directly or by surrogacy, directly into the Middle East after World War I. The Balfour Declaration had covert imperial origins and intentions. Its actual author, Lord Milner, was a noted colonialist who had been associated with the business and military interests of Cecil Rhodes, who sought to advance British interests in South Africa and elsewhere. Doubtlessly the British in 1948 were influenced not only by revulsion at the Holocaust and a genuine desire to make amends for it, but also by the wish to replace their expired Palestine mandate by the establishment of a new Middle Eastern power, Israel, that could be counted on to be friendly, and both militarily and commercially useful, not to speak of being a collector of indispensable intelligence information.

After 1948, the United States began to take the diplomatic lead with similar, if differently managed, imperial intentions. It is vital to understand the U.S. good offices in assisting peace negotiations after each phase of Israeli-Palestinian conflict have typically had two objectives beyond simply making peace. On the one hand, the growing domestic power of the so-called "Jewish lobby" (actually a loose coalition of several different Jewish groups) has continually pressed the United States to underwrite Israel's military and economic security almost without limits. Besides raising large sums of money both for lobbying efforts at home and direct aid to Israel, this lobby, composed of a variety of American Jewish organizations, has successfully pressed each administration since 1948 to take hard diplomatic positions wherever Israel's security as a nation seemed to be threatened. Helping repeatedly to devise peace arrangements has been part of this process, as has, in the case of Hezbollah in Lebanon, delaying peace initiatives in order to permit Israel's military to do maximum damage to a neighboring country.

Hence American Middle Eastern diplomacy, like that of the British of old, has aimed at managing certain features of U.S. internal politics and also at furthering America's own economic and political ambitions in the region. The so-called "roadmap" based, with variants, on the failed proposals of Camp David and Oslo is an instrument for the furthering of American interests that awaits favorable circumstances for another push. As this chapter is being finally revised, some commentators are saying that such a favorable alignment of diplomatic planets across the region may soon be at hand, and with it the possibility once again of adding peace between Israel and Palestine to the American foreign policy agenda.[2]

But any such resolution would need to involve a just settlement of rival land claims, including contiguity of Palestinian territory and possible acceptance by Israel of a "right of return" in some form. There would also need to be resolutions of the question of Israeli settlements on the West Bank and in East Jerusalem "neighborhoods," combined with adequate security guarantees for both nations. Under any such arrangement, the "security fence" would be likely to be completed and would remain as a deterrent both to Palestinian suicide bombers and to Israeli bulldozers.

I believe that Western diplomacy can at least temporarily break such deadlocks. But I do not believe that such diplomatic efforts alone can bring genuine reconciliation among Israelis and Palestinians. For one thing, there remain many groups whose members do not want to see any such diplomatic accommodation. These will drench both Israel and Palestine with blood in order to keep bringing security fears on both sides to the fore and see that these worries express themselves in various sorts of intransigence. Such circumstances virtually guarantee that if negotiations show signs of success, they will be sabotaged by acts of violence and revenge. And, if successfully concluded, their results will be undermined both by those who stand to lose out in the wake of them, and by those who feel that the accords in question have not gotten to the bottom of deeply felt questions of religious identity.

The paradox about depending on Western initiatives to instigate peace talks is that the instigation may well be needed, along with the protection Western powers can give, but such interventions comport poorly with traditions of Middle Eastern relationships among hostile tribes that nevertheless share among themselves certain similar cultural assumptions. This poor fit is exacerbated by the fact that one side, Israel, is far better acquainted with Western political conceptions than are most Palestinian Arabs, so that outside interventions are justifiably viewed in Palestine as one-sided and suspect. And remember, too, that Israel's population contains a strong element of Sephardic Jews from North Africa and Eastern European Ashkenazic Jews, both of whose very different cultures stand at some distance from Western European models.

Diplomacy, obviously, is not to be dismissed just because its predominant models come from outside the situation of application. Patiently talking things through is one of the best of Enlightenment traditions, provided the diplomats have sufficient intercultural awareness not to impose their own models but also to listen. But diplomacy, being a form of politics, all too easily does become, as Clausewitz (and others before him) said, a continuation of war by other means. After all, Western intervention in Arab-Israeli matters does not happen unless the intervening nations see it as in their own best interests to make such moves. Middle Eastern diplomatic traditions understand differential power considerations very well, but they respond more readily to face-to-face compacts in which personal and tribal honor are the values most at stake. It is important to remember that conservative elements of all three faiths are in agreement that Western "great power" diplomacy is deficient in the dimension of personal honor. The organized modernity that mounts such diplomacy is viewed as morally suspect, so that "roadmaps" from this source may be of immediate practical use but in the long term are not trusted. In such a situation, accepting a peace arrangement brokered by the Western powers means accepting something from this putatively bankrupt civilization. Worse, the nation representing this civilization is the patron of one of the contending powers, Israel. Making peace with Israel could mean signing on to Western ambitions, becoming dependent on U.S. support, trusting Palestinian lives to a culture not credited with honor and integrity as those qualities are understood in the Middle East.

Western nations, furthermore, bring to that part of the world sets of historically rooted assumptions about the role of religion in the public order. These views are embedded in the work of political philosophers who bring out what lies behind them. Western diplomats may not have read these authors, but they nonetheless may take for granted ideas about what "religion" is in relation to politics that are foreign to Middle Eastern cultures. So to make peace on Western diplomatic terms can mean implicitly to accept some version of an American, or British, notion of reconciliation between religious communities and the modern world that fits poorly into the cultural situation in which reconciliation is sought.

Perhaps this poor fit between Western diplomatic assumptions and the religio-social customs represented in the lives of many Israelis and Palestinians, especially cultural conservatives in powerful positions, accounts in part for diplomacy's repeated failures in this part of the world. Holy places and the holy territories on which they stand have a sacredness, an intrinsicality, however those qualities are expressed, that are not part of the usual Western diplomatic vocabulary. A different sort of diplomacy based on face-to-face meetings, the giving and receiving of forgiveness, the evolution of interpersonal trust, and lived affirmations of solidarity, is needed.

How such diplomacy can produce frameworks acceptable in such a varied patchwork quilt of civil societies is not a matter for conceptual analysis in advance, but a matter for historians of the future to describe, if indeed some such meeting of civil and diplomatic worlds has successfully been negotiated and ratified. But one can say now that the importance of this question will increase as the implications of a "two-state solution" for Israel-Palestine begin to become clear. The question of the kind of two-state arrangement that emerges is a vital one. And that question, I think, turns on the kind of civil society that exists in each nation, and across the boundary between the two nations, at the moment when the nature of the peace agreement, or armature, is chosen.

The Question of "the Land"

But all this remains abstract until both civil society groups and members of the diplomatic corps wrestle with the question of "land." One must ask what, exactly, is the role of "land" in the religious imaginations of the different faiths. Clearly it is important beyond being disputed living space. It is of enormous religious importance, but not the same kind of importance, for Jews, Christians, and Muslims. This land, with Jerusalem at its symbolic and ritual center, is the point of meeting of all three religious eschatologies and of the identity narratives that activate eschatological ideas for the present. What the land stands for is at least as important as its material resources or strategic location for military purposes.

It is useful, in tempering our own perhaps undue idealism, to be reminded of what these eschatological land claims are like. In all three cases we have a mixture of peaceful and violent notions of the consummation of human history. A vision in which the final unity of humankind is achieved by the victory of the particular faith concerned often stands alongside, or is combined with, a vision in which the different "families" of humankind achieve their fulfillment or "blessing/blessedness" in response to the presence of the faith community in question, but not in being conquered by it or forced into fealty to it. And, in all three cases, the eschatology, implicit or explicit, shapes interfaith behavior in present time.

All three faiths make clear that they intend—over the historical long haul—to offer "blessings" to humankind. But the question is what this means, and on what terms. The hope that a genuinely mutual covenantal humanism might emerge out of Abrahamic dialogues is put in serious question by the often violent nature of their eschatological narratives. Mutual imagination of one another's moral worlds often discloses things we today do not want to see. As has often been observed, these faiths' proclivities to violence, either generated from within or drawn out of them by various forms of political cooptation, lie to a very large extent in these sectarian and largely self-serving eschatologies. The different claims to the land of Israel-Palestine stand within these larger stories of final triumph. Each of the three faiths approaches this issue in its own way. Each builds an historical claim into an eschatological narrative, or an eschatological narrative into a historical claim.

The Hebrew Scriptures

The Hebrew Scriptures contain the most theologically elaborated claims, but not all claims within Hebrew scripture are of the same kind. The claims made in Torah are unequivocally tied to the original covenantal promise. See, for example, Genesis 15:18: "To your descendants I give this land, from the river of Egypt to the great river, the river Euphrates." Also Genesis 17:8: "And I will give to you and to your descendants after you, the land of your sojournings, all the land of Canaan, for an everlasting possession, and I will be their God." The promise is repeated differently, but with the same effect, in Exodus 6:8 and Deuteronomy 1:7–8.

The promise is made again after the land has been lost to the Babylonian conquest. See Amos 9:15, and numerous passages in Ezekiel: see 37:12, but also 11:14–21; 20:39–44; 36:16–36. One notes that while references to the land in the prophetic writings identify that land as having been promised to Abraham and his descendants, that original promise is not made the basis for its restoration after the Exile. Rather the postexilic criterion is Israel's righteousness and justice. See on this point Jeremiah 18:1–12. The promise of blessing now refers to more than land alone. It has to do also with a communicable quality of life.

Furthermore, passages begin to appear in which the reference is to the earth with all its inhabitants. The theme now is more than Israel's restoration to its former territory. It becomes a matter of summoning Israel to live up to the terms of the covenant. The fulfillment of the covenant promise is now portrayed in an inclusive mode. Isaiah 11 offers images of the consummation well-known in Western literature: "with righteousness he shall judge the poor, and decide with equity for the meek of the earth" (v. 4). "The wolf shall dwell with the lamb" (v. 6). "They shall not hurt nor destroy in all my holy mountain; for the earth shall be full of the knowledge of the LORD as the waters cover the sea" (v. 9). And "in that day the root of Jesse shall stand as an ensign to the peoples; him shall the nations seek" (v. 10). A very similar vision of universal blessing, achieved not by conquest but by attraction, is found in Micah 4: "The mountain of the house of the LORD shall be established as the highest of the mountains ... and peoples shall flow to it" (v. 1). "For out of Zion shall go forth the law, and the word of the LORD from Jerusalem" (v. 2b). "And they shall beat their swords into plowshares, and their spears into pruning hooks; nation shall not lift up sword against nation, neither shall they learn war anymore" (v. 3).

The promise concerning the land also receives expression in the apocalyptic mode. An eventual triumph of Israel comes through battles fought both on earth and in heaven. A very good example is the apocalypse occupying chapters 7 through 12 of the book of Daniel. The imperial powers—Babylon, Syria, Persia—are encoded as great beasts. The hosts of heaven fight on Israel's side. If one waits long enough, vindication and well-being will come. And that in itself will be blessing.

Blessed is he who waits and comes to the thousand three hundred and thirty-five days. But go your way to the end; and you shall rest, and shall stand in your allotted place at the end of the days. (Dan 12:12–13)

The words "your allotted place" are a possible (but disputed) reference to the gift of the land to the descendants of Abraham, now drawn into the context of world-historical struggle. Expectations of the latter sort, taken literally today by fundamentalist scripture interpreters, have led to political visions that are applied to the contemporary State of Israel and its policies. The fulfillment of the Zionist vision (in contrast to the universalist hopes of the early Zionists themselves) is attached to the recovery of these boundaries, by violent means if necessary, making the question of "the land" an especially incendiary topic in present-day Israeli-Palestinian politics. The contemporary political consequences of literal adherence to this kind of eschatology need no rehearsal here.

The Christian Scriptures

In view of the prominence of the "land" theme in all these very different strands of Hebrew Scripture,[3] it is remarkable how little use of this theme is found in early Christian writings. The question of why this is so preoccupies W. D. Davies in his controversial book *The Gospel and the Land*.[4] Studying the evidence exhaustively, Davies traces this neglect to Jesus of Nazareth himself, as depicted in the Gospel accounts. Jesus pays little attention to the "land" theme. Rather this motif is "spiritualized" or "transcendentalized." Davies writes, "[In place of] the holiness of space, Christianity has fundamentally, though not consistently, substituted the holiness of the Person: it has Christified holy space."[5] One can even speculate that the phrase "in Christ," so frequent in Paul, is a Christian amendment of the Hebrew term "in the land."

The Greek noun *ge*, meaning "land" or "earth" (hence the term "geography" and many other English words), is quite frequent in the New Testament, but never with the meaning of specific territory promised to the children of Israel. Often it appears in the phrase *epi tes ges*, meaning "on the earth," as in "Thy will be done, On earth as it is in heaven" (Matt 6:10). Here the meaning is close to that conveyed in Genesis 12:3, "And by you all the families of the earth shall bless themselves." But in this Genesis passage the Hebrew term for earth is *adamah*, rather than *eretz*. The latter term usually means "land" in the sense of "promised land" (although this is not the case at Genesis 1:1, where God creates the heavens and the earth, using for "earth" the word *eretz*). *Adamah* in Genesis 12:3 is the earth in the sense of the red soil, the whole fertile habitation of living things.

So we may say that not only do the Christian scriptures "Christify" the land, as W. D. Davies puts it, but they universalize it. But Christian tradition retains the specific "land" reference in at least the symbolic form represented by the city of Jerusalem. Revelation 21 sees an eventual triumph over the great "beasts"—Egypt, Babylon, Assyria, Rome—as leading to the rise of the holy City of God pictured as a commonwealth of perpetual peace. Here we have the very definition of blessing: "He will wipe away every tear from their eyes" (v. 4). With this apocalyptic claim to the significance of Jerusalem, the symbol of the land reenters Christian faith in a new form. This fact could call renewed attention to the significance of Jerusalem in the Gospel treatments of Jesus' life. The Gospel of John, indeed, is organized around a series of journeys to Jerusalem. Here we find not a territorial, but certainly a spiritual claim.

One dangerous modern variant of Christian apocalypticism is the "Christian Zionism" approach. Here conservative Christians exploit, while they despise, the Jewish struggle, seeing in it a set of signs of the Christian apocalyptic fulfillment that ironically leaves unconverted Jews out in the cold. Here is another example of an interpretation of biblical eschatology taking over contemporary policy. "Christian Zionism" is the belief that the end of history will come soon, and that events in the Middle East, specifically those involving Israel and Palestine, are signs of the proximity of the final cosmic battle between good and evil, the battle of Armageddon (Mount Meggido) foreseen in the book of Revelation (16:16ff). The biblical children of Israel, in this account, will return to possess their ancient homeland, and lo, this is happening as we speak. It is thought necessary, then, to make a policy of aiding the present State of Israel to achieve its territorial aims—involving even more territory than it now claims—say the whole Solomonic Empire of biblical times—in order to fulfill biblical prophecy. Since this Christian Zionism is associated with the "dispensationalist" theology of the series of *Left Behind* books by Tim LaHaye and Jerry Jenkins, in which evangelical believers, in the last day, are to be "raptured" to heaven while unbelievers will be "left," it is evident what is to happen to Israeli citizens who fail to convert quickly to evangelical Christianity in time to be on the right side for the final act.[6]

Islam: The Qur'an

Islamic claims to the land of Palestine have a somewhat different basis. The Qur'an supplies an account that attributes Allah's gift of territory to Muslims through a different narrative that overlaps with and yet amends the story in Hebrew Scripture. The Qur'an picks up the Ishmael stories from Genesis, giving them a different reading, and implicitly claims the territory "to the East" occupied by him and his descendants for Islam. But this claim is more historical and traditional than theological. Nothing in the Qur'an makes any of this a specific divine gift of territory. Rather we are dealing with the scenes of traditional, and perhaps legendary, events, such as Mecca, Medinah, and, of course, Jerusalem.

In Islam, again, we find the notion that this faith offers a gift of blessing to all humankind contingent on the spread of this faith in particular. Islamic texts use the category of "blessing" extensively, above all to say that Islam itself is a "blessing" to humankind, as is the Qur'an itself. Reading it and devotion to it yield personal "blessings." Allah grants "blessings" or favors. Eventually Allah does this for the whole human race. The question is how this last, universal blessing is offered, whether by conquest and domination, a gift imposed, or as a gift freely given. Is there here an intended justification of the Islamic empire at the height of its geographical reach, constituting a land claim of stupendous proportions?

In any case, Islamic conceptions of the end-time, like those of Judaism and Christianity, include the notion of fulfillment of the human story under God. From the beginning, human beings are conceived as "vicegerents" of Allah on earth: beings called to act in Allah's place, to represent his purposes in the universe. There is a rough parallelism here with the notion of the human being as *imago Dei* and of the "Son of Man" as the new human being, the beginning of a new race of human beings. For some, perhaps a minority of, Muslims who hold this view, our vicegerency on earth is eventually to find focus in the coming person of the Mahdi, a figure parallel in many ways to the Christian figure of Jesus the Messiah in his second coming, and in some texts actually identified with Jesus.[7] Some depictions of the Mahdi see him as resorting to violence to restore the full extent of medieval Islamic domination from Indonesia west to Spain and the Pillars of Hercules. Whether this result is achieved by violent conquest or won through the intrinsic attraction of the Muslim way of life depends on the specific strand of Islam in which the vision in question has arisen, and therefore no doubt on what that sect of Islam is experiencing historically at the time.[8]

Jerusalem: Focus of Curse and Blessing

Of the iconic importance of "Jerusalem" for all three faiths there can be no doubt. This place name has both literal and symbolic power. It stands for the whole of what is at stake in the Israeli-Palestinian dispute. It is also literally the site of many of the land issues characteristic of that dispute. Jerusalem, as point of focus of Israel-Palestine situation, with all the practical and symbolic importance of the city, is a case of immense importance not only to the three faiths, but to the human race. Not only is there the question of "the land" as such, but also the symbolic importance of the fact that major shrines of all three faiths are located here within a few hundred yards of one another. These are places of pilgrimage, of devotion, of prayer, and sometimes of defiance, as in Ariel Sharon's provocative walking tour of the Temple Mount. So whatever happens is an event—of blessing or of curse—in the history not only of the politics of the Middle East, but of the history, even the "holy history" of three world religions.

The Temple Mount at the heart of Jerusalem is the traditional place of Abraham's near-sacrifice of Isaac, the place of Mohammed's ascension into heaven and of the appearance of the Mahdi or Islamic messianic figure. It stands near the place of the crucifixion and resurrection of Jesus. All this symbolism is the product of these three faiths reasoning diversely on the authority of their interrelated scriptures to produce stories that intersect in Jerusalem. These faiths understand themselves to have been given (in their conceptions of a covenanting God, in the unfolding of tradition, in their imaginative constructions of the present situation) distinctive yet conflicting notions of responsibility for the well-being of Jerusalem, at the heart of the land of promise, for what it is and is to be.

If parallel and interactive hermeneutical study of the "land" passages in all three faiths were to be carried on among many communal units of an Israeli-Palestinian civil society (a move requiring much attention to forgiveness, trust, and solidarity), a possible outcome might be the conviction that the blessing or gift of a "holy land" to some must be instrumental to a larger blessing intended for all human beings. If we explore the theme of "blessing" in these passages, we will see that it includes much more than territory or other possessions. Blessing is the condition of deep *well*-being, not mere subsistence, that God intends in creation. It means deep well-being for all. A place to live is surely one indispensable form of blessing, but not the only meaning of the word. The full range of meanings is much richer. The texts read together suggest that the blessing is the gift of responsibility for forming an exemplary commonwealth, existing not in some utopia but "on the ground." Jerusalem as the ultimate "city of refuge" for those denied justice elsewhere. Hence Jerusalem is the place where a convergence of political visions needs to take place, where civil society needs to be realized in the context of a social contract embodying justice for all citizens of the city and its surroundings. The point of the gift of the land is to require the vision of justice to become concrete. All the history of Israel—and its successor covenantal communities of Christianity and Islam—is a struggle for the right kind of concretion of political achievement under God to which the "nations" will flock.

Exploring Different Moral Worlds in Civil Discourse

How might this happen? The issue of Israel/Palestine, with Jerusalem embodying all the issues in miniature, is a perfect test case for the proposition that the Abrahamic faiths might learn—on some sort of Walzerian basis involving the mutual exploration of moral worlds—to lay groundwork for a comprehensive civil society, involving various sorts of democratic institutions, across the whole region. This could make possible provisional accords on some issues leading to accords on other issues until the resulting political armatures became clothed with a workable political culture. Crucial to any such process is not only a workable diplomatic "roadmap," but also the growth of an underlying interfaith consciousness of mutual recognition and mutual responsibility. And crucial to the latter is some reconciliation of the different sacred and quasi-sacred narratives that shape the reality-sense and the actions of those whose narratives they are. One thinks of Jews and Palestinian Arabs as the main actors. But some Israeli citizens, as well as some Arabs, are Christians. And, on the larger stage, there are very powerful Christian interests in what goes on in Israel/Palestine.

Imagine politically alert and covenantally rooted inter-Abrahamic groups all over Israel-Palestine, some of them straddling the present security boundary. What difference in the public world might their activities make? Indeed, this question is not merely theoretical. Such groups do exist in large numbers, including those sponsored by Yehuda Stolov's Interfaith Encounter Association, which claims to have involved around four thousand people in inter-Abrahamic activities of various descriptions during the year 2007.[9] Other such groups exist in Israel-Palestine under other auspices, notably universities and other academic bodies, religious, civic, and political-economic-social research institutions, specialized organizations representing each of the three faiths, coalitions of local congregations, religious retreat centers, spontaneously organized conversations among neighbors, and so forth. The dialogues in question obviously reflect the orientations of the groups that sponsor them. But they are all also panels in the patchwork of discourse that represents civil society, as distinct from governmental and economic structures, across the region.

The analysis I have borrowed (in chapter 7) from Michael Walzer applies. These dialogues bring together groups with "thick" religious and moral traditions, offering one another entry as guests into their respective value-worlds. They are able to wring out of such processes certain tentatively agreed minimal frameworks, which I have called "armatures," on which thicker cultural flesh may eventually grow. In this case, as in all such cases, the search for minimal agreements does not begin *de novo*. There is always some inherited framework, whether embraced gladly or reluctantly, that makes the culture-growing discourse possible. That framework may be supplied by sponsoring institutions or even by neighborhood assumptions that simply facilitate conversation. Or it may be something larger: say the political yield of everything that has taken place since 1948 (or long before) establishing the terms on which these particular people of these three faiths are living close together here in this territory of Israel-Palestine. Were there to be a peace agreement, say one according to a diplomatically devised "roadmap," that agreement would likewise become part of the political-social framework within which interfaith "civil society" discussions could continue.

Some sort of framework is always "given" from the past, or just now devised to meet present purposes, or some of each. It may or may not have a philosophical (say Rawlsian or Habermasian) justification. Inter-Abrahamic dialogue both depends for its possibility on the framework and brings the framework under criticism. Such dialogue asks, explicitly or not, whether the given framework does or does not resemble the armature that emerges from mutual Walzerian exploration of moral worlds. If so, such discourses can present the structural givens with gifts of responsibility that help the givens to become more far-sighted, sensitive, and just. If not, civil society can become a breeding ground for revolutionary ferment. Obviously, the question in Israel-Palestine today is whether such elements of civil society as exist in these territories are supportive of the frameworks proposed in peace agreements. Does each "roadmap" resulting from diplomacy resemble an armature grounded in practices of mutual hospitality among "thick" moral worlds? If so, that particular roadmap's chances for political success are materially increased.

Matters on the ground, of course, are never so simple as this. "Civil society" may be an attractive theory, but in Israel-Palestine it is a reality so unevenly represented as to make our simple definition of it problematic. In fact, part of that situation is already Western in culture and familiar with the civil society tradition, and part is not. There are at least three ideal-typical "situations" in Israel-Palestine for the formation of "civil society" groups. Each is distinct and each poses its own set of problems for productive three-faith conversations.

Jewish secular liberals in Tel Aviv, Haifa, and West Jerusalem will know what is being called for here, but perhaps be disinclined, given their secularity, to see value in meeting around the scriptural and postscriptural land traditions. To these folk, Muslim Arabs who live among them and hold Israeli citizenship are not fully accepted as part of the culture, yet they are precisely the sorts of persons with whom they should be engaged in genuine civil society relationships. Here class differences and in-group/out-group distinctions stand in the way of, but do not preclude, success.

Religiously observant Jews understand much better where religiously observant Muslims, either their fellow citizens or Palestinian citizens, are coming from. The far-right orthodox Jews of Mea Shearim in long black coats, fur hats, and long side curls will usually have little to do with either Israeli or Palestinian Muslims. Yet when these meet such ones, they know exactly who these people are as orthodox believers like themselves. The possibility of genuine civil society relationships may actually be greater among the traditional Jewish and Muslim believers than among the Tel Aviv secularists and the few religious Muslims they see on their streets. Here, at least, similar kinds of seriousness with respect to different traditions meet. Mutual respect and interactive responsibility could be the long-term result.

As to interfaith relationships between Jewish settlers and Palestinians either in the towns or on the lands of the West Bank or in East Jerusalem, dialogical ties may be the most difficult of all to manage. Here the Jewish settlers are seen by Palestinians as armed occupiers, backed up by Israeli troops, whose presence destroys the contiguity and integrity of Palestinian territory. Palestinian homes are seen by Jews as possible bases for terrorism, with explosives stashed and parents encouraging sons and daughters to be martyrs for the faith. Discourse about different scriptural or traditional justifications of land tenure is likely to be all but impossible. Yet it needs to be tried. There will be the occasional success to learn from.

Civil society dialoguers may nonetheless be wise not to raise the land question per se too early in their deliberations. Without realized relationships of forgiveness, trust, and solidarity, discussion of land claims can be incendiary, as the writer knows from personal experience. But this subject cannot be indefinitely ignored. Traditional claims generate feelings of identity and loyalty: strong enough to derail the wisest diplomatic efforts to fashion just frameworks for peace in this part of the world. While for some secular Israelis and Arabs the question of land is a matter of simple possession—"my" house, "my" olive trees—even these people will justify their assertions of rights by resort to their respective scriptures and traditions.

The question is how to treat such claims in search of just political frameworks for peace. It seems that they need to be treated at levels closer to the land itself. Few of the questions about land are likely to be answerable without preparing the cultural soils of Israel and Palestine for the emergence of civic relationships among the different faith communities. The conflicting eschatologies, the many essentially tribal identity-narratives, the diplomatic initiatives that embody largely Western imperial stories of their own: none of these things will yield, or yield to, a long-lasting result without some sort of reconciliation of conflicting histories and worldviews close to the land on which people live.

The need is for encounters happening very close to the homes and hearths of all concerned. Peaceful, mutual responsibility generating meetings among people representing radically different worldviews and varieties of historical consciousness need to happen repeatedly until the deeply contested visions of the land where all this goes on begin to converge sufficiently for forgiveness, trust, and solidarity to begin to emerge as plausible political themes.

This could begin to happen when all three faiths begin to talk about land not as something possessed for self-interested exploitation but as a gift of living space for responsible promise keeping. The Hebrew prophets in particular see the gift of land as an opportunity for founding the first truly righteous and just commonwealth. Failure to do so constitutes grounds for revocation of the promise. Indeed, many of the "land" passages in Hebrew scripture call not only for social justice but also echo the theme of care for the earth. The promised land is a space for the symbolic enactment of the fate of the earth itself. It is to be cultivated and redeemed as a blessing to all earth's families.

The Land as Space of Justice and Blessing: The "Two-State Solution"

Such hermeneutical discoveries, if they come at all, will be the result of long dialogical experience enacting forgiveness, trust, and solidarity as covenantal virtues that act as lenses for seeing scripture anew. Serious agreement on any of these progressive propositions is likely beyond the reach of the present generation of dialoguers, and maybe of the generation after that. Old assumptions die hard. But once the dialogue has begun, diplomacy aimed at interim political solutions may become easier. Long before the dialogue reaches its ultimate goals, it may help create the conditions for a "two-state solution" for the Israel-Palestine question.

But much depends on the *kind* of two-state solution that might be possible. This question can usefully be reduced to asking whether we want our two states with or without the "security barrier" or some other way of keeping the two populations apart. Many will say that any two-state solution, while very likely the best short-term answer we can reach in diplomatic terms, is bound to remain unstable and vulnerable to various sorts of political mischief by those who will continue to believe that Israel's very existence is an affront to Islam and to Islamic nations, or that Palestine will forever be a threat to Israel's security.

It follows, very logically in the minds of many, that even after a successful diplomatic settlement, the "security barrier" would need to remain in place.

We would have two very separate states, perhaps interdependent economically, but remaining distinct entities to pursue their own separate political and cultural visions. But I want to argue for a two-state solution in which the security barrier would eventually come down, and in which there would be much greater interaction between the two populations. Two sovereignties, yes, but vigorous interaction at every level, especially that of civil society. The basis of my argument is that both Israel and Palestine are already culturally and religiously diverse nations, and likely to become more so. A long-term two-state solution based on two ethnically homogeneous (I will not say "cleansed") nations separated by a security barrier could be achieved only by a mass exchange of populations, generating bitterness on both sides.

Let us look more closely at each of these states as they are now and as they might be with the conclusion of a stable peace agreement.[10] In the State of Israel, we have universalistic (i.e., Kantian, Rawlsian) terms of citizenship mediated through membership in many ethic and religious subcommunities. All citizens are theoretically equal, but Jewish European (Ashkenazic), Jewish North African (Sephardic), and Palestinian Arab citizens of the State occupy different civic, civil universes despite being complexly interspersed geographically. As Adam Seligman writes, "Insofar as Israel is a Jewish state (so defined by language, culture, educational criteria, and the allocation of resources) the Palestinian inhabitants of Israel proper (i.e., citizens of the state) are not full members of society."[11] The continued existence of different national and cultural identities and loyalties undermines Israel's ability to construct a model of citizenship and participation in the nation along lines of liberal-individualist ideology. There lies a conflict, even within the Jewish majority, between a more secular and universalistic concept of civil society and a more religious and particularistic one.

What, after all, would make a post–peace agreement State of Israel remain "Jewish?" Not, after all, its present, precarious Jewish majority. Jews have reason to fear that the birthrate among Israeli Muslims, combined with some honoring of the "right of return" of Palestinian families displaced by the establishment of the Israeli state and its subsequent expansionist moves, would make Israel no longer predominantly "Jewish."

Some strands of early Zionism, among other things, had universalistic goals, believing that the formation of a Jewish nation would do something for humankind as such. But a different Zionist logic has inevitably led to policies that amount to "ethnic cleansing" of increasing swaths of Palestinian territory. Since 1967 and the continuing occupation of the West Bank and the Gaza Strip and, more especially, since the rise of Likkud in 1977, the early universalistic assumptions have increasingly given way to an ethno-religious definitions of political life and practice.

What would it mean for the State of Israel to return to the universalism of early Zionism and seek to express this vision in the form of an Abrahamic commonwealth in which Judaism would be the host partner, giving hospitality (as did Muslim leaders in medieval Andalusia) to citizens continuing to be of other cultures and faiths? Would we here begin to see the fulfillment of the prophetic vision concerning the real meaning of the "land"? One is tempted to say that such would be a greater fulfillment of the hope of a "Greater Israel" than the expansionist, largely geographic meaning given that expression by its militant proponents today.

And what of the anticipated new state of Palestine? Would the Jewish settlers now in certain neighborhoods of East Jerusalem and on the West Bank return to Israeli territory, or would they become Palestinian citizens much as many Palestinian Arabs are Israeli citizens? Unless the Israeli settlements were dismantled to become part of a giant population exchange with Israeli Arabs returning to a newly independent state of Palestine, Palestine would need to offer the Jews within their sovereign territory the right of Palestinian citizenship.

The ideal of a "greater Palestine," in the sense of pushing Israel into the sea, would be sure to remain in the minds of some. The danger is that, without anti-Israeli propaganda feeding on the justified grievances of the occupation, Palestinians could find even less sense of common identity than they do now. A revival of specifically Islamic self-awareness could help, provided it did not turn out to be of the militant Wahabist kind. A revival of religious consciousness gained in conversation with Jews who shared a search for the meaning of their own faith in a nonpolemical, nondefensive mode could greatly help toward a parallel reinterpretation of Islam for life in the modern world. The task for Palestinians, as for Israelis, would be to become "rooted cosmopolitans," not somewhere in the West but in their own lands.

But, as matters stand, the possibilities of forming a civil society are even more complex and fraught in Palestine than they are in Israel. There is far less experience of Western political culture in Palestine than there is in the "Tel Aviv" segment of the Israeli population. The Palestinian parliament seems no more effective than the Iraqi parliament. Fatah and Hamas represent different visions for Palestinian society (as, of course, do the Liberal Party and Likkud in Israel). One can imagine different segments of the Palestinian population having different reactions to Israelis in their midst, just as different segments of Israeli society already have different reactions to Palestinian Arabs on Israeli territory. Once their hostile intentions toward Israel became less of a priority (and, of course, we cannot count on that happening very soon), Fatah and Hamas—not precisely but perhaps approximately representing these different attitudes—could become still more effective political parties, bringing to bear their respective visions for Palestinian society as such. Extensive experience in delivering social services could help immensely in a peaceful transition from terrorism to democratic politics.

Both liabilities and possibilities considered, the development of civil society in Palestine could be more difficult, but by no means impossible. Ironically, it could be easier to achieve with arrangements permitting serious and extended dialogue with Israeli participants. The current map of the borderlands between Israel and Palestine shows an interspersal of residential neighborhoods, especially in East Jerusalem. The same is true of the present placement of Israeli settlements on the West Bank, extending like fingers into Palestinian territory. A peace agreement without "the wall," leaving these populations where they are, could do much for the growth of civil society in both nations as well as between them. Arabs exercising the "right of return" to Israeli territory, alongside those already there, could balance out Israeli settlers wishing to remain deep in Palestinian territory, not as occupiers but as Palestinian citizens. The two regions of overlap would not be entirely symmetrical as political realities. Questions of citizenship would probably be handled differently, but the relationship, if one can think in figurative terms, might not be unlike the overlapping of different identity narratives between the Hebrew and Islamic scriptures.

In all such cases, and especially for a future interspersal of "Israeli" and "Palestinian" peoples, the phenomenon of a shared civil society is critical to the enterprise. The more citizens of the different entities have experience of dialogue with one another and realize the power of such potent conversation for nurturing expressions of common weal, the greater the possibility that parallel and interactive political-economic interdependency, where peoples travel side by side on the same path, where they can gain insight into one anothers' moral worlds, the more a peaceful "two state" solution can achieve stability and foster blessing or well-being on both sides.[12]

I see myriad interreligious dialogue groups responding to common issues of shared human well-being, as seeds of the sort of civil society capable of laying groundwork for such results. This is why I think a dialogue on the subject of what is human well-being on a shared earth can be fruitful, because, people being what they are, there is likely to be some agreement about these things, not only out of scripture but out of common human experience. All this explains why I think attention needs to be given to the people of these two states interacting with one another in a continuous, border-transcending civil society network.

Could such a conception of two sovereign states linked in a shared civil society—surely a form of "parallel and interactive hermeneutics" of people's different identities in the political social realm—actually come into existence and maintain itself? Some might argue that Palestinians and Israelis should be kept apart as much as possible to avoid sparks that could escalate into new conflicts. Others would say that only through civic interaction in equal partnership could the two populations learn enough about their respective religio-moral worlds to live in peace.

I do not expect anything like the latter to happen anytime soon. I set it forth as a possibility beyond a negotiated two-state solution in order to lend such an achievement promissory power for the future. For the moment, it appears that partitions of various kinds represent the ultimate in diplomatic achievement. Even to accomplish this much with some measure of fairness and justice has proved of late to require maximum effort. Yet such partitioning arrangements seem eventually to break down into further conflict. One should not denigrate such arrangements, for they seem to make for fitful forms of peace, and that is worth doing. But think, too, of walls coming down: of new social realities emerging out of the fragmentation of the old. Think of the "security fence" being recycled into paving stones for streets and building blocks for homes, with appropriate celebrations (like those at the Brandenburg Gate in 1989, or those at Nelson Mandela's inauguration in 1995) heard joyfully around the world.

Notes

1. "Resentment" or *"ressentiment"* in Nietzsche meant blaming others for one's own sense of weakness or frustration, justifying one's own story while rejecting the other's story. I do not go so far as to claim with Nietzsche that the notion of morality itself goes back to inferiority feelings, but "resentment" may partly explain the production of moral worlds in which the Other is systematically reviled. These views are developed in *Beyond Good and Evil* (New York: Vintage, 1966) and *On the Geneaology of Morals* (New York: Random House, 1969).

2. A current (December 2007) account in the American press of this possible diplomatic opening goes somewhat as follows. Iran, representing Shi'a Islam, is not only gaining influence in eastern and southern Iraq, but it is also supporting and arming both Hezbollah on Israel's northern border, and Hamas, the winner of the last parliamentary election in Palestine and now in control of Gaza, on the south. The electoral triumph of Hamas as well as the military success of Hezbollah have brought the broad cause of Jihadi militancy into Palestine, where it was not there before. Saudi Arabia, where Sunni Islam is dominant, now sees Iran, with its geopolitical expansionist and militarist tendencies, to be as much a threat to itself as Israel, if not more so. Meanwhile Sunni sheiks are assisting U.S. forces in Anbar province against Al Qaeda, and will certainly not pass up any opportunity to limit Shi'a influence, as the Shi'ite-dominated Iraqi government shows its incompetency and beholdenness to politicians who control militias of their own. The opportunity could be for the United States to try to exploit this situation by bringing together a conference that could link Sunni interests, including those of Abbas's Palestine Authority, with the interests of the Israeli state against the Shi'a Iran-influenced militancy of Hezbollah and Hamas. In short, the cause of Palestinian statehood

could become part of a coalition of Sunni interests against Shi'ite-Iranian nuclear ambitions and related strategies. Israel and the United States, in combination with with Saudi Arabian and other Sunni interests, would then be aligned against Iran. The price for Saudi cooperation could be a sizeable armaments package. Statehood, at least for Fatah-dominated Palestine, in which the people of Gaza might quickly see their own interests involved, could come as the product of a large-scale realignment of interests across the Middle East as a whole.

3. The "land" theme is overwhelmingly prominent. A computer count yields the following results. Land is mentioned 311 times in Genesis, 197 times in Deuteronomy, 271 times in Jeremiah, and 290 times in Ezekiel. For the whole of Hebrew Scripture, the total is 2,504 references. See Martens, op. cit., 9.

4. W. D. Davies, *The Gospel and the Land: Early Christianity and Jewish Territorial Doctrine* (Berkeley: University of California Press, 1974).

5. Ibid., 368.

6. Such a disreputable and dangerous eschatology would not be worth mentioning except for its profound current influence on the politics of the United States and the likelihood that, translated into policy terms, it could actually help bring about Huntington's "clash" of religiously motivated civilizations. Dipping into material such as this and appreciating its power to shape the worldview of millions, what thinking person, religiously inclined or not, would not be on the side of enlightened modernity? Who would not prefer Fukuyama's notion of history's "end" to this? Who would not devoutly hope that José Casanova, as this writer has interpreted him in chapter 1, is right in thinking that there can be such a thing as an enlightened form of religion capable of saving *the* Enlightenment from itself?

7. It is important to note that the Mahdi figure nowhere appears in the Qur'an. Belief in his coming has more the status of a folk belief, more prominent in Shi'ite than in Sunni Islam.

8. One contemporary playout of this eschatology can be seen in the Iraqi Shi'ite militia known as the "Mahdi army" loyal to Moqtada al-Sadr, a force whose very name has obvious apocalyptic implications. It is not clear exactly how the relation between an Islamic conception of the end-time is conceived to be related to the conflict going on in Iraq at the time of writing. But clearly this naming increases the proclivity to violent solutions deemed precursor to or part of the apocalyptic fulfillment. Such nomenclature testifies to the contemporary political potency of apocalyptic visions, just as is the case for Judaism and Christianity.

9. This information is contained in Rabbi Stolov's 2007 end-of-year e-mail summary of IEA activities for 2007.

10. I am indebted to Adam Seligman, *The Idea of Civil Society* (New York: Free Press, 1992), for central features of this social analysis of Israeli society, especially to pages 145 ff., his case study of the city of Jerusalem.

11. Ibid., 152.

12. There is in Palestine increasing doubt that a "two-state solution," however desirable, can come about. Israel will not likely agree to its terms: i.e. pre-1967 borders, dismantling West Bank settlements and outposts, sharing East Jerusalem, the right of return, and so forth. Palestinians will not accept anything less. Talk about a "one-state solution" is increasingly heard, with what is left of Palestinian land to be annexed by Jordan, or with Palestinians giving up their claim to be a sovereign state in return for Israeli citizenship. The latter step would begin a long struggle for equality in an *apartheid* situation, probably with new international "human rights" support. I am indebted for this insight to Dr. Walt Davis.

9

Toward a Covenantal Humanism

What can it *mean* that inter-Abrahamic discourses like those modeled in these chapters today proliferate across the globe? What can it mean that many of these relationships thrive in otherwise conflicted situations where they might be least expected to gain footholds? Toward what ends may these dialogues move us? Even toward peace between Israel and Palestine? Or is the mutual anger and resentment there too great to yield to mere talk? Nietzsche probably would have thought so. But besides violence, what is there other than talk?

I have tried in this book to construct a frame of reference for tackling these questions of meanings and ends and possibilities. I have done so by modeling parallel-hermeneutical and interactive treatments of Abrahamic and other scriptural passages in a variety of practical settings. I interpret the work of today's dialoguers, whatever the terms they may actually use, as implying some form of discernment and acceptance of a shared gift of responsibility to the scriptural promise of covenantal blessing to "all the families of the earth." I have argued that the sense of such a responsibility-gift, in whatever activity or language it is expressed, can energize Jews, Christians, and Muslims as they struggle together to overcome their own mutual estrangement and hostility. I believe that this sense of shared responsibility for human blessing could release social forces that might counter, and eventually help heal, secular modernity's betrayals of its own promises to humanity.

Modernity's Shortcomings Revisited

My analysis of these betrayals and accompanying flaws argued that modernity's central problem has been a conception of human relationships that allows social actors, particularly but not exclusively in the economic realm, to be irresponsible to one another as persons and also irresponsible where the social consequences of their actions are concerned. This has meant giving normative value to maximizing *possessions*, whether these consist of land or other material goods (*Habsucht*), power over others (*Kraftsucht*), or social status and regard (*Ehrsucht*).[1] Of course such drives were not first-time inventions of the Enlightenment. They have been characteristic of the human condition from the dawn of history. But the Enlightenment put its particular stamp upon them, connecting them with projects for autonomously refashioning human nature and society that eventually produced a world of many competing interests without significant social "steering currents," a world of entrepreneurs clambering independently for advantage, or riding on one another's backs, in search of wealth and power. All this, it began to be claimed by theorists, took place through market mechanisms alleged to be self-regulating and hence not subject to ethical critique. Even more recently, these mechanisms have been analyzed through "game theory," "rational choice theory," and the study of economic institutions that improve free-market efficiency, all seemingly thought to embody the good for society by their internal logic alone, without external moral inputs. Such models analyze both competition and cooperation: cooperation to enable competition and competition as a form of cooperation.

I find that my treatment of the human condition in these terms to be largely consistent with the analysis of democracy's disintegration by Jeffrey Stout in his book *Democracy and Tradition*.[2] Genuine democracy requires intentional and articulate value inputs, not merely market mechanisms. Democratic institutions are what I have called "armatures" arising out of various cultural accords and in turn providing structures on which and within which additional cultural flesh may take on a certain consistency and shape. But democracy itself is a tradition, not merely a theory, and it takes different forms in different places. Democracy's character as lived tradition is what gives it a reality prior to the critiques of (but still able to learn from) proceduralist liberals like Rawls, Rorty, and Habermas, and at the same time able to resist (yet also learn from) neo-traditionalists like John Milbank and Stanley Hauerwas. The health of the broad tradition of democratic currents and practices (not merely *theories* of democracy), flowing into the still wider stream of "modern culture," is in Stout's view (and my words) undermined by failures of mutual responsibility among its citizens and of shared responsibility to whatever is regarded as its promise. In Western culture, particularly that of North America, people are irresponsible toward one another because they go their separate, and often mutually destructive, ways without exchanging publicly persuasive *reasons* for what they want and what they do. For there to be democracy, the reasons given must embody responsible relationships, and the responsible relationships need also to be reasonable, and all needs to be combined with mutual recognition of one another as personal agents representing valued traditions of shared life. A good society in Stout's sense is one in which persons are responsible to one another in the sense of giving reasons and hearing reasons in return, hence placing democratic deliberation at the heart of social relationships that in turn steer the capabilities characteristic of "modernity." Here is what Stout says.

> The community at issue ... is that constituted by our mutual recognition of one another as those to whom each one of us is responsible in the exchange of reasons.

And a few lines earlier:

> Its [this community's] central and definitive component is the discursive practice of holding one another responsible for the actions we commit, the commitments we undertake, and the sorts of people we become.[3]

It is from failing to be this sort of society, and from the consequences of such failure, that modernity needs help in saving itself. Mutual recognition, reciprocal responsibility, and reason: these words describe for Stout the root reality of a civil community functioning within an ongoing stream of democratic tradition and practice.

But this description also resembles what I have called "parallel and interactive hermeneutics" with the emphasis on mutual responsibility for interpretations of our traditions and the consequences of these interpretations. My argument is that all three Stoutian characteristics—"mutual recognition," "reason-giving," and "responsibility"—in democratic discourse *must come from somewhere*, must themselves be grounded in traditions of life that give them meaning. But, as Stout makes clear, the stream of democratic tradition bearing such values is drying up. Could that be for lack of significant cultural tributaries, religious or otherwise, flowing into that stream? An impulse to refresh the stream must come from sources that still maintain its fundamental symbols and motivations. Stout's rearticulation of the democratic tradition offers a significant clarification of what these symbols and motivations need to be. My argument, following Casanova, has been that they can come from religious traditions that have internalized the Enlightenment critique of religion in order to become theologically conscious of the social realities they represent. I have argued in this book that the tradition of a modernity grounded in democratic participation can use the help of religious traditions that offer orienting and motivating perspectives. These can be unlocked if they seek to give their reasons and be mutually responsible for considering them together. The way in which the Abrahamic faiths and others can "help modernity save itself" is through a resourcing and empowering of the sorts of mutual recognition, reason-giving, and responsibility for consequences that are needed to support and maintain a good society. Inter-Abrahamic discourse about public issues can *model* the sorts of discourse that must characterize the good society by demonstrating that these faiths possess the resources and motivations to bring values they hold in common to the discourses of that commonwealth.

Much of this book has already been devoted to showing how this can happen. Our cases have been described with full awareness of the difficulties and compromises so often involved. What have we learned from these cases? We have learned that religious communities can contribute a gift of inter-human responsibility that brings shared well-being or blessing. This makes humanity possible as a community of moral discourse or open exchanges of "reasons." Otherwise human reasoning becomes mainly calculation designed to get the better of our neighbors. We justify such a calculative approach to life with the assumption that invisible social mechanisms will turn the pursuit of private advantage into social weal. The result is more often curse than blessing.

We are speaking here of conceptions of humanity in its social form: notions of the kind of humanity we represent in our lives together. The question, then, is where such different conceptions of the human lead in our present historical situation. Does the notion of a religiously founded gift of reason-giving responsibility make sense in the light of what is now happening to our global society? Can we speak convincingly of shared responsibility to a promise of blessing as fulfillment of the human odyssey?

Competing Contemporary Conceptions of the Human

The Abrahamic faiths are encountering one another in a unique concurrence of their respective experiences of time and space. Like a rare conjunction of the planets, they meet in a new "axial age" accompanying the emergence of a global sense of human community. Other conceptions of the meaning of this time exist in relation to which we need to compare our own understanding of it.

Let us take a few pages to paint the background against which this question needs now to be highlighted. The secular world has offered us not a few portraits of expected or achieved well-being, as well as of threats or curses that have materialized, or could materialize, instead. Francis Fukuyama, a few years back, gave us what scripture scholars would call a "realized eschatology," meaning an argument that the future is now, the reign of God, *has* come. He titled his book *The End of History,*[4] meaning by this term that with the 1989 collapse of the former Soviet Union and the Berlin Wall, and the seeming political victory of the West, a liberal democratic capitalist world order had come into being that put an end to history's bloody strivings after the meaning of social existence, an end to competition between visions of political and economic life, and the prospect of a forever stable mode of existence on this planet.

The word "end" in Fukuyama's title, of course, could be read in two ways: "end" as purpose, and "end" as termination. The liberal democratic capitalist world order emerging in the nineties had for Fukuyama fulfilled history's purpose or *telos,* and also terminated the sorts of passions and struggles associated with the very idea of "history." It is only fair to say, of course, that Fukuyama subsequently realized that even if history as ideological struggle has ended, the march of science has not. In his more recent book *Our Posthuman Future,*[5] he sees an overall diminishment of the capabilities of our species. Fukuyama argues here, among other things, that the increasing use of mood-altering drugs may diminish the rich variety of human character, thereby impoverishing the race. Fukuyama worries that this might go so far that we would no longer be fully human. Such a development alone would bring unpredictable developments stretching out into an unknowable future. But there is always the opposite possibility. It would take only a very few people with severe personality difficulties and access to nuclear weapons to incinerate the earth.

Religious traditions seem to play little or no role in Fukuyama's arguments for judging what has happened to us and for discerning what may happen next. Convinced that the West had won, he did not take seriously enough the rise of radical Islam, or the possibility that this development, combined with the rise of fundamentalism in other faiths, could mount a global challenge to Enlightenment assumptions. Others are more open to the current influence of religious and cultural traditions. The Harvard theologian Gordon Kaufman, for example, has approached the twenty-first century with full awareness of its serious demands but still with confidence that the future *can* be one to which specific life traditions may contribute as they try to survive. With another vision of blessing, Kaufman writes:

> The various cultural streams of humanity seem to be converging rapidly into a single interconnected human history. At this portentous moment, perhaps more than ever before, we need conceptions of the human and visions of history that will facilitate our movement toward an ordering of life and history that is at once humane and universal, an ordering in which the integrity and significance of each tradition and each community are acknowledged and the rights of every individual are respected.[6]

Kaufman's argument, in the end, proclaims his confidence in the triumph of tolerant, humane liberal values. His optimism concerning human fulfillment is buoyed by the flowing together of the once separate streams of human history on the basis of opportunities for travel, the communications revolution, the coming of a global economic order. Kaufman counts on support for these hopefully common values by contemporary, sophisticated human beings who are able to come to terms with their own religious traditions in the progressive manner by which Kaufman comes to terms with his own Christianity. There is little sense here that religious communities themselves are destined to play a major role on the twenty-first-century public stage, but Kaufman thinks that faith can deepen the liberal value scheme that he shares with other members of Western elite academic culture.

It is fascinating that such a convergence of cultures into a single interconnected history dominated by liberal values is just what Kaufman's Harvard colleague Samuel Huntington, two decades ago, did *not* see. Or, rather, Huntington saw the convergence as ultimately conflictual: not pointing at all to "an ordering of life and history ... at once humane and universal." Huntington, as we well know, became famous for his forecast that the world of the twenty-first century would be dominated by a conflict of major civilizations, often fueled by powerful religious conviction.[7] After a period of disfavor, and under the current pressures of war in Iraq and global terrorism, Huntington's views are beginning to regain currency. We are urged, not to seek common liberal values, but to reach practical accommodations among the world's religiously constructed civilizations in a maintainable balance of power. Religion as public phenomenon (rather than simply private faith) plays a larger role on the world scene for Huntington, the secular writer, than they seem to do for Kaufman the theologian. For Huntington, the coming of technological and economic "modernization" to previously undeveloped traditional societies (Iran is an example), far from drawing such societies ever further into a liberally homogeneous world, tends, after a first liberalizing stage, to provoke traditionalist reactions. As such a country gains confidence, it becomes proud of its heritage and its traditional culture. As its people experience secular *anomie* (i.e., "normlessness"), they seek to rediscover traditional values. If local religious traditions cannot adapt themselves to these opportunities, other religious traditions will be borrowed. This, for Huntington, accounts on the one hand for the resurgence of militant Islam across the Middle East and for the continuing successes of evangelical Christianity in Korea, Africa, and Latin America. Of the last-named areas, Huntington writes in a passage less often quoted than some:

> In these societies the most successful protagonists of Western culture are not neo-classical economists or crusading democrats or multinational corporation executives. They are and most likely will continue to be Christian missionaries. Neither Adam Smith nor Thomas Jefferson will meet the psychological, emotional, moral and social needs of urban migrants and first-generation secondary school graduates. Jesus Christ will not meet them either, but He is likely to have a better chance. In the long run, however, Mohammed wins out. Christianity spreads primarily by conversion. Islam by conversion and reproduction.[8]

Whichever picture of the world one chooses, there may well be threats to life today before which human beings, in their own power, religiously sourced or otherwise, are all but helpless. There may not *be* for very long a habitable human world in which either Kaufman's or Huntington's, or our own scenario could be lived out. This sort of threat can be perceived today in at least two arenas of human research activity, genetic engineering and cosmology.

More than ever before, science is now addressing itself directly to the question of life's fundamental nature, and hence also to the question of its value. If the twentieth century was the age of physics, the twenty-first may turn out to be the heyday of biology. It has been said that our genetic code *is* both who and what we *are*. Genetic engineering linked to medical practice seems poised to place capabilities in our human hands that we have never had before. These capabilities, once activated, will raise profound moral questions. We are about to be able to do things with the human genome that could turn out to be either blessing or curse to our species.

The fields of cloning, stem-cell research, and the manipulation of the human genome are on the brink of delivering diagnostic capabilities and therapies about which new sorts of ethical decisions will need to be made. Life-extension capabilities today have to do with using stem cells, made compatible with our tissues by therapeutic cloning, to repair human tissues such as damaged pumping chambers in the heart, or with using knowledge of the individual genome to foresee dangerous illnesses in time to head them off. All of this is blessing so far as personal life extension is concerned, provided always that there are no serious unforeseen side effects. But are there hidden *moral* drawbacks here or even long-term social woes? Does it make a moral difference to us, for example, to realize that such therapies in our present system are available mainly to rich families in rich countries? Or take a different moral concern. Would most of us be prepared to forego a proven stem-cell therapy for ourselves or for family members because we have reservations about how these cells were obtained? In short, are we ready to refuse personal blessing because we believe that this healing potential has been achieved at the cost of denying the possibility of some other potential human life? It is one thing to oppose a public policy that permits certain kinds of stem-cell research, but another to renounce potential healing for ourselves once such research has been made legal in our country or is effectively pursued in some other country. We are now on the brink of having to ask the second kind of question while still being preoccupied with the first. How is this combination of policy issues with personal issues likely to affect our judgment?

Or, still in the category of life extension, what about gene-based diagnosis and therapy? Again, there are great potential blessings here. We might come to be able to avoid certain diseases altogether if a proclivity toward them could be detected in our particular genomes and the actual disease is therefore caught early enough to treat it successfully, or if the dangerous gene can be eliminated, or bred out (see below) in the first place. But is it a blessing, or might it be a curse, to know what one is likely to die of when that information carries with it little present possibility of avoidance or cure (e.g., pancreatic cancer)? And what of the possible use of personal genetic information by insurance companies and government agencies to discriminate against individuals with certain genetic patterns? Do we refuse health insurance on the basis of diseases people do not yet have? Do we limit civil liberties for crimes that have not yet been committed?

And then, as citizens, we need to ask how radical life extension may impact the health-care policies of nations. What may be its impact on pension plans, health insurance, Medicare, or other forms of entitlement spending? What will be the personal cost and social cost of having increasing numbers of people living to what is now for us extreme old age? Can we adjust our ideas about "retirement" and find ways of encouraging older persons to continue as productive members of society?

And there is more. Life extension clearly involves the beginning of life manipulation, a blessing in some cases but a potential curse in others. What about using genetic techniques for effecting what we judge to be improvements in the organisms of our offspring: what used to be called "eugenics" or, in the animal world, selective "breeding"? It is already possible to detect certain diseases and genetic defects in fetuses at a very early stage of gestation. Some of these problems can already be treated before or after birth. In other cases, such defects are seen as grounds for abortion.

But our capabilities will soon exceed these, if they have not done so already. Couples will soon be able to select the characteristics they wish to see in their children. Biomedical entrepreneurs will quickly make such capabilities available for a price, no doubt a price excluding the vast majority of the population from access. But what characteristics will most people choose, and with what result? The mental image is rather like the saying concerning Lake Woebegone, a place where "all the children are above average." What will many parents in fact look for? Light skin, above average height, good looks, high intelligence, athletic ability? Frequently expressed desires for such qualities will contribute to the social marginalization of those who do not have them. The formula resembles that of the "super race" or "master race" eugenics of Hitler's Germany.

In all likelihood such a program, if successful, would gradually enhance the existing social advantages of well-to-do families, much as already do the laws of inheritance, costly college entrance coaching, "legacy" admissions to prestigious colleges, or networking among graduates who can help one another succeed. Extended over myriad generations, as we gradually manipulated our own evolution, such a program might indeed begin to produce a super race where there is none today. Having learned that what we now call "race" is not a genetic category (even if it has certain genetic markers), might our preferential use of eugenic science eventually lead us, inadvertently or not, to reinvent the notion of "race" as, for the first time, a discernible genetic distinction?

The consequences of such eugenic manipulation, extended over sufficient time, could begin to turn genetically advantaged and genetically unadvantaged persons into distinctive *species*. The manipulated human organisms could begin to differ from the unmanipulated ones like early *homo sapiens* differed from the Neanderthals, although presumably at a higher and therefore more lethally consequential level. We could along such a path be entering what certain writers have called a "post-human world." Or we could find ourselves engineering another fork in the evolution of our species: the one the inadvertent result of our scientific progress. From a few centuries of global apartheid, one could move to global enslavement or even eugenic exterminations of the genetically weaker groups. Would not such an outcome turn alleged blessings available to today's rich into curses imposed on society as a whole, indeed global moral catastrophe?

Similar far-reaching questions are now emerging in the field of cosmology. In his book *Our Final Century*[9] the Cambridge cosmologist Sir Martin Rees looks particularly at the power, for either blessing or curse, that twenty-first-century technology, extended potentially to embrace the universe, is already beginning to place in human hands. He chillingly catalogues the sorts of things that could go wrong, arguing that humanity has no better than a fifty-fifty chance of surviving another hundred years. The scientific progress we are making very likely exceeds our wisdom for managing the likely consequences. It follows for Rees that this century could prove to be as important as the moment of the big bang for the long-term future of the universe. We are at a point in time that could determine whether technology will go on to seed the cosmos with transcending robotic intelligence (we do not know yet whether such intelligence will include "consciousness," which we know directly today only as we experience it in our individual selves or infer it from the functioning of brain tissue), thus fundamentally changing its character, or whether technological advance will soon cease where it is with the destruction of the civilization that has up to now supported it. For planet earth to become the source of a cosmic intelligence network will require further centuries of scientific development, which will, in turn, require centuries of peace that must begin now.

Religious communities will clearly play some role in determining the way the twenty-first century turns out. They will either generate or legitimate finally catastrophic episodes of conflict, or they will contribute mightily to peaceful outcomes of our present-day perils. One may think it pretentious and dangerous for religious communities to believe for these new, scientific reasons that they are now fighting the battles of the "last days." After all, they have believed this for other reasons on many earlier occasions to the great detriment of everyone within reach of their swords. But humanity has now reached a point at which decisions made on earth tomorrow could alter the state of affairs in this galaxy or beyond a million or more years from now. They could do so by determining whether or not this universe will be seeded with some form of intelligence, whether self-replicating thinking, deciding, cybernetic organisms that had their far-off origins on planet earth will be present in and among the galaxies with the capability of lending them order and purpose. One can argue, of course, that there are likely to be other worlds in which similar decisions have been faced, and perhaps successfully negotiated. If we fail, others may already have succeeded. But we do not know this to be true for sure, or that communication with such other worlds will take place anytime soon. To assume that it is and thereby let ourselves off the hook would be the height of cosmic irresponsibility.

Indeed, Martin Rees's cosmology of a possible final triumph of intelligence through wise human actions is a way of speaking about a gift of responsibility far more stupendous than any discerned earlier in this book: the responsibility of determining whether or not this cosmic consummation, or something like it, will take place. This is a responsibility that has come to us through the evolutionary process. But it is a responsibility needing recognition and actualization through eschatological narratives placed in our hands for helping us grasp what such responsibility means. The consummatory presence of meaning and intelligence throughout the universe itself could therefore hinge in part on the ways Jews, Christians, Muslims, and others deal with their destructive differences now in order to lend humankind their contexts of meaning.

It is not justifiable for theologians of these faiths to assume that, having given us such potential responsibility for the future of our species and of the universe, God will not allow the worst to happen. Perhaps Jews and Muslims have arrived at perceptions similar to those of some contemporary Christian thinkers. The Swiss Christian ecumenist Lukas Vischer has argued that we are still employing the methods and assumptions of the optimistic sixties in confronting what has become a global crisis: literally a crisis of human survival. For Vischer, our sense of the urgency of the present crisis has been blunted by being seen by most people as only a *management* challenge: something they can deal with if they act intelligently before it is too late. So proportioned to our human capacities, threats to life are not allowed to undermine prior theological assumptions. Perhaps, Vischer argues, such threats should shake up conventional religious certainties. Theologians and ethicists have been all too sure that "God will lead humanity to the kingdom; injustice, degradation and destruction will not have the last word; God is already acting in history; darkness will be overcome; the church's calling is to side with God's purpose of life in history."[10] Vischer remonstrates, "Can this view be maintained? Is there any justification for the expectation of a gradual realization of God's purpose in history? Does not the Bible rather offer a contrary scenario? But above all, *how do we cope with the evidence of an increasing degradation in history*? Do we not have to admit that the historical future is radically hidden from our eyes? We must always be prepared for life *and* death."[11]

Articulating a Covenantal Humanism

A major thesis of this book has been that the best, the most worthy-to-be-preserved, features of modernity, and of modernity's global ramifications, are found today, not in economic or political life as such, but in religious traditions that have internalized the Enlightenment's criticisms of religion without compromise of their central convictions, and thus become sometimes unwitting contributors to a democratic restoration of modernity's best values. So the question that must now be asked is this: What vision of humanity's future does an enlightened religious consciousness teach? What have the Abrahamic faiths at their best to say to a compromised modernity in danger of self-destruction? All the preceding chapters of this book have been devoted to responding to this question in its different facets.

The term that seems best for summing up these chapters and grasping their import rests on an Abrahamic vision of what I will now call a "humanism of covenantal blessing" or "covenantal humanism." This is my version of the alternative eschatology for which we are looking. It should be clear that by "humanism" here I do not mean what this word has often meant in the history of Western thought, and still means to some, namely a vision of humankind without God or of conscious rejection of the very idea of God. I mean, rather, a theistic form of humanism cosponsored by the Abrahamic faiths acting together in cooperation with other initiatives in which the "God" reference may or may not be explicit but whose objectives for the human race seem compatible with the Abrahamic promise.

William Schweiker has already coined the very similar term "theological humanism" (see chapter 4). I acknowledge his authorship of this idea and thoroughly endorse its apparent intention. Still, my idea differs from his in certain important ways.[12] Schweiker's expression refers to a form of engagement, before God, with common human problems by members of many, if not all, faiths who realize that they share a humanness that is in danger from its own distortions and excesses, and affirm that God has a mission to the human race as a whole. Their respective faiths, they know, are *representations of* this divine purpose, not final *definitions* of it. The term "theological" confirms the explicit God-reference in a way that a term such as "religious" might not. Taking this direction, with its intention of embracing all religious traditions and not just Abrahamic ones, one of course is bound to encounter the same resistance Hans Küng met from those whose faiths are not "theological" in this sense[13]: for example, Buddhists, and in another sense, even Jews or Muslims. On one way of thinking, it is only Christians who have developed the idea of "theology" as systematic or constructive religious reflection by a community of faith. There probably exists no word with any serious valency that does not run into questions of this kind posed by different conceptions of the meaning of God-language.

My own preferred term, "covenantal," is obviously chosen because it arises from the experience of the "religions of the Book."[14] But the word "covenantal" gives my form of humanism an at least partly coherent historical context. And it implies something else: namely that amid all the Christian talk of old covenants and new covenants, covenants of works and covenants of grace, it is possible to defend the position that there is but one covenant of which "all the families of the earth" are members in principle. It is that covenant implied in the notion of God's dealing with and purposes for the human race as such.

But why the word "humanism"? Because the meaning of the term and the practices that constitute it have to do with common human experience. I take this commonality to be inherent in the very idea of blessing as it first appears in conjunction with responsibility for the earth at Genesis 1:28. The link between the Abrahamic faiths is not some sort of "religious" mixture. It is a link running through the human situation, appropriable by anyone but best seen through the lenses of Abrahamic traditions sharpened to discern what is going on among human beings today.

A stimulus for such discernment can be found by comparing this view with the combined work of the economist Amartya Sen and the classicist Martha Nussbaum. They argue that our common humanity should be defined in terms of our *capabilities* for various sorts of action and fulfillment.

Amartya Sen[15] developed his "capabilities" approach as an alternative to the standard way of calculating "gross national product" or GNP: the sum, over a period of time such as a year, of the goods and services produced by a given country, a strictly quantitative measurement compatible with globalized practices of capital formation. Sen desired to humanize statistical calculations of this kind by proposing to measure, instead, the degree to which a nation made possible the realization of human "capabilities" among its citizens. What are the people of a given nation able to do or be? Nussbaum early formed an academic partnership with Sen, but more recently she has proceeded on her own.

Nussbaum's[16] mature work shows significant links with that on justice by John Rawls, on whose thinking we drew in chapter 7 in formulating a view of the role of religious communities in promoting just social contracts. Human beings, Rawls taught, are of equal dignity and worth owing to the power of moral choice they possess. This alone entitles them to be treated in ways we call "just" or "fair." Nussbaum presses further. She asks, with Aristotle, what activities of human beings are so central as to seem definitive of a life that is truly human. Or, to put it the other way around, what changes can occur in a human life without calling into question a person's continued membership in the human community? Such questions lead her to offer an elaborate list of distinctively human "capabilities" that justice demands we should respect and enhance. Some of these are life itself, bodily health and integrity, minimally intact sensory abilities, capacities for imagination and thought, emotions and attachments, practical reason, affiliation, concern for other species, control over one's surroundings, opportunities for play. Access to the exercise of such capabilities could be offered as among the human rights that must be respected in any just society. Such capabilities clearly help to form the horizon of human expectation. Expectations of this sort constitute a kind of eschatology, of fulfillment, at least for the individual human person.

Nussbaum's work has been criticized along many lines. Among these is the claim that her conception of "capability," given those she lists as examples, is excessively individualistic and incapable of application to the capabilities of a society as a whole. That is, it is not clear how these capabilities belong in what other thinkers would call "social capital." She is also challenged to explain why the activation of certain capabilities should be regarded as "good," and whether there is any hierarchy of such "goods" among her listed capabilities. What notion of the "good," and what philosophical defense of that notion, does she believe to be implicit in her theory? It seems to this author that it is easier to think of Nussbaum's capabilities as "blessings" than to integrate them into any theory of "the good."

But, be all this as it may, we have here a genuine alternative to the assumptions of global capitalism guided by "rational choice theory" and "market mechanisms" that seem to dehumanize human beings to the point that they become only representatives of competing interests whose fulfillment can be measured only in terms of relative accumulations of wealth or power or preferment. Yet, for all the attractiveness and strength of Nussbaum's work, one capability that she fails to mention is precisely that which Hannah Arendt thought was the most important for human society as a whole: the human capability of receiving, making, and keeping promises.[17] This capability points toward the gift of responsibility that we, in chapter 5, derived from the Abrahamic covenant narratives, and developed in different contexts in the subsequent chapters. Arendt had hold of a distinctive and definitive human capability that Nussbaum apparently does not recognize.

But we, in turn, while recognizing the virtue of "promise keeping" in Abraham and elsewhere in the scriptures of the three faiths, want to make the point more fully in covenantal language. Promise keeping is not merely a virtue or character trait in itself. We keep promises because doing so acknowledges our gift of responsibility to a larger promise: a promise of blessing for all earth's families. Nussbaum's capabilities seem to be gifts that anyone should want. But something more needs to activate them. Something needs to ignite the desire for them, needs to plant their implied promise in the heart as living hope.

Short of this sense of promise, capabilities are often thought of simply as personal possessions to be used in the pursuit of various forms of acquisition or achievement. Capabilities are often equated with earning power. What we are able to do and be is potential "money in the bank." The economists' term "human capital" seems to reflect this level of understanding, even if not all Nussbaum's capabilities fit this commercial model. There is an analogy here to "land," which is also a possession that enlarges the capability of the possessor. Land resources and personal resources, both submit to the same metaphors of possession or property. The "properties" of an element are things that "belong" to it in the sense of what it will do, or of that to which it will relate. They are its capacities. A person's "properties" are possessions that fund capacities for action in whatever form they occur, gold coins or derivatives and hedge funds or intellect or bodily strength.

One senses that for Nussbaum people have the capacity to invent or reinvent themselves by the choices they make for using their capabilities. The element of responsibility to a promise that is *not* "our own" does not enter her picture, and hence the possibility of curse rather than the expected reward does not enter her picture either. But the land analogy shows that we, with our capabilities, are not our own.[18] Some Power must call each person by name and in effect give the gift of an energizing *expectation* that this person will take responsibility for uniquely actualizing these capabilities in him or herself to the greatest extent possible. This gift of person-focused expectation is what each of the three faiths, if in different ways, calls *blessing*. In the Qur'an, a comparable meaning is conveyed by the term translated "grace."

Seeing this ignition of human capability, uniquely among all the other capabilities, as a gift and identifying the promise concerned as that of God to the human race, builds on both Arendt and Nussbaum *and* carries the discussion to a higher level, a theological or covenantal level. Here is the larger context in which promise keeping as a human capability indispensable to just societies can be put by the Abrahamic faiths acting together. We have identified living responsibly *to* the promise—discerned in scripture as historically given to human beings, or intuited in our created nature as conscious actors to be inherent in the human way of being under God or before God. Lived out in and through all the many practices of modern societies, the shared exercise of this promise-bearing capability is what we call "covenantal" humanism, participation in the fulfillment of human capability within a covenant of blessing. More simply put, "covenantal humanism" describes or names a state of affairs in which human beings can be recognized as such by the fact that they are gifted to make and keep promises to themselves and to one another as exercises of responsibility to a larger promise.

Put this in a slightly different way. A covenantal humanism is therefore not a hubristic *theory of human self-creation* but a shared way of life on this planet in which we interpret our different but linked religious symbols in such a way that we can walk side-by-side in doing so, seeking to generate a parallel and interactive hermeneutic of human fulfillment or blessing. We can ask what each symbol says about our deep well-being before God.

We can ask how to interpret each symbol responsibly *in the presence of the other*. Our deep well-being or blessing is symbolized *in many different ways*. But they *sufficiently* (i.e., not identically) point to the same things, the same gifts of human capability to be used responsibly to promise, to permit us to walk along the same way even if we see the passing landscape differently. Thus we participate in a concrete lived universality, not a mathematical or conceptual universality. We act out a *covenantal* (or side-by-side) humanism, not or an ideological humanism, or a scientifically reductionist humanism.

It needs to be stressed, of course, that this covenantal humanism is not a self-standing position independent of the particular religious tradition through which we identify it as a possibility for ourselves. Covenantal humanism is a *way* of being Jewish, or Christian, or Muslim. It is a lived *interpretation* of one or another of these faith traditions, and conceivably of other faith traditions as well. Although a Jewish covenantal humanist can learn from Christians and Muslims, and Christians may learn from Jews and Muslims, and Muslims may learn from Jews and Christians, I do not see such reciprocal learnings as a form of syncretism or as leading to syncretism. There is no covenantal humanism without substantial grounding in some distinctive confessional expression of the covenant, despite our conviction that the covenant is in the end one. Indeed that very conviction can only be expressed in *terms* of one covenantal tradition or another.[19] The one covenant does not have its own distinctive expression independently of the different faith traditions that participate in it.[20]

A Concluding Untriumphalistic Postscript

But on what grounds are we to believe in such a covenantal promise of blessing, that we should act responsibly toward it? Much in human experience strongly suggests that the promise is not believable and hence that the notion of consistently living *this* sort of humanism is not plausible. What reason have we for supposing that the sorts of things I have just described can happen, or that they can be sustained for long enough to make a difference? Responsibility to promise involves wrestling with the unpleasant truths about us that our scriptural narratives describe so well. In Hannah Arendt's terms, these are the "darkness of the human heart," and "the basic unreliability of men who never can guarantee today who they will be tomorrow, and the impossibility of foretelling the consequences of an act within a community of equals where everybody has the same capacity to act."[21] Other secular writers agree. André Gide is reported to have said, "All things human, given time, go badly." Isaiah Berlin wrote a book around the metaphor of "the crooked timber of humanity."[22]

Today, "rational choice theory," as the logical-mathematical instrument of totalization, can be seen precisely as an attempt to rationalize, and thus to foreclose, the uncertainties of human behavior that go with freedom. Promising in freedom, Arendt said, is "the only alternative to a mastery which relies on domination of oneself and rule over others."[23] This is a mastery that relies on reducing both others and oneself to calculating machines playing games designed to get the best of one another. How are we to escape from such domination and open ourselves to the power of the promise?

But there is another side to this story. There is evidence of the possibility of such escape from domination into freedom in many lives that are, in fact, lived in fidelity to promises explicit and implicit, with quite tangible confidence that so to live is ultimately to be in harmony with the God-given purposes of the universe. These lives, and moments within them, are "signs" of the eschatological fulfillment in midst of the present.[24] The signs or traces of the presence of such a possibility in history appear most often in situations, relationships, or events in which some fragmentarily fulfilled reality of the promise becomes manifest, or in which some egregious contradiction of the promise is identified and resisted. The simple shared sense that "something is wrong" sets us on the road to overcoming and constitutes in itself a sign or trace of the promise. William Schweiker sees such events as engendering "axiological surprise," coming upon moments of ethical value, or for that matter, moral failure, that take our breath away. Such moments point beyond mere common wisdom to something more. Such traces move us, shake us, enable us. So does something like receiving Schweiker's "last, lingering touch of a dying parent" as the promised blessing is passed forward to a new generation. These are the Lévinian "traces" of the transcendent. Scripture interpretation done together by members of the Abrahamic faiths helps us see such moments of eschatological meaning more clearly and to reason from them to larger implications.

The devoted work of activists to improve the human condition, successful or not, is also sign-bearing and implicatory in this sense. There is sign value in the fact that people labor to achieve justice for women, the eradication of disease, protection for the environment, and so forth for a hundred other specific projects. Always the question is, Why are we doing all this? What is it about the human future that we expect that lends sense to a hundred different efforts to make the present human situation better? To what end sacrificial efforts to resolve intertribal conflicts in Darfur or elsewhere in Africa? To what end more reliable and cheap water supplies for all? Obviously it means something that desert people, or people anywhere, survive. One commonly takes such meaning for granted. It will not do to let this sort of "upstream" question impede the actual efforts concerned. But such questions do not go away. I argue that the least we can say is that efforts to better the human condition deserve to be considered among the signs of the coming of what I am calling a covenantal humanity, a humanity gifted by its capacity for giving reasons to one another rather than throwing bombs. To foresee such a coming, and to devote one's life to fostering its signs in the world, is to share a covenantal humanism of responsibility to that promise of blessing—or deep well-being—for all earth's families.

Notes

1. These terms were used by European existentialist philosophers of the 1930s and 1940s to describe dimensions of human striving. They are found, for example, in Paul Ricoeur's earlier works on the philosophy of the will.

2. Jeffrey Stout, *Democracy and Tradition* (Princeton, NJ: Princeton University Press, 2004).

3. Ibid., 303–4.

4. Francis Fukuyama, *The End of History and the Last Man* (New York: Free Press, 1992).

5. Francis Fukuyama, *Our Post-Human Future: Consequences of the Biotechnology Revolution* (New York: Farrar, Straus and Giroux, 2002).

6. Gordon Kaufman, *In Face of Mystery: A Constructive Theology* (Cambridge, MA: Harvard University Press, 1993), 407.

7. Samuel P. Huntington, *The Clash of Civilizations and the Remaking of World Order* (New York: Simon and Schuster, 1996), quoted in William H. McNeil, "Decline of the West?" *The New York Review*, January 9, 1997.

8. Ibid., 18.

9. Martin Rees, *Our Final Century: Will Civilization Survive the Twenty-First Century?* (London: Arrow Books, 2004).

10. Lukas Vischer, "Koinonia in a Time of Threats to Life," in *Costly Unity*, ed. Thomas Best and Wesley Granberg-Michaelson (Geneva: World Council of Churches, 1995), 72.

11. Ibid., 72f. Vischer's italics.

12. I prefer the term "covenantal humanism" to Schweiker's "theological humanism" because I wish to see this idea invested with certain qualities of relationship that begin in the practices of parallel hermeneutics among the Abrahamic faiths as such and extend to the social-historical results of such hermeneutical practice. The relational qualities of covenanting—forgiveness, trust, and solidarity among them—can be expressed in terms that are not abstractly "theological," as if to refer to God as God is in Godself. Rather, I am speaking of God as God is in the historical process, of God in God's involvement with the human race. I see such divine involvement as intimately interwoven with the stuff of common human experience. I am tempted to use the four Chalcedonian adverbs, or to devise a version of the Eastern concept of the "economic" Trinity in which God, in the power of the Spirit, has implicated Godself in the unfolding of human events and institutions. Mine is a more immanental, or perhaps panentheistic, view than that implied by Schwieker's more traditional notion that we stand "before God."

13. This Buddhist objection to God-language was one of the obstacles Kung encountered in the Parliament of the World's Religions meeting in Chicago, August 28–September 4, 1993, as he argued for adoption of his "Declaration of the Religions for a Global Ethic." A revised version of the Declaration was adopted and proclaimed on September 4.

14. I take the term "religions of the Book" to include Islam, despite the fact that it originated as an Islamic expression for Jews and Christians only.

15. See Amartya Sen, *On Ethics and Economics* (Oxford, UK: Blackwell, 1987), and *Development as Freedom* (New York: Knopf, 1999).

16. See Martha Nussbaum and Jonathan Glover, eds., *Women, Culture and Development: A Study of Human Capabilities* (New York: Oxford University Press, 1995), and Martha Nussbaum, *Women and Human Development* (New York: Cambridge University Press, 2000).

17. Hannah Arendt, *The Human Condition* (Chicago: University of Chicago Press, 1958), 219ff.

18. The words "we are not our own" have resonance for Christians of the Reformed or Calvinistic tradition. They appear repeatedly as a kind of litany in Calvin's *Institutes of the Christian Religion* (1559) and were incorporated in the *Declaration of Debrecen,* a litany used to close the 23rd General Council of the World Alliance of Reformed Churches meeting in Debrecen, Hungary, August 8–20, 1997.

19. As a Christian theologian, I can argue the case for one covenant expressed in Jewish, Christian, and Muslim forms, knowing that there are other views such as those based on the "new covenant" passage of Jeremiah 31:31. But Paul's argument in Romans 9–11 that the Gentiles are like wild olive branches grafted into a cultivated olive tree points strongly in the direction of a single covenant. But I find a most fascinating angle on this question in chapter 7 of the *Westminster Confession of Faith* (1647), a confessional document of my own Presbyterian community. Titled "Of God's Covenant with Man," already a rather inclusive expression (forgiving the seventeenth-century patriarchalism), this chapter describes a "covenant of works" promised to Adam, followed after the Fall by a remedial "covenant of grace." The latter covenant then is said to have been administered in two ways: under the law of Israel as recounted in the Hebrew Scriptures, and in Jesus Christ as signified in the Christian Scriptures. One and the same covenant of grace under "various dispensations." This final word "various," where one might have expected to read "two," has opened the door to several lines of reasoning. One interpretation of "various," long after the time of Westminster, has led to a Christian position known as "dispensationalism" that sees the history of salvation deployed in several historic "dispensations" leading up to the present millennial period of Armageddon and the "rapture." But another equally *ex post facto* interpretation is also possible. Could the word "various" open the way for saying that yet another dispensation of the one covenant is possible, and that Islam could claim to represent that expression? So far as I know, no Muslim scholar has made such a claim, nor has any Christian theologian seriously suggested it. I owe the thought of raising this question to a conversation with Dr. Ronald J. Kernaghan.

20. To put thus perspective further in Christian theological terms, one might say that the primordial "covenantal humanist" is God, who, as Karl Barth famously said, has determined Godself *for* us, the members of the human race. God, in all three faiths, can be seen as the One who has so high a regard for human potential as to entrust some part, at least, of the universe's consciousness of itself to the evolutionary success of our species. This can stand as

a contemporary interpretation of the Islamic idea of "vicegerency." We become covenantal humanists by intentionally identifying ourselves with this narrative and by acknowledging a gift of responsibility before God for what happens to this historic and cosmic experiment.

21. Arendt, *Human Condition*, 219.

22. Isaiah Berlin, *The Crooked Timber of Humanity: Chapters in the History of Ideas*, ed. Henry Hardy (New York: Knopf, 1991).

23. Arendt, *Human Condition*, 220.

24. We human beings come to our awareness of such signs in our lives, and of the question of their authenticity, largely when the hermeneutic of symbol and experience that has articulated our "effort to exist and desire to be" (Ricoeur, after Jean Nabert) continues to interact hermeneutically with the other-than-self. This works best and most profoundly when the Other is the radically other, the very different. And likewise we bring into such encounter the tradition of signs, the "scriptural" traditions that have formed us as we interact with Others, and through them with other, different scriptural traditions. This relationship with the Other is inherently an ethical relationship, as Lévinas asserts. In such a profound ethical relationship with difference, the orientation to promise that is in my tradition gets substantiated: precisely as we see the promise taking shape also in different traditions.

Bibliography

Allen, Charles W. "The Primacy of *Phronesis*, A Proposal for Avoiding Frustrating Tendencies in Our Conceptions of Rationality." *The Journal of Religion* 69 (July 1989): 359ff.

Appiah, Kwame Anthony. *Cosmopolitanism: Ethics in a World of Strangers.* New York: W. W. Norton, 2006.

Arendt, Hannah. *The Human Condition.* Chicago: University of Chicago Press, 1958.

Arkoun, Mohammad. *The Concept of Revelation: From the People of the Book to the Societies of the Book.* Claremont, CA: Claremont Graduate School, 1987.

Armstrong, Karen. *Islam: A Short History.* New York: Random House, 2000.

Arrow, Kenneth. *Social Choice and Individual Values.* Cowles Foundation Monograph Series. 2nd ed. New Haven, CT: Yale University Press, 1970.

Barth, Karl. *Church Dogmatics.* Edinburgh: T and T Clark, 1938.

———. *The Humanity of God.* Richmond, VA: John Knox Press, 1960.

Becker, Carl L. *The Heavenly City of the Eighteenth-Century Philosophers.* New Haven, CT: Yale University Press, 1932.

Becker, Gary. *The Economic Approach to Human Behavior.* Chicago: University of Chicago Press, 1976.

Bellah, Robert, et al. *The Good Society.* New York: Alfred A. Knopf, 1991.

Bennett, John. *Christian Ethics and Social Policy.* New York: Scribner's, 1946.

Berlin, Isaiah. *The Crooked Timber of Humanity: Chapters in the History of Ideas.* Edited by Henry Hardy. New York: Knopf, 1991.

Bernstein, Richard. *Philosophical Profiles.* Philadelphia: University of Pennsylvania Press, 1986.

Biggar, Nigel, ed. *Burying the Past: Making Peace and Doing Justice after Civil Conflict.* Washington, DC: Georgetown University Press, 2001.

Braaten, Carl E. and Robert W. Jenson, eds. *Jews and Christians: People of God.* Grand Rapids, MI: William B. Eerdmans Publishing Company, 2003.

Brueggemann, Walter. "Law as Response to Thou." In *Taking Responsibility: Comparative Perspectives.* Edited by Winston Davis. Charlottesville: University of Virginia Press, 2001.

Caputo, John D. *The Prayers and Tears of Jacques Derrida: Religion without Religion.* Indianapolis: Indiana University Press, 1997.

Casanova, José. *Public Religions in the Modern World.* Chicago: University of Chicago Press, 1994.

———. "Rethinking Secularization: A Global Comparative Perspective." *The Hedgehog Review: Critical Reflections on Contemporary Culture* 8, nos. 1 and 2 (Spring and Summer 2006): 7ff.

Chittister, Joan, Murshid Saadi Shakur Chisti, and Arthur Waskow. *The Tent of Abraham: Stories of Hope and Peace for Jews, Christians and Muslims.* Boston: Beacon Press, 2006.

Cohen, Jean L., and Andrew Arato. *Civil Society and Political Theory.* Cambridge, MA: MIT Press, 1992.

Colbourn, Trevor, ed. *Fame and the Founding Fathers.* New York, Norton, 1974.

Corrigan, John, et al. *Jews, Christians, Muslims: A Comparative Introduction to Monotheistic Religions.* Upper Saddle River, NJ: Prentice Hall, 1998.

Davies, W. D. *The Gospel and the Land: Early Christianity and Jewish Territorial Doctrine.* Berkeley: University of California Press, 1974.

Davis, Winston. *Taking Responsibility: Comparative Perspectives.* Charlottesville: University Press of Virginia, 2002.

de Gruchy, John. *Christianity and Democracy.* Cambridge, UK: Cambridge University Press, 1995.

Dennett, Daniel C. *Breaking the Spell: Religion as a Natural Phenomenon.* New York: Viking, 2006.

Derrida, Jacques. *Given Time.* Chicago: University of Chicago Press, 1992.

———. *The Gift of Death.* Chicago: University of Chicago Press, 1995.

———. "To Forgive: The Unforgivable and Imprescriptible." In *Questioning God.* Edited by John D. Caputo, Mark Dooley, and Michael J. Scranton. Bloomington: University of Indiana Press, 1999.

Eck, Diana. *Encountering God: A Spiritual Journey from Bozeman to Banaras.* Boston: Beacon Press, 1993.

Edwald, Francois. "Solidarite." In the *Dictionnaire d'ethique et de philosophie morale*. Edited by Monique Sperber. 3rd ed. Paris: Presses Universitaires de France, 2001.

Esack, Farid. *Qur'an, Liberation, and Pluralism: An Islamic Perspective of Interreligious Solidarity Against Oppression*. Oxford: Oneworld Publications, 1997.

———. *The Qur'an: A Short Introduction*. Oxford, UK: Oneworld Publications, 2002.

———. *On Being a Muslim: Finding a Religious Path in the World Today*. Oxford, UK: Oneworld Publications, 1999.

Feiler, Bruce. *Abraham, A Journey to the Heart of Three Faiths*. New York: Harper Collins, 2002.

Flannery, Austin, ed. *Vatican Council II: The Conciliar and Post-Conciliar Documents*. Northport, NY: Costello Publishing Company, 1998.

Forward, Martin. *Inter-Religious Dialogue: A Short Introduction*. Oxford, UK: Oneworld Publications, 2001.

Frankfort, Henri. *Before Philosophy: The Intellectual Adventure of Ancient Man*. Baltimore: Penguin Books, 1974.

Frankfurt, Harry G. *The Reasons of Love*. Princeton, NJ: Princeton University Press, 2004.

———. *On Bullshit*. Princeton, NJ: Princeton University Press, 2005.

Freeman, Samuel. *John Rawls: Collected Papers*. Cambridge, MA: Harvard University Press, 1999.

Friedman, Thomas L. *From Beirut to Jerusalem*. New York: Farrar Strauss and Giroux, 1989.

———. *The Lexus and the Olive Tree*. New York: Farrar Strauss and Giroux, 2000.

———. *The World Is Flat: A Brief History of the Twenty-First Century*. New York: Farrar, Strauss and Giroux, 2005.

"From Culture Wars to the Global Question of Religion," an unsigned editorial, *Respublica Newsletter*, December 2005.

Fukuyama, Francis. *The End of History and the Last Man*. New York: Free Press, 1992.

———. *Our Post-Human Future: Consequences of the Biotechnology Revolution*. New York: Farrar, Straus and Giroux, 2002.

———. *Trust: Social Virtues and the Creation of Prosperity*. New York: Free Press, 1995.

Gadamer, Hans Georg. *Truth and Method*. New York: Seabury, 1975.

Geertz, Clifford. *Islam Observed*. New Haven, CT: Yale University Press, 1968.

———. "Which Way to Mecca? Part II," *The New York Review of Books*, July 3, 2003, 36.

Girard, René. *Things Hidden Since the Foundation of the World*. Stanford, CA: Stanford University Press, 1987.

Gopin, Marc. *Between Eden and Armageddon: The Future of World Religions: Violence and Peacemaking*. New York: Oxford University Press, 2000.

Goudzwaard, Bob, "The Modern Roots of Economic Globalization." In *Beyond Idealism: A Way Ahead for Ecumenical Social Ethics*. Edited by Robin Gurney, Heidi Hadsell, and Lewis Mudge. Grand Rapids, MI: Eerdmans, 2006.

Gulen, M. F. *Essays, Perspectives, Opinions*. Rutherford, NJ: The Light, Inc., 2002.

Habermas, Jürgen. *The Theory of Communicative Action: Reason and the Rationalization of Society*. Translated by Thomas McCarthy. Boston: Beacon Press, 1984.

Halevi, Yossi Klein. *At the Entrance to the Garden of Eden: A Jew's Search for Hope with Christians and Muslims in the Holy Land*. New York: Perennial, 2002.

Hallencreutz, Carl F. *Dialogue and Community: Ecumenical Issues in Inter-Religious Relationships*. Uppsala: Swedish Institute of Missionary Research, 1977.

Hallie, Philip. *Lest Innocent Blood Be Shed*. New York: Harper and Row, 1979.

Hand, Sean, ed. *The Levinas Reader*. Oxford: Blackwell, 1989.

Haring, Herman, Janet Martin Soskice, and Felix Wilfred, eds. *Learning from Other Faiths*. London: SCM Press, 2003.

Harris, Lee. *The Suicide of Reason: Radical Islam's Threat to the West*. New York: Basic Books, 2007.

Hashmi, Sohail H. "Cultivating a Liberal Islamic Ethos: Building an Islamic Civil Society." *The Journal of the Society of Christian Ethics* 27, no. 1 (Spring/Summer 2007): 3–16.

Heft, James L., ed. *Passing on the Faith: Transforming Traditions for the Next Generation of Jews, Christians and Muslims*. New York: Fordham University Press, 2006.

Heim, S. Mark. *Salvations: Truth and Difference in Religion*. Maryknoll, NY: Orbis Books, 1995.

———. "Sharing Our Differences: Koinonia and the Theology of Religious Plurality." In *Faith and Order at the Crossroads, Kuala Lumpur, 2004*. Faith and Order Paper 196. Geneva: WCC Publications, 2005.

Hick, John. *Problems of Religious Pluralism*. New York: St. Martin's Press, 1985.

———. *The Second Christianity*. London: SCM Press, 1983.

———, ed. *Truth and Dialogue in World Religions: Conflicting Truth Claims*. Philadelphia: Westminster Press, 1974.

Hick, John, and Edmund S. Meltzer, eds. *Three Faiths—One God: A Jewish, Christian, Muslim Encounter*. Albany: State University of New York Press, 1988.

Huntington, Samuel P. *The Clash of Civilizations and the Remaking of World Order*. New York: Simon and Schuster, 1996.

Idinopulos, Thomas A. *Jerusalem Blessed, Jerusalem Cursed: Jews, Christians and Muslims in the Holy City from David's Time to Our Own*. Chicago: I. R. Dee, 1991.

Johnson, Mark. *Moral Imagination: Implications of Cognitive Science for Ethics*. Chicago: University of Chicago Press, 1993.

Jonas, Hans. *The Imperative of Responsibility*. Chicago: University of Chicago Press, 1984.

Juergensmeyer, Mark. *Terror in the Mind of God: The Global Rise of Religious Violence*. Berkeley: University of California Press, 2000.

Karabell, Zachary. *Peace Be Upon You: The Story of Muslim, Christian and Jewish Coexistence*. New York: Alfred A. Knopf, 2007.

Kaufman, Gordon. *In Face of Mystery: A Constructive Theology*. Cambridge, MA: Harvard University Press, 1993.

Kelsay, John, ed. *The Annual of the Society of Christian Ethics*. Washington, DC: Georgetown University Press, 1998.

Kepnes, Steven. *Reasoning after Revelation: Dialogues in Postmodern Jewish Philosophy*. Boulder, CO: Westview Press, 1998.

Kinnamon, Michael, and Brian E. Cope. *The Ecumenical Movement: An Anthology of Key Texts and Voices*. Grand Rapids, MI: Eerdmans, 1997.

Knitter, Paul F. *Introducing Theologies of Religions*. Maryknoll, NY: Orbis Books, 2002.

———. *Jesus and the Other Names: Christian Mission and Global Responsibility*. Maryknoll, NY: Orbis Books, 1995.

———. *The Myth of Religious Superiority: Multifaith Explorations of Religious Pluralism*. Maryknoll, NY: Orbis Books, 2005.

———. *No Other Name? A Critical Survey of Christian Attitudes toward the World Religions*. Maryknoll, NY: Orbis Books, 1985.

———. *One Earth, Many Religions: Multifaith Dialogue and Global Responsibility.* Maryknoll, NY: Orbis Books, 1995.

———. *Towards a Protestant Theology of Religions: A Case Study of Paul Althaus and Contemporary Attitudes.* Marburg: N. G. Elwert, 1974.

Kohlberg, Lawrence. "From Is to Ought." In *Cognitive Development and Epistemology.* Edited by Theodore Mischel. New York: Academic Press, 1971.

Koshul, Basit Bilai, and Steven Kepnes, eds. *Scripture, Reason, and the Contemporary Islam-West Encounter: Studying the "Other," Understanding the "Self."* New York: Palgrave, 2007.

Krutch, Joseph Wood, ed. *Walden and Other Writings by Henry David Thoreau.* New York: Bantam Books, 1981.

Kung, Hans. *Global Responsibility: In Search of a New World Ethic.* New York: Crossroads, 1991.

Kung, Hans, and Helmut Schmidt, eds. *A Global Ethic and Global Responsibilities: Two Declarations.* London: SCM, 1998.

Kuschel, Karl-Josef. *Abraham: Sign of Hope for Jews, Christians and Muslims.* New York: Continuum, 1995.

LaCocque, André. *Commitment and Commemoration: Jews, Christians, Muslims.* Chicago: Exploration Press, 1994.

Lakoff, George. *Moral Politics: How Liberals and Conservatives Think.* Chicago: University of Chicago Press, 2002.

Lakoff, George, and Mark Johnson. *Metaphors We Live By.* Chicago: University of Chicago Press, 1980.

Leaman, Oliver. *Jewish Thought: An Introduction.* London: Routledge, 2006.

Levenson, Jon D. *The Death and Resurrection of the Beloved Son: The Transformation of Child Sacrifice in Judaism and Christianity.* New Haven: Yale University Press, 1993.

Lévinas, Emmanuel. "Ethics as First Philosophy." In *The Levinas Reader.* Edited by Sean Hand. Oxford: Blackwell, 1989.

———. *Totality and Infinity: An Essay on Exteriority.* Translated by Alphonso Lingis. Pittsburgh: Duquesne University Press, 1969.

Lilla, Mark. "The Great Separation," *New York Times Magazine*, August 19, 2007, cover.

Lindbeck, George A. *The Nature of Doctrine: Religion and Theology in a Postliberal Age.* Philadelphia: Westminster Press, 1984.

Luhmann, N. "Familiarity, Confidence, Trust: Problems and Perspectives." In *Trust: Making and Breaking of Cooperative Relations.* Edited by Diego Gambetta. Oxford: Basil Blackwell. 1988.

MacIntyre, Alasdair. *After Virtue.* Notre Dame, IN: Notre Dame University Press, 1981.

Mamdani, Mahmood. *Good Muslim, Bad Muslim: America, the Cold War, and the Roots of Terror.* New York: Pantheon Books, 2004.

Mardin, Sherif. "Civil Society and Islam." In *Civil Society: Theory, History, Comparison.* Edited by J. A. Hall. Cambridge, MA: Polity Press, 1995.

Margalit, Avishai. *The Decent Society.* Translated by Naomi Goldblum. Cambridge, MA: Harvard University Press, 1996.

Mendenhall, George. *The Tenth Generation: The Origins of the Biblical Tradition.* Baltimore: Johns Hopkins University Press, 1973.

Milbank, John. *Theology and Social Theory.* Oxford: Blackwell Publishers, 1988.

Mittleman, Alan R. "The Modern Jewish Condition." *First Things* (October 1994): 30–34.

Mouw, Richard, and Sander Griffioen. *Pluralisms and Horizons: An Essay in Christian Public Philosophy.* Grand Rapids, MI: Eerdmans, 1993.

Mudge, Lewis. *The Church as Moral Community: Ecclesiology and Ethics in Ecumenical Debate.* New York: Continuum, 1998.

Müller-Fahrenholz, Geiko. *The Art of Forgiveness: Theological Reflections on Healing and Reconciliation.* Geneva: WCC Publications, 1997.

Niebuhr, H. Richard. *The Responsible Self.* New York: Harper and Row, 1963.

Nussbaum, Martha. *The Fragility of Goodness: Luck and Ethics in Greek Tragedy and Philosophy.* New York: Cambridge University Press, 2001.

———. *Women and Human Development.* New York: Cambridge University Press, 2000.

Nussbaum, Martha, and Jonathan Glover, eds. *Women, Culture and Development: A Study of Human Capabilities.* New York: Oxford University Press, 1995.

Ochs, Peter. "Abrahamic Theo-Politics: A Jewish View." In *The Blackwell Companion to Political Theology.* Edited by Peter Scott and William T. Cavanaugh. Hoboken, NJ: Wiley-Blackwell, 2003.

———. *Peirce, Pragmatism, and the Logic of Scripture.* New York: Cambridge University Press, 1998.

Ochs, Peter, ed. *The Return to Scripture in Judaism and Christianity: Essays in Postcritical Scripture Interpretation.* New York: Paulist Press, 1993.

———. *Understanding the Rabbinic Mind: Essays on the Hermeneutic of Max Kadushin.* Atlanta, GA: Scholars Press, 1990.

Ochs, Peter, with Eugene Borowitz, eds. *Reviewing the Covenant: Eugene Borowitz and the Postmodern Revival of Jewish Theology.* Albany: State University of New York Press, 2000.

Ochs, Peter, and Nancy Levene, eds. *Textual Reasonings: Jewish Philosophy and Text Study at the End of the Twentieth Century.* Grand Rapids, MI: William B. Eerdmans Publishing Company, 2003.

Outka, Gene, and John P. Reeder, eds. *Prospects for a Common Morality.* Princeton, NJ: Princeton University Press, 1993.

Oxtoby, Willard G., ed. *World Religions.* 2 vols. New York: Oxford University Press, 2002.

Peters, F. E. *Judaism, Christianity and Islam.* Princeton, NJ: Princeton University Press, 1990.

———. *The Monotheists: Jews, Christians and Muslims in Conflict and Competition.* Princeton: Princeton University Press, 2002.

———. *The Voice, the Word, the Books: The Sacred Scripture of the Jews, Christians and Muslims.* Princeton: Princeton University Press, 2007.

Putnam, Robert. *Making Democracy Work: Civic Traditions in Modern Italy.* Princeton, NJ: Princeton University Press, 1993.

The Qur'an: A Modern English Version. Translated by Majid Fakhry. Reading, UK: Garnet Publishing, 1997.

Rahman, Fazlur. *Islam.* Chicago: University of Chicago Press, 1979.

———. *Islam and Modernity: Transformation of an Intellectual Tradition.* Chicago: University of Chicago Press, 1982.

———. *Major Themes of the Qur'an.* Minneapolis, MN: Bibliotheca Islamica, 1980.

———. *Prophecy in Islam: Philosophy and Orthodoxy.* Chicago: University of Chicago Press, 1979.

———. *Revival and Reform in Islam: A Study of Islamic Fundamentalism.* Oxford, UK: Oneworld Publications, 2000.

Ramadan, Tariq. *In the Footsteps of the Prophet: Lessons from the Life of Muhammad.* New York: Oxford University Press, 2007.

Rasmussen, Larry. *Moral Fragments and Moral Community.* Minneapolis: Fortress Press, 1993.

Rasmusson, Arne. *The Church as Polis.* Notre Dame, IN: University of Notre Dame Press, 1995.

Rawls, John. "Kantian Constructivism in Moral Theory." *The Journal of Philosophy* (September 1980): 77.

———. *Political Liberalism.* New York: Columbia University Press, 1993.

———. *A Theory of Justice.* Cambridge, MA: Harvard University Press, 1971.

Reeder, John P., and Gene Outka, eds. *Prospects for a Common Morality.* Princeton, NJ: Princeton University Press, 1993.

Rees, Martin. *Our Final Century: Will Civilization Survive the Twenty-First Century?* London: Arrow Books, 2004.

Ricoeur, Paul. *Essays on Biblical Interpretation.* Edited by Lewis S. Mudge. Philadelphia: Fortress Press, 1980.

———. *History and Truth.* Translated by Charles A. Kelbley. Evanston, IL: Northwestern University Press, 1965.

———. *Interpretation Theory: Discourse and the Surplus of Meaning.* Fort Worth, TX: Texas Christian University Press, 1976.

———. *Oneself as Another.* Translated by Kathleen Blamey. Chicago: University of Chicago Press, 1992.

———. *The Symbolism of Evil.* Boston: Beacon Press, 1967.

Rorty, Richard. *Philosophy and the Mirror of Nature.* Princeton, NJ: Princeton University Press, 1979.

Rothberg, Robert I. *The Founder: Cecil Rhodes and the Pursuit of Power.* New York: Oxford University Press, 1988.

Sacks, Jonathan. *The Dignity of Difference: How to Avoid the Clash of Civilizations.* New York: Continuum, 2002.

———. *The Persistence of Faith: Religion, Morality and Society in a Secular Age.* London: Continuum, 2005.

———. *The Politics of Hope.* London: Jonathan Cape, 1997.

———. *To Heal a Fractured World: The Ethics of Responsibility.* New York: Schocken Books, 2005.

Sajoo, Amyn. *Civil Society in the Muslim World: Contemporary Perspectives.* New York: St. Martin's Press, 2002.

Samartha, S. J. *Courage for Dialogue: Ecumenical Issues in Inter-Religious Relationships.* Geneva: World Council of Churches, 1981.

Santa Ana, Julio de, et al. *Beyond Idealism: A New Way Forward for Ecumenical Social Ethics.* Edited by Robin Gurney, Heidi Hadsell, and Lewis S. Mudge. Grand Rapids, MI: Eerdmans, 2006.

Schell, Jonathan. *The Fate of the Earth.* New York: Knopf, 1982.

Schreiter, Robert J. *The New Catholicity: Theology Between the Global and the Local.* Maryknoll, NY: Orbis Books, 1997.

Schweiker, William. Lecture in Prague, Czech Republic, Summer 2003.

———. *Mimetic Reflections: A Study in Hermeneutics, Theology and Ethics.* Bronx, NY: Fordham University Press, 1990.

———. *Power, Value and Conviction: Theological Ethics in the Postmodern Age.* Cleveland, OH: Pilgrim Press, 1998.

————. "Religious Conviction and the Intellectual's Responsibility," *Criterion* (Autumn 2003): 12.

————. *Responsibility and Christian Ethics*. New York: Cambridge University Press, 1993.

————. *Theological Ethics and Global Dynamics: In the Time of Many Worlds*. Malden, MA: Blackwell, 2004.

Schweiker, William, Michael A. Johnson, and Kevin Jung, eds. *Humanity Before God: Contemporary Faces of Jewish, Christian and Islamic Ethics*. Minneapolis: Augsburg Fortress, 2006.

Schweiker, William, et al., eds. *Cities of Gods: Faith, Politics and Pluralism in Judaism, Christianity and Islam*. Westport, CT: Greenwood Press, 1986.

Seligman, Adam B. *The Idea of Civil Society*. New York: Free Press, 1992.

————. *The Problem of Trust*. Princeton, NJ: Princeton University Press, 1997.

Seidman, Naomi. *Faithful Renderings: Jewish-Christian Differences and the Politics of Translation*. Chicago: University of Chicago Press, 2006.

Sen, Amartya. *Development as Freedom*. New York: Knopf, 1999

————. *On Ethics and Economics*. New York: Blackwell, 1987.

Sherwood, Yvonne. "Binding-Unbinding: Divided Responses of Judaism, Christianity, and Islam to the 'Sacrifice' of Abraham's Beloved Son." *The Journal of the American Academy of Religion* 72, no. 4 (December 2004): 821ff.

Shriver, Donald W., Jr. *An Ethic for Enemies*. New York: Oxford University Press, 1995.

Smith, Adam. *An Inquiry into the Nature and Causes of the Wealth of Nations*. New York: The Modern Library, 1937.

————. *Theory of Moral Sentiments*. Indianapolis: Liberty Classics, 1982.

Solomon, Norman, Richard Harries, and Tim Winter, eds. *Abraham's Children: Jews, Christians and Muslims in Conversation*. New York: T&T Clark, 2005.

Stout, Jeffery. *After Babel: The Languages of Morals and Their Discontents*. Boston: Beacon Press, 1988.

————. *Democracy and Tradition*. Princeton, NJ: Princeton University Press, 2004.

Swidler, Leonard, ed. *Theoria>Praxis: How Jews, Christians and Muslims Can Together Move from Theory to Practice*. Leuven: Peeters, 1998.

Taylor, Charles. *Sources of the Self*. Cambridge, MA: Harvard University Press, 1989.

Thomas, M. M. *Man and the Universe of Faiths*. Madras: Christian Literature Society, 1975.

The Torah: A Modern Commentary. Cincinnati, OH: Union of American Hebrew Congregations, 1981.

Tracy, David. *Dialogue with the Other: The Inter-Religious Dialogue*. Leuven: Peeters Press, and Grand Rapids, MI: William B. Eerdmans Publishing Company, 1991.

Vaux, Kenneth L. *Jew, Christian, Muslim*. Eugene, OR: Wipf and Stock Publishers, 2003.

Vischer, Lukas. "Koinonia in a Time of Threats to Life." In *Costly Unity*. Edited by Thomas Best and Wesley Granberg-Michaelson. Geneva: World Council of Churches, 1995.

Visser 't Hooft, W. A., and J. H. Oldham. *The Church and Its Function in Society*. London: George Allen and Unwin, 1937.

Walzer, Michael. *Thick and Thin: Moral Argument at Home and Abroad*. Notre Dame, IN: University of Notre Dame Press, 1994.

Weber, Max. *The Protestant Ethic and the Spirit of Capitalism*. Translated by Talcott Parsons. New York: Charles Scribner's Sons, 1930.

White, Stephen K. *The Recent Work of Jürgen Habermas: Reason, Justice, and Modernity*. Cambridge: Cambridge University Press, 1988.

Wickeri, Philip L., ed. *The People of God Among All God's People: Frontiers in Christian Mission*. London: Christian Conference of Asia/The Council for World Mission, 2000.

Wickeri, Philip L., Janice K. Wickeri, and Damayanthi M. Niles, eds. *Plurality, Power and Mission: Intercontextual Theological Explorations of the Role of Religion in the New Millennium*. London: The Council for World Mission, 2000.

Wiles, Maurice. *Christian Theology and Inter-Religious Dialogue*. Philadelphia: Trinity Press International, 1992.

Williams, Rowan. Address at the Ninth Assembly of the World Council of Churches, Porto Alegre, Brazil, February 14–23, 2006.

Wolfe, Alan. *Whose Keeper? Social Science and Moral Obligation*. Berkeley: University of California Press, 1989.

Yoder, John Howard, with Michael Cartwright and Peter Ochs, eds. *The Jewish-Christian Schism Revisited*. Grand Rapids, MI: William B. Eerdmans, 2003.

Index